THE CAMBRIDGE COMPANION TO TWENTIETH-CENTURY LITERATURE AND POLITICS

For a long time, people had been schooled to think of modern literature's relationship to politics as indirect or obscure, and often to find the politics of literature deep within its unconsciously ideological structures and forms. But twentieth-century writers were directly involved in political parties and causes, and many viewed their writing as part of their activism. This *Companion* tells a story of the rich and diverse ways in which literature and politics over the twentieth century coincided, overlapped – and also clashed. Covering some of the century's most influential political ideas, moments, and movements, nineteen academic experts uncover new ways of thinking about the relationship between literature and politics. Liberalism, Communism, fascism, suffragism, pacifism, federalism, different nationalisms, civil rights, women's rights, sexual rights, Indigenous rights, environmentalism, neoliberalism: twentieth-century authors wrote in direct response to political movements, ideas, events, and campaigns.

CHRISTOS HADJIYIANNIS has written widely on modern literature and art, including on the avant-garde, fascist literature/politics, Julia Kristeva, Djuna Barnes, and the afterlives of Byzantium in modern British and North American literature. He is the author of *Conservative Modernists: Literature and Tory Politics in Britain, 1900–1920* (Cambridge University Press, 2018).

RACHEL POTTER writes on modernist literature and culture. Her work has focused on literature, censorship, free expression, and writers' organisations. Her books include *Obscene Modernism: Literary Censorship and Experiment, 1900–1940* (Oxford University Press, 2013); *The Edinburgh Guide to Modernist Literature* (Edinburgh University Press, 2012); and *Modernism and Democracy: Literary Culture, 1900–1930* (Oxford University Press, 2006).

THE CAMBRIDGE COMPANION TO TWENTIETH-CENTURY LITERATURE AND POLITICS

EDITED BY

CHRISTOS HADJIYIANNIS

University of Cyprus

RACHEL POTTER

University of East Anglia

CAMBRIDGE
UNIVERSITY PRESS

CAMBRIDGE
UNIVERSITY PRESS

University Printing House, Cambridge CB2 8BS, United Kingdom

One Liberty Plaza, 20th Floor, New York, NY 10006, USA

477 Williamstown Road, Port Melbourne, VIC 3207, Australia

314–321, 3rd Floor, Plot 3, Splendor Forum, Jasola District Centre, New Delhi – 110025, India

103 Penang Road, #05–06/07, Visioncrest Commercial, Singapore 238467

Cambridge University Press is part of the University of Cambridge.

It furthers the University's mission by disseminating knowledge in the pursuit of education, learning, and research at the highest international levels of excellence.

www.cambridge.org
Information on this title: www.cambridge.org/9781108840521
DOI: 10.1017/9781108886284

© Cambridge University Press 2023

First published 2023

A catalogue record for this publication is available from the British Library.

ISBN 978–1–108–84052–1 Hardback
ISBN 978–1–108–81419–5 Paperback

Contents

v

Figures

Notes on the Contributors

GERSHUN AVILEZ is Professor of English and Director of Graduate Studies at the University of Maryland, College Park. He is a cultural studies scholar specialising in contemporary African American and Black Diasporic literatures and visual cultures. Much of his scholarship explores gender and sexuality in artistic production. He has published two books: *Radical Aesthetics and Modern Black Nationalism* (University of Illinois Press, 2016) and *Black Queer Freedom: Spaces of Injury and Paths of Desire* (University of Illinois Press, 2020). He has written essays on a range of historical and cultural subjects, including the Cold War, segregation narratives, early African American writing, race and terror, social death, queer life, experimental poetry, Black women's writing, the Harlem Renaissance, Black Power gender politics, and the Black Arts Movement.

PETER BOXALL is Professor of English at the University of Sussex. He has written books on Samuel Beckett, on Don DeLillo, and several books on the novel, including *Twenty-First-Century Fiction* (Cambridge University Press, 2013) and *The Value of the Novel* (Cambridge University Press, 2015). His most recent book is *The Prosthetic Imagination: A History of the Novel as Artificial Life* (Cambridge University Press, 2020). He has edited a wide range of work, including a collection on Samuel Beckett's politics entitled *Beckett/Aesthetics/ Politics*; a collection on poetry entitled *Thinking Poetry* (with Peter Nicholls); *1001 Books You Must Read Before You Die*; *The Cambridge Companion to British Fiction, 1980–2018*; and a Faber edition of Beckett's novel, *Malone Dies*. He is also co-editor of volume 7 of *The Oxford History of the Novel in English* (with Bryan Cheyette), editor of the book series 'Cambridge Studies in Twenty-First-Century Literature and Culture', and editor of the UK journal *Textual Practice*. He is currently writing a book about the twentieth-century novel and the current crises in Western culture, entitled *Fictions of the West*.

RACHELE DINI is Senior Lecturer in English and American Literature at the University of Roehampton, where she works on post-1945 US literature and culture. She is the author of *Consumerism, Waste, and Re-Use in Twentieth-Century Fiction: Legacies of the Avant-Garde* (Palgrave Macmillan, 2016) and *'All-Electric' Narratives: Time-Saving Appliances and Domesticity in American Literature, 1945–2020* (Bloomsbury, 2021), and the editor of *Queer Trash and Feminist Excretions: New Directions in Literary and Cultural Waste Studies* (SUNY Press, 2022). She is also the founder of the International Literary Waste Studies Network. Her current projects include a study of the politics of postmillennial nostalgia for mid-century interior design, and a British Academy and Leverhulme funded study, 'Cleaning Through Crisis: Political Upheaval and the Advertising of Domestic Hygiene, 1963–2023', about the politics of domestic cleaning product ads.

ALISON DONNELL is Professor of Modern Literatures in English and Head of the School of Literature, Drama, and Creative Writing at the University of East Anglia. She has published widely on Caribbean, diasporic, and Black British writings, focusing specifically on challenging orthodox literary histories and on recovering women's voices. She is the General Editor of the three-volume publication *Caribbean Literature in Transition, 1800–2015* (Cambridge University Press, 2020). Her latest book, *Creolized Sexualities: Undoing Heteronormativity in the Literary Imagination of the Anglo-Caribbean*, appeared in the Critical Caribbean Studies series (Rutgers University Press, 2021). She is also leading a major research project funded by the Leverhulme Trust: 'Caribbean Literary Heritage: Recovering the Lost Past and Safeguarding the Future' (www.caribbeanliteraryheritage .com).

CHARLES FERRALL is Associate Professor in the School of English, Film, Theatre, Media Studies, and Art History at Te Herenga Waka Victoria University of Wellington, New Zealand. He is the author of *Modernist Writing and Reactionary Politics* (Cambridge University Press, 2001) and, with Dougal McNeill, of *Writing the 1926 General Strike: Literature, Culture, Politics* (Cambridge University Press, 2015), and editor of *British Literature in Transition, 1920–1940* (Cambridge University Press, 2018).

CHRISTOS HADJIYIANNIS is Research Fellow at the Centre for Medieval Arts & Rituals at the University of Cyprus and Visiting Research Fellow at the Institute of English Studies in London. He is the author of *Conservative Modernists: Literature and Tory Politics in Britain, 1900–1920* (Cambridge University Press, 2018). He has published widely on modernist art and literature. His current project, hosted by the Centre for Medieval Arts & Rituals at the University of Cyprus, explores the afterlives of Byzantium in Anglophone modernism.

CLARA JONES is a Senior Lecturer in Modern Literature at King's College London. She is the author of *Virginia Woolf: Ambivalent Activist* (Edinburgh University Press, 2016), a book which explores Woolf's involvement with organisations including the People's Suffrage Federation and the Women's Co-operative Guild. Her new project focuses on the politics of interwar women writers and activists such as Sylvia Townsend Warner, Amabel Williams-Ellis, and Ellen Wilkinson.

DONNA V. JONES is an Associate Professor in the Department of English at the University of California, Berkeley. She is the author of *The Racial Discourses of Life Philosophy: Négritude, Vitalism, and Modernity* (Columbia University Press, 2010).

BÁRBARA GALLEGO LARRARTE is a Postdoctoral Visiting Research Fellow at the Institute of English Studies, University of London. Her research interests fall broadly within the interwar period, with a special focus on the ideological impact of the Spanish Civil War. In 2019, she completed a PhD at Wolfson College, Oxford, on T. S. Eliot, Virginia Woolf, E. M. Forster, and their networks. She is currently working on a monograph about intergenerational dynamics in the 1930s based on this doctoral work.

DOUGAL MCNEILL is Senior Lecturer in the School of English, Film, Theatre, Media Studies, and Art History, Te Herenga Waka Victoria University of Wellington. He is the author, with Charles Ferrall, of *Writing the 1926 General Strike: Literature, Culture, Politics* (Cambridge University Press, 2015).

EMER NOLAN is Professor of English at Maynooth University, Ireland. She is author of works on Irish literature and culture, including *James Joyce and Nationalism* (Routledge, 1995); *Catholic Emancipations: Irish Fiction from Thomas Moore to James Joyce*

(Syracuse University Press, 2007); and *Five Irish Women: The Second Republic, 1960–2016* (Manchester University Press, 2019).

RACHEL POTTER is Professor of Modern Literature at the University of East Anglia. She has written extensively on modernist literature and culture. More recently, her work has focused on literature and censorship, free expression, and writers' organisations, most notably International PEN. She is currently the Principal Investigator of a four-year AHRC-funded project on free expression and writers' organisations. Her books include *Modernism and Democracy: Literary Culture, 1900–1930* (Oxford University Press, 2006); *The Edinburgh Guide to Modernist Literature* (Edinburgh University Press, 2012); and *Obscene Modernism: Literary Censorship and Experiment, 1900–1940* (Oxford University Press, 2013).

ANINDYA RAYCHAUDHURI is Senior Lecturer in English at the University of St Andrews. He is the author of two monographs: *Homemaking: Radical Nostalgia and the Construction of a South Asian Diaspora* (Rowman & Littlefield, 2018) and *Narrating South Asian Partition: Oral History, Literature, Cinema* (Oxford University Press, 2019). In 2016, he was named one of the BBC/AHRC New Generation Thinkers. His research interests include critical theory and Marxism, postcolonial studies, and memory studies.

CORINNE SANDWITH is Professor of English at the University of Pretoria, South Africa and is the author of *World of Letters: Reading Communities and Cultural Debates in Early Apartheid South Africa* (University of KwaZulu-Natal Press, 2014) and, with M. J. Daymond, editor of *Africa South: Viewpoints, 1956–1961* (University of KwaZulu-Natal Press, 2011). Her research interests include African print and reading cultures and the history of dissident reading and cultural debate in early apartheid South Africa. Her recent work focuses on early twentieth-century Black South African newspapers as an index of Black intellectual life. Particular focus areas include the life and form of the newspaper, counter-political framings, aesthetic debates, and the circulation and citation of texts across disparate reading contexts.

JOS SMITH is Lecturer in Contemporary Literature at the University of East Anglia. His research explores the relationship between literature and the environmental movement through cultural history and is informed by environmental criticism, literary and cultural geographies, postcolonial ecocriticism, and archipelagic criticism. He is the author of *The New Nature Writing: Rethinking the Literature of Place* (Bloomsbury, 2017) and co-editor with Nicholas Allen and Nick Groom of *Coastal Works: Literatures of the Atlantic Edge* (Oxford University Press, 2017).

MATTHEW TAUNTON is Associate Professor of Literature at the University of East Anglia. Alongside numerous articles and chapters, mostly about modern literature and politics, he is the author of *Fictions of the City: Class, Culture and Mass Housing in London and Paris* (Palgrave Macmillan, 2009) and *Red Britain: The Russian Revolution in Mid-Century Culture* (Oxford University Press, 2019). With Benjamin Kohlmann, he is co-editor of *A History of 1930s British Literature* (Cambridge University Press, 2009), *The People: Belonging, Exclusion and Democracy* (Cambridge University Press, forthcoming), and of a special issue of *Literature & History* called *Literatures of Anti-Communism* (2015). He is also co-editor, with Rachel Potter, of *The British Novel of Ideas: George Eliot to Zadie Smith* (Cambridge University Press, forthcoming). He is Senior Deputy Editor of *Critical Quarterly*.

CHRISTINA TURNER is a Social Sciences and Humanities Research Council Postdoctoral Fellow in English, Theatre, Film, and Media at the University of Manitoba, and an honorary Grant Notley Memorial Postdoctoral Fellow in English and Film Studies at the University of Alberta. She holds a PhD in English from the University of Toronto, where her doctoral research analysed how contemporary works of Indigenous literature interrogate the legal recognition of Indigenous rights in Canada's 1982 Constitution Act. Her next research project examines how works of Anishinaabeg, Cree, and Métis speculative fiction operate as crucial sites for reimagining core principles of Indigenous law. She is the co-editor with Sophia Reuss of *Everything on (the) Line*, an essay collection about progressive social movements in recent Canadian history (Between the Lines, 2021) and has essays published and forthcoming in *Canadian Literature, Law and Literature*, and *Studies in American Indian Literatures*. She is a white settler of English and Norwegian heritage who was born in Toronto, where she currently lives with her husband.

RYAN WEBERLING is a Contingent Lecturer in English Literature at Boston University. His book project, 'Constituting Decadence: Anglophone Modernist Fiction and the Politics of Federation', explores how disruptions and innovations in narrative form mediated the changing constitutional form of states across the Anglophone world, as federalism became both a national norm and an international ideal. His essays and reviews have appeared in the *Modernist Archives Publishing Project* (MAPP), *Modern Fiction Studies*, and *The Virginia Woolf Miscellany*.

JO WINNING is Professor of Modern Literature and Critical Theory in the Department of English, Theatre, and Creative Writing at Birkbeck, University of London. She has written extensively on gender, sexuality, and modern literature, from early twentieth-century modernisms through to contemporary twenty-first-century literatures in English. She is currently working on the 'Dorothy Richardson Scholarly Editions Project', producing a new critical edition of Richardson's modernist canonical series, *Pilgrimage* (Oxford University Press, 2021).

Acknowledgements

For their advice and support, we'd like to thank the late, great Laura Marcus, Rebecca Beasley, Hermione Lee, Ato Quayson, Jarad Zimbler, Edward Doegar, and Lina Protopapa. Thanks also to Edgar Mendez at Cambridge University Press and, of course, Ray Ryan, whose idea this book was and without whose input and energy it simply wouldn't have happened. We thank Rose Bell for her incredibly attentive copyediting, and Ann Barrett for her expert indexing skills. We would like to acknowledge Martha Rosler, who has generously granted us rights to use two of her images, 'Red Stripe Kitchen' and 'Cleaning the Drapes', from *House Beautiful: Bringing the War Home* (1967–72) (originals in colour and reproduced here – in Chapter 14 – in black and white). Our deepest gratitude is to our contributors; we thank them for their diligence, patience, and collaborative spirit.

Chronology

Any book about literature and politics will tell different stories and histories – stories and histories that no chronological table could ever capture. In the chronology below, we have flagged the key political events referenced in the eighteen chapters that make up this book, events that are as interrelated as they are singular, sensitive to time and place, and which impacted (and still do) on different people at different times and places differently.

1900: First Pan-African Conference organised in London.

1903: Women's Social and Political Union (WSPU) founded by Emmeline Pankhurst and others in Manchester, UK to campaign for women's right to vote.

1905: The Liberal Henry Campbell-Bannerman replaces the Conservative Arthur Balfour as Prime Minister, forming a minority government. The next year, at the 1906 election, the Liberal Party wins a landslide majority. Twenty-nine Labour MPs are elected.

1908: Women Writers' Suffrage League (WWSL) established by Cicely Hamilton and Bessie Hatton.

1909–11: After the House of Lords in the UK sends back David Lloyd George's 'People's Budget', the Liberals pass a Parliament Act removing the Lords' power to veto money bills. Many Tories see this as an attack on the constitution.

1914–18: First World War.

1914: No-Conscription Fellowship (NCF), the main pacifist organisation in Britain during the war, is founded in November by Clifford Allen and Fenner Brockway. A year later in Geneva, the International Committee of Women for Permanent Peace is formed.

1915: In Georgia, US, William Joseph Simmons founds the second Ku Klux Klan.

1916: Easter Rising in Ireland. Rebels in Dublin hold out against the British forces for six days.

1917: The Balfour Declaration promises to establish a Jewish 'national home' in Palestine.

1917: Bolshevik Revolution in Russia.

1918: Representation of the People Act gives the vote to women (over thirty) in Great Britain and Ireland for the first time.

1919: Treaty of Versailles marks the formal end of the First World War.

1919–1922: Alceste de Ambris and Filippo Marinetti publish *The Manifesto of the Italian Fasces of Combat*. Mussolini becomes Prime Minister of Italy in October 1922.

1920: Foundation of the League of Nations. In the UK, the Communist Party of Great Britain is founded in London in July.

1921: Anglo-Irish Treaty of 1921 concludes the Irish War of Independence, mostly conducted through a guerrilla-style campaign in the countryside. Government of Ireland Act partitions the country into the Irish Free State in the south and the six-county territory of Northern Ireland in Ulster.

1922: The League of Nations agrees Britain's mandate of Palestine.

1924: First Labour government in UK elected under Ramsay MacDonald.

1926: General Strike in the UK fails to force government to act to prevent wage reduction amid worsening conditions for coalminers.

1928: Representation of the People Act gives suffrage to women aged twenty-one and over.

1932: British Union of Fascists formed by Oswald Mosley.

1933: In January, Adolf Hitler becomes Chancellor of Germany.

1934: The Bolsheviks centralise control of literature within the Union of Soviet Writers.

1934–8: Wave of strikes and social unrest in West Indian islands.

1935: All-India Progressive Writers' Association (AIPWA) founded at the Nanking Restaurant in London. AIPWA's manifesto attacks bourgeois modernism and signals a commitment to socialist realism. In India, the British Parliament imposes a colonial constitution on India that emerged out of the all–white Simon Commission.

1936–9: Spanish Civil War.

1937: International African Service Bureau founded in London to address issues relating to the African diaspora.

1939–45: Second World War.

1941: Foundation of the Southern Rhodesia Communist Party.

1945: George Orwell coins the term 'Cold War' to describe the chilling global effects of the atomic bomb. The following year, Winston

Churchill speaks of a metaphorical 'Iron Curtain' in Europe that extends from 'Stettin in the Baltic to Trieste in the Adriatic'.

1947: The post-war breakup of the British Empire begins. The India Independence Act of 1947 partitions British India into two independent Dominions: India and Pakistan. In the same year, the British partition Palestine. In the US, the CIA takes control of the international cultural programme from 1947, ploughing significant government funds into the arts.

1948: The National Party government in South Africa introduces apartheid, a political-economic system of institutionalised racial discrimination. The same year, the Universal Declaration of Human Rights is proclaimed by the United Nations in Paris.

1950: Congress for Cultural Freedom (CCF) launched at a 1950 Berlin Congress of artists and intellectuals from across the anti-Communist West.

1950–3: Over 1,500 political prisoners are interned in Recsk, a forced labour camp in Hungary.

1955: Sudan declares independence.

1956: Suez crisis. Hungarian revolt suppressed by the Soviets and Soviet invasion of Hungary. In Venice, at the European Cultural Association conference, Soviet and Western European intellectuals meet for the first time since Stalin's death.

1957: The Food and Drug Administration (FDA) in the US approves the use of the pill to 'regulate menstruation' for the first time; three years later, in 1960, Enovid, one type of the pill, is approved as an oral contraceptive.

1958: Establishment of short-lived West Indies Federation by the British in response to Caribbean nations demanding independence. The Federation would fall apart after Jamaica would withdraw. Jamaica becomes independent in 1962, as does Trinidad and Tobago. Barbados gains its independence in 1966; the Bahamas in 1973; Grenada in 1974; Dominica in 1978; St Lucia and St Vincent and the Grenadines in 1979; Antigua and Barbuda in 1981; and St Kitts and Nevis in 1983.

1958–62: Anti-nuclear weapons demonstrations – the Aldermaston Marches – take place in the UK.

1960: France agrees to Ivory Coast becoming independent.

1961: Erection of Berlin Wall.

1962: Rachel Carson publishes *Silent Spring*, issuing a dire warning about the dangers of synthetic agricultural pesticides.

1963: Kenyan independence. In the US, Martin Luther King Jr. delivers his 'I Have a Dream' speech during the March on Washington for Jobs and Freedom. A year later, the Civil Rights Act of 1964 outlaws discrimination based on race, colour, religion, sex, and national origin. Jim Crow laws do not go away, though. Selma to Montgomery marches follow in 1965.

1963: US Equal Pay Act prohibits unequal pay between men and women.

1964: US Civil Rights Act outlaws discrimination on the basis of 'race, color, religion, sex, national origin'.

1964: Malcolm X is assassinated.

1965: UK Race Relations Act prohibits discrimination on the grounds of 'colour, race, or ethnic or national origins' in public places.

1965: First US active combat troops arrive in Vietnam; by 1969 there are more than half a million US military personnel stationed in Vietnam. US combat troops would withdraw by 1973.

1966–67: Black Panther Party founded in Oakland, California; a year later, Stokely Carmichael and Charles V. Hamilton's volume *Black Power* (1967) defines Black Power nationalism in terms of a new consciousness rooted in 'a sense of peoplehood'.

1967: Abortion legalised in UK and homosexual acts between consenting adults are decriminalised. In the US, a combination of mass casualties in Vietnam and the mounting power of the Civil Rights struggle lead to the clear emergence of the American New Left as a mass movement.

1968: Martin Luther King Jr. is assassinated.

1968: US Civil Rights Act amends and updates the 1964 Act to incorporate the Indian Civil Rights Act, which applies to Native American tribes in the US.

1969: Police in New York storm the Stonewall Inn, a gay bar in Greenwich Village.

1968–9: Non-violent protest marches against sectarian discrimination in housing and local government in Ireland are set upon by organised Protestant mobs and by the police. In 1969, in response to widespread disorder in Belfast and Derry, the British army is sent into Northern Ireland. Three years later, on 'Bloody Sunday', thirteen unarmed Catholics at a protest in Derry are shot dead by soldiers from the Parachute Regiment. A reorganised 'Provisional IRA' emerges more emphatically with the initial priority of defending Catholic areas from attack.

1970: UK Equal Pay Act prohibits unequal treatment between men and women in terms of pay and employment.

1970: Senator Gaylord Nelson in the US organises the first Earth Day on 22 April. Friends of the Earth had been established a year earlier by David Brower in San Francisco. A year later, in 1971, Greenpeace is set up by a group of people including Irving and Dorothy Stowe, initially in opposition to the American testing of nuclear weapons underground on the island of Amchitka at the north-western tip of Alaska.

1971: The US withdraws from the Bretton Woods agreement that kept the US dollar pinned to a notional gold standard. Capital is freed from any of the regulatory frameworks imposed upon it by the state.

1972: UN Conference on the Human Environment.

1975: UK Sex Discrimination Act protects men and women from discrimination on the grounds of sex or marital status in employment, education, the provision of goods, and services.

1976: UK Race Relations Act prohibits discrimination on the grounds of 'colour, race, nationality or ethnic or national origin' in employment, the provision of goods and services, education, and public functions. That same year, the UK Commission for Racial Equality is established to oversee the Race Relations Act.

1978: Scottish and Welsh Devolution Acts.

1979: Margaret Thatcher is elected Prime Minister in the UK. Her premiership, lasting until 1990, will be characterised by support for freedom of economic competition and privatisation, and opposition to trade unionism and workers' rights.

1981: In the face of Thatcher's refusal to negotiate, ten IRA members die on hunger strike in prison for the right to be treated as political prisoners.

1981: The US Centers for Disease Control and Prevention (CDC) publishes for the first time a report mentioning the disease AIDS. Start of the AIDS epidemic in the West.

1984–5: Miners' strike in the UK: the major industrial action which defined the increasing class divisions in Thatcher's Britain.

1985: Mikhail Gorbachev begins his *perestroika* reforms.

1986: Chernobyl nuclear disaster.

1988: In an amendment to the Local Government Act 1986, Thatcher's Conservative government in the UK introduces Section 28, setting a prohibition upon the 'teaching' of homosexuality in schools.

1989: Fall of the Berlin Wall.

1990: In February, Nelson Mandela is released from prison and, over the next two years, apartheid is dismantled. That same year, Ken Saro-Wiwa founds the Movement for the Survival of Ogoni People (MOSOP) in Nigeria.

1991: Gulf War and collapse of the Soviet Union.

1992: Bill Clinton is elected President of the United States.

1995: UK Disability Discrimination Act makes it unlawful to discriminate against people in respect of their disabilities in relation to employment, the provision of goods and services, education, and transport.

1998: Good Friday Agreement signed by the UK and Ireland, bringing an end to most of the violence of the Troubles.

2001: 11 September attacks in the US. George W. Bush declares 'war on terror'. The US, joined by its allies, invades Afghanistan.

Literature and *Politics*

Christos Hadjiyiannis and Rachel Potter

The history of literature has long been viewed in its relationship to politics. But while neither literature nor politics are easy to define or demarcate, there has also never been a consensus about what it is that connects them. Different approaches to the 'and' in this Companion's title produce distinct understandings of both literature and politics, and different views on what unites and what separates them. The eighteen essays that make up this volume tell a story of the diverse ways in which literature and politics over the twentieth century coincided, overlapped, and clashed: a story of the *and* that connects them and which also keeps them apart.

***

For much of the century, discussions about politics and literature centred around that century's dominant literary aesthetic: modernism. One of modernism's key legacies was to test whether literature's politics lay in its autonomous forms or thematic engagements with history. For Georg Lukács, the formal fragmentations and subjectivism of modernist literature constituted a retreat from political engagement and interpretation.[1] Ernst Bloch countered that modernist fragmentation was a response to the discontinuous nature of reality, and Theodor Adorno insisted that the formal properties of modernist literature expose 'whatever is veiled', as he put it, 'by the empirical form assumed by reality', an uncovering that is only possible through 'art's own autonomous status'.[2] Lionel Trilling, whose liberal politics was distinct from this Marxist debate, also argued that, despite the illiberal political views of many modernist writers, their writing constituted the fullest expression of a liberal imagination he connected to 'variousness, possibility, complexity and difficulty'.[3]

Shifting the debate, in her 1973 Foreword to *Sula*, Toni Morrison registered the ongoing force of these various ways of seeing literature's politics as disconnected from political commitment. While the conventional wisdom had been (still is?) that 'political fiction is not art', Morrison, countering this assumption, made clear that 'since my sensibility was highly political *and* passionately aesthetic, it would unapologetically inform the work I did'.[4] Though this Companion gives space to several different takes on literature *and* politics, the essays in it all take their cue from Morrison's unapologetic political-and-literary sensibility. Being the works of individuals who have been politically active, and who channelled their politics through their writing, the texts considered in this book are all political in specific and direct ways. This is not to say that these writers did not question literature's relationship to politics, nor that they didn't quiz literature's ability to affect politics. It is rather to say that the twentieth-century texts considered in this volume engage with politics openly, obviously, and directly: with ideas and movements aiming at influencing the way a country or a people is governed, and with distinct political ideologies. Liberalism, Communism, fascism, suffragism, pacifism, federalism, different forms of nationalism, civil rights, women's rights, sexual rights, Indigenous rights, environmentalism, neoliberalism: twentieth-century authors wrote in direct response to political movements, ideas, events, and campaigns, and many were activists for or against them.

***

To view literature's relationship to politics in this fashion is to question some dominant twentieth- and twenty-first-century critical paradigms. Much twentieth-century Marxist and deconstructive criticism has schooled us to find the politics of literature not in its acknowledged commitments, but, as in Adorno, as lying deep within its unconsciously ideological structures and forms. Adorno emphasised the condition of alienation in the administered world of late modernity and insisted that the novel form must register what he called 'everyday estrangement'. In the context of what he described as a 'society in which human beings have been torn from one another and from themselves', the idea that a novel should have 'any message with ideological content', or that a narrator should write as though they were 'directly capable of something', is 'ideological in itself'.[5] The critic's task, for Adorno and for those influenced by his work, was to seek literature's politics not in its direct messages but in its autonomy from ideology, its buried ideological commitments and presuppositions. Fredric Jameson, in his foundational work on the political 'unconscious', sought to demystify and unmask the ideological narratives and forms of literary objects – what he described as restoring to the 'surface of the text the repressed and buried reality' of the fundamental history of class struggle.[6]

Adorno's theory of the autonomous art object was also a theory of history: bourgeois art separated from empirical society at the very moment that it became powerless to exert political or social agency. The agentless nature of literature within the totalising administered worlds of late modernity has become a truism for many of the dominant twentieth-century theories of power and knowledge. Michel Foucault sees literary texts as part of the discursive and institutional formations of disciplinary and biopolitical power.[7] Giorgio Agamben, in his extension of Foucault's work, reads literary texts with reference to their position within a modernity of the state of exception and the politicisation of 'bare life', politically construed as a continuum involving totalitarianism, the Nazi death camps, and liberal democracy.[8]

These very different constructions of literature's relationship to politics would seem nevertheless to share what have been called 'symptomatic' or 'paranoid' interpretative approaches to and readings of literary texts. But what if we were to attend to literature's political surfaces instead? And what if we saw politics as less monolithic than Jameson's 'fundamental history' of class struggle or Agamben's modernity that encompasses totalitarianism and liberal democracy? The recent critical turn to what has been called 'post-critique', which has questioned the surface-depth model of knowledge underpinning 'paranoid' or 'symptomatic' interpretations to attend to literary surfaces, carries significant implications for the study of literature and politics, for what constitutes politics, how literature might be political, and where its politics might be seen to take place.

Honing in on the philosophy and proceduralism of liberal theory, for instance, allows Amanda Anderson to trace what she calls an aesthetics of 'bleak liberalism', a liberal tradition entailing 'the dedication to argument, debate, and deliberative processes of legitimation and justification'. For Anderson, these commitments constitute a 'tradition of liberal aesthetics' distinct from, for example, socialist aesthetics, which serves to open up the form and content of works by Richard Wright, Lionel Trilling, Doris Lessing, and others.[9] Elizabeth Anker and Rita Felski, meanwhile, question the assumption that a political commitment to 'leftist resistance' resides in critique as a method of reading, following Bruno Latour in arguing that a 'hermeneutics of suspicion has become the preferred weapon of conservative thinkers and conspiracy theorists alike'. As they put it, 'the shift away from suspicion may conceivably inspire a more nuanced vision of how political change comes about'.[10]

As in the works by Anderson and Anker and Felski, in this book politics is also construed less as a totalising ideological structure: more an activism energised by distinct political philosophies and with different aims. Put differently, the literary politics discussed in this Companion involves attending to the collective forms of the political party, organisation, or manifesto – to literature's constructive 'cultural agency', in the sense of the term given to it by Doris Sommer – and, specifically, to a collective activism defined by the mobilisation of literature as a form of political activism.[11] Politics, always a fiddly term, is thereby identified as much with ideas as with government process and political parties, with new nations, and with non-governmental organisations and rights activism.

Twentieth-century writers have been directly involved in both govern-mental and non-governmental political organisations, whether the British Liberal, Conservative, or Labour parties, or through organisations such as the Fabians, the British and American Communist parties, the suffragettes, Black civil rights movements, anti-colonial nationalist parties and organ-isations, the women's and LGBTQ+ rights movements, ecological organ-isations, and many more. The essays that follow show that such commitments have not been incidental to the content and form of literary texts, and the understanding of what literary knowledge is or should be. Governmental and non-governmental political activism tends to entail the argument, debate, and deliberative processes identified by Anderson, and involves both aspirational beliefs and a set of methods, procedures, and actions. These methods presuppose and enact theories of historical change, literary agency and collective activism, and sometimes democratic account-ability, normative ethics, and free speech. The literary text entails a dialogue between past and present in which political commitments and activities fuel literary meaning. In just the same way, twentieth-century writers and texts covered in this volume maintained a critical distance towards politics and political literature alike, questioning literature's polit-ical potential.

✳✳✳

The scope and energy of writers' political commitments also has a history, and this Companion acknowledges this history in its structure and focus. The story it tells – inevitably selective as it may be – is about literature's political commitments in which the location of political activism itself also shifts ground. The first section attends to the politics of governance, political parties, and parliamentary process. The writers focused on in this part of the book were engaged with both the twentieth century's 'big' political ideas – liberalism, fascism, Communism – and with political party struggles to take control of governmental power. The initial focus is on European-based political movements and ideas as they played out in Britain. As we move through the twentieth century, however, the geographical focus shifts outwards beyond Britain and Europe to consider anti-colonial political activism, anti-racist Black politics, the Cold War, Afropolitanism, and eco-cosmopolitanism. And so the second section shifts ground, geographically and politically, to consider politics in its global dimensions. Here politics involves the international struggles leading to the end of colonialism, the birth of independent nations, and the Cold War, *and* the political ideas of anti-colonial nationalism, federalism, cultural nationalism, and the state-sponsored literature of the cultural cold war. The third part of the book alters focus again, zooming in on grassroots political activism with a transnational reach, and often entailing the assertion of rights. While the end of the Cold War brought about what David Scott calls the 'reengineering of empire, with its distinctive self-congratulatory discourse of transitional justice and human rights', this third and final section attends to the grassroots mobilisation and group activism of, amongst other things, environmentalism, women's rights, sexual rights, and Indigenous rights.[12] Our concluding chapter on neoliberalism is interested in the late twentieth century's dominant political formation of governance, taking us back, as almost in a circle, to the book's first chapter on liberalism.

***

The book begins in Edwardian England at the opening of the century and at the intersection of Edwardian liberalism and early twentieth-century literary modernism. Christos Hadjiyiannis considers how E. M. Forster, Ford Madox Ford, T. E. Hulme, and T. S. Eliot engaged in their critical and creative works with Edwardian liberalism: with the reformist policies of the Liberal Party (which came to power in 1906), with the New Liberal ideas on which these policies were based, but also and more broadly with the much older philosophical and political outlook of liberalism. The works and theories of these early modernists were written in direct response to liberal ideas old and new, with even anti-liberal 'classical' modernists such as Hulme and Eliot embracing fundamental liberal values (while of course rejecting many others). As Hadjiyiannis shows, much as with many other contradictory facets of literary modernism, the relationship of modernism to liberalism was close, uneasy, and, certainly, foundational.

In this sense, the relationship of modernism to liberalism was not unlike its relationship to Communism. Matthew Taunton makes a strong case for a much more nuanced understanding of the relationship between

Communism and twentieth-century literature than is still sometimes put forward. Communist writing has been traditionally associated with socialist realism, the officially sanctioned aesthetic approach of Communism, which Adorno later dismissed as art that concedes that the world is bad and which in turn uses this judgement as a form of consolation, Adorno's point being that socialist realism allows the writer to rest easy in the knowledge that reality has been grasped in the correct way. Taking works by Sylvia Townsend Warner, Mulk Raj Anand, and Lewis Grassic Gibbon as his case studies, Taunton reveals committed Communist writers to have used the novel form to test the relationship between ideology and reality, without, however, either falling back on the consoling judgement that the world is bad or assuming that the real can be unproblematically grasped once the heroic Marxist has cut through the fog of ideology. As Taunton puts it, in the works of these Communists, 'the false certainties of ideological enchantment give way . . . to complexity, contradiction, and debate'.

The case is much different when it comes to fascism. Charles Ferrall and Dougal Mcneill's opening statement – that 'Fascism produced no significant literature' – might seem provocative to some, but, as Ferrall and McNeill explain, while fascism found uses for cinema, the visual arts, architecture, and music, it left no memorable literary record. That's not to say that fascism did not impact literature, for it generated a complex culture of opposition and engaged work, including by women writers who, as is so often and still sadly the case, have not received due scholarly attention. Considering a current of anti-fascist circulating journals, newsletters, tensely aligned writers, and writers' organisations, Ferrall and McNeill show the different and fascinating ways in which anti-fascist writers – from W. H. Auden and Virginia Woolf to Naomi Mitchison, Ellen Wilkinson, Langston Hughes, Winifred Holtby, Katharine Burdekin ('Murray Constantine'), and Dorothy Livesay – channelled politics in and through writing.

Just as fascism spawned a complex set of literary responses, so suffrage campaigns in the early twentieth century generated writing that, as Clara Jones argues in her chapter on suffragism, was in its quantity and generic diversity unprecedented. Women activists were novelists, poets, playwrights, letter, speech, and pamphlet writers: 'The written word', as Jones puts it, 'was an integral political tool for those fighting for the vote.' Reflecting on the history of the twentieth-century suffrage movement, the work of the Women Writers' Suffrage League (WWSL) and of the Women's Co-operative Guild, and bringing in suffragettes such as Elizabeth Robins, Virginia Woolf (then Stephen), Selina Cooper, and

Margaret Llewelyn Davies, Jones details how the suffrage movement in Britain was ridden with disagreements and conflicts. These tensions and oppositions are captured neatly in Constance Maud's 1911 novel, *No Surrender*, a campaigning work that, however, never relinquishes awareness of the limitations of the campaign's political imagination. Yet again, the relationship between literature and politics is revealed as unstraightforward.

Turning to another social movement that took to the street and to the text, Bárbara Gallego Larrarte considers pacifism: not as writing and politics complementary or responsive to war, but as politics and writing *about* peace. The advent of the twentieth century saw the rise of widespread peace movements that reconceived pacifism from a moral, faith-based position into a political and humanitarian stance, culminating in the Universal Declaration of Human Rights in 1948. Pacifist writing and politics as they developed out of the First World War and the Spanish Civil War, by writers and activists like Wilfred Owen, Sylvia Pankhurst, Bertrand Russell, John Maynard Keynes, Beverly Nichols, A. A. Milne, Vera Brittain, Canon Dick Sheppard, Julian Bell, Aldous Huxley, Cecil Day Lewis, George Orwell, and Stephen Spender, campaigned for peace as an aspiration and an ideal. Though pacifism is in many ways always bound to fail – and it failed by not preventing the Second World War – it did succeed in converting an individualist, faith-based belief into a political position that legitimised civic activism and promoted social change. Its vital democratic legacy has influenced landmark struggles, from the American Civil Rights movement in the 1960s to anti-nuclear demonstrations in the 1970s, to present-day climate activism and Black Lives Matter protests. As Gallego Larrarte shows, to study peace writing in the first half of the twentieth century is to engage with texts that have radically shaped what it means to be a democratic citizen today.

Perhaps no other event disturbed the possibility for balance in the twentieth century as much as partition, which, as Anindya Raychaudhuri shows, has been the century's most characteristic political instrument during transition from colonial rule to independence. Raychaudhuri takes issue with the way partition studies has been made part of regional studies. Pushing instead for a more macro, more comparative approach, Raychaudhuri brings into focus Bapsi Sidhwa's *Ice-Candy-Man*, Amitav Ghosh's *The Shadow Lines*, Saadat Hasan Manto's short story 'Toba Tek Singh', and Auden's poem 'Partition', to reveal partition as both an event with a specific set of historical and geographical contexts and a pattern repeated across time and space. Highlighting different ways in which partition literature channels and upholds trauma and grief, Raychaudhuri calls for a literature and a scholarship of partition that move beyond simply responding to the politics of partition, and which will instead help to create a newly imagined politics that can combine trauma and agency: a politics 'that makes space for and respects the almost unimaginable grief that many suffered, but which does not allow them to be defined entirely by their grief'.

One of the systems of political organisation that spread in response to partitions – and in the post-Second World War era more broadly – was federalism. In different and often competing versions, federalism guided political reforms in the British and French empires, the Soviet Union, international organisations such as the United Nations, and in a host of African and Asian nations during decolonisation. To consider the way literature and federalist politics overlapped, Ryan Weberling brings into view the federalist views of Virginia Woolf, Gertrude Stein, Wyndham Lewis, Evelyn Waugh, George Orwell, W. H. Auden, and Salman Rushdie. The federal formula, Weberling shows, involves a balance between homogeneity and variety, between centralisation and decentralisation. Taking Rushdie's 1981 novel, *Midnight's Children*, as his main case study, Weberling unveils how Rushdie's book fuses individual character with national history to dramatise and critique the influence of 'loose federalism' on Pakistan, Bangladesh, and especially India – now the world's largest federal state.

During this time – the time of the Cold War – authors caught up in it asked important questions about the function of literature, its supposed commitment or autonomy, as well as questions about the relationship between individual and state. As Rachel Potter explains, not only was the Cold War long, dominant, and traumatic, but it also shaped an evolving critical debate about literature's relationship to politics. Potter is interested in the transition from the 'First Cold War', during which the key actors in the conflict – the Soviet Union and the United States – explicitly and covertly funded writers and networks, to the late 1960s grassroots activism of the Civil Rights movement and the New Left. In the era of nuclear paranoia, state secrecy, and concealed state funding for anti-Communist and anti-American propaganda alike, writers and literary texts depicted the political state itself as a totalising and opaque system against which literature pitched its energies. Both Stephen Spender and Doris Lessing engaged with and questioned state-sponsored literary values and forms of the 'cultural cold war' while at the same time experimenting with literary form to capture the psychological responses of paranoia, disintegration, and terror in the face of nuclear conflict. Cold War literature voices the conflict between abstract political ideals and the lived reality of experiences as much as it questions the relationship between literary form and political commitment.

This close but difficult relationship between writers and politics is explored also by Emer Nolan, this time in the context of Irish nationalism. Towards the end of her chapter, which charts the long history of Irish nationalism from the modern Irish separatist republicanism that emerged in the wake of the French Revolution to the financial crash of 2008, and which covers Irish writers from Jonathan Swift to Eavan Boland, Nolan quotes lines from a 1984 work by Seamus Heaney, *Station Island*. Heaney, a poet who explored, to much acclaim, colonial, sectarian, and intra-communal violence in Ireland, has his speaker reassured by the ghost of James Joyce that his artistic vocation need not involve any sense of commitment to an oppressed community: 'That subject people stuff is a cod's game'.[13] As Nolan explains, perhaps only with the loud exception of W. B. Yeats, who found in Ireland symbols and myths that underlie Western culture, modern Irish literature's engagement with politics is also an engagement with failure. For Heaney, as for Joyce and Samuel Beckett before him, political critique and failure of politics are one and the same thing. In fact, as Nolan shows, this overlap stretches back to Swift and Edmund Burke, both of whom questioned the benefits of civility and modernity. We find this estrangement in Oscar Wilde and in Elizabeth Bowen too, and, of course, in Beckett, whose works are pervaded by a sense of catastrophe deeply rooted in Irish history and politics.

The relationship between the state and the self is examined also by GerShun Avilez in his chapter on Black nationalism. Charting the transition from Civil Rights activism to Black Power nationalism following a barrage of disappointments and setbacks for Black rights in the 1960s, Avilez details the ways in which modern Black nationalism envisaged creating a radically different relationship to the state and to the self. Much as for colonial and post-colonial activists, for writers associated with Black nationalism in the US – Amiri Baraka, Stokely Carmichael, Charles V. Hamilton, and others – the struggle for political autonomy could not be separated from the process of 'decolonising the mind'. This is all familiar territory; as Avilez stresses, however, the reappraisal of racial identity demanded by Black nationalism carried an accompanying assessment of gender identity that is part-and-parcel of the nationalist redefinition. Correcting those interpretations of Black nationalism that have written out women, and focusing on Alice Walker's 1973 short story collection, *In Love and Trouble: Stories of Black Women*, Avilez demonstrates how the interface of Black nationalist literature and politics becomes a space for exploring and disrupting gender ideologies, and how in this interface critiques of the state 'become explorations of embodied power differentials and the social construction of masculinity and femininity around such differentials'. In Avilez's reading, Walker's collection exemplifies the artistic engagement of Black nationalist thought insofar as it showcases Black nationalism's transformative potential – and the limits of its social logic.

In her own discussion of the logic of nationalism, but in the Anglophone Caribbean region, Alison Donnell similarly emphasises its complexities and limits, and also the key and understated part played by women in politically engaged literary traditions. The nationalisms that delivered the first wave of independent nation states in the 1960s in the Anglophone Caribbean (known then as the West Indies), Donnell shows, were from the outset plural and interconnected, and literary works were critical to political anticipations towards non-colonial sovereignty. While we tend to focus on canonical fictions of male Windrush novelists who wrote at the mid-century (think George Lamming, Roger Mais, V. S. Naipaul, and Samuel Selvon), Donnell takes us back to the nascent nationalism invoked by a number of literary projects at the turn of the century. Moving chronologically onwards, Donnell considers how Pan-African and Black Atlantic movements shaped the decolonial literary imagination in the early twentieth century, and the crucial role assigned to the writer in the short-lived project of Anglophone regional Federation between 1958 and 1962, which pre-dated the constitution of nation states. Her chapter calls attention to the role that women played in what have been inscribed as male-centred histories, and in politically engaged literary traditions: Caribbean women writers like Una Marson and Vera Bell, Donnell demonstrates, took up the persistent challenge to 'imagine, craft, and cultivate a national consciousness that did not reinscribe hierarchies of belonging'.

While all national identities and nation states are complex, vexed things, they are particularly so in Africa, where, as Donna V. Jones explains, the nation state was from the outset experienced as a mode of disorganisation. The work of nationhood in Africa was 'a shock imposition', Jones shows, and this shock was captured by African writers in and as storytelling of fragmentation, disruption, and the eventual dissociation of the protagonists from the project of national and individual psychological development. African writers' turn to the interior – in novels, epics, or praise-songs – was, in fact, a political gesture, for 'intimate depictions of the profound mental and emotional toll on an individual life under colonialism provide the requisite work towards decolonisation as well'. This was, after all, Chinua Achebe's objection to Joseph Conrad's *Heart of Darkness*: that Conrad is a racist not because he portrays Africa negatively but because he attributes to his African characters a silent impassivity. Bringing into discussion writers from René Maran to Ngũgĩ wa Thiong'o, Ousmane Sembène, Chinua Achebe, and Amos Tutuola, to Ahmadou Kourouma, Maryse Condé, as well as writers associated with the Afropolitan, like Chris Abani, Taiye Selasi, and NoViolet Bulawayo, Jones demonstrates how twentieth-century African literature fought to find a space in which the complex dialectic engagement between the individual psyche and the world could be staged and reimagined.

In apartheid South Africa, political struggles were frequently articulated in cultural terms and forms of political critique that often took shape as arguments about culture and the reading of texts. Corinne Sandwith departs from more conventional histories of the celebrated oppositional texts and figures of the anti-apartheid canon to explore what she calls 'the hidden transcript of cultural-political debate and the dissident public sphere', meaning the debates in and across periodicals, discussion groups, and little magazines. Venues and networks such as *Trek*, *Fighting Talk*, *The Classic* and the *New Classic*, *Staffrider*, *The Voice*, and *The Torch* approached questions of racial 'advancement', cultural exclusion, pre-colonial culture, creolisation, the social function of art, Western academic authority, the figure of the artist, the role of the audience, the reading of literary texts, and the relationship between politics and aesthetic value, through a series of different strategies and ideologies. While in reading communities of the Stalinist Left the literary-cultural text was approached as a site of political emancipation and education, intellectuals associated with *The Torch* (a publication of the Non-European Unity Movement) were more interested in developing an oppositional critical practice and in drawing out the social implications of literary texts – irrespective of their political provenance – as a means of engaging with the contemporary political scene. And while some networks advocated the literature of rampant opposition, others cautioned against didacticism and spectacle. As Sandwith shows, literary criticism in apartheid South Africa was explicitly fashioned as a mode of political engagement, and the practice of literary analysis was the means through which to attack and expose apartheid politics.

In the US, literature was fighting another battle. As Rachele Dini shows, in the aftermath of the Second World War, second-wave feminists like Betty Friedan and Sheila Ballantyne took to dismantling the idea of the 'all-American' housewife and the patriarchal, heteronormative, right-wing forces that proliferated her myth. Just as the frustrated housewife became in the US a topic of national concern, it also became a theme for literature – and the impetus for grassroots activism like the National Organization for Women (NOW), which was founded in 1966 by Friedan and which lobbied for women's rights. Soon, however, writers such as Angela Davis, bell hooks, and Audre Lorde were challenging the movement for its exclusion of Black, working-class, and immigrant women, who had long had to work outside the home and so did not fit the bill of 'housewife' – happy or repressed. Feminist fiction of the 1970s and 1980s serves as a record of this heterogeneity and conflict, capturing experiences of sexual awakening, activism, and failed attempts at liberation, some of which explicitly contradict each other. In the wake of the publication of Judith Butler's revolutionary *Gender Trouble* (1990), feminist literature, more committed than ever before to challenging universalist accounts of history, was no longer interested in presenting women's history through the eyes of the white middle-class housewife. It was now time to see through the eyes of Asian American, Latina, Black, working-class, and queer women, as well as of those who don't identify as women at all. Surveying a great amount of literature and incorporating close readings of Whitney Otto's *How to Make an American Quilt* and Paule Marshall's *Daughters* (both published in 1991), Dini shows how the literature of women's rights undoes formal and political boundaries alike, drawing attention to the role of American literature itself, feminist fiction included, in perpetuating racist oppression, and how women's rights are inextricably connected to the rights of other marginalised groups: non-whites, immigrants, working-class, genderqueer, butch and femme lesbians, and trans men and women.

Literary writing and activism merge once again in the work of writers campaigning for sexual rights in the 1970s and onwards. That it does so is not surprising: for, as Jo Winning explains, writing has always formed the bedrock of sexual rights movements, both in terms of self-expression and self-definition and in terms of community-building and consciousness-raising. Scottish poet Jackie Kay contested the prohibition (in 1986) of the 'teaching' of homosexuality in schools through richly textured, intimate reimaginings of family. Thom Gunn performed through his poetry a political act of representation in the context of the HIV/AIDS epidemic in San Francisco in the 1980s. In Gunn's case, the poet-activist speaks up; and because when it comes to AIDS 'Silence=Death', Winning argues, 'finding a vocabulary through which to narrate the epidemic' is a political act, a way of 'repudiating death' and 'defying cultural silence'. Jeanette Winterson's *Written on the Body* (1992) brings literature and sexual rights together when it employs a neutral narratorial gender identity showing that gender is a fabrication. The novel further correlates sexuality and textuality in its description of writing on/of the body, which turns the lover's body into a book. The high-energy LGBT activism of the 1990s meets literature once more in Sarah Waters's *Tipping the Velvet* (1998). And, finally, *Trans: A Memoir* (2016), by British author Juliet Jacques, and Jordy Rosenberg's *Confessions of the Fox* (2018), demonstrate literature's transformative and political potential for trans self-authoring. There is a 'tight knot', Winning writes, 'between LGBT history, sexual rights, and the role of literature in representing LGBT lives and imagining pasts, presents, and futures beyond their oppression'.

Turning to Canada and to Indigenous rights, Christina Turner shows how, despite the relative gains in Indigenous rights over the last several decades (the 2007 United Nations Declaration on the Rights of Indigenous Peoples finally formalised a set of rights seen as belonging to Indigenous peoples worldwide), Indigenous rights have yet to be substantively recognised, either at the international or national level. For Turner, the gap between formal and substantive recognition stems from the disaggregation of Indigenous rights from Indigenous law. It is this chasm that Indigenous literary activists have sought to flag and emphasise, and literature has again a role to play in this battle as both a medium and a tool. Turner's discussion focuses on the Indigenous legal context of the Mississauga Anishinaabeg. Leanne Betasamosake Simpson's 2013 book, *Islands of Decolonial Love*, illuminates the consequences of the disparity between rights and law and highlights the gravity of ongoing violations of Indigenous law. Simpson uses storytelling, translation notes, and radical experimentation with form to demonstrate how settler legal systems that operate without regard for Indigenous law suppress Indigenous rights – and why Indigenous rights and law must be recognised together. In her poem 'jiibay or aandizooke', Simpson extends a welcoming hand to the settlers, warning them, however, not to stay too long. This welcome is for Turner a 'riposte to the ideology of settler colonialism that positions the settler as the new, permanent inhabitant of Indigenous lands'. To be welcomed as anything other than visitors, settlers have to give up their subject position of white settlers and learn to respect Anishinaabeg law. In Turner's reading, Simpson's work and Indigenous literature more broadly ontologically reorient the position of the settler. The realisation of Indigenous rights requires settler-colonial nation states to obey the Indigenous laws structuring the territories they inhabit rather than merely 'accommodate' them.

Equally inseparable is the relationship of literature and politics when it comes to the literature and politics of nature: in fact, as Jos Smith notes, these emerged together. Environmental politics is not homogeneous, of course, nor had literature always embraced this politics unquestioningly. From the close of the nineteenth century and the foundation in the US of the Sierra Club up to contemporary eco-cosmopolitanism, the literature of nature has encompassed various kinds of values, pursuits, aesthetics, and politics that range from liberal to fascist, conservative to anarchist, and which, as Smith explains, have often overlapped in the most surprising of ways. Smith focuses mostly on New Environmentalism, a political and literary movement that rose in the 1960s in tandem with the anti-Vietnam War protests, the Campaign for Nuclear Disarmament, and the Civil Rights movement. What marks out New Environmentalism from the conservative preoccupation with preservation and national heritage is its international collaborative reorientation. As Smith points out, however, literature of nature has also thought critically about the nature of this global politics. In testing the early optimism of the 'Global North' and in putting emphasis on the politics of poorer and more vulnerable countries, the literature of nature demonstrates how literary work has always had a capacity for agency and an ability to illustrate and provoke changes in thought and action. One of the places in which this politics found its literary voice was in science fiction, a genre that, according to Ursula K. Le Guin, has always sought to challenge conventional ways of thinking. In his reading of Le Guin and of Ernest Callenbach's *Ecotopia* (1975), Smith demonstrates the striking ways in which the literature of science fiction has negotiated environmental rights. Poets too (Smith focuses on the collaborative work between the poet Aka Niviana and the poet and filmmaker Jetñil-Kijiner) have challenged Western nature politics's lack of engagement with postcolonial and Indigenous perspectives. This is what eco-cosmopolitanism is seeking to do: amplify messages spoken in isolation by seeking to speak them together in solidarity and to ground environmental politics in place, not 'nature'.

The ongoing battles for rights are being fought within neoliberalism, a nebulous term that describes the politics that has dominated in most the world over the closing decades of the twentieth century. In his chapter, the last of our book, Peter Boxall investigates literature's response to the pervasive phenomenon of neoliberalism and, more specifically, the response to neoliberalism of the late twentieth-century novel. To understand the novel of the late twentieth century, Boxall argues, one needs to understand relations between surface and depth, between shallowness and intensity. And to understand these relationships, one has to look to the economic, political, and aesthetic effects of the new cultural-economic logic that rose to dominance in the 1970s. Boxall defines neoliberalism as the economic process whereby capital is freed from the constraints of nation states in order to act as its own kind of sovereign agent. There is a clear correlation between this delinking of capital from any monetary base with the delinking of word from world, and text from body, that we see in Muriel Spark's *The Takeover* or Philip Roth's *The Human Stain* (both closely examined by Boxall), as well as in J. G. Ballard's *Crash*, Angela Carter's *The Bloody Chamber*, Salman Rushdie's *Midnight's Children*, Don DeLillo's *White Noise*, Toni Morrison's *Beloved*, and Chris Kraus's *I Love Dick*. All these novels are touched by a close relation between narrative form and the anti-representational logic of neoliberalism. Postmodernist critics produced a theoretical language that sought to account for this anti-representational logic: a language that laid transparent the 'postmodern condition'. Other critics, such as Walter Benn Michaels, lamented the novel's loss of critical power. For Boxall, the onus is on the critic to develop a new way of understanding critique and the novel's contemporary capacity to perform it. The late twentieth-century novel is, according to Boxall, capable of doing exactly that. An example of such a novel is James Kelman's *How Late It Was, How Late* (1994), whose shallowness and loss of traction, Boxall argues, is an affect that requires us to develop a new way of understanding how perception materialises itself; it is a novel that contains within itself the very substance of fiction, which is its own form of seeing, a seeing that adjusts the relations between the subject and the object, between the shallow and the intense.

Notes

1 Georg Lukács, 'Realism in the Balance', in Ernst Bloch, Georg Lukács, Bertolt Brecht, Walter Benjamin, Theodor Adorno, *Aesthetics and Politics*, trans. and ed. Ronald Taylor (London: Verso, 1977), pp. 28–59.
2 Ernst Bloch, 'Discussing Expressionism', in Bloch et al., *Aesthetics and Politics*, pp. 16–27; Theodor Adorno, 'Reconciliation Under Duress', in Bloch et al., *Aesthetics and Politics*, pp. 151–76 (p. 162).

3 Lionel Trilling, *The Liberal Imagination: Essays on Literature and Society* (Harmondsworth: Penguin, 1950), p. 14.
4 Toni Morrison, *Sula* (London: Vintage, 2004), p. xi.
5 Theodor Adorno, 'The Position of the Narrator in the Contemporary Novel', *Notes to Literature*, Vol. 1, trans. Shierry Weber Nicholsen (New York: Columbia University Press, 1991), pp. 30–6 (pp. 32, 31).
6 Fredric Jameson, *The Political Unconscious: Narrative as a Socially Symbolic Act* (London: Methuen, 1981), p. 20.
7 See, for instance, Michel Foucault, *The Order of Things: An Archaeology of the Human Sciences* (London: Routledge, 1970) and *Discipline and Punish: The Birth of the Prison*, trans. Alan Sheridan (London: Penguin, 1977).
8 See, for example, Giorgio Agamben, *Homo Sacer: Sovereign Power and Bare Life*, trans. Daniel Heller-Roazen (Stanford, CA: Stanford University Press, 1998).
9 Amanda Anderson, *Bleak Liberalism* (Chicago, IL: University of Chicago Press, 2016), p. 3.
10 Elizabeth S. Anker and Rita Felski, 'Introduction', *Critique and Postcritique* (Durham, NC: Duke University Press, 2017), p. 15.
11 See Doris Sommer, 'Introduction', in *Cultural Agency in the Americas*, ed. Sommer (Durham, NC: Duke University Press, 2006), pp. 1–28 (pp. 2–14).
12 David Scott, *Omens of Adversity: Tragedy, Time, Memory, Justice* (Durham, NC: Duke University Press, 2014), p. 173.
13 Seamus Heaney, 'Station Island', *Station Island* (London: Faber, 1984), p. 93.

PART I

1900–1945: *Ideas and Governance*

CHAPTER 1

Liberalism

Christos Hadjiyiannis

Modern literature and liberalism have always been the best of frenemies. Modern literary movements we think of as subversive, iconoclastic, even anti-democratic, were often built on liberal values. In fact, not only did many such movements develop and thrive in liberal democratic systems, but they had liberal democracies to thank for their success and appeal.[1] This is true of several continental avant-gardes, and it is also the case with various Anglophone high modernist projects. It is so like high modernism to send mixed signals: to antagonise the individualist values of liberalism (and liberal democracy more specifically) while at the same time embracing them in redressed forms. Liberal democracy is, of course, beset by its own contradictions. If we believe Lionel Trilling, liberalism also has a record for letting modern literature down, what with its anodyne emphasis on reason, its glorification of pleasure-as-affluence, and its denial of imagination.[2] The relationship between modern literature and liberalism, it's safe to say, has always been complicated.

This essay explores the uneasy but close relationship between modern literature and liberal democracy by focusing on how some early twentieth-century modernists in England – E. M. Forster, Ford Madox Ford, T. E. Hulme, and T. S. Eliot among them – engaged with Edwardian liberalism: with the reformist policies of the Liberal Party (which came to power in 1906) and the New Liberal ideas on which these policies were based, but also and more broadly with the much older philosophical and political outlook of liberalism. A popular though discredited historiography of liberal democracy in Britain runs as follows: liberalism, thriving in the opening years of the twentieth century, was during the Edwardian period (roughly 1900–14) steadily moving towards a 'strange death'.[3] A similarly incomplete yet equally persistent reading finds that many modernists had little or no time for liberal democracy, which was inherently antithetical to their thinking and writing.[4] This essay challenges both these narratives, showing that liberalism did not die with modernism but

19

that, on the contrary, even anti-liberal 'classical' modernists embraced fundamental liberal values (though certainly not all of them).

Liberalism

Much like modernism, liberalism is a notoriously nebulous category. Subject to historical and geographical particularities, it is difficult to define. From the time it emerged in the fourteenth and fifteenth centuries, it was associated with an extraordinary emphasis on innerness, empiricism, and the demise of feudalism.[5] That's not to say that it was directly oppositional to royal absolutism (which grew increasingly in the sixteenth and seventeenth centuries), nor that it was necessarily curtailed by feudalist rule. As Larry Siedentop has explained, 'By claiming a monopoly of legal authority, sovereigns deprived many traditional attitudes and practices of legal status', yet within these absolutist systems there lay 'the seeds of individual liberty.' For 'What royal commands did not positively enjoin or forbid', Siedentop maintains, 'defined – at least potentially – a sphere of choice and personal freedom.'[6] Even so, liberalism would always side against all forms of authoritarian rule. John Gray has traced its roots as far back as the Sophists, Pericles, and Protagoras, but he too found that it was in the late seventeenth century that liberalism really began to flourish.[7] In Britain, its chief exponent was John Locke, who wrote about a civil society made up of individuals in 'a state of perfect freedom to order their actions . . . A state also of equality, wherein all the power and jurisdiction is reciprocal.'[8] Over subsequent centuries, liberalism came to stand for individualist, egalitarian, universalist, and meliorist values. Yet internal varieties and disputes remained, with liberals, then as now, holding onto different ideas about individual liberty, progress, and the virtues of popular democracy. So, while Jean-Jacques Rousseau (in *The Social Contract*, 1762), William Godwin (in *An Enquiry Concerning Political Justice*, 1793), and Nicolas de Condorcet (in *The Progress of the Human Mind*, 1795) all promoted the inevitability of progress, post-revolutionary French liberals, the Scottish founders of classical liberalism, and some of America's 'Founding Fathers' were more pessimistic about the possibilities for true liberty. Moreover, many liberals were apprehensive of popular democracy, with even household names like Alexis de Tocqueville and John Stuart Mill worried about 'majority tyranny'.[9]

   In the long and intricate history of modern liberalism in Britain, the event that most stands out is Jeremy Bentham's new philosophy of Utilitarianism in the nineteenth century, which decisively breached classical liberal doctrines of laissez-faire and non-interventionism in favour of social engineering. Much to the chagrin of later classical liberals like Friedrich Hayek, who would caution against 'the constructivist fallacy', Bentham introduced into British liberal thought the idea that social institutions could be rationally redesigned to serve the greater good.[10] Mill later tried to shift the emphasis of Utilitarianism back to liberal individualism (in *On Liberty*, 1859) and recognised (in *Utilitarianism*, 1863) qualitative distinctions among pleasures, but he too promoted interventionism. In *Principles of Political Economy* (1848), Mill drew a distinction that would stay at the basis of later liberal interventionist calls between production and distribution. Distributive arrangements were a matter of social choice, Mill showed, and so classical liberal ideas that treated productive and distributive activities as relational, mixed, and therefore not to be interfered with, were wrong. In the wake of Mill, revisionary liberals such as T. H. Green and Bernard Bosanquet argued even more forcefully against negative conceptions of freedom (as non-interference). As Gray surmises in his survey of liberalism, 'This more positive view of freedom led naturally in the writings of these Hegelian liberals to a defence of enhanced governmental activity and authority and to support for measures limiting contractual liberty.'[11] By the time Hulme, Eliot, and co. began concocting their respective modernisms in the early twentieth century, classical conceptions of liberalism had been supplanted with ideas of distributive justice and social harmony. L. T. Hobhouse, J. A. Hobson, and their New Liberal allies were now campaigning for a more 'constructive' liberalism. The modern British liberal democratic state was to be involved and interventionist. Individual liberty was no longer seen as negating governmental intervention; on the contrary, real liberty presupposed corrective measures. Nothing was off limits: not education, not pensions, not health, not the constitution, and (eventually) not who had the vote. As Rachel Potter has shown, British liberalism at the time of modernism was steadily moving away from a Gladstonian politics of anti-collectivist individualism towards an ever-greater emphasis on social reform.[12]

Liberalism at the Time of Modernism

Even though liberal reformism was fast gathering pace, when the Liberals in Britain surged to power in the elections of 1906, they did so with a comparatively moderate manifesto for social reform. This was soon to change, however. In 1908, Henry Herbert Asquith replaced Henry

Campbell-Bannerman as Liberal Party leader, and became Prime Minister in a cabinet united behind a much more radical programme. In terms of popular vote distribution, the 1906 Liberal victory was not exactly the landslide win many still make it out to have been, but it was certainly a resounding victory, and the greatest in the party's history.[13] There were 400 Liberals elected, as against 157 Conservatives (including 24 Liberal Unionists), in a parliament that now also had 29 Labour MPs. Having lost 245 seats, the Tories – increasingly split between Tariff Reformers and Free Traders, Chamberlain's supporters and Balfourites – were in disarray, giving the new Liberal administration a strong mandate to govern. The Conservative Party was not far behind in the polls, though, and would anyway regroup in time for the 1910 elections, while the Liberal Party was far from united itself, not least in its attitude towards social welfare.[14] At the January 1910 election, the Conservatives bounced back, winning 116 seats, or 2 short of the Liberals; in December, the balance remained unchanged. What's often lost in modernist historiographies of liberalism is not only the fact that parliament continued throughout the period to hang in a delicate balance between Liberals and Conservatives, and that opposing attitudes to national and international questions meant that policies often crossed party lines, but also the fact that there were various internal tensions and conflicts within Edwardian liberalism.[15]

    With New Liberals such as David Lloyd George (who replaced Asquith as Chancellor of the Exchequer), Winston Churchill, Herbert Samuel, and Charles Masterman in the cabinet, Asquith's 1908 administration began pressing for sweeping reforms. These included proposals for old-age pensions (which the Tories had promised in 1895 but never delivered), health and unemployment insurance, school meals, increases in income and excise duties, taxes on cars, petrol, and land, and a super-tax on incomes over £5,000. Tories were particularly horrified by Lloyd George's 1909 'People's Budget', which proposed a hiking up of redistributive taxation in an attempt to ease the burden of old-age pensions on public finances. The budget proceeded on the principle of 'unearned increment', which, as the historian E. H. H. Green explained, 'allowed the State, acting on behalf of society, to appropriate wealth which had been wholly or mainly created by social factors for redistribution for the benefit of society'.[16]

    What was for many Tories even more alarming was that, in order to force through their radical agenda, this new cabinet of reformist Liberals was willing to attack the most sacred of English institutions: the upper chamber of the House of Lords. It all came to a head when the Lords sent back Lloyd George's 'People's Budget' in late 1909. This was the first time the House of Lords had vetoed a budget in two centuries, and the Liberals responded with the 1910 Parliament Bill, designed to limit the Lords' powers to veto legislation. The budget was eventually passed following the January 1910 election, which confirmed the Liberals' mandate, but the government saw an opportunity to press for constitutional reform, with Asquith prompting Liberals 'to treat the veto of the House of Lords as the dominating issue in politics'.[17] After the December 1910 election, the Liberals, who retained control, were able finally to pass a Parliament Act removing the Lords' power to veto money bills. They now had the power to veto other public bills, but only for a maximum of two years. While a sensible measure, it antagonised many in the country, including the classical modernists who felt that curbing the power of the 'ancient Chamber' was an attack on the founding principles of the British political system. It also irrevocably linked social change to constitutional reform, and so brought to the fore key questions about the role of the state and who was best suited to govern; about individuality and progress as against external constraints, continuity, and tradition: in short, questions about the relation of the new to the old. These sticky questions would never cease to yank and pull liberalism – and modernism – in different and often opposing directions.

Progress

For all its newness, modernism never felt comfortable with progress. The idea of progress or, to be more precise, the belief that humans can expand their consciousness indefinitely and so endlessly improve the conditions of life, lay for a long time at the centre of many liberalisms. As we've seen, it was promoted by Rousseau, Condorcet, and Godwin in the eighteenth century. In late nineteenth-century Britain it was popularised by Paul Carus, Jane Hume Clapperton, Lester Frank Ward, and Herbert Spencer. All of them agreed that, in Spencer's words, 'life is on the way to become such that it will yield more pleasure than pain' – even if they disagreed over how betterment was possible.[18] In the early twentieth century, progress was invoked anew by New Liberals to add historical, scientific, and philosophical credence to their 'progressive' proposals for social reform. As John Burrow has argued, New Liberals followed Mill in emphasising *Bildung* (over pleasure and happiness) and so in imagining the liberal self as achieving 'the fullest possible realization of human potentialities'.[19] In his manifesto for New Liberalism in 1911, Hobhouse followed up on Mill's idea to argue that 'The foundation of liberty is the

idea of growth', while Hobson had written two years earlier of the 'illimit-
able process of Liberalism, based on the infinitude of the possibilities of
human life', describing liberalism as a 'progressive achievement' that can
never quite lead to fulfilment.[20]

Many early modernists were not, however, convinced. Even thinkers
and writers sympathetic to liberal ideas, Edwardians like Alfred Orage
(who edited *The New Age*) and Allen Upward, questioned melioristic
and perfectibilist views of human nature: what Upward described as
'anthropolatry', meaning the idea that 'man is born without sin, and that
he has been deliberately enslaved and degraded by kings and priests'.[21] Late
Victorian and Edwardian notions of perfectibility were also challenged, as
Nathan Waddell has shown, by Joseph Conrad, even, at times, by
H. G. Wells (who was otherwise an advocate of meliorism).[22] Despite his
later reputation as a liberal doyen, we find sceptical attitudes towards
progress in the early writing of E. M. Forster, too. Those who tested
Forster's liberalism found it melancholic and conscious of its own
frailty.[23] Forster's ambivalent attitude towards progress is evident in one
of his lesser-studied texts, a short story from 1904 called 'The Other Side of
the Hedge'. An unnamed protagonist is trudging along a dusty road with
'brown crackling hedges on either side'. Feeling the 'monotony of the
highway', he forces his way through to the other side of the hedge. While
this side is green and paradisal – 'wreathed over with dog-roses and
Traveller's Joy' – to the protagonist it looks like 'a prison for all its beauty
and extent'. As he tells his companion:

> 'This is perfectly terrible. One cannot advance: one cannot progress. Now
> we of the road –'
> 'Yes. I know.'
> 'I was going to say, we advance continually.'
> 'I know.'
> 'We are always learning, expanding, developing. Why, even in my short
> life I have seen a great deal of advance – the Transvaal War, the Fiscal
> Question, Christian Science, Radium [. . .].'

At just this moment, the protagonist finds out that he has not, in fact,
advanced any further: he is still the same age, and his pedometer has
stopped. And so Forster pokes fun at once at those who, like the protagonist, feel the urge to 'advance continually', but also at those who believe in
a communal heaven-on-earth. For there might be 'singing', 'talking', and
'gardening' on the other side of the hedge, but it all feels standardised,
lethargic, and unfulfilling.[24]

Ford (then known as Ford Madox Hueffer) was another writer sceptical of any prospect of ameliorating the human condition. Robert Green finds Ford 'a pessimist, who saw history as a decline from a distant glory' and therefore as 'aligned with that section of the Conservative Party most hostile to reform'; but Ford was, in fact, a perfect example of an anti-liberal liberal: a modernist whose politics crossed party lines.[25] He pronounced himself a 'Tory' on several occasions, and supported many Conservative policies, yet he also claimed never to have voted for the party, and he supported numerous policies that were distinctly liberal. He was in favour of old-age pensions and pensions for widows and dependants, as well as of sickness and unemployment benefits. He was in favour of Irish Home Rule, and he supported the right of women to vote. Moreover, he saw many positive elements in Lloyd George's 'People's Budget', with which, he said, he was 'in comparative agreement'. But that did not stop him from wondering, 'How can a man, an educated man ... any man who can read at all ... hold the vast number of contradictory opinions that are necessary to a "Progressive" of to-day?'[26]

Ford's suspicion of progress is on display in his articles in *The English Review* between 1909 and 1910, in novels such as *The Inheritors* (1901), the *Fifth Queen* trilogy (1906–8), *An English Girl* (1907), and *The Good Soldier* (1915), but is most succinctly expressed in 'Süssmund's Address to an Unknown God', a Browningesque poem of 1912.[27] In it, the displaced persona 'Carl Eugen Freiherr von Süssmund' pleads that he be given 'no management in this great world, / No share in fruity Progress'. The poem concludes with the following plea:

> God, you've been hard on me; I'm plagued with boils,
> Little mosquito-stings, warts, poverty!
> Yes, very hard. But when all's catalogued
> You've been a gentleman in all your fun.
> No doubt you'll keep your bargain, Unknown God.
> This surely you will never do to me –
> Say I'm not bitter. That you'll never do.
> T'would be to outpass the bounds of the Divine
> And turn Reformer.[28]

The idea ridiculed here – that humanity is able to progress ever closer to perfection – is found by Ford to be at the basis of Edwardian Liberal proposals for social reform. The poem also links progress and reform to that romantic heresy of mistaking oneself for God that the early modernists who fashioned themselves as 'classical' found both reprehensible and at the heart of liberalism. As Hulme put it memorably in the contemporaneous 'Romanticism and Classicism', 'Here is the root of all romanticism: that man, the individual, is an infinite reservoir of possibilities; and if you can so rearrange society by the destruction of oppressive order then these possibilities will have a chance and you will get Progress.'[29]

Meanwhile, at this very early stage of his career, and while still in the US, T. S. Eliot was independently quizzing the idea of progress, dismissing all attempts to base politics on 'biological theory' or 'theories of knowledge' in general. In 'The Relationship between Politics and Metaphysics', an essay he read to the Harvard Philosophical Club in spring 1914, Eliot argued that 'Any attempt to found politics on a metaphysical basis must be confusing and fallacious', and that it is the 'weakness of Socialism' that it relied on metaphysics for support and verification.[30] Eliot regarded all celebration of progress as 'uncritical', 'blind', and based on 'political enthusiasm' rather than upon a disinterested understanding of metaphysics or biology.[31] Though he did not deny the utility of progress – as 'an incentive to endeavour' – he objected to the way that it came to carry 'an alcoholic or stimulant value'.[32]

Eliot's critique of progress in 1914 hinged on his perception that it was an abstraction which did not allow for social and historical realities. This was his problem with Walter Lippmann, whose book *A Preface to Politics* (1913) he discussed extensively in this early student paper. Lippmann was a liberal who held, however, to a pessimistic view of democracy. In *A Preface to Politics*, Lippmann made several claims with which many classical modernists would agree: for instance, that 'human nature is a rather shocking affair if you come to it with ordinary romantic optimism', or that the Whig theory of government was mechanical in its thinking and limited by its rationalism, which, Lippmann believed, ignored the true nature of humans.[33] But Lippmann was nonetheless a progressive who had invoked, as Eliot rightly observed, evolution in order to show that 'in politics . . . you cannot recover what is passed' – and in doing do, Eliot objected, he committed 'the fallacy of Progress'.[34]

In Defence of the House of Lords

A much more concerted – because openly partisan – attack on liberal ideas of progress came from the young Tory Imagist, Edward Storer, and his better-known friend and ally, T. E. Hulme. Both Storer and Hulme wrote for *The Commentator*, a hard-line Tory weekly set up in London in May 1910 in the midst of the constitutional crisis forced by Lloyd

George's 'People's Budget'. Crucially for understanding the extent to which early modernist poetics was imbricated with Tory politics, first Storer and then Hulme responded to *The Commentator*'s calls for improving the Conservative Party's rhetoric and propaganda strategy by mobilising their proto-Imagistic theories for the composition of poetry: modern poetry and Tory propaganda alike ought to be definite, precise, and stir visual images in the minds of their audience. It was also as part of this campaign that the distinction between romanticism (or Liberalism) and classicism (or Conservatism), which became so foundational for classical modernism, emerged in its modernist context.[35]

Hulme found that it was progress that allowed the Fabians to demand the delegation of political power to the lower classes, the idea being that, given sufficient education, everyone could progress – personally, socially, and financially.[36] But history offered us a different interpretation, Hulme argued: it did not prove that civilisations continuously progress or that they progress in a better direction; what history taught us instead was that types of civilisation recur and are constant. This put paid to the 'naïve belief in inevitable progress which enables the intellectual to welcome with enthusiasm the sweeping away of all the checks' that existed in a controlled democracy.[37] And so, like others in his modernist circle (not least Ford, whose support for the Lords was, however, linked to an almost mawkish support for aristocracy), Hulme sided against reform of the House of Lords. Intriguingly, he drew on traditional liberal demands for constitutional constraints in this defence.[38] Rejecting 'unrestrained' democracy in favour of a democracy with controlling powers, he explained how discipline and order were necessary for the correct function of democracy: 'There must be a hierarchy, a subordination of the parts, just as there must be in any other organisation.' History made clear that discipline was needed for harmonious cooperation between the various parts of the state, he maintained, and 'shows that it is only by the action of certain checks that a democratic State can continue to exist in a healthy condition'.[39]

To back up his point, Hulme appealed to the sanity of the Constitution of the United States, which distributed powers between two chambers and in this way regulated democracy by restraining it. The Senate, Hulme stressed, was the strongest second chamber in the world. This invocation should not surprise us, given what has been called the 'conservative' leaning of the US Constitution, in the sense that it is based on the supposition that humans are fallible and limited beings. One of the Federalist Papers – the collection of essays published by Alexander Hamilton, James Madison, and John Jay under the pseudonym 'Publius' in support of the United States

Constitution in 1787–8 – states that any government must be 'a reflection on human nature', adding that, owing to the inherent limitations of human nature, 'external' and 'internal' controls and 'auxiliary precautions' were necessary.[40] The American model worked, Hulme wrote more than a century later, because it ensured a 'centre of authority . . . to a certain extent independent of the people governed', a separation of powers that nullified the possibility for populist decisions while also guaranteeing that 'The wielders of authority must have a tenure which, while it may depend partially, must not depend entirely upon their popularity with the governed.'[41]

Tradition and the Liberal Mind

Behind the modernists' misgivings about 'progressive' social reforms and their concerns about unfettered democracy lay a confidence, a hope, and a fantasy that, as writers and artists, they were invested with extraordinary powers. This belief took many forms; it was often delivered in the manner of polemical barbs intended to shock, but it also bore on their attitudes towards liberal democracy. Ford wrote of 'a very few . . . who have a certain originating power whether in the provinces of thought or of action', and of an 'immense proportion of entirely unnecessary people, whose only function in the world would appear to be to become the stuff to fill graveyards'.[42] Hulme described the classical poet in 'Romanticism and Classicism' as someone engaged in a 'terrific struggle with language', which is 'by its nature a communal thing', has 'its own conventions', and is the result of 'compromise', a description which recalls Ezra Pound's own definition of his ideal poet as someone who 'perceives at greater intensity, and more intimately, than his public' and who writes against 'conventional symbols'.[43] Even modernists like H.D. (Hilda Doolittle) defined writers against the crowd. As Potter has shown, while H.D.'s poems 'violate Pound's rules about poetic objectivity and impersonality, she concurs with his belief that the artistic self is defined through its ability to assert its difference from modernity'. Moreover, as Potter also shows, H.D.'s early poetry shared with D. H. Lawrence 'an interest in an aristocratic band of poetic legislators who stand above the crowd'.[44]

What John Carey saw as the myth of the modernist intellectual as a natural aristocrat is also at work in writers we think of as 'liberal'.[45] Michael Levenson found Forster in general agreement with his character Margaret Schlegel in *Howards End*, who distinguishes between 'a few human beings' and the 'universal gray' of humanity; while, as Douglas

Mao has argued, the idea that the modernist artist possessed a capability for 'individuation manifested as critical intelligence' was also pursued by W. H. Auden.[46] Comparing Auden to that most anti-liberal of thinkers, Wyndham Lewis, Mao finds in both a 'commitment to certain core tenets of liberalism ... inseparable from a vision of the liberal intelligence as a kind of virtuous badness'. Mao is right to see the possession of critical intelligence as 'part of liberalism's self-definition'.[47] He cites (in a footnote) Locke, Paley, and Voltaire on toleration and religious dissent to make his point, but he could as easily have cited those New Liberals who, at the time of modernism, were emphasising both dissent and superior intelligence as core liberal values.[48] Take New Liberal journalist William Clarke, for example: 'But the community is growing in knowledge and intelligence? Assuredly; but the great innovating thinkers and artists will always be ahead of it, and if they were not, they would be of no value.'[49] Or the anonymous reviewer in *The Nation*, who wrote of the 'need for an apostolic succession of thinking men who will constantly restate political principles in terms of the living needs of each generation'.[50] The reviewer here had in mind J. A. Hobson, who conceived of the liberal thinker as (in Michael Freeden's words) 'a man with a living and practical function, exercising a deep and lasting influence on the nation'.[51] Hobhouse similarly felt that a 'complete and wholehearted absorption in public interests is rare', and that such absorption 'is the property not of the mass but of the few'. In keeping with Mao's reading of Auden and Lewis, but also anticipating Chantal Mouffe's more recent view of democracy as an energetic debate requiring conflict and dissent, Hobhouse also insisted that 'the most liberally-minded democracy is maintaining a system which must undermine its own principles'.[52]

Eliot has, of course, long been seen as the spokesperson for the need for a 'disinterested exercise of intelligence'.[53] In his later life, he would write of a community of 'more conscious, more spiritually and intellectually developed' individuals who 'form the conscious mind and the conscience of the nation' (*The Idea of a Christian Society*), and of an elite whose job is to 'bring about a further development of the culture in organic complexity' and who are, therefore, capable of embodying more of the whole than their fellows (*Notes Towards the Definition of Culture*).[54] But at this early stage of his career, he was still debating the exact function of critical intelligence and, what was more important to him, the nature of the relationship between autonomous individuals and history, tradition, and community. These questions have always been central to Eliot's cultural programme, but they were and remain also crucial for liberalism, whose history, as

Levenson put it, 'is itself a history of negotiations between part and whole'.[55]

'Tradition and the Individual Talent' (1919) is accordingly a manifesto for impersonal art, an apology for Eliot's elitist brand of modernism, and a negotiation of a central tension within liberalism. In this programmatic essay, Eliot calls on the individual talent to exercise erudition, historical sense, and a heightened poetic sensibility to filter and reformulate tradition, work that, as Michael North has noted, requires both a conscious and an unconscious effort.[56] But Eliot also made it clear that the individual was always and necessarily part of a community. And so, by some sort of dialectical trick, the individual talent and tradition were found to be, in fact, the same. Eliot's neat solution was designed to correct the ills of modern disunity (soon to be explicitly associated with liberalism), but his emphasis on organicity and reciprocity in this early essay echoed Hobhouse's argument in *Liberalism*.[57] Appreciative of ancient Greeks who 'governed themselves subject only to principles and rules of life descending from antiquity and owing their force to the spontaneous allegiance of successive generations', Hobhouse envisaged the liberal state as an organic whole, in which progress is the result of 'conscious or unconscious co-operation' and in which individuality is always kept in check.[58] 'A thing is called organic', Hobhouse wrote in 1911, 'when it is made up of parts which are quite distinct from one another, but which are destroyed or virtually altered when they are removed from the whole.' In the new liberal society he had in mind, 'there are no actions which may not directly or indirectly affect others'; in fact, 'even if there were they would not cease to be matter of concern to others'. That was because the common good included 'the good of every member of the community, and the injury which a man inflicts upon himself is matter of common concern, even apart from any ulterior effect upon others'. Hobhouse's liberal state was therefore to be 'self-governing' and 'at once the product and the condition of the self-governing individual'.[59] While Eliot and his fellow classical modernists would agitate for rule by a select few, however, Hobhouse was led to a distinctly different conclusion. Ultimately, and even though he felt that 'the life of the average man must be organized for his own good', Hobhouse concluded that responsibility must be given to the individual, and hence was why he supported enlarging the franchise.[60]

After the War

In 1918, the Representation of the People Act, backed by a Liberal-Conservative coalition government, extended the franchise to unpropertied men over twenty-one and to women over thirty who were householders or married to a householder. The masses, long gendered feminine, were now over the gates, and the classical modernists, who had long felt paranoid about their insignificance as cultural producers, would only grow more alienated and incensed.[61] Yet, the war did push many of them closer to, not further away from, liberal values. At least this was the case with Ford and Hulme, both of whom followed the Liberal government (and of course the Tory opposition) in supporting the war. Hulme claimed the war was necessary to protect British institutions and ideals, which were under threat from 'bureaucratic' and 'anti-Liberal' Germany. Taking democracy in its broadest sense possible, to mean freedom rather than the electoral system, he warned that 'All we mean by democracy will certainly take a second place in our daily lives if the Central Powers have their way.'[62] As regards Ford, he continued to feel that in practice liberal democracy amounted to plutocracy, yet he wrote of his hope that the war might bring a 'revaluing of democracy'.[63]

It may have been that, as Bertrand Russell argued, when war broke out, reactionaries who were once extremely critical of democracy began to speak of the danger of Germany to democracy. 'They were not insincere in so speaking', Russell wrote: 'the impulse of resistance to Germany made them value whatever was endangered by the German attack. They loved democracy because they hated Germany.'[64] Or else it may have been that, in line with the Tory leaders, Hulme and Ford found after 1914 common cause with the Liberal government. This much is clear, though: while the war may have pushed Hulme, Ford, and the other modernists caught up in it to test further the viability of their anti-liberal politics, modernists before, during, and after the war were only too comfortable calling on several liberal democratic values. In true modernist – and liberal – form, twentieth-century writers freely embraced central values of liberal democracy just as they rejected others.

Notes

1 See Sascha Bru, *Democracy, Law and the Modernist Avant-Gardes: Writing in the State of Exception* (Edinburgh: Edinburgh University Press, 2009), pp. 2–5, 11–12.
2 See Lionel Trilling, *The Liberal Imagination: Essays on Literature and Society* (Harmondsworth: Penguin, 1970), pp. 13–14, and *Beyond Culture: Essays on Literature and Learning* (Harmondsworth: Penguin, 1967), pp. 74–5.

3 This diagnosis was famously issued by George Dangerfield in his 1935 book, *The Strange Death of Liberal England* (Stanford, CA: Stanford University Press, 1997). For two different criticisms of this interpretation, see Alan Sykes, *The Rise and Fall of British Liberalism, 1776–1988* (London: Routledge, 1997), pp. 177–99, and Gabriel Hankins, *Interwar Modernism and the Liberal World Order: Offices, Institutions, and Aesthetics After 1919* (Oxford: Oxford University Press, 2019), pp. 26, 165–6.

4 On this point, see Janice Ho, 'The Crisis of Liberalism and the Politics of Modernism', *Literature Compass* 8.1 (2011), pp. 47–65 (pp. 51–2).

5 See Larry Siedentop, *Inventing the Individual: The Origins of Western Liberalism* (London: Allen Lane, 2014), pp. 335, 338, 340.

6 Ibid., p. 347.

7 John Gray, *Liberalism*, 2nd edition (Minneapolis, MN: University of Minnesota Press, 1995), pp. xii, 10.

8 John Locke, *Two Treatises of Government*, ed. Mark Goldie (London: J. M. Dent, 1993), p. 116.

9 Gray, *Liberalism*, pp. 20–5.

10 Cf. F. A. Hayek, *Law, Legislation and Liberty*, Vol. 1: *Rules and Order* (London: Routledge & Kegan Paul, 1973), p. 17. On Bentham committing the 'constructivist fallacy', see Gray, *Liberalism*, p. 23.

11 Gray, *Liberalism*, pp. 31–2.

12 Rachel Potter, *Modernism and Democracy: Literary Culture, 1900–1930* (Oxford: Oxford University Press, 2006), pp. 28–9.

13 See Walter L. Arnstein, 'Edwardian Politics: Turbulent Spring or Indian Summer?', in *The Edwardian Age: Conflict and Stability, 1900–1914*, ed. Alan O'Day (London: Macmillan, 1979), pp. 60–78 (p. 70). The Conservatives got 2,451,454 votes (or 43.6 per cent) and the Liberals 2,757,883 votes (or 49 per cent).

14 Ibid., p. 61.

15 One example of a policy that received Liberal *and* Conservative support was 'National Efficiency'. See G. R. Searle, 'The Politics of National Efficiency and of War, 1900–1918', in *A Companion to Early Twentieth-Century Britain*, ed. Chris Wrigley (Oxford: Blackwell, 2003), pp. 56–71.

16 E. H. H. Green, *The Crisis of Conservatism* (London: Routledge, 1995), p. 144.

17 Quoted in Arnstein, 'Edwardian Politics', p. 71.

18 Herbert Spencer, 'The Great Political Superstition', *Contemporary Review* 46 (July/December 1884), pp. 24–48 (p. 39).

19 John Burrow, *The Crisis of Reason: European Thought, 1848–1914* (New Haven, CT: Yale University Press, 2000), p. 131. Cf. John Stuart Mill, *Utilitarianism, Liberty and Representative Government* (London: J. M. Dent, 1964), p. 115.

20 L. T. Hobhouse, *Liberalism* (London: Williams & Norgate, 1911), p. 122; J. A. Hobson, *The Crisis of Liberalism: New Issues of Democracy* (London: P. S. King, 1909), p. 95.

21 Allen Upward, 'Anthropolatry', *The New Age* (13 January 1910), pp. 249–50 (p. 249). On Orage's anti-melioristic views, see Wallace Martin, *The New Age under Orage* (Manchester: Manchester University Press, 1967), p. 214.

22 Nathan Waddell, *Modernist Nowheres: Politics and Utopia in Early Modernist Writing, 1900–1920* (Basingstoke: Palgrave Macmillan, 2012), pp. 45–54.

23 See, for example, David Medalie, 'Bloomsbury and Other Values', pp. 32–46 (p. 33); Dominic Head, 'Forster and the Short Story', pp. 77–91 (pp. 85–6); and David Bradshaw, 'Howards End', pp. 151–72 (p. 171), all in *The Cambridge Companion to E. M. Forster*, ed. David Bradshaw (Cambridge: Cambridge University Press, 2007).

24 E. M. Forster, 'The Other Side of the Hedge', *Collected Short Stories* (London: Penguin, 1972), pp. 35–7.

25 Robert Green, *Ford Madox Ford: Prose and Politics* (Cambridge: Cambridge University Press, 1981), pp. 40–1.

26 Ford Madox Ford [Didymus], 'A Declaration of Faith', *The English Review* 4 (February 1910), pp. 543–51 (p. 547); and Ford Madox Ford, 'Literary Portraits – XVIII. Mr. A. G. Gardner and "Pillars of Society"', *Outlook* 33 (10 January 1914), pp. 46–7.

27 On Ford's suspicion of progress in these writings, and in others, see Max Saunders, *Ford Madox Ford: A Dual Life, Vol. 1: The World before the War* (Oxford: Oxford University Press, 1996), pp. 416–17.

28 Ford Madox Ford, *Selected Poems*, ed. Max Saunders (Manchester: Carcanet, 1997), p. 67.

29 T. E. Hulme, 'Romanticism and Classicism', *The Collected Writings of T. E. Hulme*, ed. Karen Csengeri (Oxford: Oxford University Press, 1994), pp. 59–73 (p. 61).

30 T. S. Eliot, 'The Relationship between Politics and Metaphysics', *The Complete Prose of T. S. Eliot, Vol. 1: Apprentice Years, 1905–1918*, ed. Jewel Spears Brooker and Ronald Schuchard (Baltimore, MD: Johns Hopkins University Press, 2014), pp. 90–105 (p. 100).

31 Ibid., p. 91.

32 Ibid., p. 95.

33 Walter Lippmann, *A Preface to Politics* (New York: Mitchell Kennerley, 1913), pp. 39, 14–15.

34 Eliot, 'The Relationship between Politics and Metaphysics', p. 95. Cf. Lippmann, *A Preface to Politics*, p. 313.

35 For more on how Imagist poetics was imbricated with Tory rhetoric, and on the distinction between romanticism and classicism as it emerged in its modernist context, see Christos Hadjyiannis, *Conservative Modernists: Literature and Tory Politics in Britain, 1900–1920* (Cambridge: Cambridge University Press, 2018), pp. 21–30, 45–51.

36 T. E. Hulme, 'Theory and Practice', *The Collected Writings*, pp. 226–31 (p. 230).

37 T. E. Hulme, 'On Progress and Democracy', *The Collected Writings*, pp. 219–25 (p. 224).

38 Hobhouse, *Liberalism*, p. 52.

39 Hulme, 'On Progress and Democracy', pp. 220, 225.

40 [Publius], Federalist Paper 51, 'The Same Subject Continued with the Same View and Concluded', in Alexander Hamilton, James Madison, and John Jay, *The Federalist Papers*, ed. Lawrence Goldman (Oxford: Oxford University Press, 1987), pp. 256–60 (p. 257).

41 Hulme, 'On Progress and Democracy', pp. 220–1.

42 [Didymus], 'A Declaration of Faith', p. 545.

43 Hulme, 'Romanticism and Classicism', p. 68; Ezra Pound, 'Psychology and the Troubadours', *Early Writings: Poems and Prose*, ed. Ira B. Nadel (London: Penguin, 2005), pp. 195–208 (p. 195).

44 Potter, *Modernism and Democracy*, pp. 105, 118.

45 John Carey, *The Intellectuals and the Masses: Pride and Prejudice among the Literary Intelligentsia, 1880–1939* (London: Faber, 1992), p. 71.

46 Michael Levenson, *Modernism and the Fate of Individuality: Character and Novelistic Form from Conrad to Woolf* (Cambridge: Cambridge University Press, 1991), pp. 88, 90; Douglas Mao, 'A Shaman in Common: Lewis, Auden, and the Queerness of Liberalism', in *Bad Modernisms*, ed. Douglas Mao and Rebecca L. Walkowitz (Durham, NC: Duke University Press, 2006), pp. 206–37 (p. 230).

47 Mao, 'A Shaman in Common', pp. 207, 228.

48 Ibid., p. 234 n.16.

49 *William Clarke: A Collection of His Writings*, ed. Herbert Burrows and J. A. Hobson (London: Swan Sonnenschein, 1908), p. 39.

50 'The Restatement of Liberalism', *The Nation*, 8 January 1910. Cited in Michael Freeden, *The New Liberalism: An Ideology of Social Reform* (Oxford: Clarendon Press, 1978), p. 254 n.20.

51 Ibid., p. 254.

52 Hobhouse, *Liberalism*, pp. 230, 42. Cf. Chantal Mouffe, *The Democratic Paradox* (London: Verso, 2000), pp. 15–16.

53 T. S. Eliot, 'The Perfect Critic', *The Complete Prose of T. S. Eliot*, Vol. 2: *The Perfect Critic, 1919–1926*, ed. Anthony Cuda and Ronald Schuchard (Baltimore, MD: Johns Hopkins University Press, 2014), pp. 263–72 (p. 268).

54 T. S. Eliot, *The Idea of a Christian Society*, in *The Complete Prose of T. S. Eliot*, Vol. 5: *Tradition and Orthodoxy, 1934–1939*, ed. Iman Javadi, Ronald Schuchard, and Jayme Stayer (Baltimore, MD: Johns Hopkins University Press, 2017), pp. 683–747 (pp. 705–6); T. S. Eliot, 'Notes Towards the Definition of *Culture*', *The Complete Prose of T. S. Eliot*, Vol. 7: *A European Society, 1947–1953*, ed. Iman Javadi and Ronald Schuchard (Baltimore, MD: Johns Hopkins University Press, 2018), pp. 194–287 (p. 213).

55 Levenson, *Modernism and the Fate of Individuality*, p. 92.

56 Michael North, *The Political Aesthetic of Yeats, Eliot, and Pound* (Cambridge: Cambridge University Press, 1991), p. 91.

57 See *After Strange Gods* (1933), where Eliot argued that 'the struggle of our time' was how 'to re-establish a vital connexion between the individual and the race;

the struggle, in a word, against Liberalism', in Eliot, *Complete Prose*, Vol. 5, pp. 15–55 (p. 37).

58 Hobhouse, *Liberalism*, pp. 11, 133.

59 Ibid., pp. 125, 142–3, 153–4.

60 Ibid., p. 170.

61 As David Trotter has suggested, this was a symptom shared by many in the 'non-capitalist middle class' that emerged during the nineteenth century. See his *Paranoid Modernism: Literary Experiment, Psychosis, and the Professionalization of English Society* (Oxford: Oxford University Press, 2001), p. 83. For the gendering of mass culture as feminine, see Andreas Huyssen, *After the Great Divide: Modernism, Mass Culture, Postmodernism* (Bloomington, IN: Indiana University Press, 1986), pp. 39–57.

62 T. E. Hulme, 'War Notes', *Collected Writings*, pp. 331–415 (p. 334).

63 Ford Madox Ford, 'Literary Portraits – XLVIII. M. Charles-Louis Philippe and "Le Père Perdrix"', *Outlook* 34 (8 August 1914), pp. 174–5 (p. 175).

64 Bertrand Russell, *Principles of Social Reconstruction* (London: Routledge, 1997), p. 16.

CHAPTER 2

Communism

Matthew Taunton

The story of British writers' engagement with Communism in the interwar period is tangled up with those writers' own accounts of their failure. When W. H. Auden famously characterised the 1930s as a 'low, dishonest decade', he referred to the moral corruption he and his 'gang' suffered as a result of their (for the most part) temporary flirtations with Communism. As well as totting up the moral cost of becoming apologists for Stalinism, they often lamented that their art had suffered by its dogmatic commitment to a political cause, or else that it had been condemned by Party hacks as 'a reflection of bourgeois, individualistic tendencies'.[1] As Ben Harker explains, in the Communist Party of Great Britain (CPGB), '"Intellectualism" was a dirty word even in the notional "United Front" period.'[2] The Party retained a proletarian orientation, and middle-class intellectuals were viewed with suspicion. The post-war trajectories of prominent literary ex-Communists such as Stephen Spender and Arthur Koestler, tended to suggest that – in line with an emerging Cold War liberal consensus – literature and radical politics ought to be kept separate.

Yet a wave of fascinating recent scholarship in this field has revealed a more ideologically various interwar Communism that includes a wider and more diverse cast of characters, is not so trapped in the binary logic of the cultural cold war, and whose Marxism could flexibly adapt itself to the specifics of the historical conjuncture.[3] Where literary historians had sometimes (like Spender or Orwell) seen Communist ideas through the lens of the youthful flirtations of a group of upper-middle-class, Oxbridge-educated, male, white poets, this new scholarship has refocused attention on writers who do not fit that mould, and for whom Marxist ideas were not a straightjacket or a recipe for rote conformism, but a way of seeing the world that proved fertile for their literary art.

To understand Communist writing afresh inevitably involves a reckoning with socialist realism – the officially sanctioned aesthetic approach of the Communist International. One of the defining moments in the development of Communist theories of literature was Karl Radek's address to the Soviet Writers' Congress of 1934, entitled 'Contemporary World Literature and the Tasks of Proletarian Art'. Radek condemned modernist writers, memorably describing Joyce's *Ulysses* as 'A heap of dung, crawling with worms, photographed by a cinema apparatus through a microscope.' Instead of this 'literature of decadence', Radek called for a socialist realism that could 'comprehend the tremendous whole' of contemporary reality, 'not only knowing reality as it is, but knowing whither it is moving'.[4] Communist writers responded to this call in a variety of ways – including by resisting or rejecting it. Nevertheless, the urgent call for a literature that would facilitate an understanding of the world 'as it is' and 'whither it is moving' is a vital context for understanding Communist writing in this period.

Reading Communist literature one has to navigate an inbuilt hostility to socialist realism, which is heavily institutionalised in literary studies. In his influential essay 'Commitment', Theodor Adorno suggested that politically committed realist art readily arrives at the 'judgment that the way of the world is bad', but that this judgement is merely 'consoling', allowing the writer to rest easy in the knowledge that reality has been grasped in the correct way.[5] Stephen Spender similarly complained that Communist writers were too confident that they had escaped from the distortions of ideology and arrived at an unproblematic grasp of reality. 'Somehow', Spender wrote, 'I had expected that when I joined the Party I would soon become endowed with that blessed sense of being right about everything which most Communists seemed to feel. But this did not happen.'[6] Taking works by Sylvia Townsend Warner, Mulk Raj Anand, and Lewis Grassic Gibbon as its case studies, this chapter shows how these committed Communist writers used the novel form to test the relationship between ideology and reality without falling back on the consoling judgement that the world is bad, and without assuming that the real can be unproblematically grasped once the heroic Marxist has cut through the fog of ideology.

With this in mind, I focus on one important strand of Communist fiction that I will call 'the conversion narrative', which sees a protagonist making the journey from false consciousness and ideological deception to fuller self-knowledge and political awareness. The end point of this journey often involves the protagonist actually becoming a Communist, or moving towards an explicitly Marxist position. Such narratives mobilise Marxism as a suspicious hermeneutic capable of exposing fundamental contradictions in modern society. They remind us that Communism was not just a political movement, but also a way of seeing the world, with distinct aesthetic possibilities. Conversion narratives allowed Communist writers to explore how it feels for a protagonist to inhabit a state of false consciousness, and then to show how cracks begin to appear in the ideological carapace in which that character is enclosed. The twinned promises of self-knowledge and political emancipation come into view.

Marx's theory of ideology was designed to account for the fact that the proletariat – whose concerted political action was required to effect the necessary revolution – often held beliefs (religious, moral, nationalistic, etc.) which were contrary to their material interests. It is a fertile idea for the novelist because it allows writers to exploit discrepancies between a protagonist's immersion in false consciousness and that of the reader, and also to play with the ironic distance between narrators and characters who think and speak ideologically. The writers I discuss here all test this theory of ideology against new situations, where the primacy of class in Marxist analysis jostles for position with gender, sexuality, race, national identity, and rural identity – each with its own cluster of mentalities and institutional structures.

Sylvia Townsend Warner

Along with her partner and political comrade-in-arms Valentine Ackland, Sylvia Townsend Warner conjugated her defiantly lesbian private life with her political commitment to Soviet Communism, evolving a stance that Glyn Salton-Cox has labelled 'queer vanguardism'.[7] Ackland and Townsend Warner were active members of their local branch of the Communist Party of Great Britain (CPGB), and also went to Spain to support the anti-fascist cause in the Spanish Civil War, working for the Red Cross. As Salton-Cox argues, it has often been assumed that 'The thoroughgoing antinormativity of queer life . . . is completely incompatible with the po-faced puritanism of Communist discipline, particularly in the increasingly sexually conservative atmosphere of the 1930s left.'[8] Townsend Warner's work, as Salton-Cox shows, can help us to undo this apparent antinomy.

Townsend Warner's *Summer Will Show* (1936) brings elements of queer vanguardism to the conversion novel, exploring the contours of bourgeois false consciousness from a Marxist perspective but also a critically queer one. The novel's central protagonist, Sophia Willoughby, is from the English gentry, and the beginning of the novel finds her living with her two children as the mistress of Blandamer House in Dorset. Her husband Frederick has deserted her to take up with his Jewish lover, Minna, in bohemian Paris. After her two children die, a bereft Sophia travels to France with a view to getting her husband to give her another child. Instead, she falls in love with Minna, who also provides a conduit for the ideas of the 1848 revolution (which forms the backdrop to their lesbian affair). Initially, Sophia is somewhat complacent as she resists the call of politics, and her attitudes remain entrenched in those of the English gentry. These attitudes soften towards the end of the novel, then Minna is violently killed. The novel concludes as Sophia reads the opening of Marx and Engels's *Communist Manifesto*, itself first published in 1848.

The turn towards Marxist politics is accompanied by a rejection of bourgeois heteronormativity (a rejection prefigured in Townsend Warner's first novel, *Lolly Willowes*, published in 1926, whose protagonist evades the snares of the marriage plot to become a witch instead of a wife). Following Minna's death, Sophia's Great-Aunt Léocadie tries to convince her to return to respectable society. 'I cannot possibly return … to anything like my old manner of living', Sophia replies. 'I have changed my ideas. I do not think as I did.'[9] Queer theorists such as Michael Warner have sought to extend the Marxist notion of false consciousness to cover the ideology of sexual life.[10] This is reflected in *Summer Will Show*, where the path out of ideology and false consciousness entails a necessary break with the ideology and the constitutive heterosexuality of the bourgeois family.

As conversion narratives go, *Summer Will Show* retains a fair portion of ambiguity at its conclusion – not least due to the way it balances sexual politics with class politics. Communism has often been caricatured as a rigidly normative, disciplined, and puritanical creed, and, as Salton-Cox demonstrates, Townsend Warner's novel puts that characterisation into dialogue with an inherently anti-normative queerness. Such a dialogue is built into the novel's character system, which sees the cold, hard-line Marxism articulated by Ingelbrecht played off against the more romantic and bohemian socialism embodied by Minna. This opposition emerges when we first encounter Ingelbrecht at Minna's party, which continues as the barricades go up outside. Minna continues to discuss orchestral music, and Ingelbrecht objects:

> 'There is a barricade in your street, Minna. And revolutions have no second flute-players to spare,' said the man with the shawl.
> 'Why not, Ingelbrecht? A revolution must have music to match it.'
> 'Street songs. But not symphonies.'
> 'Symphonies! Are the people, a free people, to have nothing better than a tune on the hurdy-gurdy? My dear, the truth is, you don't like music.'

Her change of voice might have wheedled open a strongbox, and he smiled and grunted, pleased to have his lack of taste recognised.[11]

Inglebrecht wears his philistinism with pride: the revolution cannot afford to indulge in artistic distractions, which he sees as part of the cloudy veil of bourgeois ideology which a dedicated revolutionary must strive to break through. Minna's more expansive (or, from an orthodox point of view, dilettantish) conception of revolution gives a prominent role to culture.

Later in the novel, Ingelbrecht articulates his differences with Minna in a treatise he is writing 'on the proper management of revolutions' which includes an account of Minna's 'defects, in so far as they are typical and instructive'.[12] He reads to Minna and Sophia an extract that savagely criticises various shades of romantic socialism – mocking the '*appeal to bourgeois sympathies*', complaining of '*undesirable recruits from the bourgeoisie, sentimentalists, sensation-seekers, idealists, etc.*'[13] These arguments echo the famous invectives of Marx and Engels against romantic and utopian socialists in *The Communist Manifesto*, which will fall into Sophia's hands at the very end of *Summer Will Show*.

Minna is the key figure who facilitates Sophia's break from the moral and sexual norms of the patriarchal bourgeois family. But the way Townsend Warner presents this suggests a distinct tension between Sophia's newfound sexual freedom and the politics of the 1848 revolution. Happily ensconced with Minna, it is only with 'some outlying part of her brain' that Sophia 'recognised that a revolution was going on outside':

> News of it was brought by hurried visitors; and as though a semi-awakening had blurred the superior reality of a dream, she listened drowsily to tidings of a fallen ministry, a stormed building, a palace in terror and disarray. They went. And instantly she began to talk once more to Minna, caressing her hand.[14]

Her intimacy with Minna, at least at this stage in the novel, seems to constitute a 'superior reality' as compared with the events of the revolution taking place outside. But it is paradoxically only the superior reality 'of a dream', with the possibility of a 'semi-awakening' clearly linked to the political violence on the streets below.

In *Summer Will Show*, Sophia's sexual awakening is both indispensable to her rejection of bourgeois ideology and a potential barrier to it. Sexual liberation appears to have elements of the bold political gesture, but at times it also acts as a distraction from politics. There is no easy solution to be found in Sophia's journey from false consciousness to enlightenment. Even as the novel narrates Sophia's passage from bourgeois family life to queer vanguardism, there remain underlying polarities within the novel's character system which are not resolved simply because Sophia takes up a new position within it. Minna's bohemian socialism and Ingelbrecht's austere critique of it express a dialectic that is invigorated by the novel's plot, rather than finally resolved.

Mulk Raj Anand

The Indian novelist Mulk Raj Anand was a 'committed Marxist', who became the first president of the All-India Progressive Writers' Association (AIPWA), which was founded at the Nanking Restaurant in London in autumn 1934.[15] Ralph Fox – the author of a fascinating foray into Marxist literary theory, *The Novel and the People* (1937), and an important figure in British literary Communism – was present at the meeting, alongside left-wing Indian writers Sajjad Zaheer and Jyotirmaya Ghosh. Following the inaugural meeting in the Nanking, Anand was tasked with drafting the AIPWA's manifesto, which was then published in 1936 in the *Left Review* (the intellectual organ of the CPGB) and translated into Hindi to be printed in the journal *Hans* (Swan) the same year. Its vocabulary is recognisably Communist, and its arguments draw on the debates triggered by Radek's speech at the 1934 Soviet Writers' Congress (discussed at the beginning of this chapter):

> It is the object of our association to rescue literature and other arts from the priestly, academic and decadent classes in whose hands they have degenerated so long; to bring the arts into the closest touch with the people; and to make them the vital organ which will register the actualities of life, as well as lead us to the future.[16]

The manifesto clearly signalled a frustration with bourgeois modernism, and a commitment to socialist realism – the literary mode most capable of registering 'actualities' as well as showing the way to the future. As Carlo Coppola has shown, the manifesto became 'the most basic document in the development of socialist realism in India'.[17]

Yet despite his close involvement in producing this literary manifesto, Anand has more often been read as a modernist than as an adherent of socialist realism. As Jessica Berman has rightly pointed out,

> Anand secretly determined to pattern himself after Joyce, taking specific instruction not merely from Joyce's mode of narration and his representation of self-development but also from his rejection of religion and

mysticism, his use of sound to transmit extralinguistic meaning in prose, and his complex cosmopolitan perspective.[18]

Anand's first novel, *Untouchable* (1935), uses the modernist trick of being set on a single day, immersing the reader in the minutiae of its protagonist's shifting thoughts and impressions (like *Ulysses* and *Mrs Dalloway*). Anand, like the other writers I focus on in this chapter, helps us to undo a Cold War opposition between socialist realism and bourgeois modernism: Townsend Warner, Anand, and Grassic Gibbon can all be described as at once modernists and Communists. Ulka Anjaria and John Connor have separately emphasised how Anand's political aesthetic took its bearings from international Communism and socialist realism, without implying that it was politically doctrinaire or rigidly traditional in form.[19] Indeed, Anjaria situates Anand's work in a rich tradition of self-reflexively realist Indian novels:

> realism in the colony is highly metatextual, founded on variegated textual fields and constituted not by ideological certainties but by contradictions, conflicts, and profound ambivalence as to the nature of the 'real' world being represented, and the novel's ability to represent it.[20]

This is a realism that understands the real not as some kind of epistemological certainty, but as caked in ideology. *Untouchable* depicts a day in the life of Bakha, a sweeper and a Dalit (untouchable) in the Hindu caste system. It is a version of Communist conversion story that foregrounds the functioning of false consciousness, infuses its Marxism with anti-colonialism, and where the enlightenment that the protagonist achieves is itself presented as a set of unresolved contradictions.

Alongside his Marxism, Anand's politics were also defined by his opposition to British rule in India, and his critique of the Hindu caste system. In a sense, *Untouchable* extends aspects of the Marxist theory of ideology to account for the ways both the Empire and the caste system were legitimated among the Indian population. Before I show how the novel achieves this, it is worth noting that such a project presents distinct difficulties. Proletarian 'class consciousness', for Marx, meant the knowledge that the workers were the wealth creators (and therefore wielded a certain power). As Marx saw it, the Dalits were not the wealth creators, and he argued that they constituted a residuum of a pre-capitalist mode of production 'contaminated by distinctions of caste and by slavery'.[21] Bakha sweeps in exchange for the scraps off the tables of higher-caste Indians who deride him as 'eater of your masters': not a creator, but a destroyer of wealth.[22] In relation to pre-capitalist India, Marx tended to emphasise the progressive nature of British imperialism, suggesting that by introducing railways, modern machinery, and capitalism to the colonies, the British Empire had (while exploiting Indian workers and land) laid the foundations for Communism, however inadvertently. *Untouchable* does not resolve the tensions between Marxism and anti-colonialism, but ingeniously articulates them: as Bakha begins to break out of various forms of false consciousness, he encounters not an unmediated 'reality', but a set of distinct and mutually incompatible diagnoses, which draw on Marxist, nationalist, and anti-colonial discourses. Anand's *Untouchable* is undeniably committed literature, of the type Adorno meant to criticise, but Bakha's ideological awakening does not present him with the consolation of a simple moralising analysis. Anand's realism is complex and self-reflexive enough to avoid what Adorno called 'the element of ratification which lurks in resigned admission of the dominance of evil'.[23]

Untouchable explores how Bakha holds beliefs and social attitudes that are against his own interests, and how his contact with new experiences and ideas might bring him to a fuller consciousness of his social position and a greater awareness of where his interests lie. This is evident, for example, when Bakha is entrusted with a task that untouchables are generally felt to be too unclean to do. Charat Singh wants to smoke his hookah, and asks Bakha to fetch him coal. Bakha is 'wonder-struck' by the idea that 'a Hindu should entrust him with the job of fetching glowing charcoal in the chilm that he was going to put on his hookah and smoke!' The narrator reports that Bakha is 'grateful to God that such men as Charat Singh existed' and that he is inclined to 'worship' a man who could 'entrust him, an unclean menial, with the job'.[24] The passage concerns a partial violation of the accepted rules of the caste system, but one that validates the essential hierarchy that underpins it. Bakha has internalised the caste system to the extent that he is merely grateful when someone allocates him to a position marginally above his own. He is spared the humiliation (for now) of being deemed too filthy and low to carry out these menial tasks. But the reader clearly perceives another humiliation – just as deep in its way – in Bakha's fawning attitude of excessive gratefulness, which reaches an intense pitch when Charat Singh gives him a hockey stick. 'He [Bakha] couldn't look at so generous a person. He was overcome by the man's kindness. He was grateful, grateful, haltingly grateful, falteringly grateful, stumblingly grateful, so grateful that he didn't know how he could walk the ten yards to the corner to be out of the sight of his benevolent and generous host.'[25] The narrator only gives us Bakha's subjective thoughts, but we understand nevertheless that his excessive gratefulness – ironically signalled by an excess of repetition and a piling up of adjectives – is misplaced. The reader is invited to think critically about the social dynamics at work, without such a critique being set out either by a character or the narrator.

In other places, Bakha's ideological assumptions are more explicitly tested, both by the narrator and by other characters. One of the first things we learn about Bakha, at the very beginning of *Untouchable*, is that he has an engrained Anglophilia, believing that the 'Tommies' (in contrast to the higher-caste Indians) 'had treated him as a human being'.[26] He imitates the English style of dress, in a vain attempt to escape his position within the caste system. The narratorial discourse functions in a different way here as compared with the encounter with Charat Singh. Instead of exaggerating Bakha's thoughts in a way that encourages the reader to identify them as ideological, the narrator makes explicit the error in Bakha's attitude: 'The clear-cut styles of European dress had impressed his naïve mind.'[27] Bakha is effectively at the mercy of two interlocking hegemonic ideologies: the colonial system of the British Empire and the Indian caste system. Anand wants us to see through both ideologies – and in the service of this double unmasking makes explicit that Bakha's embrace of the 'European' in response to the iniquities of the caste system is no solution at all. By temporarily stepping out of the closely focalised presentation of Bakha's inner thoughts – precisely in order to label these 'naïve' – the narrator pivots towards a more omniscient form of narration, opening up a gap between reality as the narrator implicitly understands it, and Bakha's limited, ideological perspective on events.

This effect is amplified later in the novel. Bakha is more able to become critical of the caste system than he is to break through the more potent racial ideology of British colonialism, as is demonstrated in the scene where Bakha is pricked with shame when he realises that his very presence displeases a white woman. The narrator explains that Bakha is learning to direct his anger against the caste system and those of his 'brown countrymen' who enforce it, but that the 'mem-sahib was more important to his slavish mind': 'He dared not think unkind thoughts about her. So he unconsciously transferred his protest against her anger to the sum of his reactions against the insulting [brown] personages of the morning.'[28] Here, the narrator offers to the reader an explanation of Bakha's mental processes that goes beyond Bakha's own limited self-knowledge. The anger that Bakha is storing up against the caste system and the 'insulting personages' who mistreat him in its name, seems like a step towards consciousness. But the narrator stresses that this growing realisation of the iniquities of caste also involves burying any awareness of the injustices of colonialism deep in his unconscious mind. In this way, the reader is invited to view Bakha's path towards self-knowledge and political awareness with scepticism.

So far, I have focused on the negative critique which *Untouchable* brings to its exploration of Bakha's false consciousness, showing how the novel depicts a deficit in his understanding of the world. The reader is encouraged to see through the veil of ideology even when Bakha cannot. Towards the end of *Untouchable*, however, as Bakha begins to understand for himself, Anand brings explicitly political arguments onto the novelistic stage, which pose distinctive and positive challenges to the engrained ideological attitudes that tend to naturalise Bakha's subjection. First, there is the figure of Gandhi, whose public oration Bakha attends towards the end of the novel. Gandhi speaks against the British Empire, asking for 'freedom from a foreign nation', but also against untouchability as 'the greatest blot on Hinduism'.[29] This speech is preceded by a discussion that Bakha overhears in the crowd, as the audience awaits Gandhi's appearance and argues about his religious and political significance. By framing Gandhi's speech with these opinionated tirades (often mixed with rumour, superstition, and false supposition), Anand presents it not as a revelation of truth, but as an entry point into dialogue and debate.

Bakha listens to Gandhi very much in this spirit. Though he approves of much of what he hears, when (for example) Gandhi argues that the untouchables must 'rid themselves of evil habits, like drinking liquor and eating carrion', the narrator records Bakha's response: 'But now, now the Mahatma is blaming us, Bakha felt. "That is not fair!"' After Gandhi's oration, there follows a debate between Iqbal Nath Sharshar, a poet and editor of the *Nawan Jug* (New Era), and R. N. Bashir, an Anglicised Indian and barrister. Bashir condemns Gandhi for 'running counter to the spirit of our age, which is democracy' and for being stuck 'in the fourth century with his *swadeshi* and his spinning-wheel'. The poet is more sympathetic to Gandhi, but also feels that India has 'suffered for not accepting the machine': he argues for a more modernising approach than the Mahatma would countenance. Sharshar's ideas are closer to a Marxist analysis, and, indeed, Bashir caricatures them as 'greater efficiency, better salesmanship, more mass-production, standardization, dictatorship of the sweepers, Marxian materialism, all that!'[30]

In Colin MacCabe's definition of the 'classic realist text', the omniscient narrator constitutes a 'metadiscourse' that 'functions simply as a window on reality'. For MacCabe, the narrator's claim to a privileged access to reality is a purely ideological feature of the realist novel.[31] The narrator of *Untouchable* is often close to Bakha's limited perspective, but occasionally moves to a more omniscient position to label Bakha's thoughts 'naïve' or discuss the operations of his unconscious mind. Yet if Bakha has broken free of certain ideological preconceptions by the end of the novel, that is not to say that he has achieved the omniscience towards which the narrator occasionally gestures. Rather, he enters a dialogic space where different discourses and analyses are articulated and debated.

Lewis Grassic Gibbon

Lewis Grassic Gibbon had started to call himself a Communist in 1917, at the age of only sixteen, when he left the rural life of his upbringing to try to become a journalist in Aberdeen. Grassic Gibbon's trilogy of novels, *A Scots Quair* (1932–4), begins in a rural crofting community in the north-east of Scotland, and follows its female protagonist, Chris Guthrie, through her education, two marriages that end in the deaths of her husbands, and eventually the emergence of her son, Ewan Tavendale (confusingly named after his father, Chris's first husband), as a leading Communist organiser in the fictional city of Duncairn. Like *Summer Will Show* and *Untouchable*, the trilogy sketches a route out of false consciousness towards self-knowledge and Communist commitment, while also similarly complicating the conventional Marxist narrative. *Sunset Song* (1932), the first book of the trilogy, is set in the fictional estate of Kinraddie and its action straddles the Great War. The agricultural community in which the trilogy begins seems to inhabit a timeless and ahistorical space, threatened by both capitalist modernity and the imperialist conflict of the First World War. *Sunset Song* is a story of false consciousness, but Chris is positioned outside of the imperialist ideology that begins to take root as the country goes to war, and indeed the rural community's sense of attachment to the soil provides one source of resistance to it – at least potentially.

The people of Kinraddie are divided by British imperialist ideology, whose main spokesman is Reverend Gibbon. In his sermons, he argues that the Germans were sent by God as a 'curse and a plague on the world', and that 'the Kaiser was the Antichrist, and that until this foul evil had been swept from the earth there could be neither peace nor progress again'.[32] Chris resists Reverend Gibbon's nationalistic and warlike rhetoric, and this resistance is rooted in the rhythms of the agricultural seasons: 'The minister might be right or wrong with his Babylons and whores and might slobber Attila every night of the week, Blawearie [their croft] had its crop and that was all what mattered.'[33] When her husband Ewan is finally drafted, he is brutalised by his experiences and forced to take an interest in the war. A rift opens up between the couple, and Chris looks to the land to restore their lost equilibrium: 'when the War was done, they'd forget and forget, busy themselves in new hours and seasons, there would never be fire and gladness between them again but still undying the labour of the fields in which she now buried her days'.[34] When news comes that Ewan has been killed, Chris cannot initially accept it: 'he was never dead for those things of no concern, he'd the crops to put in and the loch to drain and her to come back to'.[35] Chris responds angrily to those in the village who attempt to fit Ewan's death into a heroic narrative of British imperialism, and her resistance to this ideology is rooted in the daily experience of the crofter. This anti-heroic perspective is soon vindicated when Chris learns that Ewan did not die heroically in battle, but was in fact shot for desertion. The night before his execution, Ewan had explained to Chae Strachan, another soldier from Kinraddie, his reasons for leaving the front: '*It was that wind that came with the sun, I minded Blawearie, I seemed to waken smelling that smell. And I couldn't believe it was me that stood in the trench, it was just daft to be there. So I turned and got out of it.*'[36] Their close connection to the land, to the timeless cycle of the seasons, is what allows Chris and (in due course) Ewan to see through the jingoistic nationalism of wartime. The central ideological assumptions of capitalist imperialism are portrayed as a form of false consciousness, and it is because Ewan's attachment to the land endures that he is able to 'waken' from this state.

The persistence of an older, agrarian way of life proves to be a valuable vantage point from which to articulate a critique of capitalist ideology, and suggests the real possibility of seeing this from the outside. *A Scots Quair* therefore throws a spanner in the works of a traditional Marxist teleology that identifies the rural with the past, and sees modernity and political emancipation emanating exclusively from the industrial cities. Marx and Engels were quite explicit in *The Communist Manifesto*:

> The bourgeoisie has subjected the country to the rule of the towns. It has created enormous cities, has greatly increased the urban population as compared with the rural, and has thus rescued a considerable part of the population from the idiocy of rural life.[37]

For some Communists (especially those inspired by Stalin's collectivisation drive), the industrialisation of the countryside is a necessary step in the direction of Communism, and any peasant resistance implicitly falls into the category of backward, reactionary 'idiocy'. Others have argued that peasant resistance to the onset of agricultural capitalism was not simply reactionary, but potentially radical, for example in Eric Hobsbawm's famous 1952 essay,

'The Machine Breakers', or E. P. Thompson's *The Making of the English Working Class* (1963).[38] Because it seeks to acknowledge and respect peasant resistance to capitalism, Grassic Gibbon's work can be aligned with this second group: the crofter's critical perspective on the advance of capitalist modernity is seen as neither reactionary nor idiotic.

In Nick Hubble's fascinating reading of *A Scots Quair*, the 'pre-capitalist social relations' depicted in the first half of *Sunset Song* (before the Great War disrupts the scene) represent a form of 'organic rural community' which becomes the basis for a radical critique of capitalism. Hubble sees Chris as 'advancing an alternative set of social values that are not entirely rooted in class relations because they still contain the trace of unalienated experience'.[39] I would suggest that in *A Scots Quair*, the land itself is also gradually exposed as an ideology, perhaps necessary to the development of a critique of capitalism, but in the end not sufficient. The idea that the community is 'organic' and that crofting is 'unalienated' labour is certainly thematised in the novel. However, it arguably forms part of a tissue of false consciousness that Grassic Gibbon's trilogy seeks to disrupt.

The idea of the 'organic' and 'unalienated' rural community is bound up in *A Scots Quair* with the idea of its timelessness. A central theme of Marx's theory of ideology is that it makes historically contingent phenomena appear as eternal verities. So we should pause to ask whether Grassic Gibbon – a committed Marxist – really means to suggest that a particular way of inhabiting and working agricultural land is organic, and the crofter's labour unalienated. The strongest image of an ancient and organic resistance to capitalism in *A Scots Quair* is the site of the Standing Stones, to which Chris returns from time to time to 'come and stand back a little from the clamour of the days'.[40] The Standing Stones mentality hinges on an assumption that the land stands outside of historical process and change:

> nothing endured at all, nothing but the land she passed across, tossed and turned and perpetually changed below the hands of the crofter folk since the oldest of them had set the Standing Stones by the loch of Blawearie and climbed there on their holy days and saw their terraced crops ride brave in the wind and sun. Sea and sky and the folk who wrote and fought and were learnéd, teaching and saying and praying, they lasted but as a breath, a mist of fog in the hills, but the land was forever, it moved and changed below you, but was forever, you were close to it and it to you, not at a bleak remove it held you and hurted you. And she had thought to leave it all![41]

Chris's thoughts, conveyed in free indirect discourse, beautifully compress Grassic Gibbon's central theme. The writing powerfully communicates the appeal of a rooted identification with the soil. The slightly oxymoronic notion of the land as 'perpetually changed' emphasises the cyclical nature of crofting as a way of life, and the Standing Stones in turn suggest the unchanging pattern of life that persists as generations of particular individuals are born and then die.

However, *A Scots Quair* also suggests that the Standing Stones mentality is itself an ideological formation. The 'Proem' that begins the second part of the trilogy, *Cloud Howe* (1933), takes the reader through nearly a millennium of violent Scottish history, from the reign of Kenneth III (c.966–1005), through the time of Robert the Bruce and the Battle of Bannockburn (1314), up to the 'Killing Time' (when Presbyterians were persecuted by Charles II and James VII), and later the growth of the railway and with it modern manufacturing and trade.[42] This millennium of history is packed into six pages, in which the apparently timeless rhythms of the crofting life – which had provided a powerful vantage point from which to refuse the ideology of British imperialism in *Sunset Song* – are revealed not to be timeless at all, but the historically contingent product of violent conflict. The Proem complicates any nostalgia for the unchanging rural past, and suggests that the whole history of Kinraddie is one painfully disruptive social change. What is so remarkable about Grassic Gibbon's writing is that the satisfactions of rooted rural life are palpably deep and real, but also and at the same time ideological.

It is in the concluding part of the trilogy, *Grey Granite* (1934), that the full emotional cost of an awakening into Communism becomes clear. Chris has moved with her son Ewan Tavendale to Duncairn. Chris nudges Ewan towards college and university but he resists, taking instead an apprenticeship in Gowans and Gloag, smelters and steelmakers, where he becomes a vocal trade unionist. Initially, he forms the 'League', which attempts to unite Communists and Labourites against the capitalist enemy. But when he is arrested and savagely beaten by the police, he loses faith in 'the slobberings of middle-class pacifists, the tawdry promisings of Labourites, [and] Douglasites'.[43] Echoing Ingelbrecht's critique of bourgeois socialists in *Summer Will Show*, Ewan moves towards an uncompromising Communism. The hardening of Ewan's political views models a transition from ethical socialism towards Communist commitment, which is also represented as a passage towards epistemological certainty. Bandaged after his beating by the police, and released with a small fine, Ewan addresses the workers of Duncairn at a rally in his honour (his words are conveyed indirectly by the narrator):

> One thing he had learned: the Communists were right. Only by force could we beat brute force, plans for peaceful reform were about as sane as hunting

a Bengal tiger with a Bible. They must organize the masses, make them
think, make them see, let them know there was no way they could ever win
to power except through the fight of class against class, till they dragged
down the masters and ground them to pulp –
Then he fainted away on the Windmill Steps.[44]

The violence of Ewan's rhetoric echoes his treatment at the hands of the
police (even if his fainting fit seems to cut across it in some ways). It is
a visceral and remorseless violence, from which many readers will recoil.
Reviewing *Grey Granite* for the *Left Review*, John Lehmann wrote that one
of the book's 'obvious faults' was that, 'for all his moral passion and
courage', Ewan 'never becomes a really sympathetic character', being 'too
humourless, and at times even priggish'.[45]

There is a contrast to be drawn here with *Sunset Song*. In the earlier
novel, Chris's education allows her to see through the drudgery and
confinement of rural life, and yet that same education makes her painfully
aware of what she is losing. Hubble recommends reading *Grey Granite* not
as an enthusiastic endorsement of Ewan's hardening Communism, but as
'a trenchant critique of narrow proletarian politics'.[46] This involves taking
more seriously the trajectory of Chris, who follows a more winding path
from the false certainties of the organic community to a tentative embrace
of uncertainty, of an anxious and ambivalent relationship to modernity. As
Matti Ron writes in a compelling reading of Grassic Gibbon's trilogy,
'*A Scots Quair* centres and legitimises the experience of a non-politicised
character, thus foregrounding the agency of the working class in societal
transformation rather than the ideologies or organisations of political
representatives.'[47] For Ron, this distinguishes Grassic Gibbon's work
from much other committed left-wing fiction of the period.

Conclusion

The novels I have focused on in this chapter show how a Marxist account of
ideology can be adapted to thinking about gender and sexuality, colonialism,
nationalism, and the relationship between the country and the city. They
clearly draw on the traditions of socialist realism as they seek to peel back the
veils of ideology and false consciousness. Yet the reality that the protagonists
then confront is more fraught with epistemological doubt than are the decep-
tive certainties of false consciousness. Writing in 1936, the Communist novelist,
classicist, and polymath Jack Lindsay analysed the route to self-knowledge in
several recent left-wing novels, comparing this to 'Recognition' (*anagnorisis*) in
ancient Greek literature. '*Now*', Lindsay writes (i.e., in the Communist novel),

'Recognition appears as the point where the shell of the old self cracks and the new self is born, breaking into new spaces of activity and achieving fullness of social contact.'[48] Lindsay's description could be aptly applied to the character trajectories of the protagonists of *Summer Will Show*, *Untouchable*, and *A Scots Quair*. Townsend Warner, Anand, and Grassic Gibbon are Communist writers who evade Adorno's condemnation of politically committed art. If they stage a modernised version of 'Recognition', inflected with Marxist theories of ideology, then they do not do so in order to console us with epistemological and moral certainty, as Adorno suggested. Instead, in these fascinating novels, the false certainties of ideological enchantment give way to an intensification and deepening of social and intellectual activity – to complexity, contradiction, and debate.

Notes

1 Arthur Koestler, *The Invisible Writing: The Second Volume of an Autobiography: 1932–40* (London: Vintage, 2005), p. 283.
2 Ben Harker, *The Chronology of Revolution: Communism, Culture, and Civil Society in Twentieth-Century Britain* (Toronto, ON: University of Toronto Press, 2021), p. 17.
3 See, for example, John Connor, 'Anglo-Soviet Literary Relations in the Long 1930s', in *A History of 1930s British Literature*, ed. Benjamin Kohlmann and Matthew Taunton (Cambridge: Cambridge University Press, 2019), pp. 317–30; Benjamin Kohlmann, *Committed Styles: Modernism, Politics, and Left-Wing Literature in the 1930s* (Oxford: Oxford University Press, 2014); Harker, *The Chronology of Revolution*; Ben Harker, '"Communism is English": Edgell Rickword, Jack Lindsay and the Cultural Politics of the Popular Front', *Literature & History* 20.2 (2011), pp. 16–34; Ben Harker, 'Politics and Letters: The "Soviet Literary Controversy" in Britain', *Literature & History* 24.1 (2015), pp. 41–57; Glyn Salton-Cox, *Queer Communism and the Ministry of Love* (Edinburgh: Edinburgh University Press, 2018); Matthew Taunton, *Red Britain: The Russian Revolution in Mid-Century Culture* (Oxford: Oxford University Press, 2019); and Elinor Taylor, *The Popular Front Novel in Britain, 1934–1940* (Leiden: Brill, 2018).
4 Karl Radek, 'Contemporary World Literature and the Tasks of Proletarian Art', in Andrey Zhdanov et al., *Problems of Soviet Literature: Reports and Speeches at the First Soviet Writers' Congress,* ed. H. G. Scott (London: Martin Lawrence, 1935), pp. 73–182 (pp. 153, 171, 157).
5 Theodor Adorno, 'Commitment', *New Left Review* 1.87/88 (September/December 1974), pp. 75–89 (p. 87).
6 Stephen Spender, *World Within World* (London: Faber, 1977), p. 211.
7 Salton-Cox, *Queer Communism*, p. 79.
8 Ibid., p. 5.

9   Sylvia Townsend Warner, *Summer Will Show* (New York: New York Review Books, 2009), pp. 326–7.
10 Michael Warner, *The Trouble with Normal: Sex, Politics, and the Ethics of Queer Life* (Cambridge, MA: Harvard University Press, 2000), p. 105.
11 Townsend Warner, *Summer Will Show*, pp. 113–14.
12 Ibid., pp. 212, 219.
13 Ibid., p. 221. The extract from Ingelbrecht's treatise is presented in italics in the original.
14 Ibid., p. 129.
15 Ulka Anjaria, *Realism in the Twentieth-Century Indian Novel* (Cambridge: Cambridge University Press, 2012), p. 66; Carlo Coppola, 'The All-India Progressive Writers' Association: The European Phase', in *Marxist Influences and South Asian Literature*, Vol. 1, ed. Coppola (East Lansing, MI: Asian Studies Center, Michigan State University, 1974), pp. 1–34; Rudrani Gangopadhyay, editorial note to Mulk Raj Anand, 'Manifesto of the Indian Progressive Writers' Association', in *Global Modernists on Modernism: An Anthology*, ed. Alys Moody and Stephen J. Ross (London: Bloomsbury Academic, 2000) pp. 248–9 (p. 248). As John Connor has pointed out, Anand's role as a 'leading activist in the Indian cultural front' has been obscured by his 'late-career autobiographical writing, which cast his one-time socialist humanism in looser, more liberal, terms, and his aesthetics as an almost exclusive debt to high modernism' (Connor, 'Anglo-Russian Literary Relations', p. 326). His first novel, *Untouchable* (1935), came packaged with a foreword by E. M. Forster, which coloured its British reception with the tinge of Bloomsbury liberalism. The effects of Forster's introduction to the novel are explored in Anna Snaith, 'Introducing Mulk Raj Anand:The Colonial Politics of Collaboration', *Literature & History* 28.1 (2019), pp. 10–26.
16 Anand, 'Manifesto of the Indian Progressive Writers' Association', p. 249.
17 Coppola, 'The All-India Progressive Writers' Association', p. 5.
18 Jessica Berman, *Modernist Commitments: Ethics, Politics, and Transnational Modernism* (New York: Columbia University Press, 2011), pp. 90–1.
19 Anjaria, *Realism*; Connor, 'Anglo-Russian Literary Relations'.
20 Anjaria, *Realism*, p. 5.
21 Karl Marx, 'The British Rule in India', *Karl Marx on India*, ed. Iqbal Husain (New Delhi: Tulika Books, 2006), pp. 11–17 (p. 16).
22 Mulk Raj Anand, *Untouchable* (London: Penguin, 2014), pp. 60–1.
23 Adorno, 'Commitment', p. 87.
24 Anand, *Untouchable*, p. 92.
25 Ibid., pp. 94–5.
26 Ibid. p. 3.
27 Ibid., p. 4.
28 Ibid., p. 118.
29 Ibid., pp. 128–9.
30 Ibid., pp. 132, 134, 137.
31 Colin MacCabe, *James Joyce and the Revolution of the Word* (London and Basingstoke: Macmillan, 1978), p. 15.

32 Lewis Grassic Gibbon, *Sunset Song*, in *A Scots Quair* (Edinburgh: Canongate, 2008), pp. 193–4.

33 Ibid., p. 193.

34 Ibid., pp. 229.

35 Ibid., pp. 235.

36 Ibid., pp. 237–8. Ewan's speech is reported in italics in Grassic Gibbon's text.

37 Karl Marx and Friedrich Engels, *The Communist Manifesto*, trans. Samuel Moore (London: Penguin, 2002), p. 224.

38 E. J. Hobsbawm, 'The Machine Breakers', *Past & Present* 1.1 (February 1952), pp. 57–70; E. P. Thompson, *The Making of the English Working Class* (London: Penguin, 2013). I have explored debates about Communism and rural life in greater depth in Taunton, *Red Britain*, pp. 162–215.

39 Nick Hubble, 'Transformative Pastoral: Lewis Grassic Gibbon's *A Scots Quair*', in *Rural Modernity in Britain: A Critical Intervention*, ed. Kristin Bluemel and Michael McCluskey (Edinburgh: Edinburgh University Press, 2018), pp. 149–64 (p. 156).

40 Grassic Gibbon, *Sunset Song*, p. 108.

41 Ibid., p. 119.

42 Lewis Grassic Gibbon, *Cloud Howe*, in *A Scots Quair* (Edinburgh: Canongate, 2008), pp. 1–6.

43 Lewis Grassic Gibbon, *Grey Granite*, in *A Scots Quair* (Edinburgh: Canongate, 2008), p. 137.

44 Ibid., p. 145.

45 John Lehmann, 'Grey Granite', *Left Review* 1.5 (1935), pp. 190–1 (p. 190).

46 Nick Hubble, *The Proletarian Answer to the Modernist Question* (Edinburgh: Edinburgh University Press, 2017), p. 114.

47 Matti Ron, 'Representing Revolt: Working-Class Representation as a Literary and Political Practice from the General Strike to the Winter of Discontent', unpublished PhD thesis, University of East Anglia, 2020, p. 137.

48 Jack Lindsay, 'Man in Society', *Left Review* 2.15 (1936), pp. 837–40 (p. 837).

CHAPTER 3

Fascism

Charles Ferrall and Dougal McNeill

Fascism produced no significant literature. And how could it? Contemptuous towards individual creativity; intellectually incoherent; cynically opportunistic in its deployment of revolutionary rhetoric, fascism destroyed the very conditions of possibility for writing. Poetry and narrative, in the early to mid-twentieth century (the era of the first media age), offered few possibilities for spectacle. Fascism found uses for cinema, the visual arts, architecture, and music, but left no memorable literary record. However much particular authors may have fancied their chances as exemplary *Übermenschen*, fascist *politics* had little use for individualist thinkers in its ranks. There were plenty of connections between modernist writing and reactionary politics, to be sure: D. H. Lawrence pursued the theme of leadership in his novels of the mid-1920s; W. B. Yeats flirted with the Blueshirts towards the end of his life; T. S. Eliot remained scandalously indifferent to the realities of antisemitism and fascist murderousness across continental Europe; and Ezra Pound, notoriously, broadcast for Mussolini's regime throughout the Second World War. All of these examples, disgraceful enough on a biographical level, illuminate little about the achievements of their writing as literature. Pound's reputation persists despite, and not as a result of, the political ideas that seep into the *Pisan Cantos*. Lawrence's flirtation with fascist ideas was eccentrically individual and not connected to any political movement. Yeats's personal involvement with the Blueshirts prompted nothing more than some forgettable songs. The literary fields of fascism are barren ground.

What fascism generated in literature, instead, was a complex culture of opposition irreducible to its component parts. *Anti-fascism*, a current of circulating journals, newsletters, tensely aligned writers, and writers' organisations, channelled politics through writing. Fascism, Jason Stanley argues, is not so much a coherent ideology as a way of doing politics, a set of 'tactics as a mechanism to achieve state power'. He lists among these, mobilisation of 'the mythic past, propaganda, anti-intellectualism, unreality, hierarchy, victimhood, law and order, sexual anxiety, appeals to the heartland, and a dismantling of public welfare and unity'.[1] Born out of Europe's 'Thirty Years War' (1914–45) as a counter-revolutionary response to workers' revolutions in Russia and Germany, anti-colonial revolts, and insurgent workers' mobilisations in Italy, France, and Spain, fascism deployed its tactics inconsistently and opportunistically. Italian fascism, the earliest to take state power, stressed from the start anti-socialist violence, corporatist solutions to class conflict through national unity, and intense, masculinist nationalism. Racist from its beginnings, Italian fascism only codified racial laws in the late 1930s, as part of its alliance with Nazism. Drawing on, and radicalising, deep structures of anti-Jewish racism in European culture, fascism relied on racism everywhere. Fervently nationalist, and combining self-pitying accounts of national humiliation with dreams of national superiority, fascism could prioritise sectarian violence over nationalist assertion, as with the Rashtriya Swayamsevak Sangh in India, an anti-Muslim fascism that isolated itself from the anti-colonial movement, or move between bigotries as the moment demanded, as happened with Italian fascism's shifting targets. Combining revolutionary rhetoric with a loyalty, once in power, to stabilised capitalist social relations, fascism is best understood, unlike other groupings in this Companion, not as a distinct political philosophy, but as the generation and mobilisation of racialised passions for political ends. Japanese fascism, for example, dreamed of 'overcoming modernity' while frantically modernising army, navy, and industry, rhetoric and reality running in parallel.[2] 'There is not yet a satisfactory definition of what Fascism is', the novelist and anti-fascist activist Ellen Wilkinson noted in 1934; 'the Fascists themselves have not been able to produce an intelligible definition.'[3] This was a strategically useful ambiguity, the fascist deployment of passions itself a substitute for the usual business of politics. If the Leader and his people were one, and the Leader knew the people's wishes through instinct and racial affinity – the non-people, whether Jewish, Muslim, homosexual, or Roma, having been purged from the national body – what need then of political deliberation? 'Fascists held that elections, parliaments, and discussions about public affairs – in short the stuff of politics – were incapable of representing a "general will"', Dylan Riley argues; in place of this public sphere, fascism offered itself as a total state-party-people.[4] Instead of the contestation of class politics pursued by trade unions and Socialist and Communist parties, or the deliberative transformations of liberal democracy and universal suffrage, fascism offered myths of a unitary people redeemed through violent redemption and purged of politics.

Anti-fascism was a public sphere forged out of the international movement in opposition to this sham redemption. Fascism, unlike more traditional authoritarianisms, stood not for the suppression, but the complete annihilation of its opponents, dreaming of a world not just without social conflict but without Communists, socialists, Jews, or dissidents as a physical reality. Anti-fascism thus, from its beginning, saw its struggle in existential terms. Literature was at the heart of this struggle from its inception. The first anti-fascist group in Britain was formed by a novelist, Ethel Carnie Holdsworth, and the networks of writers created through shared anti-fascist commitments created both new venues for literature and new, productive, pressures on literary forms. Naomi Mitchison, in her anti-fascist *Vienna Diary* (1934), called this anti-fascist writers' alliance 'the bad girls of the Labour movement, always playing with the naughty boys and getting away with it'.[5] The bad girls' contribution is not reducible to its component parts of Communism, Labour politics, and feminism, however. Anti-fascism was a new, creative, and unstable compound, its differing parts pulling, at times, in different directions, as writers sought to address strategic questions: Was fascism an outgrowth of existing social relations or something new? Did it represent the negation of modern society or its consummation? Would anti-fascist resistance draw on tradition or reject it for revolutionary transformation? Literary texts both circulated in new arrangements, as anti-fascist networks created new publics through mass-movement journals, and felt different pressures, as authors worked to draw artistic forms into dialogue with the urgencies of a threat to art itself. As Enzo Traverso puts it:

> In the mid twentieth century [. . .] this return to the Enlightenment and the values of 1789 took on a new dimension, drawing the main lines of a *European public space* defined by cultural, ethical and political frontiers. Antifascism included all the constitutive elements of a 'public sphere' in the most traditional sense of the term: literature, science, the arts, the press. The antifascist cause was defended above all by a constellation of writers [. . .] It was expressed in a broad network of magazines and duplicated bulletins, side by side with certain mass-circulation press organs [. . .] antifascism was a public space in which choices crossed paths that were inevitably fated to come into conflict once this threat had dissipated.[6]

New networks formed, as refugee intellectuals such as Ernst Toller socialised with anti-fascist British and American writers and anti-colonial thinkers such as Krishna Menon. New patterns of literary connection became possible, as when Nancy Cunard organised *Les Poètes du monde défendent le people espagnol! The Poets of the World Defend the Spanish*

People!, a series of trilingual poetry pamphlets publishing together English, French, and Spanish poems, including, most famously, W. H. Auden's 'Spain' (1937), to raise funds for the Spanish Republic.[7] These new connections and networks would, in turn, shape post-1945 literature, as the movements of new worlds and new nations drew, in their critiques of colonialism, on the uncomfortable questions anti-fascism had raised about the relationship between European states and cultures, racism, and Empire. Key anti-fascist figures, from Langston Hughes in the United States to Naomi Mitchison in Britain, would continue the core tasks of the anti-fascist project in their post-war anti-colonial work.

Much of this creative energy was, until recently, obscured by critical histories that tended to focus either on individual, and unrepresentative, biographical histories – the 'Auden generation' of Samuel Hynes's famous study – in which a small group of upper-middle-class male writers' affiliation to, and then defection from, anti-fascism was taken as *the* narrative of interwar literary politics. Cold War histories, in addition, reduced anti-fascism to Communism. This chapter, drawing on more recent critical work, emphasises the range, distinction, and importance of writing produced within 'the populist anti-fascist politics of the years leading up to the war'.[8]

Fascism posed a representational problem for oppositional writers. It combined an unprecedented destructiveness and violence, murdering opponents and annihilating trade unions and democratic publications and organisations, with aestheticised displays of spectacular power: mass rallies, feverish processions, carefully choreographed film and posters. How could writing both acknowledge the urgency of this threat and reality while also piercing the screen of fascism's spectacular display? How might anti-fascism combine political *commitment* with fidelity to doubt, questioning, and reservation as democratic virtues in the face of fascist belief, obedience, and authority? If writers found themselves in new activist situations ('police-charges are not things that one can take as placidly as tea parties', Sylvia Townsend Warner wrote to a friend after she was beaten at a counter-demonstration protesting Oswald Mosley's Blackshirts in 1936), anti-fascism needed to find ways to avoid mirroring fascist aesthetics and affect.[9] Mia Spiro has identified this as the dilemma of 'anti-Nazi aesthetics', those anti-fascist attempts to account for the peculiar appeal of fascist spectacle while resisting its temptations.[10] Mitchison attempted to solve this problem by aesthetic distance, writing *We Have Been Warned* (1935) as 'an historical novel of [her] own time', historicising fascism's rise and potential trajectory.[11] Virginia Woolf, in turn, made the image and the spectacle the organising conceit of her anti-fascist polemic, *Three Guineas* (1938), both evoking and resisting the power of the violent image. In the process, she fuses fascism's *external* threat and its resonances with injustices *internal* to British society:

> consider these photographs: they are pictures of dead bodies and ruined houses. Surely in view of these questions and pictures you must consider very carefully [. . .] what is the aim of education, what kind of society, what kind of human being it should seek to produce. At any rate I will only send you a guinea with which to rebuild your college if you can satisfy me that you will use it to produce the kind of society, the kind of people that will help us to prevent war.[12]

How might literature make new people and prevent war while also fostering doubt and openness, an openness that will 'combine doubt with action, will direct mistrust usefully'?[13] This was the challenge of anti-fascism.

Fascism Elsewhere

Fascism emerged in reaction to the revolutionary left-wing advances across Europe that ended the First World War, and it sought to eradicate their example and legacy. If socialist and feminist thinkers welcomed the revolutions in Germany, Hungary, and Russia, the 'Biennio Rosso' and factory occupations in Italy (1919–20), and the anti-colonial insurgencies from China (1925–7) to Ireland (1916–22), the counter-revolutions of fascism in Italy, Germany, Spain, and, via Japanese invasion, China, stood as the cancellation of a possible future. Anti-fascist writing first sought to document fascist outrages in texts such as Mitchison's *Vienna Diary*, communicating the realities of life under fascist rule that were rarely documented in mass-circulation newspapers, many of which were owned or edited by figures sympathetic to Italian and German fascism until the late 1930s. Fascism's development abroad, however, challenged writers to represent the threat of a politics both distant and present. Distant, because elsewhere, but also present because those faraway places shared the same world as the inhabitants of Britain. The threat was felt as at once immediate and displaced. Fascism's triumphs occurred, spatially, in places away from Britain, and yet that shared the same world as its inhabitants. As Auden put it, 'maps can really point to places / Where life is evil now: / Nanking, Dachau.'[14] At the same time, however, *temporally*, fascist rule was, for anti-fascist writers, a combination of the past and the future. In its barbarisms – its anti-Jewish pogroms, its reactionary campaigns to return women to

Kinder, Küche, Kirche anti-Enlightenment irrationalism – fascism represented a move *backwards*. Its examples in space were also visions of other *futures*, and writers produced warnings of what might come elsewhere. This scrambling of space, time, the past, and the future produced an unstable temporal order as a defining feature of anti-fascist writing. Auden's twentieth sonnet, in the sequence 'In Time of War', for example, begins in the tones of reportage, describing something happening to others: 'They carry terror with them like a purse'. After two stanzas describing 'them', however, its next two speak of 'us', the poem's speaker shifting from someone observing the Chinese war to a figure caught in a moment in history: 'We live here. We lie in the Present's unopened / Sorrow; its limits are what we are.'[15]

Nowhere was that sorrow and those limits felt more intensely than in Spain. The Spanish Revolution, in Traverso's phrase, 'condensed conflicts of continental and global significance on the scale of a single country'.[16] Spain was, in politics and literature, synecdoche. When General Franco's attempted coup against the Republican government failed, German and Italian fascisms sent military aid to his counter-revolution, while volunteers, including many writers, rallied to serve in defence of the Republic. Spain was poetic occasion, with appeals, fund-raising pamphlets, and poems produced as part of a wider movement in which any perceived split between artistic autonomy and popular audience was rendered meaningless. Spain also tightened the tensions between thinking of fascism temporally or spatially almost to breaking point. The revolutionary war represented an absolute temporal break, 'Yesterday all the past' – in Auden's 'Spain' – and a spatial reminder, elsewhere, of a reality almost denied in pre-fascist Britain and America, as in Muriel Rukeyser's 'Mediterranean' (1938), where Spain is 'our home country' that 'fights our war':[17]

> If we had not seen fighting,
> if we had not looked there
> the plane flew low
> the plastic ripped by shots
> the peasant's house
> if we had stayed in our world
> between the table and the desk
> between the town and the suburb
> slowly disintegration
> male and female[18]

The particular details of the Spanish conflict matter less in this poetry than its role as a part standing in for the fascist whole: what was happening in

Spain would happen to Britain, just as it had happened in Austria and Germany, were writing not to move its readers to action. Anti-fascism, in organising public aid for Spain, addressed the distant as the universal – 'Barcelona / everywhere, Spain everywhere', Sylvia Townsend Warner announced.[19] At its best, however, anti-fascist literature found ways of connecting the linkages of solidarity with an awareness of difference and specificity, the risk of the emptied time of a fascist victory with a sense of complex continuity. Nancy Cunard's 'Yes, It Is Spain', for instance, in poetic dialogue with Auden's line 'Yes, I am Spain', deploys an irregular, broken rhyme scheme and metre to match its dialectical account of the returns of imperial history and the 'Thirty Years Crisis' in the Spanish fight:

You, man, mumbling that misplaced, ridiculous 'spot of bother',
O brother contemporary, and some of you the salt of the earth –
What else could you do but go? We shall not forget you,
(And that's a fact, humanly not officially said),
Not forgive the present Flanders-Poppy flaunting ahead towards the next one,
By La-Der-des-Ders into La Prochaine. I have not forgot my dead.

You think this is something new? No; this too becomes Spain,
All of it, all of it's Spain with the dial set at Revenge –
No past pageantry of wan mothers and lovers weeping,
Ruined, undone forever, that Spain cannot avenge.[20]

Fascism Here

Cunard's scorn towards 'Flanders-Poppy flaunting ahead towards' the next war gestures at anti-fascism's more disquieting, and productive, affinities. If, elsewhere, war 'is simple like a monument', organising against racism, misogyny, and anti-democratic mobilisations abroad drew many writers to question what traits fascism might share with society closer to home.[21] In the political sphere, anti-fascism confronted a strategic problem: was fascism an *aberration* from 'normal' life, and thus best confronted with alliances comprising as wide a swathe of society as possible, or was it the *outgrowth* of class society, thus requiring revolutionary opposition to its causes? Different parts of the anti-fascist alliance stressed different elements of this dilemma, with the official Communist parties, for example, travelling from the latter analysis to the former as the 1930s progressed. Anti-fascist literature, however, kept these options in imaginative relation by interrogating fascism's shared features with those based in Britain and the United States. This interrogation was both a literary-representational problem, as writers struggled to find ways of expressing the enormity of fascism's threat while remaining believable, and an exercise in extending solidarity, as anti-fascism linked European dissent to wider networks of anti-colonial thinking. What began as a formal, literary problem of representation, developed into a wider challenge to what in the everyday practices of Empire was invisible from the colonial centre. Mitchison, in her *Vienna Diary*, summarised the problem:

> I keep thinking how apt one is to skip atrocity stories (after all, one must live, and such stories, if one begins to allow the imagination to vivify them, are shattering) [...] Everyone – here and abroad – says that the Austrians would never be as beastly and brutal as the Germans. And so *we* say about the possibilities of Fascism in England. It is the kind of line one can't help believing, for it goes so well with one's inclinations.[22]

In *We Have Been Warned*, Mitchison uses generic discontinuity, shifting from a realist mode to a speculative, future-history in order to challenge these inclinations and complicities. Her narrative of Britain after a fascist coup makes its affiliations to the Empire explicit:

> 'We are not like your rebels. We are not concerned with what the foreigner thinks. We are concerned with our English Empire. These executions are necessary. They are a purging. Our country has gone rotten. Now it will be England again!'
> 'Is it English to shoot prisoners? Wounded men?'
> 'It was their doing. They began the revolution. We have to crush them. In a week we shall have order again. We cannot afford any mercy and weakness now!'[23]

Shooting prisoners was, as Mitchison knew, one of the many atrocities committed by the British Empire against independence fighters abroad, and the example of the Empire had itself inspired fascist ambitions for racialised conquest in Europe.[24] Anti-fascism provided a bridge between pre-1914 suffrage campaigning, interwar leftist organisation, and post-war anti-colonial writing. If, as Priyamvada Gopal documents, anti-colonial 'black counterculture in London drew on actually occurring resistances', these resistances were in turn inspired by the challenge of anti-colonial critique.[25] Nancy Cunard, Ellen Wilkinson, and Victor Gollancz were all patrons of the International African Service Bureau at the same time as they built anti-fascist alliances. Wilkinson's uncomfortable reminder, in her work with Edward Conze, that 'the whole Empire has been built up on the firm conviction of the superiority of the Anglo-Saxon race', as she analysed fascism's racial mythology in Germany, drew intellectual sustenance from the Bureau's recognition that:

> Fascism, which is the most brutal form of imperialism, puts a firm break on all liberal ideas, all freedom, on every concept of human equality and fraternity. In Germany, it bases itself on fanatical nationalism, and exaggerated racial arrogance. Its inhuman persecution of the Jews is a sop to national discontent and a convenient distraction from the real issues at stake. With giant strides it stalks all over the world. In Italy, Germany, Poland, Romania, in diverse forms, it raises its head everywhere. It has appeared in Britain and in the British House of Commons.[26]

This complex solidarity, combining affiliation with European forces opposing fascism alongside a firm insistence on liberal democratic Europe's complicity with colonialism, found its most challenging literary expression in Langston Hughes's poetry. Across a series of poems, Hughes prompts readers to imagine fascism at home ('Air Raid Over Harlem', 1936), to link with Ethiopian, Spanish, and German workers facing fascist threats, and in his 'Letter' and 'Postcard' from Spain (1937), connects experiences of Spanish colonialism with African American oppression. But when Hughes describes Czechoslovakia as 'lynched on a swastika cross!' he complicates these affinities.[27] To 'lynch' is an American verb describing an American white supremacist violence, and, by translating European suffering into American terms, and with the 'swastika cross' evoking the burning cross of the Ku Klux Klan, Hughes evokes continuities between everyday American life and states of fascist emergency. His 'Beaumont to Detroit: 1943', written after the United States' entry into the Second World War and after the Communist Party had dropped its anti-fascist militancy in favour of wartime unity, draws out this affinity more starkly:

> Yet you say we're fighting
> For democracy.
> Then why don't democracy
> Include me?
>
> I ask you this question
> Cause I want to know
> How long I got to fight
> BOTH HITLER – AND JIM CROW.[28]

Hughes's speaker's suggestion that Hitler 'took lessons / From the Ku Klux Klan' and that 'everything that hitler / And mussolini do, / Negroes get the same / Treatment from you',[29] draws anti-fascist critique out, without losing any of its initial impulse, into wider reflection. Gopal has described this process as the shared 'unlearning of paternalism as an anti-colonial disposition in favour of constructing working solidarities', and it played out across countless fundraising readings, editorial meetings, and journal subscription drives through the anti-fascist movement.[30]

Fascist Psychology

Virginia Woolf's *Three Guineas* (1938), in terms less direct but no less polemical than Hughes's, traces affinities between fascism's reactionary gender politics and the assumptions structuring British society. Positioning the early twentieth-century feminists who 'were fighting the tyranny of the patriarchal state' as the 'advance guard' of the movement 'fighting the tyranny of the Fascist state', Woolf uses modernist juxtaposition to show the uncomfortable parallels between the two, insisting that 'we are merely carrying on the same fight that our mothers and grandmothers fought'.[31] Placing unattributed quotes from Hitler and Mussolini on women's proper social role next to excerpts from a letter to *The Times* opposing women's work in the Civil Service, Woolf directs her readers' attention to their shared assumptions. 'Where is the difference?', she asks:

> Are they not both saying the same thing? Are they not both the voices of Dictators, whether they speak English or German, and are we not all agreed that the dictator when we meet him abroad is a very dangerous as well as ugly animal? And here he is among us, raising his ugly head, spitting his poison, small still, curled up like a caterpillar on a leaf, but in the heart of England still.[32]

Woolf's questions, and her determination to refuse the 'unreal loyalties' of nationality and 'sex pride' in patriarchal Englishness, prompt answers around fascism's appeal, and its connections to those most intimate areas of subject formation – the family, sexuality, gender – that organise social relations.[33] Anti-fascist writers set themselves the task, in imaginative fictions, of analysing the psychological dynamics of fascism and its attractions.

Woolf insists that 'the public and the private worlds are inseparably connected, that the tyrannies and servilities of the one are the tyrannies and servilities of the other', but insists also that anti-fascist rejection of these twinned tyrannies must generate a world of human freedom.[34] Freedom 'from unreal loyalties' of nationality and gendered roles is, for Woolf, a freedom to reimagine human motivations and relationships.[35] What, then, sustains fascist loyalties? Anti-fascist writing, Woolf's *Three Guineas* above all, concerned itself with accounting for the psychology of fascism in order to better counter its appeal. Fascism was, Wilkinson wrote, more than just 'sadistic tyranny' or the confidence trick of an all-powerful leader, and it was only by understanding the ways that those 'who seem at critical moments to ride the storm and direct the whirlwinds, are themselves no more than light conspicuous corks, showing in which way the deep hidden waves of human feelings are flowing', that anti-fascism might organise opposition.[36] Literary anti-fascism thus joined and advanced ongoing modernist adaptations of psychoanalysis, and offered particular feminist and gendered insights and critiques of psychoanalytic theories of the fascist crowd.

Strategic questions around the relationship between public and private life link Woolf's feminism, fascist strategy, and psychoanalytic theory. Anti-fascism constructed alternative public spheres to fascism's all-encompassing reach. As Paul Corner observes of fascist ideology, society was

> no longer autonomous in respect of the state but was merged with the state in a single unitary body politics. It was axiomatic that there was no longer a 'public sphere' where some kind of mediation between state and society took place. But equally and rather paradoxically [. . .] neither was there a private sphere where the state had no right to intrude. By denying the private sphere of the individual, everything thus became public.[37]

Corner describes this fascist 'public', where 'politics' has been abolished, as 'street theatre', or as 'being fundamentally about aesthetics'.[38] But as Peter Nathan observed in 1943, Hitler was not concerned with public policy and he 'stated quite clearly that the aim of his movement is a psychological one'.[39] Fascism not only aestheticises but psychologises politics, and inter-war feminist and literary interest in psychology, pioneered by the Woolfs' Hogarth Press publishing translations of Sigmund Freud, thus informed anti-fascist thinking.

One influential account, Freud's 'Group Psychology and the Analysis of the Ego' (1921), was published before Mussolini's March on Rome, but, as Theodor Adorno argues, it 'clearly foresaw the rise and nature of fascist mass movements in purely psychological categories'.[40] According to Freud, a 'primary' social group consists of 'a number of individuals who have put one and the same object in place of their ego ideal and have consequently identified themselves with one another in their ego'.[41] Freud has in mind social groups such as the church and the army, and Adorno argues that such narcissism is also characteristic of the relationships between fascist followers ('egos'), the fascist leader ('ego ideal'), and what he calls the 'outgroup' (and Freud the 'outer object'). The followers identify both with each other through what Adorno calls a form of 'repressive egalitarianism' as well as with a 'superman [who] must still resemble the follower and appear as his "enlargement"'.[42] When it comes to the role women play in this psychological triangle, however, both Freud and Adorno have little to say. During the 1930s, it was three women writers – Woolf, Winifred Holtby, and Katharine Burdekin ('Murray Constantine') – who analysed respectively the three axes of this triangle, with women rather than men at two of its points. Whereas for Freud and Adorno the gendered nature of the fascist psychological dynamic goes unremarked, these anti-fascist authors complicate and contest its patriarchal-domestic axes. For two of these writers, Woolf and Burdekin, fascism is both the cause and effect of the exclusion of women from the public sphere, whereas for Burdekin one of its consequences is the abolition of both spheres.

Woolf claimed not to have read Freud until 1939, but, as Elizabeth Abel notes, *Three Guineas* 'rewrites the Oedipus concept by situating both love and hatred in the daughter', though it is actually focused not on the daughter but the father.[43] Whereas Freud's emphasis is on the son's hostility towards his father, Woolf looks instead at the father's 'infantile fixation' towards his daughter. This is a double substitution of daughter for son and father for son. The final consequence of the 'infantile complex' – patriarchy – shares the logic of fascism and, like fascism, leads inevitably to war. Woolf's text, in keeping with an anti-fascist aesthetic of doubt, proceeds by a series of spirals, interruptions, digressions, and returns, rather than through explicit statement, but has, perhaps alarmingly, a simple, challenging conclusion. Fathers 'possess' – in all senses of that word – their daughters by denying them access to a public sphere, and the 'law of England' denies women 'the full stigmata of nationality'.[44] Since the main way in which their brothers gain access to the public sphere is through education, in particular that of the university, then the education of women, albeit in a radically reformed system, could prevent war. Whereas Freud and Adorno believe that psychoanalysis can dispel the 'hypnotism' of individuals within the social group, Woolf uses the same word – 'hypnotism' – to describe the effect of the 'medals, ribbons, badges, hoods, gowns' of the militarist patriarchy that can be deflated by education.[45] *Three Guineas*'s coolness towards Woolf's own society, the source of much of the controversy in its subsequent reception, is, in a crucial sense, its anti-fascist message: British masculine society, infantilising its daughters, shares fascist states' gendered order.

In contrast to Woolf, Holtby's emphasis in her play *Take Back Your Freedom* (1935) is on the relationship between mother and son, or, in Freud's terminology, 'ego' and 'outgroup', and the relationship, as Vera Brittain summarised the play, between loss of liberty and 'illusory visions of power and prestige'.[46] Holtby tracks the development of an English dictator, Arnold Clayton, as he grows into his role while trying to escape maternal domination, a domination that 'overshadows, and finally destroys, his career'. Early in the play, Clayton reveals that his 'clever' mother had given up her job when she married and let loose her 'superfluous power' on him as a form of 'Achievement by proxy'.[47] Clayton's fascist Movement represents 'My independence, my autonomy, my genesis!' He claims that his mother 'trained me so well in detachment and integrity that I was nearly impotent for action'. Because 'Reason divides men into a thousand parties, but passion unites them', his Movement therefore abolishes the realm of liberal democracy whose rationality he associates with his politically progressive mother.[48] In Freudian terms, instead of loving a feminine object (or 'whore') in the place of an idealised mother (or 'Madonna'), he transforms himself as subject, from a man of reason to one of action. Whereas for Woolf the daughter's relegation to the private sphere ultimately leads to paternal fascism, in Holtby's play it is the mother's exclusion from the public sphere which produces a fascist son.

The third axis of the triangle we have been describing is that between the dictator figure and the 'outgroup', which Adorno, who makes no reference to either misogyny or antisemitism, largely ignores. In Burdekin's dystopia, this 'outgroup' consists of women and Christians, the Germans having 'killed all the Jews off' long ago. Set 700 years in the future, when the Nazis control most of the world and 'Holy Hitler' is a religion, *Swastika Night* (1937) imagines total fascist triumph.[49] In this future, fascism figures women (and Christians) as dirt and animals, with 'no will, no character, and no souls'.[50] But unlike in Aldous Huxley's *Brave New World* (1932), women are still necessary for procreation, though sons are taken away from their mothers at the age of eighteen months. Fascism 'was entirely male, the worship of a man [Hitler] who had no mother, the Only Man', someone who was 'exploded' rather than born, a fantasy of self-parturition. In Burdekin's previous novel *Proud Man* (1934), one narrator claims that 'the root-jealous male had felt a certain terror of the extraordinary biological powers of the female'.[51] The fascist male fantasies of power combine with a rhetoric of male victimhood – 'the rejection-right of women was an insult to Manhood' – in Burdekin's narrative, in ways that echo wider fascist hostility to politics itself.[52] Male unity comes through the exclusion of women. With this exclusion, the fascist homosocial community, as in Holtby, is represented as inherently homosexual, though in reality fascism was murderously homophobic. In such a world the public and private spheres are conflated: the 'public' world is charged with 'private' homosexual desire and mothers' only 'private' function is to provide sons for the public fascist state. Woolf's *Three Guineas* mapped the common ground of fascism and traditional British social roles; Holtby dramatised the dangers of women's exclusion from the social as a domestic parable of fascism's drives; and Burdekin imagined fascism's gendered order completed and worldwide, a dystopia on a global scale. All three try to account for, rather than merely to condemn, fascism's power.

Conclusion

Did anti-fascism fail? Axis forces lost the Second World War, certainly, but, in the era of the atomic bomb, apartheid, and the Cold War, it was not anti-fascist energies that prevailed in the new order. If, as Traverso suggests, after the war 'antifascism was transformed into a kind of "civil religion" for many of the democratic regimes that had experienced the resistance', in Britain and the Anglosphere, without wartime resistance traditions, the anti-fascist contribution was marginalised in Cold War histories.[53] 'For all of us', Mitchison remembered, 'whatever the outcome of the war, we felt ourselves, deep inside, already defeated. Stalin and Chamberlain had seen to that.'[54] Dorothy Livesay, writing at the outbreak of the war, found little to recover from anti-fascism:

> No one has come from the fronts we knew –
> Shanghai and Yenan – for a long session:
> Silent now the Madrid broadcasts. So was Vienna once
> Blotted out. We remember her voices fading.[55]

The devastation of Nazi rule, almost destroying Jewish life in Europe, was not fully clear to Livesay yet, and it would take a new generation, radicalised by the American war in Vietnam, to rediscover the anti-fascist archive and legacy. If the abundance of new narrative forms and technologies – from popular music to digital games – makes literature less central to the politics of contesting fascism now, the record of anti-fascism provides rich resources for those resisting the growing reactionary nationalisms of the twenty-first century. Auden may have concluded that 'History to the defeated / May say Alas but cannot help nor pardon', but the ongoing interest in anti-fascist literature, and the ongoing threat of fascism, suggests that, while there may be no pardon, literature offers prompts to help.[56] 'The issue', as the poet F. R. Scott put it in response to Auden, in his 'Spain 1937' (1945), 'is not ended with defeat.'[57]

Notes

1 Jason Stanley, *How Fascism Works* (New York: Random House, 2018), p.xiv.
2 See Harry Harootunian, *Uneven Moments: Reflections on Japan's Modern History* (New York: Columbia University Press, 2019), chap. 7.
3 Ellen Wilkinson and Edward Conze, *Why Fascism?* (London: Selwyn & Blount, 1934), p. 70.
4 Dylan Riley, *The Civic Foundations of Fascism in Europe: Italy, Spain, and Romania 1870–1945* (Baltimore, MD: Johns Hopkins University Press, 2010), p. 5.
5 Naomi Mitchison, *Vienna Diary* (London: Victor Gollancz, 1934), p. 15.
6 Enzo Traverso, *Fire and Blood: The European Civil War, 1914–1945*, trans. David Fernbach (London: Verso, 2016), p. 264.
7 See Lois Gordon, *Nancy Cunard: Heiress, Muse, Political Idealist* (New York: Columbia University Press, 2007), chap. 11.
8 Elinor Taylor, *The Popular Front Novel in Britain, 1934–1940* (Leiden: Brill, 2018), p. 5.
9 Sylvia Townsend Warner to Julius and Queenie Lipton, 23 March 1936, in *Sylvia Townsend Warner: Letters*, ed. William Maxwell (New York: Viking, 1982), p. 38.
10 Mia Spiro, *Anti-Nazi Modernism: The Challenges of Resistance in 1930s Fiction* (Evanston, IL: Northwestern University Press, 2013), p.10. That temptation was not always so easy to avoid, as Tyrus Miller documents in his essay 'Representing Fascism in 1930s Literature', in *A History of 1930s British Literature*, ed. Benjamin Kohlmann and Matthew Taunton (Cambridge: Cambridge University Press, 2019), pp. 241–56.
11 Naomi Mitchison, *We Have Been Warned* (London: Constable, 1935), n.p.
12 Virginia Woolf, *Three Guineas*, ed. Naomi Black (Oxford: Blackwell, 2001), p. 32.
13 Esther Leslie, 'Anti-Fascism, Anti-Art, Doubt and Despair', *Third Text* 33.3 (2019), pp. 293–313 (p. 313).
14 W. H. Auden, ' Sonnet XVI', in W. H. Auden and Christopher Isherwood, *Journey to a War* (London: Faber, 1939), p. 279.
15 W. H. Auden, 'Sonnet XX', in ibid., p. 278.
16 Traverso, *Fire and Blood*, p. 45.
17 W. H. Auden, ' Spain', *Selected Poems*, ed. Edward Mendelson (New York: Vintage, 1979), p. 51.
18 Muriel Rukeyser, *Collected Poems* (New York: McGraw-Hill, 1978), pp. 139, 140.
19 Sylvia Townsend Warner, 'Journey to Barcelona', in *Women's Poetry of the 1930s: A Critical Anthology*, ed. Jane Dowson (London: Routledge, 1996), p. 155.

20 Auden, 'Spain', p. 52; Nancy Cunard, *Selected Poems*, ed. Sandeep Parmar (Manchester: Carcanet, 2016), p. 141.

21 Auden, 'Sonnet XVI', *Journey to a War*, p. 274.

22 Mitchison, *Vienna Diary*, pp. 36–7.

23 Mitchison, *We Have Been Warned*, p. 550.

24 See Mark Mazower, *Hitler's Empire: Nazi Rule in Occupied Europe* (London: Allen Lane, 2008), chap. 18.

25 Priyamvada Gopal, *Insurgent Empire: Anticolonial Resistance and British Dissent* (London: Verso, 2019), p. 322.

26 Wilkinson and Conze, *Why Fascism?*, p. 90; Ellen Wilkinson, 'An Open Letter to West Indian Intellectuals', *International African Opinion* 1.7 (May/June 1939), quoted in Gopal, *Insurgent Empire*, p. 343.

27 Langston Hughes, *Collected Poems*, ed. Arnold Rampersad and David Roessel (New York: Vintage, 1995), p. 207.

28 Ibid., p. 281.

29 Ibid. Hughes's claim needs to be read as factual as much as rhetorical. See James Q. Whitman, *Hitler's American Model: The United States and the Making of Nazi Race Law* (Princeton, NJ: Princeton University Press, 2018).

30 Gopal, *Insurgent Empire*, p. 249.

31 Woolf, *Three Guineas*, p. 94.

32 Ibid., pp. 50–1.

33 Ibid., p. 75.

34 Ibid., p. 130.

35 Ibid., p. 75.

36 Wilkinson and Conze, *Why Fascism?*, p. 14.

37 Paul Corner, 'Habermas, Fascism, and the Public Sphere', in *Mass Dictatorship and Modernity*, ed. Michael Kim, Michael Schoenhals, and Yong-Woo Kim (London: Palgrave, 2013), pp. 101–16 (p. 104).

38 Ibid.

39 Peter Nathan, *Psychology of Fascism* (London: Faber, 1943), p. 105.

40 Theodor W. Adorno, 'Freudian Theory and the Pattern of Fascist Propaganda', *The Culture Industry* (London: Routledge, 2001), pp. 132–57 (p. 134).

41 Sigmund Freud, 'Group Psychology and the Analysis of the Ego', *The Standard Edition of the Complete Psychological Works of Sigmund Freud*, Vol. 19, ed. James Strachey (London: Hogarth, 1955), p. 136.

42 Adorno, 'Freudian Theory and the Pattern of Fascist Propaganda', p. 135.

43 Elizabeth Abel, *Virginia Woolf and the Fictions of Psychoanalysis* (Chicago, IL: University of Chicago Press, 1989), p. 108.

44 Woolf, *Three Guineas*, p. 76.

45 Ibid., p. 46.

46 Winifred Holtby, *Take Back Your Freedom* (London: Jonathan Cape, 1939), p. 9.

47 Ibid., p. 35.

48 Ibid., pp. 60, 58.

49 'Murray Constantine' [Katharine Burdekin], *Swastika Night* (London: Gollancz, 2016), pp. 73, 5.
50 Ibid., p. 70.
51 Katharine Burdekin, *Proud Man* (New York: Feminist Press, 1993), pp. 29, 325.
52 Ibid., p. 81.
53 Traverso, *Fire and Blood*, p. 10.
54 Naomi Mitchison, *You May Well Ask* (London: Victor Gollancz, 1979), p. 221.
55 Dorothy Livesay, 'The Lizard: October 1939', in *Sealed in Struggle: Canadian Poetry and the Spanish Civil War*, ed. Nicola Vulpe and Maha Albari (Madrid: Centre for Canadian Studies, 1995), p. 141.
56 Auden, *Selected Poems*, p. 55.
57 F. R. Scott, 'Spain 1937', in *Sealed in Struggle*, ed. Vulpe and Albari, p. 222.

CHAPTER 4

Suffragism

Clara Jones

The writing generated by the suffrage campaigns of the late nineteenth and early twentieth centuries was unprecedented both in its quantity and generic diversity. Novelists, playwrights, poets, and, of course, polemicists, paid tribute to and parodied the first wave of the women's movement in print. The motivations behind writers' engagement with the campaign varied. Many nailed their colours to the mast. Sylvia Pankhurst remembers how 'Evelyn Sharp, May Sinclair, Violet Hunt and other women writers rattled collecting-boxes at street corners. John Galsworthy, E. V. Lucas, [Henry] Nevinson and others gave autographed copies of their books [to be auctioned].'[1]

As well as rattling 'collecting-boxes', Sharp and Sinclair wrote short fiction and essays for suffrage periodicals, while Elizabeth Robins and Cicely Hamilton wrote novels, plays, and pageants for the stage celebrating the bravery of suffrage activists.[2] On the other hand, 'anti-suffragist' writers caricatured the 'shrieking sisterhood' in order to warn the public against votes for women. The founding president of the Women's National Anti-Suffrage League was none other than the novelist Mary Augusta Ward, whose works *The Testing of Diana Mallory* (1908) and *Delia Blanchflower* (1914) are stalwarts of the anti-suffrage canon.[3] That the campaign roughly coincided with a revolution in print media and the development of new and more diverse reading publics is something that those on both sides of the debate capitalised upon.[4] Moreover, some writers simply seized on the passion and drama of the cause as timely material that might help to sell books.[5] The formal, generic, and ideological diversity of the writing inspired by the campaign makes it difficult to discuss suffrage literature in the singular.

The written word was an integral political tool for those fighting for the vote. The spectacular politics of the suffrage campaign utilised pageantry and choreographed processions, as well as the imagery of its posters and banners. Textual activism played a profound and related role. As Sowon

Park puts it, 'the suffrage movement prompted women to write, publish, and read'.[6] Much of the work of women writers for the suffrage campaign was organised through the Women Writers' Suffrage League (WWSL), established in 1908 by Cicely Hamilton and Bessie Hatton, while suffrage periodicals offered new venues for publication.[7] These were novel, in so far as they were frequently administered and edited by women.[8] Reflecting upon the status of the woman writer in an essay originally published in just such a journal, Elizabeth Robins, first president of the WWSL, points out the pressures and inequities regularly experienced by women writing for male 'publishers', 'professional readers', and 'advisers':

> Let us remember it is only yesterday that women in any number began to write for the public prints. But in taking up the pen, what did this new recruit conceive to be her task? To proclaim her own or other women's actual thoughts and feelings? Far from it. Her task, as she naturally and even inevitably conceived it, was to imitate as nearly as possible the method, but above all the point of view, of man.[9]

Robins's diagnosis of the strictures of a male-dominated culture industry and the withering effect this has on 'woman's art' closely anticipates the insights Virginia Woolf would offer years later in her essays *A Room of One's Own* (1929) and 'Professions for Women' (1931).[10]

Woolf, then Virginia Stephen, also engaged in what she called the 'humbler work' of grassroots activism in a suffrage office in 1910:

> I spend hours writing names like Cowgill on envelopes. People say that Adult Suffrage is a bad thing; they will never get it owing to my efforts. The office, with its ardent but educated young women, and brotherly clerks is just like a Wells novel.[11]

Stephen's account may not ring with enthusiasm, but it does remind us of the bread-and-butter work upon which the campaign depended. It also offers another slant on the relationship between the politics of the campaign and contemporary literature. Stephen imagines her experiences in the office through the prism of literature, 'a Wells novel', which suggests that perhaps it was not simply suffrage activism providing subject matter for fiction, but fiction itself shaping and even offering a model through which suffrage activists could imagine their work.

Just as recent suffrage historians have complicated and diversified narratives of the campaign, attention to its literary culture has also flourished.[12] Barbara Green's *Spectacular Confessions* draws attention to the generic range of the textual documents of the campaign – 'novels, letters, speeches and diaries' – and shows the dynamic relationship between this writing and the spectacular political activism of the campaign.[13] Suffrage theatre and the organisations that made possible its grand-scale productions and pageants are the subject of rich discussion.[14] The rise of feminist periodical studies and the research of scholars including Green and Maria DiCenzo, among others, into suffrage print cultures has nuanced our understanding of the suffrage campaign as a literary movement, and one with a keen eye on the marketplace.[15] The new availability of suffrage texts has had a powerful impact on the field, which had historically to contend with a scarcity of primary materials.[16]

Questions of literary value loom large in the critical reception of suffrage writing. Elaine Showalter suggests that despite the 'enormous quantity' of suffrage writing, 'relatively little of this work is distinguished as fiction', its value instead lying in its historical interest.[17] As critics have noted, Showalter's pitting of aesthetic quality against historical content has influenced the terms of the debate around suffrage literature.[18] Ann Ardis argues that the practice of literary scholars, principally concerned with 'the appreciation and evaluation of the individual text, and the individual great writer's work', has made suffrage writers easier to overlook as their 'texts are arguably less impressive individually than in the aggregate'.[19] Park addresses the lack of formal experimentation in suffrage literature explicitly: 'In order for suffrage fiction to reach a wide audience, and remain intelligible, it had to use the form most familiar to the majority of readers. [. . .] Thus the novels were experimental and radical in content rather than in form.'[20] The experiments of 'high modernism' still appear to set the aesthetic standard in these arguments. Park's suggestion that the suspension of 'normative criticism of suffrage fictions' allows critics to see this material 'not only as literary *texts* but also as historically situated sociocultural *acts*' retrenches this binary, even as it makes the case for recognising the politically motivated textual strategies at work in suffrage fiction.[21] With the increased availability of suffrage literature and the integrity of literary categories less taken for granted by critics of modern literature, now may be a moment to revisit the question of the relationship between form and content in suffrage writing, and to consider whether the idea that one instrumentally serves the other is necessarily borne out by an encounter with suffrage texts.[22]

Constance Maud's 1911 novel, *No Surrender*, conforms to many characteristics of suffrage fiction. It plays on romance conventions, uses tropes of conversion, and integrates only lightly fictionalised episodes from the real-world campaign in order to persuade the reader of the righteousness of the women's movement. But even as *No Surrender* is a campaigning novel that propagandises to its audience, it is also a novel of a campaign that registers and reflects upon the tensions and disagreements that characterised the movement. The issue of social class was deeply contentious in the campaign. The degree to which suffragists and suffragettes could have been said to be fighting in the interests of women of all classes was fiercely debated, and the position of working women in the campaign was a vexed one. The following section will supply some of the context for these debates, which are central to my reading of Maud's novel.

Suffrage and Social Class

Virginia Stephen's desultory letter about her suffrage work offers insights into the class politics of the campaign. On first reading, it appears edged with snobbish detachment: her sniffiness about the Wellsian atmosphere of the office and her ironic amusement at 'names like Cowgill' – a name native to the North of England – hints at both a classist and regionalist strain in her thinking. Such attitudes were not particular to Stephen. A version of the suffrage movement as dominated by middle-class women campaigning in their own interest was widely accepted and resulted in the jibe 'Votes for Ladies'.[23]

Class tensions were felt to varying degrees across the different wings of the movement. There is some justification for thinking of the National Union of Women's Suffrage Societies (NUWSS) as primarily a middle-class organisation, particularly in its early moment, while the role of working-class women in the Women's Social and Political Union (WSPU) and its leadership's (un)willingness to address social class as a political question were influenced by that organisation's roots in and subsequent break with the Labour movement.[24] During its early years based in Manchester after its formation in 1903, the WSPU 'coexisted quite peacefully' with a group of working-class radical suffragists who campaigned for the vote as part of a portfolio of social reform demands.[25] Central to the WSPU/Labour schism was the question of who exactly would get the vote if campaigners were successful. Most suffrage activists aimed to secure the vote on the same terms as were presently granted to men, accepting the 'accumulated variety of property-based qualification' that meant, in fact, not all men had the vote at this time.[26] The limited nature of the reform bills promoted by the WSPU and NUWSS was a source of anxiety for Labour, who feared their electoral chances would be damaged by the enfranchisement of only wealthy women. Efforts were made to prove that even limited reform would result in the enfranchisement of a large proportion of working women. Investigations conducted by working-class suffragist Selina Cooper and Independent Labour Party (ILP) leader Keir Hardie in 1905, suggested that between 80 and 95 per cent of enfranchised women in a 'typical ward' would be 'working women'. As Jill Liddington notes, while these statistics gave 'comfort' to those already sympathetic to the cause, in fact 'the figures were of doubtful worth' and did little to quiet Labour concern.[27]

The question of adult suffrage was a flash point in disagreements between Labour and woman suffragists. Some Labour activists opposed limited electoral reform and felt all efforts should instead be directed into securing universal suffrage for all adult men and women. Margaret Llewelyn Davies, leader of the Women's Co-operative Guild, put the case for adult suffrage like this: 'The Limited Bill is [. . .] obnoxious to us [. . .] We feel that a personal, and not a property basis, is the only democratic one.'[28] Woman suffragists countered that 'universal suffrage was not yet practical politics'.[29] Writing in *The Englishwoman* in 1910, woman suffragist Clementina Black suggested that radical voting reform went against England's 'custom' of making 'political changes gradually' and risked complicating the position and alienating supporters.[30] There was the added complication that the concept of adult suffrage was ambiguous, as it could designate 'either universal franchise with both the property and sex disqualifications removed, or merely the extension of the existing sexually exclusive franchise to all adult males'.[31] Radical suffragist Hannah Mitchell articulates a suspicion felt against adultist campaigners in her memoir:

> We knew the Adult Suffragists [. . .], and paid little heed to their suggestions that we should work for the larger measure. 'Let those who want votes, work for them,' was our answer, having no mind to get our heads broken, as women did at Peterloo, in order to get more votes for men.[32]

Virginia Stephen's statement, 'People say that Adult Suffrage is a bad thing; but they will never get it owing to my efforts', takes on a different complexion when read in the context of these debates. As I suggest elsewhere, her letter becomes not just an expression of personal boredom but a historically specific statement that casts light on political fault lines of the suffrage movement.[33] Stephen's experiences of volunteering for an adult suffrage organisation, the People's Suffrage Federation, will have left her in no doubt that class as well as sex justice were at stake in the campaign, and her letter has something to tell us about the work adult suffragists did to keep a 'feminist-Labour alliance' alive, even when it made them unpopular with factions on both sides.[34]

When the WSPU split with Labour in 1906, it was as a result of the thorny politics of adult suffrage. The WSPU leadership took steps to sever remaining ties between their activists and the Labour movement, insisting that its members sign the following pledge: 'I endorse the objects and methods of the Women's Social and Political Union and hereby undertake not to support the candidate of any political party at Parliamentary elections until women have the vote.'[35] The autocratic behaviour of Christabel and Emmeline Pankhurst, and their perceived lurch to the Right, led to disputes within the organisation which, in 1907, saw the departure of a number of former members, including socialist Charlotte Despard and working-class organiser Teresa Billington-Greig to establish the Women's Freedom League (WFL).[36] The move to London marked a shift in the position of working women in the organisation: 'the Pankhursts soon dropped their working class support, except for a few token speakers like Annie Kenney and her sisters, in favour of influential allies among upper-and-middle-class women'.[37] Suffragette propaganda and publicity looked different as a result. As art historian Lisa Tickner observes, while working women had always played a prominent role in suffrage demonstrations, Christabel Pankhurst increasingly felt it was bad tactics to rely on 'a stage army' of 'women of the East End' when 'the House of Commons, and even its Labour members, were more impressed by the demonstrations of the feminine bourgeoisie than of the feminine proletariat'.[38] While the practical political position of working-class women in the suffrage campaign oscillated, her image remained integral to suffrage imagery and 'iconography'.[39] Suffrage propaganda deployed the figure of the working woman to various ends: in the guise of the exploited sweated labourer she represents the need for womanly protection that votes for women would bring with it, while as the dignified clogged and shawled mill-worker she reminds the viewer of 'women's importance to the economic, material and moral life of the nation'.[40]

The ethical problems raised by the use of the figure of the working woman by 'predominantly middle-class' suffrage artists points to broader questions about representation, authenticity, and appropriation, questions that have forever troubled feminist theory and practice.[41] Suffrage literature made similar use of working-class figures. It is Maud's presentation of Lancashire mill-worker Jenny Clegg that will concern me for the rest of this chapter. I want to show how a fuller familiarity with the internal debates of the campaign – particularly those between adult and women suffragists – results in a more precise sense of how the novel works as propaganda. We will see that a corollary of such a contextual approach is that more self-reflexive and self-questioning currents in *No Surrender* that run parallel to its primary propagandising ones are also made visible.

Constance Maud's *No Surrender*

No Surrender was published in 1911, at a moment of sea change in suffrage campaigning. The first forcible feeding of a suffragette prisoner took place in Holloway Prison in 1909. The spectacle of this state-sanctioned torture and the failure of the second so-called 'Conciliation Bill' led to the WSPU's adoption of more militant tactics. Yet Maud's novel takes a historical view of the campaign, concluding with the establishment of the first 1910 Conciliation Committee – a moment of hope – stopping short of these tumultuous subsequent events. It tells the story of mill-worker Jenny Clegg and her 'call' to work for the 'Women's Union'. Although Maud protests in her Preface that while the events contained in the novel are 'historically real and true', 'there are no portraits of living people in this book', prominent figures from the campaign are recognisable in the characters of *No Surrender*. Jenny is loosely modelled on Annie Kenney, while charismatic Mrs Wilmot recalls the leader of the WFL, Charlotte Despard, to whom the novel is, in fact, dedicated.

Maud's own organisational affiliations are not known, although she contributed to suffrage papers, and her novel is diplomatic in its handling of suffrage factions.[42] Jenny and other prominent characters are members of the Women's Union, but the passive resistance of the WFL also comes in for praise as does the work of erstwhile constitutionalists.[43] Given the novel's narrative dependence on real events and characters of the campaign, it might come as a surprise that the Pankhursts are barely mentioned; 'one of the leaders of the WSPU' makes just the briefest of appearances.[44] This narrative neglect, combined with Maud's earnest dedication of the novel to 'that inspired leader', Despard, invites a cautious approach to *No Surrender*'s allegiances and its advocacy of a 'line' associated with one wing of the movement or another. The fact that the novel was published by, albeit a small, mainstream publisher, Duckworth & Co., rather than one of the suffrage presses that emerged in this period, bears out my sense that the propagandist politics of the novel are not to be taken for granted. The section above concerning class and suffrage shows the difficulty of seeing suffrage politics as monolithic, and the same is true of suffrage fiction. Here, I suggest that, when read in light of the (often vexed) internal politics of the campaign, the picture becomes a great deal more mixed, and nowhere is this more apparent than in *No Surrender*'s handling of social class.

*** *** ***

No Surrender's interest in class as a political question is evident from its opening, which has the ring of a Victorian social reform novel. The narrator describes how industrial modernity – 'the Juggernaut-car of so-called progress' – 'stunted and blighted' a once green and pleasant land.[45] A move to 'Walker's great mill' triggers a tonal shift, with the narrator switching from distant and grandiloquent to immediate and matter-of-fact:

> Ventilation, in spite of inspectors and laws, is of the meagrest and most primitive description. The air, when dry, is moistened by steam lest the thread should suffer, but the lungs of the workers are not so carefully considered. There are always plenty of girls to fill a vacant place, for the textile worker is better paid than any other class of working woman.[46]

Published in 1911, five years after the WSPU's split with Labour and relocation to London, Maud's emphasis on the movement's roots in the industrial North of England and her focus on the lives of working women is significant. This becomes more apparent as the opening chapter moves from the factory where Jenny Clegg works to her family home. The narrative sustains its preoccupation with the iniquities of daily life for working people; we discover that Jenny's brother's invalid condition is the result of being hit by a shuttle in the factory weaving shed.[47] Grassroots Labour organisations are offered up as an ameliorative to an indifferent state when we discover Jenny's mother has saved enough to send Peter to a convalescent home by shopping loyally at the 'Co-op stores'.[48] The chapter concludes with the painful undercutting of this possibility when Mr Clegg discovers his wife's saved 'checks' and claims them as his legal property as her husband.

The chapter features no direct reference to women's suffrage, although the topic looms large. Chapter one accumulates examples of working women's powerlessness – improper working conditions, mothers' lack of rights over their own children and money, lack of access to divorce in the case of Jenny's domestically abused sister – to illustrate the iniquitous position of a woman living under male laws with 'no reets' of her own.[49] The logic Maud presents leads irrevocably to the vote, as the only means by which working women can hope for their lot to be improved. The false promise of the cooperative store is revealing. As we have seen, disagreements between Labour and suffragists hinged on women's status as a 'sex-class', and whether their interests were better served by socialist or feminist political agitation. Maud implies that Labour initiatives are of limited use to working women, who remain at the mercy of men. It is a narrative move that invites us to read the novel in the context of the debates about the position of working women in the campaign and the fractious relationship between Labour and woman suffragists.

No Surrender's dialogue with these debates becomes starker later in the novel when Jenny narrates her conversion to suffragism to a group of fellow prisoners. She frames this squarely in terms of disenchantment with socialism:

> It was my father made me a Suffragette – not as he meant to – but first he turned me a Socialist, hearin' him talk at home an' then goin' to the meetin's. All that talk about human rights and liberty set me thinkin' about women, the poor women – but my father an' my brothers they shut me up if I talked of liberty. 'Women ain't the same,' they said.[50]

Here, Jenny rehearses the suffragette criticisms of Labour's hypocritical failure to support women's suffrage bills. Such gestures appear elsewhere in the novel, too. A sympathetic policeman, for instance, tellingly ventriloquises Keir Hardie when he accepts a suffrage paper from Jenny: 'he took one, saying his "missus" was all for the women gettin' their vote, and he "couldn't see why any but dogs-in-the-manger was against it"'.[51] Criticising adult suffrage opposition to the Women's Enfranchisement Bill, Hardie wrote: 'Its policy is that of the dog in the manger.'[52]

The novel also stages extended exchanges between socialists and feminists: Jack Wilmot is modelled as a sympathetic man of the Left, and a conversation with his mother explicitly establishes the hierarchy of 'causes' that was so contentious to the relationship between these groups:

> 'I envy you women – yours is the only cause on earth I feel to be even a bigger one than ours!'
> 'Ah, my son,' she answered, 'the best and truest kind of Socialism will follow in the wake of the freedom of women – I am convinced of it. All true progress will be made easier.'[53]

Maud's decision to have a committed socialist character identify the suffrage as the more significant cause is obviously provocative. But Maud is, if anything, more interested in the arguments of her *opponents* on the Left; indeed, the romance plot of the novel hinges upon them. Jenny's love interest, Joe Hopton, a Labour MP, starts the novel aggressively opposed to women's suffrage, and his rapprochement with Jenny only takes place after his own conversion to the 'bigger' cause in a chapter whose title, 'Joe's Surrender', tellingly reworks romance conventions.[54] The novel's sustained interest in arguments between suffrage activists and their socialist counterparts indicates the degree to which the politics of the novel is embedded in arguments with Labour about women's suffrage. At the heart of Maud's position is Mrs Wilmot's response to her son that 'the best and truest kind of Socialism will follow in the wake of the freedom of women'. The idea that 'true progress' would be made easier if even some women were given the vote is an argument that was rehearsed throughout the campaign.

The novel reveals comparatively little interest in other political estates, who are the subject of ridicule and caricature.[55] Maud's decision to offer space to the arguments between Labour and women suffrage campaigners is significant given the fact that by 1911, the WSPU leadership were actively anti-Labour and uninterested in courting the support of working women.[56] The novel draws close attention to the links between suffrage and Labour, not just through its working-class heroine, but also through gestures to the Peterloo massacre and the politics of cooperation and trade unionism.[57] The result is a novel that reads as though directed to the Left, and in which the suffrage campaign is positioned squarely as part of a wider campaign for the reform of British society. The generic conventions of the romance do a service in this regard: *No Surrender* aims to romance a certain faction of the Labour movement represented by Joe Hopton. The union of Jenny and Joe has a proleptic quality and there is a sort of wish fulfilment at work in a novel that enacts a fantasy reunion between Labour and suffrage.

And yet it is difficult to square the confident vision of a reunion between the forces of suffrage and Labour at the end of the novel with the author's eliding of the question of how many working women will actually get votes. Mrs Wilmot reassures her anti-suffragist niece: 'For if we obtain the suffrage on the same basis as men, which is all we ask or want, only one million and a quarter women would be enfranchised as against seven million and a half men.'[58] The novel's radicalism only goes so far. As this passage illustrates, the text appears to endorse the gradualism and pragmatic necessity of a limited bill. In spite of Mrs Wilmot's concession – 'all we ask or want' – the novel insists upon the working-class credentials of the campaign: 'We are a great army of working women', Mary O'Neil insists to a conservative dinner companion.[59] Jack Wilmot also repeats the dubious statistics that caused such contention on the Left: 'This is a working women's movement [...] of the women who would be enfranchised eighty-two per cent are earning their own living.'[60]

The novel is not without an awareness of the limitations of the campaign's political imagination, and there are moments of palpable anxiety surrounding the role of working-class suffragettes. Take the comments of 'one of the leaders of the W.S.P.U' when she makes her momentary appearance in the prison courtyard. Singling out Jenny, she says to her companion:

> We shall have plenty of use for such a girl as that when she comes out – mustn't let her go back to the mill, we need that kind up here – they are worth their weight in gold to us. She shall speak at the Albert Hall meeting in October, and do some more converting.[61]

This may seem innocuous enough, but something about the leader's keen eye for that 'kind' of girl and the blunt language of utility – 'use' and 'worth' – she falls back upon stand out. They are at odds with the strong seam of spiritualism stitched through the novel, and the mystical, semi-religious language regularly used to describe people's conversion to the cause. We know the question of the 'use' being made of working women by middle-class suffragettes was an exceptionally fraught one, and Maud's choice of words here probes this problem. Elsewhere, Maud demonstrates self-awareness about the importance of the symbolism of the working woman to suffragette performative politics. During chapter ten, Jenny casts off her maid's disguise in order to present unsuspecting cabinet ministers Boulder and Weir-Kemp with a suffrage petition in 'the shawl and clogs of the mill'.[62] The chapter that follows opens with Jenny changing out of 'her mill-clothes for the ubiquitous coat and skirt', a detail that draws attention to the 'mill-clothes' as costume, and which also hints at what Morag Shiach describes as the element of 'masquerade or forced identification, in some of the ways in which the suffrage movement drew on the figure of the "working woman"'.[63] Like Annie Kenney, who 'appeared dressed in clogs and shawl long after she had ceased to earn her living in the mills', it had been some time since Jenny worked in the mill and she donned her 'mill-clothes' only for symbolic purposes.[64]

No Surrender demonstrates more awareness of class as both a political and aesthetic problem for the suffrage movement than might first appear. Jenny's rejection of Jack Wilmot's proposal is presented as an act of class-consciousness:

> 'To leave the mill, yes,' Jenny agreed, 'but not my own people or my own class. I am one with them – I belong to them and they belong to me. I suffer with them – I feel as they do, Mr. Wilmot, not as you do.'
> [. . .]

He followed her every word with his quick sympathy and artist's ready imagination:
'I can picture it,' he assured her, 'it is not necessary to have lived through it.'
'Oh yes, it is,' said Jenny. 'It's only what we've lived through as we can feel – that's what shapes our thoughts and shapes our souls. You must work in your class, God knows you're needed there, and I must work in mine.'[65]

Jenny's assertion of class in this episode can be read in two ways. On the one hand, her unwillingness to leave her 'station' by marrying into a different class appears to be a narrative reinforcement of the conservative status quo. On the other hand, Jenny's positive claim on her class identity and the importance of 'working' as a class means this scene feels charged with class solidarity rather than class hatred. The slipperiness of the treatment of class in the novel and its character in the campaign mean that both impulses – the progressive and the reactionary – may coexist in this scene. What is also striking is the way in which the artist and their imaginative powers are held up for questioning in this passage. The narrative is sympathetic to Wilmot's eagerness, but, ultimately, we are left unconvinced by his belief in his own power to 'picture' the lives of working people. This episode may gesture to Maud's own concerns as a writer of a novel about a class that was not her own, as well as reflecting on the more specific question of suffrage fiction's representation of working women.

Conclusion

No Surrender is about the promotion of the 'cause', but it is also a site for reflection on the efficacy of certain strategies and anxiety about claims and counter-claims being made within the campaign. The openly propagandist nature of much suffrage literature means it is easy to imagine the relationship between art and politics in its case as straightforward, with one being drawn simply into the service of the other. However, the relationship between literature and politics is rarely straightforward, and this is certainly the case when it comes to the suffrage campaign, a movement fraught with internal disputes: not only the well-known arguments relating to militant tactics that divided the suffragettes from the suffragists, but more profound disagreements about the relationship of the campaign to other contemporary struggles.

Notes

1 Sylvia Pankhurst, *The Suffragette Movement: An Intimate Account of Persons and Ideas* (London: Longmans & Co., 1931), p. 279.

2 For Sharp and Sinclair's suffrage writing, see Angela V. John, *Rebel Woman, 1869–1955* (Manchester: Manchester University Press, 2009), pp. 52–75, and Suzanne Raitt, *May Sinclair: A Modern Victorian* (Oxford: Oxford University Press, 2000). For more on suffrage drama, see Leslie Hill, *Sex, Suffrage and the Stage: First Wave Feminism in the British Theatre* (London: Red Globe Press, 2018); Sheila Stowell, *A Stage of Their Own: Feminist Playwrights of the Suffrage Era* (Manchester: Manchester University Press, 2002); and Katharine Cockin, *Women and the Theatre in the Age of Suffrage: The Pioneer Players, 1911–1925* (New York: St Martin's Press, 2000).

3 See Maroula Joannou's 'Mary Augusta Ward (Mrs Humphrey) and the Opposition to Women's Suffrage', *Women's History Review* 14 (2005), pp. 561–80. For further examples of anti-suffrage literature, see Lucy Delap and Ann Heilmann, eds., *Anti-feminism in Edwardian Literature* (London: Thoemmes Continuum, 2006).

4 See Patrick Collier and Ann Ardis's 'Introduction' to *Transatlantic Print Culture, 1880–1940: Emerging Media, Emerging Modernism*, ed. Collier and Ardis (Basingstoke: Palgrave Macmillan, 2008), pp. 1–13.

5 'General Introduction' to *Women's Suffrage Literature*, ed. Katharine Cockin, Glenda Norquay, and Sowon S. Park (London and New York: Routledge, 2007), p. xix.

6 Sowon S. Park, 'The First Professional: The Women Writers' Suffrage League', *Modern Language Quarterly* 58.2 (1997), pp. 185–200 (p. 186).

7 Ibid.

8 For more on the official organs of the suffrage campaign, see Maria DiCenzo, Leila Ryan, and Lucy Delap, *Feminist Media History: Suffrage, Periodicals and the Public Sphere* (Basingstoke: Palgrave Macmillan, 2011), and Maria DiCenzo, 'Militant Distribution: *Votes for Women* and the Public Sphere', *Media History* 6.2 (2000), pp. 115–28.

9 Elizabeth Robins, *Way Stations* (London: Hodder & Stoughton, 1913), p. 5.

10 Park suggests that 'all the strands of feminist literary theory found in *A Room of One's Own* or [. . .] *Three Guineas* (1938) are readily found in the suffrage writings of the decades before' (Park, 'The First Professional', p. 197).

11 Letter of 27 February 1910, *The Letters of Virginia Woolf*, Vol. 1, ed. Nigel Nicolson and Joanne Trautmann Banks (London: Hogarth Press, 1975), p. 422.

12 Sandra Stanley Holton and Jo Vellacott consider the work of democratic suffragists in Holton, *Feminism and Democracy: Women's Suffrage and Reform Politics in Britain, 1900–1918* (Cambridge: Cambridge University Press, 1986) and Vellacott, *Pacifists, Patriots and the Vote: The Erosion of Democratic Suffragism in Britain During the First World War* (Basingstoke: Palgrave Macmillan, 2007), respectively. Angela V. John and Claire Eustance

explore the contributions of male suffragists in *The Men's Share? Masculinities, Male Support and Women's Suffrage in Britain, 1890–1920* (London: Routledge, 1997).

13 Barbara Green, *Spectacular Confessions: Autobiography, Performative Activism, and the Sites of Suffrage, 1905–1938* (London: Macmillan, 1997), p. 5.

14 See Park, 'The First Professional' and Cockin, *Women and Theatre in the Age of Suffrage*.

15 See Barbara Green, 'Complaints of Everyday Life: Feminist Periodical Culture and Correspondence Columns in the *Woman Worker* and the *Freewoman*', *Modernism/modernity* 19.3 (September 2012), pp. 461–85, and Maria DiCenzo, 'Gutter Politics: Women Newsies and the Suffrage Press', *Women's History Review* 12.1 (2003), pp. 15–33. See also David Doughan and Denise Sanchez, *Feminist Periodicals, 1855–1944: An Annotated Critical Bibliography of British, Irish, Commonwealth, and International Titles* (Brighton: Harvester, 1987).

16 See, for instance, Glenda Norquay, *Voices and Votes: A Literary Anthology of the Women's Suffrage Campaign* (Manchester: Manchester University Press, 1995); Carolyn Christensen Nelson, ed., *Literature of the Women's Suffrage Campaign in England* (Peterborough, ON: Broadview Press, 2004); and Cockin, Norquay, and Park, eds., *Women's Suffrage Literature*.

17 Elaine Showalter, *A Literature of Their Own: British Women Novelists from Brönte to Lessing* (London: Virago, 1982), p. 218.

18 Cockin, Norquay, and Park, 'General Introduction', *Women's Suffrage Literature*, p. xxiv.

19 Ann Ardis, 'The Gender of Modernity', in *The Cambridge History of Twentieth-Century English Literature*, ed. Laura Marcus and Peter Nicholls (Cambridge: Cambridge University Press, 2004), pp. 61–80 (p. 78).

20 Sowon Park, 'Suffrage Fiction: A Political Discourse in the Marketplace', *English Literature in Transition* 39.4 (1996), pp. 450–61 (p. 456).

21 Ibid., p. 459; emphasis in original.

22 DiCenzo suggests as much, in her article comparing literary representations of suffrage 'newsies'. See DiCenzo, 'Gutter Politics', p. 17.

23 Alison Lee, 'Introduction' to Gertrude Colmore, *Suffragette Sally*, ed. Lee (Peterborough, ON: Broadview Press, 2007), p. 23.

24 Its character changed later in the campaign when a strategic pact with the Labour Party resulted in well-known democratic suffragists allying themselves with the NUWSS. See Holton, *Feminism and Democracy*, and Sandra Stanley Holton, *Suffrage Days: Stories from the Women's Suffrage Movement* (London: Routledge, 1996).

25 Jill Liddington and Jill Norris, *One Hand Tied Behind Us: The Rise of the Women's Suffrage Movement* (London: Rivers Oram, 2000), p. 28.

26 Writing about the introduction of adult male suffrage after the Representation of the Peoples Act (1918), Stuart Ball notes that the 'proportion of men enfranchised under the previous system varied greatly between different types of constituency', with 'the working class of industrial towns' affected

particularly negatively: 'the average level of adult male enfranchisement in England and Wales was 59.8% in the boroughs and 69.9% in the counties'. See Stuart Ball, 'The Reform Act of 1918 – the Advent of Democracy', in *The Advent of Democracy: The Impact of the 1918 Reform Act on British Politics*, ed. Ball (Chichester: Parliamentary History Yearbook Trust, 2018), pp. 1–22 (p. 3).

27 Jill Liddington, *The Life and Times of a Respectable Rebel: Selina Cooper, 1864–1946* (London: Virago, 1984), pp. 144–5.

28 Georgia Pearce, 'Miss Llewelyn Davies and the People's Suffrage Federation', *The Woman Worker* (10 November 1909), p. 437.

29 Holton, *Feminism and Democracy*, p. 58.

30 Clementina Black, 'The Year's Progress in the Women's Suffrage Movement', *The Englishwoman* (January 1910), p. 258.

31 Holton, *Feminism and Democracy*, p. 54.

32 Hannah Mitchell, *The Hard Way Up* (London: Virago, 2000), p. 139.

33 Clara Jones, *Virginia Woolf: Ambivalent Activist* (Edinburgh: Edinburgh University Press, 2017).

34 Holton, *Feminism and Democracy*, p. 6.

35 Pankhurst, *The Suffragette Movement*, p. 265.

36 Hilary Frances, '"Dare to be Free!": The Women's Freedom League and Its Legacy', in *Votes for Women!*, ed. June Purvis and Sandra Stanley Holton (London: Routledge, 2000), pp. 181–202 (pp. 182–3).

37 Liddington and Norris, *One Hand Tied Behind Us*, p. 28.

38 Lisa Tickner, *The Spectacle of Women* (London: Chatto & Windus, 1987), p. 57.

39 Morag Shiach, *Modernism, Labour and Selfhood in British Literature and Culture, 1890–1930* (Cambridge: Cambridge University Press, 2003), p. 104.

40 Tickner, *The Spectacle of Women*, p. 182; Shiach, *Modernism, Labour and Selfhood*, p. 104.

41 Tickner, *The Spectacle of Women*, p. 181.

42 Lydia Fellgett, 'Introduction' to Constance Maud, *No Surrender* [1911] (London: Persephone, 2011), p. xiii.

43 Maud, *No Surrender*, pp. 156, 318.

44 Ibid., p. 88.

45 Ibid., p. 1.

46 Ibid., p. 3.

47 Ibid., p. 6.

48 Ibid., p. 17.

49 Ibid., p. 18.

50 Ibid., p. 112.

51 Ibid., p. 127.

52 Pankhurst, *The Suffragette Movement*, p. 232.

53 Maud, *No Surrender*, p. 151.

54 Ibid., pp. 65–77.

55 Ibid., pp. 38–9, 201–7.

56 Liddington and Norris, *One Hand Tied Behind Us*, p. 18.

57 Jenny reminds Joe of women's involvement at Peterloo: 'If you would stand by us now as we women stood by you men when you came out to fight for your vote at the battle of Peterloo.' Maud, *No Surrender*, p. 134.

58 Ibid. p. 162.

59 Ibid., p. 225.

60 Ibid., p. 160.

61 Ibid., p. 89.

62 Ibid., p. 238.

63 Ibid., p. 245; Shiach, *Modernism, Labour and Selfhood*, p. 104.

64 Shiach, *Modernism, Labour and Selfhood*, p. 105.

65 Maud, *No Surrender*, pp. 171–2.

CHAPTER 5

Pacifism

Bárbara Gallego Larrarte

Writing Peace

German bomber planes circle in the sky above an English house in 1940. A woman, wide awake in the dark, lies still, fearful, listening. Although the sounds herald death and destruction, the piercing hum of the planes fire her mind into action, motivating her to 'think peace into existence'.[1] Virginia Woolf's essay, 'Thoughts on Peace in an Air Raid', complicates what we think of as 'war literature'. While the threat of aerial bombardment is central to her piece, she is using her wartime experience to consider how peace might be achieved. Woolf's short essay conveys most of the themes that characterise peace writing: anxiety over what counts as 'action' outside the confines of war; the particular role women could play in securing peace; the tension between belief and political action; a search for the causes (social and psychological) for the pervasiveness of using violence for conflict resolution; and the struggle, common to other forms of political writing, between propaganda and politically engaged literature.

With few exceptions, writing about peace is regularly examined as complementary to war writing. This can be explained by the overwhelming presence of armed conflict in the first half of the twentieth century, during which the nature of war also changed dramatically. Technological innovation resulted in an unprecedented capacity for destruction and redefined the concept of combat, as aerial warfare brought the battleground to civilian populations. Writing of this time, and the critical literature which examines it, is understandably shadowed and shaped by the expectation, experience, and memory of war. But this same period also saw the rise of widespread peace movements that created a climate where pacifism was reconceived from a moral, faith-based position to a political and humanitarian stance. Particularly in the United Kingdom, but also in the United States, peace activism was prominent, organisations around it thrived, and it was vocally supported by intellectuals and writers as varied as George Orwell, Siegfried Sassoon, Storm Jameson, and Aldous Huxley. As an idea – and an ideal – that galvanised many writers in the early decades of the century, shaping and motivating their work, this body of literature deserves to be reconsidered. How did writers bear witness to and engage with pacifism? What characterises writing for peace? This chapter investigates peace as an aspiration central to the first half of the twentieth century by examining the intersection between peace movements and peace writing in Britain, where pacifist activism was at its strongest.

Origins

> Blessed are the peacemakers: for they shall be called the children of God.
>
> (Mathew 5:9, King James Bible)

The Sermon on the Mount in the Bible often serves as a key reference for those who find the immorality of killing another human being in the teachings of Christ. In Western nations, arguments in defence of peace have been shaped by the legacy of various Christian sects, most notably the Quakers. This centuries-old history has contributed extensively to articulating the value of placing one's moral belief in the sanctity of life above all other considerations. Pacifist convictions were radical, for they challenged the power of the state – both over individual conscience and as a political entity that relied on violence to function. The Enlightenment further emphasised the inhumanity of killing, building the basis for a secular and rational justification for pacifism. Immanuel Kant's influential essay, 'On Perpetual Peace' (1795), sought a peaceful world order by encouraging cooperation between nation states and respect for individual freedoms, a political vision that guided liberal theories on responsible forms of government.

A defence of peace often aligned with arguments in favour of sociopolitical reform. Martin Ceadel, one of the leading historians in this field, identifies as formative for pacifist thought the anti-militarism of anarchists and socialists in the nineteenth century.[2] Leo Tolstoy's inspirational reform movement at the end of the 1800s championed his version of Christian pacifism, a 'non-resistance to evil' conceived as an affront to Russia's militaristic culture. Tolstoy was an important influence on Mahatma Gandhi, and their correspondence constitutes a key document in the history of peace thought. After embracing the concept of *satyagraha* (truth force) around 1906, Gandhi transformed it into a powerful tool to push for social and political change in India, becoming, in the process, a global icon for peace.

Christianity remained the main inspiration for British pacifism, but by the turn of the century Victorian optimism, with its faith in free trade and progress, took precedence. The dominant narrative, captured in 1910 in Norman Angell's bestseller *The Grand Illusion*, was that war was counter-productive in an interdependent economic environment, since military conflict was an unprofitable endeavour. The twentieth century, Vera Brittain recalled, seemed at first 'the Century of Hope'. With the outbreak of the First World War in August 1914, this vision was irrevocably altered.[3]

The First World War

As the majority of Britain was united in patriotic fervour, with many volunteers enlisting to fight, some mobilised instead to protect those who felt they could not take part. The No-Conscription Fellowship (NCF), which became the main pacifist organisation during the war, was founded for this purpose in November 1914 by two socialists, Clifford Allen and Fenner Brockway. It drew together individuals from different walks of life and with often conflicting convictions. For among those who were labelled 'pacifist' there existed a great variety of views – ranging from the strict absolutist position (which was often, but not always, religious based) of those who upheld the immorality of all wars and refused to contribute in any way to their existence (even by activities that were not directly bellicose), to those who agreed about the inherent immorality of war but who were willing to serve in non-combatant ways. Historians group these two positions as pacifist, and term 'pacifistic' those who favour peace and work towards it while accepting that force is a necessity in certain circumstances. In 1914, these divisions were not conflictive and could therefore cohabit under the broad wing of the NCF.

But the lack of clarity was actually revealing: pacifism was at a crucial juncture. Until then, it had primarily expressed a moral stance, inspired mostly by Christian doctrine, but also by a respect for human life inherited from the Enlightenment. It was when conscription was introduced in a country unaccustomed to required enlistment that the obligations of citizenship were made explicit, and pacifists were propelled into the terri-tory of politics. Defending peace in this context went beyond engaging in an ethical argument about the value of human life; it also meant embarking into the political arena to question the social contract and to address what kind of citizens, nation, and international order might best secure the conditions for peace. A belief that had been largely confined to the realm of ethics was in the process of being redefined.

When the Military Service Act was passed by Parliament in January 1916, requiring unmarried men between the ages of eighteen and forty-one to enlist, it included 'unconditional and non-religious exemption'.[4] England was practically unique in allowing for conscientious objection on secular grounds. Even though the Act recognised this right, the Military Tribunals set up to hear such cases were often severe, reflecting the public's overwhelmingly negative view of those who were derided as 'conchies'. While the legacy of civil liberties and the influence of religious pacifists opened up the government's understanding of the right not to bear arms for one's country, the tide of public opinion was clearly against it, making the example of conscientious objectors (COs) and anti-war writing particularly significant. Here, the impact of writers and intellectuals was key – they not only lent authority and publicity to the cause of peace, but they articulated a defence (often secular) of the right to stand peacefully against the will of the state.

The literary and intellectual circles of Bloomsbury presented a largely united front against the war. Ottoline and Philip Morrell offered Garsington as a refuge for friends and like-minded individuals, providing COs such as David Garnett, Duncan Grant, and Clive Bell farm jobs which satisfied the requirement for work of 'national importance'. With visits from the Woolfs, Lytton Strachey, Siegfried Sassoon, John Maynard Keynes, and Bertrand Russell, among many others, Garsington became an important nexus for anti-war exchanges. Most of them saw conscription, and the growing propaganda encouraging men to enlist, as a contradiction to the war's alleged objective of confronting the rise of militarism. 'What difference would it make if the Germans *were* here?', asked Lytton Strachey, a regular contributor of pacifist propaganda.[5] Many in Bloomsbury feared the upsurge of patriotism, with its tide of jingoism and xenophobia. There was also suspicion that the war served to perpetuate a capitalist and imperialist worldview, a case made in Clive Bell's pamphlet, *Peace at Once* (1915), which was seized and burnt by the authorities. The most vocal intellectual to speak for peace was Russell. Eschewing the religious language that pacifist rhetoric had favoured, in his many lectures, pamphlets, and essays Russell rationalised the movement, rebranding it as a secular pursuit which sought to engage with *realpolitik*. In 'War and Non-Resistance' (1915), he defended the idea that Britain should take a strict position of non-violence, even if colonies were lost or the country was invaded. His popular London lecture series, published as *Principles of*

Social Reconstruction (1916), tackled the issue of peace by suggesting structural change across the board – from education to marriage to the economy – in order to confront social conditioning towards war. Although all those associated with Bloomsbury were by no means strict pacifists, many of these individuals contributed, through their activism and writing, to the anti-war effort, making this coterie, as Christine Froula has suggested, 'an avant-garde of preemptive peace'.[6]

A long tradition connects women to pacifist work, with key figures such as the South African peace activist Olive Schreiner and the suffragette leader Sylvia Pankhurst campaigning for the pacifist cause. Women were placed in the uniquely difficult position of being on the sidelines of war – denied access to the role of combatant, politician, or CO – and yet remaining central to it, as British citizens, potential civilian targets, and as mothers and wives of the men fighting. Peace activists supported the International Committee of Women for Permanent Peace, and for those seeking a first-hand experience of the war, nursing was the main channel available. 'The only way to see war is from a hospital', wrote the pacifist novelist Mabel Dearmer, who recorded her time as a nurse in Serbia in *Letters from a Field Hospital* (1915).[7] Nursing gave women a close-up view of the consequences of war, and the suffering they witnessed drove some, such as Vera Brittain and Winifred Holtby, towards pacifist positions. Asked to sacrifice their loved ones and to see their country embroiled in violence whilst having little agency forged a strong link between pacifism and feminism in these years. This is vividly apparent in Rose Macaulay's *Non-Combatants and Others* (1916) and in Rose Allatini's [A. T. Fitzroy] *Despised and Rejected* (1918). These novels introduce disabled, homosexual, and female characters who work against the war, thus re-directing the pervasive wartime question of who was 'fit' to fight, dramatising the exclusion of women, and introducing pacifist activism as a vehicle for social change.

Resistance against conscription undoubtedly renewed the energy of pacifism in Britain, and its impact could be felt in the decades after the First World War. But, as a critique of the realities of war, nothing could compare with the words of those with direct experience of the front. Siegfried Sassoon's 'The Hero' (1917) topples this bastion of military mythology by contrasting the death of a soldier as it is narrated for the home front to his mother – in an account littered with the language of bravery, glory, and pride – with a vision of his death at the front, where a panicked soldier, desperate to escape, is 'blown to small bits'.[8] Undermining and satirising the myths surrounding war, anti-war writing by Sassoon and other soldier-poets (canonical today) dramatically changed how the warfront was envisioned. Confronting his reader with a ghastly portrait of a gassed soldier in the genre-defining 'Dulce Et Decorum Est' (written in 1917), Wilfred Owen summons us to look at him, to 'watch the white eyes writhing in his face', for only in that proximity could one recognise the underlying cruelty of the country-and-family educated forces that led him to that crisis.[9] In its search for answers to understand the unprecedented violence of this war, this witness poetry provided a crucial legacy for peace writing. The horror of the suffering they depicted gave moral authority to pacifist claims about the depravity of war; the blame directed at the home front justified the need for peace work to move beyond ethical discussions and towards practical reforms, and their testament to the futility of war legitimised the case against armed conflict.

Peace Time

After the Treaty of Versailles marked the formal end of the war on 28 June 1919, pacifist energies shifted towards finding ways to secure long-lasting peace. John Maynard Keynes's bestselling *The Economic Consequences of Peace* (1919) drew a worrying vision of the future by offering a devastating critique of the Treaty, arguing that the harshness of the reparations imposed on Germany would lead to instability within Europe. Internationalism was held up as a crucial approach to foster unity. The foundation of the League of Nations in 1920 constituted a significant step towards peace, for it advanced the cause of disarmament (popular after the war) and promoted diplomacy and negotiation as alternative methods for solving disputes. Many leading intellectuals in Britain – Goldsworthy Lowes Dickinson, Leonard Woolf, Gilbert Murray – were instrumental in organising and promoting the League of Nations Union (LNU, founded in 1918), which was a centre of pacifist activity in the interwar period.

The memory of the First World War was kept alive in a stream of publications in the final years of the 1920s. From America, e. e. cummings sang 'of Olaf glad and big / whose warmest heart recoiled at war: / a conscientious object-or', while Ernest Hemingway further showcased the tragedy of war in his semi-autobiographical novel, *A Farewell to Arms* (1929).[10] Poems, plays, and novels by ex-combatants dominated the British literary landscape: Edmund Blunden, Robert Graves, Siegfried Sassoon, Richard Aldington, R. C. Sherriff, and Ford Madox Ford were all publishing in these years. The horror of trench warfare was made widely available for the reading public to learn about and react against. This literary outpouring represented a looking back, which, though vital for memorialising the last war as futile and destructive, was limited in its engagement with contemporary challenges to peace. From the start of the 1930s onwards, these challenges would become increasingly severe.

More than a decade after the end of the First World War, disarmament had failed. In 1931, war returned with the Japanese invasion of Manchuria, a conflict that the League was unable to stop. Days before the outbreak, Gandhi, by now an inspirational icon, visited the UK. His influence was recorded in an attempt by Christian pacifists to put together a Peace Army that would intercede in the Sino-Japanese conflict. Although this idea was never realised, it formed part of an ongoing proactive approach to prevent violent conflict. Albert Einstein's argument that if 2 per cent of the world's male population refused to fight, wars could never take place, resonated with many. In February 1933, the Oxford Union sided with the motion that 'This House will in no circumstances fight for its King and Country'. Nevertheless, the odds were heavily stacked against peace. Totalitarian ideologies, which saw violence as a key tool to enact their projects of radical change, were quickly spreading across Europe. Stalin was consolidating power in the Soviet Union, the British Union of Fascists was formed in 1932, Hitler was appointed German chancellor in 1933, and Mussolini started his campaign for Italian expansion in 1934. When Leonard Woolf, who had been a central figure in conceptualising the post-war international order, reassessed efforts for peace in 'From Geneva to the next World War' (1933), he saw that the failure to achieve European disarmament was the primary cause for the escalating crisis. Another major war seemed a real possibility.

This hostile political landscape instilled a sense of urgency in the peace writing of this period. Beverly Nichols's popular *Cry Havoc!* (1933) and A. A. Milne's *Peace with Honour* (1934) both plead for peace. Narratives of personal experience remained the preferred medium through which to make a case against war. Vera Brittain conveyed the folly of war in her bestselling memoir, *Testament of Youth* (1933). She had become an indefatigable campaigner for peace and women's rights (causes she felt were intrinsically linked), but from 1933 onwards, she would use her newfound celebrity to concentrate on peace advocacy, focusing particularly on the roles played by women. In 'Can the Women of the World Stop War?' (1934), she critiqued 'a terrible, inert mass of lethargic womanhood'.[11] 'I believe', Brittain wrote, 'that the women of the world could stop war if they [. . .] began to realize that their duty to mankind extends beyond their own little doorstep.'[12] A similar case was made by the socialist and feminist novelist Storm Jameson, whose memoir, *No Time Like the Present* (1933), rebuked women for perpetuating war through their inaction. A pacifist campaigner active after the First World War, Jameson promoted anti-war writing in her collection *Challenge to Death* (1935), and emphasised that social reform was integral to peace work in her autobiographical trilogy, *The Mirror in Darkness* (1934–6). In merging their pacifism with arguments calling for a change in women's civic agency and public engagement, both Brittain and Jameson were shifting the content of peace writing from its emphasis on the horror and futility of warfare towards political activism.

Fractures

Two influential attempts to consolidate the popularity of peace in the mid-1930s paradoxically served to illustrate widening divisions within the movement. In 1934, the LNU started work on the Peace Ballot, a countrywide referendum on League membership and international disarmament. Of the adult population, 38 per cent took part, and their responses demonstrated an impressive support for the League and its work towards peace.[13] But the League did not advocate absolute pacifism. To gauge support for the more radical position, on 16 October 1934, the charismatic Canon Dick Sheppard asked the public to write to him with the following pledge: 'I renounce war and never again, directly or indirectly, will I sanction or support another.' The response was overwhelming, and writers in particular were mobilised by this call to renounce all war. Gerald Heard, Storm Jameson, Siegfried Sassoon, Aldous Huxley, Vera Brittain, Rose Macaulay, and John Middleton Murry all signed the pledge. Virginia Woolf did not sign, but she was sympathetic. The Peace Pledge Union (PPU), formed in the wake of Sheppard's call, became the strongest pacifist movement in history.

In asking the public to clarify their views on peace, divisions between pacifists that had hitherto remained secondary came to the foreground. Moreover, the spread of fascism – confirmed by Italy's attack on Abyssinia in October 1935 – precipitated a crisis for left-wing pacifists that had more or less remained latent since the 1917 Bolshevik Revolution. If war were a result of capitalist competitive structures, would a violent revolution be necessary and defensible to bring about radical change and lasting peace? The transition from pacifism to Communism was not uncommon; in fact, as Peter Brock and Nigel Young remind us, 'some of the founding members and early apostles of the British Communist Party' had been COs during the war.[14] In the US, the committed Christian pacifist

A. J. Muste turned to Marxism during these years. The example of Virginia Woolf's nephew, Julian Bell, was emblematic of this growing acceptance of armed action. Having shared the pacifist legacy of his parents' circles, in editing the anthology *We Did Not Fight: 1914–18 Experiences of War Resisters* (1935), he used his Introduction to convey how his peers were reinterpreting the use of violence. 'I believe', he concluded, 'that the war-resistance movements of my generation will in the end succeed in putting down war – by force if necessary.'[15]

Debates over peace and forms of action in the years leading up to the Second World War conveyed a broader polarisation within British culture. The publication and responses to Aldous Huxley's pamphlet, *What Are You Going to Do About It? The Case for Constructive Peace*, in April 1936, illustrate this fracture. Huxley had become a committed pacifist after his conversations with Sheppard. He would go on to publish a series of works intended to promote the value of peace, including the novel *Eyeless in Gaza* (1936), the *Encyclopaedia of Pacifism* (1937), and his theoretical tract, *Ends and Means* (1937). In *What Are You Going to Do About It?*, an early pamphlet for the PPU, which drew in many new members, Huxley emphasised the importance of profound individual change. 'Constructive Peace', he argued, 'must be first of all a personal ethic, a way of life for individuals.'[16] Influenced by Gerald Heard's 'new pacifism' and Richard Gregg's Gandhi-inspired theories of non-violent resistance, he advocated group meetings with 'spiritual exercises' to strengthen these 'athletes in training'.[17] Reactions from the post-war generation were swift and damning. In *We're Not Going to Do Nothing*, the young Communist poet Cecil Day Lewis dismissed Huxley's 'policy of final inactivity', advocated realism, and echoed Bell in articulating a pacifist stance that incorporated 'force if necessary'.[18] Stephen Spender and Christopher Caudwell joined in the critique with open letters to Huxley in the following months.

Bell's peers performed their generational identity in a rejection of their elders and in a reclaiming of the political subject. In his 'Letter to a Young Revolutionary' (1933), Day Lewis referred to 'our generation, sick to death of protestant democratic liberalism and the intolerable burden of the individual conscience'.[19] Pacifists were increasingly thought to embody an important adversary in this generational story: the individualist author, isolated in his work from the reality on the ground, was inactive and aloof. Rex Warner's poem 'Pacifist' (1935) conveys this critique: it undermines this group as dull ('pale as porridge') and docile ('who feel no fight'), casting them off as irrelevant liberals sheltered and detached in their privilege.[20] Huxley's understanding of individual commitment, with its emphasis on spiritual renewal and communal exercises, was an ideal target to contrast with their realism and the extent of their political engagement. The ideological and generational schism performed in these debates was a prelude to the profound challenge to pacifism brought about by the Spanish Civil War (1936–9).

A Challenge to Peace

The outbreak of hostilities in Spain in August 1936, coming as it did on the heels of Germany's remilitarisation of the Rhineland in March, symbolised for many the fundamental ideological battles intensifying across Europe. A Manichean view of the war spread throughout the literary culture of the period and partisanship became practically a requirement. For pacifists – whether driven by left-wing ideologies or inspired by democratic or humanitarian ideals – the Spanish conflict was a crucial test. While most sympathised with the Republican side, they were divided over how to respond when confronted with the overthrow of a democratically elected government by a military force with fascist support. There were many, particularly from the Left, who recanted or adjusted their pacifist positions. Key figures such as Fenner Brockway (founder of the NCF) or the American socialist leader Norman Thomas (an influential member of the Fellowship of Reconciliation), revised their views to support armed action, and the No More War Movement in Britain singularised this war as an exception to their pacifism. The Spanish conflict particularly roused younger generations who identified with the hope for a new future they saw in the young Republic, and who were eager to find a testing ground for their political commitment. George Orwell, John Cornford, Julian Bell, W. H. Auden, and Stephen Spender were only some of the many young writers who travelled to Spain to support the threatened government. In 'War and Peace: A Letter to E. M. Forster', Bell explained why he, 'and many more men of military age, have ceased to be pacifists'.[21] He accused Forster's generation of failing to recognise the need to use violence in order to achieve political ends. Auden's reference to 'the necessary murder' in his poem 'Spain' (1937) presented a similar argument.[22]

Those who retained their pacifist convictions had to confront this renewed willingness to embrace the use of force. This is what Virginia Woolf set out to do in *Three Guineas* (1938), probably the most sustained attempt to address the challenges raised by the Spanish Civil War. This pacifist and feminist tract, structured as an epistolary reply to a man who asks how women could prevent war, was mostly written during 1937, the year her nephew left to volunteer in Spain and the same year he was killed (at the age of twenty-nine). *Three Guineas* urged women to address the psychological forces at work driving men to respond violently to a conflict. Others debating the possibility of an enduring peace had already considered this evolutionary drive as a fundamental obstacle. The idea that human actions were largely driven by impulses rather than reason had been at the heart of Russell's *Principles*.[23] In 1932, when asked by Einstein if there was 'any way of delivering mankind from the menace of war', Sigmund Freud replied that the 'destructive element' inherent in human nature gave little cause for hope unless it were possible to divert 'humanity's aggressive tendencies' towards 'a channel other than warfare'.[24] While Woolf would have agreed, she saw this as distinctly a gendered issue: 'to fight has always been the man's habit, not the woman's'.[25] Her pamphlet identifies three reasons why men fight: 'war is a profession; a source of happiness and excitement; and it is also an outlet for manly qualities, without which men would deteriorate'.[26] If war constituted the logical consequence of a patriarchal society, finding ways for women to think beyond those oppressive structures was vital if there ever would be peace.

Woolf's proposal is set out in *Three Guineas*, where the letter's respondent asks: 'what active method is open to us?'[27] A man's form of action was irrelevant, since most of the options available to them – force, money, or influence through the church or the press – were inaccessible to women. Fighting 'intellectually' is a woman's tool of 'influence': 'she need not acquiesce; she can criticize'.[28] Women are asked to embrace their historical exclusion as outsiders, reverting this position of disenfranchisement into one of civic capital. Rather than trying to access the same channels of power, they are encouraged to form an 'Outsiders' Society' which made them immune to the logic of wars and countries, stripped of affiliations that might bias their critical thinking. Controversially, Woolf stated in *Three Guineas* that 'as a woman, I have no country. As a woman I want no country. As a woman my country is the whole world.'[29] Woolf is here suggesting a shift in loyalties away from the patriarchal structure of nations (as internationalist pacifists had tried after the war) and towards a loosely conceived network of women. This society exists as an imagined sisterhood which builds the freedom and the agency for women to use their critical thinking to prevent war. Woolf's pamphlet treats peace as an ethical aspiration that is larger than the political problems of the day. Foreshadowing the establishment of a universal code of conduct in the language of human rights after the Second World War, Woolf frames peace as a secular ethical norm which women were ideally placed to promote.

The Cost of Peace

While the outbreak of hostilities in Spain drove many to defend or embrace the use of arms, as the war advanced, returning volunteers were often deeply disillusioned, and it was not uncommon to find some embracing anti-war positions. Having served alongside anarcho-socialists in Catalonia and Aragon, Orwell came to view war as a tool to perpetuate oppression. By 1938, he was arguing that 'Anyone who helps to put peace on the map is doing useful work.'[30] His trust in 'the dislike of war that undoubtedly exists in ordinary decent people' comes across in the character of George Bowling in *Coming Up for Air* (1939), despite being written after Neville Chamberlain accepted Germany's annexation of the Sudetenland from Czechoslovakia in September 1938 in order to secure 'Peace for our time'.[31] As Steve Ellis has argued, this event shaped much literature written in its aftermath, with works such as Ruth Adam's *There Needs No Ghost* (1938) and Woolf's *Between the Acts* (1941) anticipating the pacifist doubts inspired by the Munich crisis.[32] Forster presaged the impending dilemma in his essay 'Post-Munich', where he stated: 'Sensitive people [. . .] see [. . .] that if Fascism wins we are done for, and that we must become Fascist to win.'[33]

In the first months after the outbreak of the Second World War (on 3 September 1939), most pacifists who had supported appeasement were advocating a negotiated peace. But by the summer of 1940, Germany's military advancements prompted a decisive change. The number of individuals registering as COs dropped.[34] As the brutality of Nazism became more apparent, many pacifists worried that their stance was at best counterproductive, and at worst lending support to the fascist side. Key activists either distanced themselves from the peace movement or publicly recanted their positions. Storm Jameson, Rose Macaulay, A. A. Milne, Cyril Joad, J. D. Beresford, and Russell renounced pacifism at this time. In *The End of This War* (1941), Jameson explained her new position and critiqued pacifists' false belief in reasonable options: 'What is open to us is submission, the concentration camp, the death of our humblest with our best.'[35] Pacifists were not only increasingly unpopular; they were often viewed with suspicion. After changing his stance to fully support the war in August 1939, Orwell began a series of bitter attacks against pacifists, repeatedly characterising them as 'pro-Nazi'.[36] Rebecca West made a similar case in *The Meaning of Treason* (1949), referring to the PPU as 'That ambiguous organisation which in the name of peace was performing many actions certain to benefit Hitler.'[37] By 1944, even John Middleton Murry, editor of *Peace News*, had recognised that 'The conventional pacifist conception of a reasonable or generous peace' was 'irrelevant' when confronted with 'the unspeakable crimes' of the Nazis.[38] Faced with such an uncompromisingly destructive enemy, the argument for peace at any cost lost its foothold.

Pacifist convictions were not completely crushed, particularly when they were grounded on religious foundations. Vera Brittain defended the need to negotiate peace with Germany, arguing that war destroyed the humanitarian values it set out to preserve. She outlined her views in 'What Can We Do in Wartime?' (1939), in which she encouraged pacifists to promote peace and to help with relief work. She also led by example, working to alleviate famine and to stop area bombing. Even as pacifists were progressively shunned, she continued to lecture and write for peace in publications such as *Humiliation with Honour* (1942) and *Seed of Chaos* (1944). As if responding to Woolf's call that 'to make ideas effective, we must be able to fire them off', Brittain managed to sustain a letter-writing campaign for peace from October 1939 until the end of the war, working tirelessly to lift spirits and to promote anti-war sentiments.[39]

Conclusion

Most histories of the British peace movement note that ultimately it failed because it could not prevent the Second World War. While this may be right, it did succeed in converting an individualist, faith-based belief into a political position that legitimised civic activism and promoted social change. Literature by COs, trench poets, feminist activists, anti-war campaigners, and pacifist writers gave political traction to the concept of peace by validating the right to go against the state in matters of conscience, defending civic agency in the form of peaceful protest, and emphasising the need for reforms to underpin a lasting peace. This vital democratic legacy has influenced landmark struggles, from the American Civil Rights movement led by Martin Luther King Jr. in the 1960s, to anti-nuclear demonstrations in the 1970s, to present-day climate activism and Black Lives Matter protests. To study peace writing in the first half of the twentieth century is to engage with texts that have radically shaped what it means to be a democratic citizen today. Moreover, in giving secular expression to an ethical aspiration that was partly religious in origin, the peace campaigners and writers of this period laid the groundwork for the language of rights. For even though pacifism was reframed in secular and political terms, at its core, as Ceadel has argued, it remained 'a moral creed'.[40] And after the unimaginable atrocities of the Holocaust, there was an ethical imperative to establish a shared secular morality, eventually encoded in the 1948 Universal Declaration of Human Rights.

Notes

1 Virginia Woolf, 'Thoughts on Peace in an Air Raid', *The Essays of Virginia Woolf*, Vol. 6, ed. Stuart N. Clarke (London: Hogarth Press, 2011), pp. 242–8 (p. 242).
2 Martin Ceadel, *Pacifism in Britain, 1914–1945: The Defining of a Faith* (Oxford: Clarendon Press, 1980), p. 13.
3 Vera Brittain, *The Rebel Passion: A Short History of Some Pioneer Peacemakers* (London: Allen & Unwin, 1964), p. 15.
4 Ceadel, *Pacifism*, p. 39.
5 Quoted in Michael Holroyd, *Lytton Strachey: The New Biography* (London: Chatto & Windus, 1994), pp. 341–2.
6 Christine Froula, 'War, Peace, and Internationalism', in *The Cambridge Companion to the Bloomsbury Group*, ed. Victoria Rosner (Cambridge: Cambridge University Press, 2014), pp. 93–111 (p. 108).
7 Mabel Dearmer, *Letters from a Field Hospital* (London: Macmillan & Co., 1915), p. 145.
8 Siegfried Sassoon, 'The Hero', in *The Oxford Book of War Poetry*, ed. Jon Stallworthy (Oxford: Oxford University Press, 2008), p. 176.
9 Wilfred Owen, 'Dulce et Decorum Est', in *The Oxford Book of War Poetry*, ed. Stallworthy, p. 189. The poem was published posthumously in 1920.
10 e. e. cummings, 'i sing of Olaf glad and big', in *The Oxford Book of War Poetry*, ed. Stallworthy, p. 202.
11 Vera Brittain, 'Can the Women of the World Stop War?', in *History in Our Hands: A Critical Anthology of Writings on Literature, Culture and Politics from the 1930s*, ed. Patrick Deane (London: Leicester University Press, 1998), pp. 69–73 (p. 70).
12 Ibid., p. 71.
13 Helen McCarthy, *The British People and the League of Nations: Democracy, Citizenship and Internationalism, c.1918–45* (Manchester: Manchester University Press, 2011), p. 29.
14 Peter Brock and Nigel Young, *Pacifism in the Twentieth Century* (Syracuse, NY: Syracuse University Press, 1999), p. 37.
15 Julian Bell, ed., *We Did Not Fight: 1914–18 Experiences of War Resisters* (London: Cobden-Sanderson, 1935), p. xix.
16 Aldous Huxley, *What Are You Going to Do About It? The Case for Constructive Peace* (London: Chatto & Windus, 1936), p. 33.

17 Ibid., pp. 31, 34.

18 Cecil Day Lewis, *We're Not Going to Do Nothing* (London: The Left Review, 1936), pp. 3, 30.

19 Cecil Day Lewis, 'Letter to a Young Revolutionary', in *New Country: Prose and Poetry by the Authors of 'New Signatures'*, ed. Michael Roberts (London: Hogarth Press, 1933), p. 29.

20 Quoted in Valentine Cunningham, *British Writers of the Thirties* (Oxford: Oxford University Press, 1988), p. 70.

21 Julian Bell, *Essays, Poems and Letters*, ed. Quentin Bell (London: Hogarth Press, 1938), p. 336.

22 W. H. Auden, *Spain* (London: Faber, 1937), p. 7.

23 See Jo Vellacott, *Conscientious Objection: Bertrand Russell and the Pacifists in the First World War* (Nottingham: Spokesman, 2015).

24 Sigmund Freud, 'Why War?', *Free World* 11 (1946), p. 23.

25 Virginia Woolf, *Three Guineas* [1938] (London: Hogarth Press, 1991), p. 9.

26 Ibid., p. 10.

27 Ibid., p. 15.

28 Ibid., p. 21.

29 Ibid., p. 125.

30 George Orwell, Letter to the Editor of the *New English Weekly*, *The Collected Essays, Journalism and Letters of George Orwell*, ed. Sonia Orwell and Ian Angus, 3 vols. (London: Penguin, 1968), Vol. 1, pp. 366–8 (p. 368).

31 Ibid.

32 See Steve Ellis, 'Literature and the Munich Crisis', *Literature & History* 22.2 (Autumn 2013), pp. 32–56.

33 E. M. Forster, *Two Cheers for Democracy* (London: Edward Arnold, 1972), p. 23.

34 See Ceadel, *Pacifism*, p. 298.

35 Quoted in ibid., p. 297.

36 Orwell, *Collected Essays*, Vol. 2, p. 197.

37 Quoted in Sybil Morrison, *I Renounce War: The Story of the Peace Pledge Union* (London: Sheppard Press, 1962), p. 51.

38 Quoted in Richard A. Rempel, 'The Dilemmas of British Pacifists During World War II', *Journal of Modern History* 50.4, On Demand Supplement (December 1978), pp. D1213–D1239 (p. D1227).

39 Woolf, 'Thoughts on Peace in an Air Raid', p. 242. See Vera Brittain, *Testament of a Peace Lover: Letters from Vera Brittain*, ed. Winifred and Alan Eden-Green (London: Virago, 1988).

40 Ceadel, *Pacifism*, p. 5.

PART II

1945–1989: New Nations and New Frontiers

CHAPTER 6

Partitions

Anindya Raychaudhuri

On the evening of 13 February 1986, BBC Two aired its sixth episode of the first series of the hit sit-com *Yes, Prime Minister*, featuring James Hacker, the perennially incompetent Prime Minister, and Sir Humphrey Appleby, his scheming and apparently all-controlling civil servant. This specific episode, called 'A Victory for Democracy', centres around the fictional postcolonial nation of St George's Island, and the possibility of a Marxist revolution there. In one particular scene, Sir Humphrey (the Cabinet Secretary) and Sir Richard (the Foreign Secretary) discuss the history of empire and independence in the island. Sir Richard admits that the real mistake was made twenty years ago 'when we gave them their independence', because 'we should have partitioned the island'. He says that 'that was our invariable practice when we gave independence to the colonies' and that 'it always worked'. When Sir Humphrey points out that it always led to civil war, at least it did in 'India and Cyprus and Palestine and Ireland', Sir Richard responds that at least 'it kept them busy' and that 'instead of fighting other people, they confined themselves to fighting each other'. Sir Humphrey accepts this because it 'saved us having a policy about them'.

It is an odd place to start, this, for a chapter about the literatures of partitions, but I think the underlying assumptions on which the joke is structured are useful for analysing commonly held understandings about partition. First, partition is presented as all-pervasive. Following a characteristic device for the programme, the line 'India and Cyprus and Palestine and Ireland' is repeated twice for emphasis – highlighting how common the phenomenon of colonialism transitioning to independence via partition is. We might even say that it is the twentieth century's most characteristic political instrument.

When Sir Richard suggests that the independence of St George's Island was a 'mistake', Sir Humphrey wonders if it wasn't the right thing to do because of 'Wind of change and all that'. He is, of course, referring to then

British Prime Minister Harold Macmillan's 1960 speech to the South African parliament, signalling that his Conservative government would not seek to block independence for Britain's colonies. This moment crystallises the process of decolonisation that marks the second half of the twentieth century. If the twentieth century is characterised by, in part, the dismantling of European empire, it is also, of necessity, characterised by partition. Partition, defined as the often violent reordering of national borders to realign nation states along linguistic, ethnic, religious, or other forms of identities has been a persistent feature across much of the last hundred or so years – associated with the transition from colonialism to independence, with the transition from socialist to post-socialist states in Europe after 1989, and multiple other forms of actual and potential realignments of national borders (Brexit and possible Scottish independence, for example). While modern political partitions thus cover a wide range of historical moments, political processes, and geographical contexts, they do, however, also share a certain set of features; partitions are always *productive* in that they result in new objects: new nations, new identities and polities, new memories and life experiences, and also new cultural products such as literature, cinema, art, and music. Wherever and whenever they happen, partitions fundamentally and irreversibly transform public and private life.

It is thus not a little unfortunate that the library of comparative partition studies is so relatively slender. Apart from a few important exceptions that I discuss below, it is probably generally true to say that scholarship on the history and culture of partitions has largely been limited to the silos of regional studies. Often this is for understandable reasons having to do with academic rigour when it comes to methodological and intellectual approaches, but it has nevertheless left us less able to benefit from the better understandings of partitions that could come from a more macro, more comparative approach. Abandoning the historic and geographic specificities of regional studies is, to be sure, a risky approach, but it would open up possibilities that a rigorous regional focus could not.

This is not a new claim. In 2005, Ranabir Samaddar issued a stirring challenge, asking why 'writings of partition have to be bound by nationalist reasoning and have to move only in a closure'.[1] The volume which Samaddar was introducing was not the first attempt at establishing a framework for comparative partitions studies, nor would it be the last; but I think it is fair to say that in the fifteen years since he posed this question, the cumulative scholarship of comparative partitions has arguably not moved forward as decisively to answer his challenge and to destabilise the nationalist closure that he identified as might have been hoped for.

In 2001, Joe Cleary made perhaps the first move to transgress beyond the regional focus of partition, comparing the literary cultures of partition in Ireland, Israel, and Palestine. Cleary correctly points out that 'For the most part, the partitions mentioned here tend to be studied in isolation, and there has been little sustained or extended comparative analysis of such situations.'[2] In 2003, Ghislaine Glasson Deschaumes and Rada Iveković connected the South Asian context with the post-1989 partitionings of Europe and explored the possibilities of partition as a reorganisation to prevent conflict. Deschaumes and Iveković elaborated on the idea of partition as a process, or rather as a theme that repeats itself through the century: 'the Partition of India stands out as an indispensable and instructive reference for equipping our thinking on the partition processes underway in Europe and elsewhere in the world'.[3]

This notion of partition as a recurring motif later got picked up by scholars such as Smita Tewari Jassal and Eyal Ben-Ari in their edited collection that compares the specific contexts of India/Pakistan, Israel/Palestine, and East/West Germany.[4] Radhia Mohanram and Anindya Raychaudhuri's 2019 volume extended this work in a number of directions, bringing together multi-disciplinary approaches including archival history, oral history, literary studies, and cultural studies.[5] It is, however, undeniably true that while most of these multi-author efforts succeed at placing scholarship of different partitions next to each other, they don't necessarily lead to a new discipline of comparative partition studies. Arie M. Dubnov and Laura Robson's book begins to address this lack by featuring historiographical work covering multiple partitions.[6] As a collection of transnational historiography, however, this book is not as cross-disciplinary as some of the others. Twenty years is, ultimately, not a long enough period to be able to establish a new discipline that manages to both sustain comparative analysis and incorporate intellectual and methodological approaches from multiple conventional disciplinary backgrounds. Having said that, I would argue, however, that there is an even more fundamental reason for the regional and national stratification of scholarship, and one which cuts to the heart of our understanding of partition itself.

Partition emerges from scholarship as a multiplicity of conceptions – it is an event with a specific set of historical and geographical contexts, but it is also a pattern that is repeated across time and space. It is a political instrument and an act of power; it creates identities and nations, at once generating some polities and destroying others. It is a literary and cultural trope that seems to be associated with a set of themes and images – trauma, nostalgia, homelessness, violence, pain, and loss. Partition is a contested experience that can be narrativised, and all of these incarnations can be an object of scholarship in history, geography, political science, literary and cultural studies, and more. For all of the interdisciplinary work done on various partitions, however, partition itself emerges from these pages as a surprisingly coherent moment. As Cleary puts it when comparing 1947 India/Pakistan and post-1989 Yugoslavia:

> Anyone familiar with the history of partition could not fail to be aware that the events then underway in a collapsing Yugoslavia – the massacre and rape, the exodus of terrorised populations across state borders, the creation of new national majorities and minorities by ethnic cleansing, the tented cities of refugees that were the inevitable by-product of the drive to create homogeneous national states – were uncannily similar to those that had attended the partition of places such as India and Palestine earlier in the century.[7]

Partition is a motif in the most literal sense, it is a trope that gets repeated, often uncannily, across time and space – always associated with a violence that is simultaneously all-pervasive and inexplicable, at once mundane and extraordinary. Gyanendra Pandey has argued of the India/Pakistan partition that, through its re-telling, the violence is made '"unhistorical" and inexplicable', or something that does not have to be explained because it cannot be.[8] Partition violence, she continues, is 'not industrialised slaughter, directed from a distance, but a hand-to-hand, face-to-face destruction, frequently involving neighbour against neighbour'. It is thus bracketed off, as 'non-narratable . . . as a freak occurrence, like a natural calamity', always othered so that public and private life can carry on without having to process its horrors.[9] Not for nothing does Sir Humphrey believe that it 'always led to civil war'. Jassal and Ben-Ari point out that partition is associated with 'trauma, disaster, or catastrophe . . . both as an outcome and as cause', while Deschaumes and Iveković argue that the moment of partition 'is the time of collective violence against individual destinies'.[10]

Partition represents a rupture, a time of disorder. In this, it is reminiscent of Frantz Fanon's description of decolonisation: 'Decolonization, which sets out to change the order of the world, is, obviously, a programme of complete disorder.'[11] For Fanon, this disorder comes ultimately from a complete reversal of hegemony which he believes decolonisation has to involve:

> In decolonization, there is therefore the need of a complete calling in question of the colonial situation. If we wish to describe it precisely, we

might find it in the well-known words: 'The last shall be first and the first last.' Decolonization is the putting into practice of this sentence.[12]

Where scholarly understandings of partition differ drastically from Fanon's understanding of decolonisation is in the relative optimism for the success or otherwise of the project. Fanon is defiantly optimistic about the possibility of decolonisation – 'if we try to describe it', he says, 'all decolonization is successful'.[13] Partition scholarship, on the other hand, is almost uniformly and overwhelmingly pessimistic about the project of partition (as distinct from violence). When Deschaumes and Iveković rhetorically ask of partition, 'can it really provide a long-term solution to a conflict?' – the answer, it is obvious, is to be in the negative.[14]

Partition, it seems, is not just a cause and an outcome of catastrophe, but in its moment and its afterlives, it becomes catastrophic itself – a break-up of a nation that in and of itself becomes coded as traumatic. The act of partitioning a country, then, is in effect seen *solely* as 'wrestling the other from the self, aiming at an unlikely homogeneity', rather than, say, 'the effort of a disenfranchised and politically underrepresented people to gain greater self-determination'.[15] In other words, the predominant narrative of partition is one that takes the ontological stability of the existing nation state for granted, the dismantling of which becomes an index of the essential undesirability of partition. It is not just that partition studies has largely been limited to national silos, it is that the approach to studying partition has largely and fundamentally been nation-centric. The collapse of one nation state into smaller, newer, realigned nation states as an event gets equated through much of partition scholarship with the violence that causes it, or is caused by it.

Thus, if decolonisation is always successful for Fanon, partition is mostly seen as a failure. Cleary puts it forcefully and persuasively when he argues that:

> [partition's] major deficiency is that in regions where the peoples concerned are geographically intermingled, the attempt to manufacture ethnically homogeneous states, or states with secure ethnic majorities, cannot be accomplished without extraordinary communal violence. This violence does not end with the act of partition: violence is not incidental to but constitutive of the new state arrangements thus produced.[16]

At the risk of stating the obvious, Cleary's point is based on seeing partition as a desire 'to manufacture ethnically homogeneous states' – a view which asserts the moral superiority of the existing nation state as a more heterogeneous entity. This conception of partition has little to do with a sovereignty or disenfranchisement of a minority within the nation state. The strength of Cleary's argument lies in its self-fulfilling nature – for much of partition scholarship, violence has indeed become constitutive of partition.

This connects to the next major assumption behind the extended joke in *Yes, Prime Minister*: the idea that partition is a blunder. The canned laughter that follows Sir Richard's claim that 'it always worked' serves as a prompt for the audience – a sign that they should recognise the blinkered nature of his Whitehall view, the view that the programme lampoons. The contrast between Sir Richard's characterisation of partition as 'invariable practice' and Sir Humphrey's acknowledgement that it made 'a policy' unnecessary is further proof that partition is presented as bad practice as opposed to determined policy, evidence of incompetence rather than malevolence on behalf of Whitehall. In the specific case of the India/Pakistan partition, it becomes an index of the blundering, incompetent, self-serving nature of colonial governance, 'the "bumbler" school of historiography', in Lucy Chester's words.[17] Partition becomes, according to this narrative, a fatally wrongheaded decision that is made in rooms like the one occupied by Sir Humphrey and Sir Richard, with no involvement from, or thought given to, the people who would have to live with or die as a result of these decisions. It is done by great men in high places, or, to quote from Pippa Virdee's analysis of the historiography of the India/Pakistan partition:

> The pervasive hold of the national leadership in shaping perceptions of partition . . . [has] contributed to an obsession with what happened at the top echelons. Moreover, this imbalance is reflected in the history books, which have for a long time neglected the heavy price paid by the citizens of the two new nations.[18]

Virdee is one of many historians who has acknowledged the role of literature and film in filling this gap. She has correctly pointed out that literature and cinema 'provided an outlet to express and share those emotive, traumatic and religiously sensitive subjects that . . . [were] too peripheral for mainstream history'.[19] It should also be said that a lot of this rebalancing work has been done by oral historians like Virdee herself, as well as earlier pioneering oral historians such as Urvashi Butalia, and Ritu Menon and Kamla Bhasin. This body of work has done much to recover the voices of ordinary people who had little say over the events of partition, but had to live through it and with its consequences.[20]

Arguably, however, this dichotomy ultimately still reinforces the idea of partition being enacted by 'great men', and the notion that the voices of the ordinary people need to be incorporated only to demonstrate 'how it impacted and transformed the lives of ordinary citizens' – partition remains a top-down process, imposed from above, as opposed to a contested notion that was fought for and against by 'ordinary citizens' on the streets.

My point here is not to deny that this narrative has any truth to it, but rather to explore the ramifications this historiographical narrative has had on the production and reception of partition literature. In the rest of this chapter, I will focus on a number of literary representations of the 1947 India/Pakistan partition in order to explore how they represent or deny agency to their characters when it comes to understanding the partition that they are living with. I will argue that across multiple genres of literary texts, characters are depicted as bewildered or confused by the events happening around them, and that this confusion has important political ramifications for the nature of partition, and for our understandings of the extent to which people who lived through partition experienced agency over the trajectory of their own lives.

As the British left India in 1947, the country was divided along religious lines, with Punjab in the west and Bengal in the east divided in two. West Punjab and East Bengal formed the new state of Pakistan, even though these two halves were separated by hundreds of miles of India, which had a Hindu majority but remained officially secular. Partition led to perhaps the single largest population migration in human history – with as many as 15 million people crossing the newly created borders. The level and scale of violence was unimaginable – as many as 2 million were killed and more than 75,000 women were abducted, raped and/or forced to convert – and turned the India/Pakistan partition into something like an original event, which can be seen to have then been replicated in many places since.[21]

In 1988, the Pakistani-American novelist Bapsi Sidhwa published *Ice-Candy-Man*, later republished in the United States as *Cracking India*. Semi-autobiographical in nature, this coming-of-age novel tells the story of Lenny, a young girl with polio from a rich Parsee family in Lahore who experiences the trauma of partition. The reader sees partition through Lenny's eyes, though as adult readers we always know more than she is allowed to know. When Lenny first hears of partition, her confusion is palpable: 'There is much disturbing talk. India is going to be broken. Can one break a country? And what happens if they break it where our house is? Or crack it further up on Warris Road. How will I ever get to Godmother's then?'[22] As a child, Lenny does not understand that borders aren't material objects, or that their force doesn't come from their physicality. We the adult readers know this, and are being encouraged to sympathise with Lenny because her confusion helps to locate her as a helpless victim of events beyond her control.

Lenny, however, is hardly the only literary figure who is confused by partition. Amitav Ghosh's novel of the 'other' 1947 partition in Bengal, *The Shadow Lines*, was published in the same year as *Ice-Candy-Man*. Ghosh includes a moment of confusion that is uncannily similar to Lenny's. Thamma, the narrator's grandmother, is on a flight to go and visit their ancestral homelands in what has become East Pakistan. Thamma wants to know 'whether she would be able to see the border between India and East Pakistan from the plane'. Thamma and Lenny share a common misconception regarding the tangibility of the borders. When her son points out her confusion – 'did she really think the border was a long black line with green on one side and scarlet on the other, like it was in a school atlas' – he represents the superior knowledge that the reader enjoys, but that Thamma is denied. Her son's rather patronising response does not ease her confusion:

> But if there aren't any trenches or anything, how are people to know? I mean, where's the difference then? And if there's no difference both sides will be the same; it'll be just like it used to be before, when we used to catch a train in Dhaka and get off in Calcutta the next day without anybody stopping us. What was it all for then – partition and all the killing and everything – if there isn't something in between?[23]

Partition is presented as unnatural, counterintuitive, and people living through it are not allowed to understand what is happening and why. Perhaps the most iconic example of this is 'Toba Tek Singh' (1955), the famous short story by Saadat Hasan Manto, where partition is described through the metaphor of a hospital for the insane. The story centres around the repercussions of a decision made after 'many conferences of important officials from the two sides', to the effect that 'inmates of lunatic asylums, like prisoners, should also be exchanged. Muslim lunatics in India should be transferred to Pakistan and Hindu and Sikh lunatics in Pakistani asylums should be sent to India.'[24] Like for little Lenny and the elderly Thamma, partition doesn't seem to make much sense to these people either:

> As to where Pakistan was located, the inmates knew nothing. That was why both the mad and the partially mad were unable to decide whether they were now in India or in Pakistan. If they were in India, where on earth was

Pakistan? And if they were in Pakistan, then how come that until only the other day it was in India?'[25]

The story focuses on Bishan Singh, known as Toba Tek Singh after the village he is from. His village has been assigned to Pakistan, and his family have been forced to abandon him and move to India. Like Bapsi Sidhwa and Amitav Ghosh, Manto here is using dramatic irony to great effect. The readers are allowed knowledge that is inaccessible to the characters, and the relative ignorance of the characters serves to reinforce both the violent nature of partition and their helpless victimhood in the face of these events that are beyond their control. Bishan Singh's friend Fazal Din comes to the asylum to see him and to give him news of his family:

> 'I have been meaning to come for some time to bring you news. All your family is well and has gone to India safely. I did what I could to help. Your daughter Roop Kaur . . . ' – he hesitated – 'She is safe too . . . in India.'[26]

Fazal Din's hesitation, typographically depicted through Manto's use of ellipsis, stands in for what cannot be said but what the reader knows – that Roop Kaur is almost certain to have faced horrific sexual violence on the journey to India. We the readers know this because we know what partition is, but Bishan Singh is not granted full knowledge of partition because he has to remain a victim: 'Bishan Singh kept quiet.'

Bishan Singh's speech gets more and more nonsensical as the trauma of the loss of his home hits him. In the end, he becomes the home that is denied to him; he becomes Toba Tek Singh and defiantly remains an outsider, choosing self-annihilation in the no-man's land between the two nations: 'There, behind barbed wire, on one side, lay India and behind more barbed wire, on the other side, lay Pakistan. In between, on a bit of earth which had no name, lay Toba Tek Singh.'[27]

In the face of the overwhelming force of partition, there is no room for individual agency except self-annihilation. Writing about 'Toba Tek Singh', Ayesha Jalal has correctly argued that Manto's point in the story is that 'the madness of partition was greater than the insanity of all the inmates put together. But beyond partition there were other no less farcical turns in the postcolonial movement.'[28] She is not alone in pointing out the farcical nature of partition that Manto evokes in his writing. Ramu Nagappan has described Manto's writing as 'a fiction that smashes political notions with preposterous farce'.[29] Writing in *The New Yorker*, William Dalrymple has argued that 'For all the elements of tragic farce in

Manto's stories, and the tormented state of mind of Manto himself, the reality of Partition was no less filled with absurdity.'[30]

One way in which Manto represents partition as farce is through a very effective use of bathos. The juxtaposition of the supposedly serious with the supposedly trivial in order to mock hegemonic norms becomes a key literary device with which to point out the apparently farcical nature of partition: 'One day a Muslim lunatic, while taking his bath, raised the slogan "Pakistan Zindabad" with such enthusiasm that he lost his balance and was later found lying on the floor unconscious.'[31] This bathos – a juxtaposition of the serious and the trivial – is designed to reflect what is seen as the ultimately farcical nature of partition. Multiple scholars have used the idea of farce to depict the events of partition. Thus, in *Empire in Retreat: The Story of India's Partition*, Rabia Umar Ali argues that 'The hasty British departure pre-empted the partition of India that made a farce of planning for one of the most significant developments of the twentieth century.'[32] Kavita Panjabi has argued that 'the deployment of religion as basis for the partitioning of the sub-continent was nothing short of a political farce'.[33] Tarun K. Saint has described 'this history of interminable divisive politics and unending social rifts' as 'a tragic farce'.[34] It would be true to say that this is by no means a hegemonic scholarly understanding of partition, but it is important as a commonsensical notion of the events and, as such, it has had an enduring legacy in collective memories within and outside the subcontinent.[35] This is what ultimately connects 'Toba Tek Singh' with *Yes, Prime Minister* and 'the "bumbler" school of historiography': the idea that partition was a tragic farce, the blame for which can be laid at the door of individual incompetent administrators. The most common personification of this bumbling British official ruining the lives of countless helpless Indians is Cyril Radcliffe, the lawyer who was given the responsibility for deciding the precise location of the borders between the two new partitioned countries.

Born in 1899, Radcliffe was by any measure a successful and accomplished man by the time he was picked to head the two Boundary Committees that would adjudicate the borders between India and Pakistan. He had been called to the bar in 1924 and appointed a King's Counsel in 1935. During the Second World War, he became the Director-General of the Ministry of Information. As Lucy Chester narrates, his appointment was welcomed in the subcontinent as well:

> Mountbatten informed Jinnah in confidence, that Cyril Radcliffe had been proposed ... Jinnah replied that he would need time to consider

Radcliffe's suitability ... but that he 'knew of him and of the high reputation which he held at the Bar'. The next day Jinnah wrote to Mountbatten and indicated that Radcliffe would make an acceptable boundary commission chair.[36]

In terms of literary representation, however, he is most often depicted as a bumbling fool, the personification of all that was wrong with the British Empire and partition. W. H. Auden's 1966 poem, 'Partition', uses the two devices of irony and bathos to depict partition as a farce with Radcliffe at its centre. The opening rhyming couplet depicts Radcliffe's unsuitability for the role he had been given using devastating irony:

> Unbiased at least he was when he arrived on his mission,
> Having never set eyes on this land he was called to partition[37]

Auden's bathetic description of Radcliffe's predicament is Manto-esque in its conflation of the serious and the vulgar:

> The weather was frightfully hot,
> And a bout of dysentery kept him constantly on the trot,
> But in seven weeks it was done, the frontiers decided,
> A continent for better or worse divided.[38]

Auden's depiction of a ridiculous Radcliffe who is singularly unqualified for the task that he has been given is repeated in Howard Brenton's 2013 play, *Drawing the Line*. Before he is sent to India, Brenton's Radcliffe freely admits that he knows 'Absolutely squelch!' about the place, but he believes he 'can try to offer a rational overview', and fantasises about the possibility that he 'may even personally be remembered for something good'.[39] Like many of the authors I have discussed above, Brenton deploys dramatic irony, utilising the audience's previous knowledge of partition as an unquestioned failure – knowledge that the Radcliffe on stage at this point is not allowed. He has no interest in maps but he knows that 'there is a right way and a wrong way, always in everything' because 'that's how we've run an Empire'.[40] Nor do Nehru, Jinnah, and Gandhi know of Radcliffe, but have heard that he is 'principled' and has 'a liberal reputation'.[41] When the representatives of Congress and the Muslim League argue, however, all Radcliffe can do is ineffectually request, 'please could we have some order'.[42] As he realises the impossibility of the task he has been given, he descends into a progressive physical and psychological disintegration:

> Perhaps it would be better to use a water-divining stick over the map: sideways vibrating for Hindu, up and down for Muslim, and what, circles

for Sikh? ... We are making a new reality. Out of an old. But the old reality ... I can hardly grasp what it is.[43]

Following Auden, Brenton's Radcliffe is diarrhoea-ridden as well: 'I must go mightily to the lavatory', he says.[44] He is offered either 'figs' or 'milk of magnesia' as a solution to the problem of the clichéd British reaction to the tropics, based on the understanding that there are two different philosophies: 'flush right through' or 'block up'.[45] In the end, Radcliffe is left a broken man, unable even to write his own resignation letter.

The important point here is not so much the historical accuracy or otherwise of this depiction. These representations might be unfair to Radcliffe-the-man, but literature does not necessarily have the responsibility for telling historical truths, assuming there is one simple truth anyway. The more important point is that, as the other essays in this volume also demonstrate, literature is not just imbricated with politics, but in their responses to specific political events, processes, and causes, literary texts create political narratives of their own. Brenton's Radcliffe insists that he must be 'logical' and 'indifferent' to the violence because he 'cannot become emotional', while Auden's Radcliffe 'quickly forgot / The case, as a good lawyer must'.[46] Sir Humphrey and Sir Richard might be less well-meaning and more deliciously conniving than Radcliffe, but they too are part of this same trope of partition, of the way it has been represented through culture, and therefore of the way it is remembered today. Literature creates realities which only ever tell part of the story. Focusing on the malevolence or incompetence of Sir Humphrey or Radcliffe individualises the empire – reduces all the structural inequalities and institutional violence of empire to the level of a few undesirable or ineffective individuals. Empire as a whole is not the problem; individual imperial administrators are. This political narrative is created, in part, through literary representation. The history of partition becomes the story of some individuals in high places making farcical decisions, and other individuals who figure as victims with no sense of agency in the course of events, whose victimhood demands that they cannot be allowed to know or understand, and that they remain confused by the counterintuitive act of partition. While literature is well placed (unlike historiography, perhaps) to represent the undoubted grief and trauma of partition, there is a danger in doing so as well. The danger is that we reduce grieving individuals to only their grief, and elevate partition to something akin to a sovereign process that exists beyond human agency.

Instead, if we could reconceive partition as a contested notion, an idea that people fought for and against, in many cases knowing exactly what they were doing and why, we could perhaps make room for what Virdee has described as 'the human trauma and turmoil ordinary citizens endured', or what Menon and Bhasin regard as 'the full impact of what Partition meant', without defining these assimilated voices solely through their trauma.[47] Perhaps then literature will be able to move beyond simply responding to the politics of partitions, and instead help to create a newly imagined politics that can combine trauma and agency, a politics that makes space for and respects the almost unimaginable grief that many suffered, but which does not allow them to be defined entirely by their grief. This literature would create a politics of partition that represents the people who lived through partition as fully agentic selves, allowed to know and understand just as much, and maybe even more about partition than their readers do.

Notes

1 Ranabir Samaddar, 'Introduction: The Infamous Event', in *Partitions: Reshaping States and Minds*, ed. Stefano Bianchini, Sanjay Chaturvedi, Rada Iveković, and Ranabir Samaddar (Abingdon: Frank Cass, 2005), pp. 1–12 (p. 1).

2 Joe Cleary, *Literature, Partition and the Nation-State: Culture and Conflict in Ireland, Israel and Palestine* (Cambridge: Cambridge University Press, 2001), p. 3.

3 Ghislaine Glasson Deschaumes and Rada Iveković, 'Preface', in *Divided Countries, Separated Cities: The Modern Legacy of Partition*, ed. Deschaumes and Iveković (New Delhi: Oxford University Press, 2003), p. viii.

4 Smita Tewari Jassal and Eyal Ben-Ari, eds., *The Partition Motif in Contemporary Conflicts* (New Delhi: Sage Publications, 2007).

5 Radhika Mohanram and Anindya Raychaudhuri, eds., *Partitions and their Afterlives: Violence, Memories, Living* (London: Rowman & Littlefield International, 2019).

6 Arie M. Dubnov and Laura Robson, eds., *Partitions: A Transnational History of Twentieth-Century Territorial Separatism* (Stanford, CA: Stanford University Press, 2019).

7 Cleary, *Literature, Partition and the Nation-State*, pp. 2–3.

8 Gyanendra Pandey, *Remembering Partition* (Cambridge: Cambridge University Press, 2001), p. 45.

9 Ibid., p. 46.

10 Jassal and Ben-Ari, 'The Partition Motif', p. 22; Deschaumes and Iveković, 'Preface', p. viii.

11 Frantz Fanon, *The Wretched of the Earth* (London: Penguin, 2001), p. 27.
12 Ibid., p. 28.
13 Ibid.
14 Deschaumes and Iveković, 'Preface', p. vii.
15 Ibid., p. viii; Mohanram and Raychaudhuri, 'Introduction', *Partitions and their Afterlives*, p. xii.
16 Cleary, *Literature, Partition and the Nation-State*, p. 11.
17 Lucy P. Chester, *Borders and Conflict in South Asia: The Radcliffe Boundary Commission and the Partition of Punjab* (Manchester: Manchester University Press, 2009), p. 6.
18 Pippa Virdee, *From the Ashes of 1947: Reimagining Punjab* (Cambridge: Cambridge University Press, 2018), p. 8.
19 Ibid., p. 9.
20 Urvashi Butalia, *The Other Side of Silence: Voices from the Partition of India* (London: C. Hurst & Co., 2000); Ritu Menon and Kamla Bhasin, *Borders and Boundaries: Women in India's Partition* (New Brunswick, NJ: Rutgers University Press, 1998).
21 Ian Talbot, 'The 1947 Partition of India', in *The Historiography of Genocide*, ed. Dan Stone (Basingstoke and New York: Palgrave Macmillan, 2008), pp. 420–37 (p. 420).
22 Bapsi Sidhwa, *Ice-Candy-Man* (New Delhi: Penguin, 1989), p. 92.
23 Amitav Ghosh, *The Shadow Lines* (New York: Mariner Books, 2005), pp. 148–9.
24 Saadat Hasan Manto, *Mottled Dawn: Fifty Sketches and Stories of Partition*, trans. Khalid Hasan (New Delhi: Penguin, 1997), p. 1.
25 Ibid., pp. 2–3.
26 Ibid., p. 7.
27 Ibid., p. 10.
28 Ayesha Jalal, *The Pity of Partition: Manto's Life, Times, and Work across the India-Pakistan Divide* (Princeton, NJ, and Oxford: Princeton University Press, 2013), p. 168.
29 Ramu Nagappan, *Speaking Havoc: Social Suffering and South Asian Narratives* (Seattle, WA: University of Washington Press, 2005), p. 87.
30 William Dalrymple, 'The Great Divide: The Violent Legacy of Indian Partition', *The New Yorker*, 29 June 2015. Available at: www.newyorker.com/magazine/2015/06/29/the-great-divide-books-dalrymple (accessed 10 September 2020).
31 Manto, *Mottled Dawn*, p. 2.
32 Rabia Umar Ali, *Empire in Retreat: The Story of India's Partition* (Oxford: Oxford University Press, 2012), backcover blurb.
33 Kavita Panjabi, 'Partition Violence: Self-Reckoning and the Structuring of a Modern Subjectivity', in *Cartographies of Affect: Across Borders in South Asia and the Americas*, ed. Debra A. Castillo and Kavita Panjabi (New Delhi: Worldview, 2011), pp. 217–40 (p. 219).
34 Tarun K. Saint, 'Writing and Rewriting Partition's Afterlife: Creative Re-enactments of Historical Trauma', in *The Psychological Impact of the Partition*

of India, ed. Sanjeev Jain and Alok Sarin (New Delhi: Sage Books, 2018), pp. 95–111 (p. 101).

35 See Anindya Raychaudhuri, '"Do They Want to Turn Partition into a Gilbert and Sullivan Opera?": Performing Partition as Uncanny Farce', in *South Asian Diasporic Cinema and Theatre: Re-visiting Screen and Stage in the New Millennium*, ed. Ajay K. Chaubey and Ashvin I. Devasundaram (Jaipur, India: Rawat Publications, 2017), pp. 312–34.

36 Chester, *Borders and Conflict in South Asia*, p. 36.

37 W. H. Auden, 'Partition', *Collected Poems*, ed. Edward Mendelson (London: Faber, 1994), p. 803.

38 Ibid., p. 804.

39 Howard Brenton, *Drawing the Line* (London: Nick Hern Books, 2013), pp. 9, 11.

40 Ibid., p. 22.

41 Ibid., pp. 39, 28.

42 Ibid., p. 43.

43 Ibid., p. 55.

44 Ibid., p. 60.

45 Ibid., p. 52.

46 Ibid., p. 60; Auden, 'Partition', p. 804.

47 Pippa Virdee, 'Remembering Partition: Women, Oral Histories and the Partition of 1947', *Oral History* 41.2 (Autumn 2013), pp. 49–62 (p. 49); Menon and Bhasin, *Borders and Boundaries*, p. 22.

CHAPTER 7

Federalism

Ryan Weberling

Writing in Paris at the height of the US Civil War, Pierre-Joseph Proudhon predicted that 'the twentieth century will open the age of federations, or else humanity will undergo another purgatory of a thousand years'.[1] To Proudhon's dismay, humanity seemed to choose purgatory over federation during most of the century that followed his prediction. The end of the nineteenth century saw the resurgence and formalisation of European imperialism following the 1884 Berlin Conference. Nationalism seemed a crucial factor driving the two global conflicts that defined the first half of the twentieth century, even as numerous civil wars raged around the world before, between, and after these global conflicts. Revolutionaries such as Vladimir Lenin disparaged the 'fig-leaf of "federation"' and 'the petty-bourgeois ideal of federal relationships'.[2] Yet, by the end of the twentieth century, Proudhon's prediction seemed, by some counts, and against all odds, to have come true. More than twenty-five nation states around the world, representing approximately 49 per cent of the world's population, were – or claimed to be – federations.[3] The United Nations celebrated its fiftieth anniversary in 1995, the same year that the European Union adopted the name 'Euro' for the currency of Europe's emerging economic and monetary union.

But what exactly is a federation? '[A]ll political constitutions, all systems of government', Proudhon explained in his treatise, 'fall within the scope of [this] one formula, *the balancing of authority by liberty*, and vice versa.'[4] For Proudhon, federalism meant qualifying the authority of the state with the social power of families, guilds, and other communities, within which individuals could operate freely. For other political theorists and commentators, though, the federal formula involved the balance between homogeneity and variety, or between centralisation and decentralisation of state functions. Federalism resolved such conceptual oppositions by loosening several foundational claims of modern political theory: in place of indivisible sovereignty, territorial coherence, and demographic uniformity, federalism accepted multiplicity, dispersity, and diversity as defining – even desirable – characteristics of any system of government. The state-within-a-state became the most typical manifestation of federal ideals. Nonetheless, any particular federal plan involved a new calculation and calibration between the forces or ideas opposed in the situation at hand. Federation is thus always a 'compromise formation', in the sense of political compromise and in Sigmund Freud's sense of a partial return of the repressed: 'a *compromise* between the repressed and the repressing ideas'.[5]

With its modern origins often ascribed to the imperial expansion and colonial revolt that created the United States of America, federalism played an important role in reforming and dissolving European empires across the twentieth century. Nonetheless, as an ideal articulated primarily by Anglo-American and European elites, federal compromises often worked to protect racial hierarchies and imperial interests. As George Orwell noted in a 1939 review, the many Second World War-era proposals for international federation always included an 'unspoken clause' that excluded non-white subjects and nations.[6] This racialised exclusion of much of the world from federal discussions and aspirations contributed to the turbulence of decolonisation, as many newly independent nations inherited federal or quasi-federal constitutions that had been imposed with neither the popular support nor material resources to sustain them.

***

Proudhon's prediction about the future of federalism took on new, enticingly figurative dimensions two decades following his pronouncement, after the Union victory in North America had established federation's durability as a constitutional form. In 1882, the year of his daughter Virginia's birth, Leslie Stephen adapted the federal formula to his analysis of mental order and 'individual . . . constitution':

> Man, in fact, is a microcosm as complex as the world which is mirrored in his mind; he is a federation incompletely centralised, a hierarchy of numerous and conflicting passions . . . . He is in some sense a unit, but his unity is such as to include *an indefinite number of partly independent sensibilities . . .*[7]

Stephen's understanding of mental unity as a kind of federalism suggests a particular historical and geopolitical index for the emergence of new literary techniques for representing consciousness. His metaphor of a federated self reflects contemporaneous debates about the historiography of the British Empire and the future shape of state sovereignty. In doing so, it adumbrates the range of rhetorical and conceptual innovations that would be applied to human subjectivity as federalism became a global mode of governance and structure of feeling.

As Stephen's analogy indicates, federation was more than just a category of political entities or a model for subdividing state functions. The notion of federal union provided 'a structure of thinking' derived from David Hume's associationist psychology, which viewed consciousness as aggregative rather than hierarchical.[8] As a 'political subjectivity' entailing a distinct '*geographic* imaginary', federation became a 'cultural form' when writers attempted to portray alternative models of membership and collectivity beyond the political forms of the racialised nation or the international proletariat.[9] Twentieth-century federalism developed in parallel with a philosophical pluralism that viewed reality as diverse, contingent, and too complex to be organised by traditional notions of unitary constitutionalism. As William James explained in a 1909 account of pluralism:

> The word 'and' trails along after every sentence. Something always escapes. ... The pluralistic universe is thus more like a federal republic than like an empire or a kingdom. However much may be collected, however much may report itself as present at any effective centre of consciousness or action, something else is self-governed and absent and unreduced to unity.[10]

In the pluralist constitutionalism developed over the next two decades, especially in the wake of the First World War, federation was seen not only as a 'form of state organization' but as a principle of identity and a conception of reality that revised distinctions between the political and the apolitical, between individuals and the state.[11] Theorists of federalism emphasised that federal thinking involved an expanded conception of politics, a dynamic view of political processes that not only mirrored but causally depended on the complexities of individual feeling and consciousness: 'This notion of pragmatic plurality in the compounding of consciousness, where an individual is not only himself but also the state, is the basic spirit of federalism.'[12]

Gertrude Stein slyly linked shifting literary forms to federal political forms in lectures she delivered during her 1935 US lecture tour. Echoing William James's comparison of pluralism and federalism to a long, trailing sentence, Stein evokes federalism's flexibility and expandability by contrasting the partial 'phrase' of nineteenth-century England with the all-inclusive 'paragraph' of twentieth-century America:

> [I]t was natural that in writing The Making of Americans I had proceeded to enlarge my paragraphs so as to include everything. What else could I do ...

This was inevitably because the nineteenth century having lived by phrases really had lost the feeling of sentences, and before this in English literature paragraphs had never been an end in themselves and now in the beginning of the twentieth century a whole thing, being what was assembled from its parts was a whole thing and so it was a paragraph.[13]

Unlike piecemeal and modular phrases, Stein's paragraphs can 'enlarge' to make 'a whole thing' from otherwise scattered or fragmented 'parts'.

If the geopolitical overtones of this stylistic contrast are not wholly apparent, Stein clarifies in another lecture, 'What Is English Literature', that the shift to 'whole' American paragraphs was necessitated by the anxious incompleteness of the Victorian empire, which 'did not choose a completed thing':

[I]f you have to explain the inside to the inside and the owning of the outside to the inside that has to be explained to the inside life and the owning of the outside has to be explained to the outside it absolutely is not possible that it is to be done in completed sentences . . . . *Paragraphs then having in them the quality of registering as well as limiting an emotion are the natural expression of the end of the nineteenth century of English literature.* The daily island life was not sufficient any more as limiting the daily life of the English, and the owning everything outside was no longer actual or certain and so it was necessary that these things should be replaced by something and they were replaced by the paragraph . . . . A phrase no longer soothed, suggested or confined, they needed a whole paragraph.[14]

As a compromise between emotion and order, paragraphs retain 'the feeling of sentences' but modulate them into a wider variety of purposes: 'sooth[ing]', 'suggest[ing]', 'confin[ing]', and otherwise 'limiting' emotions while still 'registering' them. Stein's paragraph form is federal in its integration of parts (phrases and sentences) within a loose and flexible new entity. Unlike English literature and the British Empire, which never managed to reconstitute themselves in federal form, Stein's American paragraphs ostensibly reconcile inside and outside, emotion and order, the certainty of 'owning everything' with the necessity of accepting change.

The years following Stein's lectures were a crucible for both federalism and American political ascendancy. In 1941, the publisher Macmillan brought out a series of 'Federal Tracts', with contributions from a range of eminent British intellectuals.[15] George Catlin, transatlantic political scientist, and husband to novelist Vera Brittain, contributed a volume to the Macmillan series and cast himself as the British defender of America's federal ideals. Catlin's version of federalism extended his quasi-racial notions of Anglo-Saxon cultural heritage into a political platform centred on the creation of an Anglo-American state to be called 'AngloSaxony' (a coinage he adopted from the English writer Wyndham Lewis):

> We should see a world where Liberalism was maintained by the power of the new Anglo-Saxon Commonwealth .... It would, I think, be entitled to compel federation in Europe and to tell States, small or great, who declined to co-operate that it would treat them as the North treated the Secessionist States of the South, until they would accept the position that the Southern States accepted after the Reconstruction era.[16]

In a much different tone than Catlin's brash boosterism, Hannah Arendt explored the idea of federation based on nationality rather than territory, as a means of securing Jewish representation in a hypothetical European parliament. For Arendt, European federation was a possible remedy for the political instabilities and imperial excesses of national sovereignty, which had led to totalitarianism and, specifically, to Nazism.[17]

Federal notions appealed to conservative traditionalists as well as liberal reformers. Speaking after the Second World War to an interviewer for *Life* magazine, Evelyn Waugh opined that 'The writer's only service to the disintegrated society of today is to create little independent systems of order of his own.'[18] In contrast to the 'stable' and 'homogeneous' societies of other times, Waugh saw in the twentieth century a dynamically ungovernable variety and variability. During such an era, writers could only hope to provide coherence and meaning at a diminished scale. As John Marx has argued, Waugh's sentiments reflected a renewed appreciation of 'local culture' amidst British imperial decline; yet they also hinted at a new aspiration for global influence, as writers took their place in 'a decentered network of places and peoples described, analyzed, and managed by a cosmopolitan cast of English-speaking experts'.[19]

The particular social arrangement described by Waugh – 'little independent systems of order' – resolves this tension between global and local, disintegration and order, with the characteristic balancing act of federalism. Waugh articulated a conservative variety of the many federalisms that proliferated in the margins of the Second World War; he was likely influenced more by the Catholic principle of subsidiarity, or preference for decentralisation, than by the utopian visions of liberal and socialist internationalists. But whereas Waugh envisioned a transition to local authorities within a decentralised cultural network, others envisioned large-scale geopolitical changes: the transformation of the British Empire into a quasi-federal Commonwealth; the federation of nations in Western Europe; and 'a Federal Union of the Democracies of the North Atlantic', as the American writer Clarence Streit advocated in his best-selling 1939 book, *Union Now* (the subject of Orwell's scathing review, mentioned above). Yet none of these political solutions produced the peace, stability, or equality that they promised.

W. H. Auden wrestled with the aspirations – and contradictions – of federalism in his great wartime poem 'New Year Letter (January 1, 1940)'. The poem's speaker looks out over crowds of New Yorkers, 'loose formations of good cheer, / Love, language, loneliness and fear'; surveys the resources available to him in 'the ideal order' of art, literature, and philosophy; and wonders finally about the sheer number of crises clamouring for his attention: 'Which of these calls to conscience is / For me the *casus foederis*[?]'[20] His final question here points subtly but specifically to the impossibility of the previous century's political optimism, as expressed by Proudhon. For Auden, witnessing the disintegration of Europe into warring nations, with the violence of their competing imperial ventures redounding on the continent in full force, questions of individual association (*casus foederis*, 'case for the alliance') take precedence over larger scales of social contract. Even as the poem mourns the destruction of local communities by an atomising industrial society that 'Replaced the bonds of blood and nation / By personal confederation', it has only diminutive sarcasm for 'teas when clubwomen discuss / The latest Federation Plan'.[21]

Yet Auden's use of the Latin term *foederis* (from *foedus*, meaning 'covenant' or 'league') invokes the same question of 'trust' that lies at the root of these political terms, 'confederation' and 'federation'.[22] Adrift between uncertain personal bonds and unsatisfying political plans, Auden distrusts but struggles to dispel the quintessential federal aspiration, *e pluribus unum* (out of many, one). Reflecting the poet's scepticism towards political plans and solutions, 'New Year Letter' begins by describing a prelapsarian domain of art and culture, in which 'local' perspectives mingle and cohere independent of the state's unitary power:

> Our minds a *civitas* of sound
> Where nothing but assent was found,
> For art had set in order sense
> And feeling and intelligence,
> And from its ideal order grew,
> Our local understanding too.[23]

This idealised view of art soon falters before the divisive and alienating influences of fascism and modernisation, and Auden even locates the provenance of such aspirations for federal order in 'The Devil', that 'great schismatic who / First split creation into two' and then 'Inspired it with the wish to be / Diversity in unity'.[24] However, the third and final section of 'New Year's Letter' revives the ideal of a future in which 'men confederate in Man'.[25] Even as Auden questions art's ability to organise experiences or to integrate parts within wholes, his poem's expansive catalogue of writers and artists finally does assemble as an ideal order, capable of preserving freedom within its 'pluralist interstices' and of yielding the 'real unity [that] commences / In consciousness of differences'.[26]

Auden's wrangling with the intellectual and affective dimensions of unity in difference exemplifies federalism's oblique influence on literature. Poems and especially novels often respond to the politics of federation figuratively or formally, conceptually, or rhetorically, in styles and techniques that can be characterised as modernist. Instead of unity being forged through public speeches and committee squabbles, as in realist versions of the protest novel or the political novel, it becomes a matter of narrative and psychological coherence. The disparate parts of a text or the discordant voices in a character's mind merge with the sphere of politics as such, and become the grounds for balancing order against chaos, control against freedom.

For example, Virginia Woolf's fiction was written during the turbulent decades in which the British Empire was refashioned as a quasi-federal Commonwealth, and much of her writing is organised around, in her words, 'moments of being ... [that] put the severed parts together ... making a character come together'.[27] The language of federation becomes more explicit in her fiction across the 1920s, in meditations on the unifying forces of vision and interpersonal sympathy. That language takes on collective and explicitly political resonances in later narratives, for example, the phonograph's declarations of 'unity-dispersity' in *Between the Acts* (1941).[28] But it is Woolf's *Orlando: A Biography* (1928) which adopts federalism the most directly. In contrast to a realist narrative such as *In the Cabinet*, Phyllis Shand Allfrey's unfinished novel about the West Indies Federation, *Orlando* rewrites the tension between English national history and British imperial violence as a single, extended life narrative. After living for centuries through transformations in government, in literary style, and in her own sex and gender, the book's protagonist comes to see herself as a pluralised system of selves and voices, each with 'little constitutions and rights of their own'.[29] Granting autonomy to her composite parts restores Orlando's mental balance, allowing her to become 'conscious of disseverment' even as she remains 'what is called, rightly or wrongly, a single self'.[30]

Triggered in the text by echoes and memories of anti-imperial resistance, this federal resolution to the story engages with the Commonwealth idea of imperial federation as it was emerging in Woolf's own day; and Woolf's model of federated character also allows her story of a life to be called, rightly or wrongly, a single 'biography'.

Woolf's model of federated character anticipates similar modernist experiments across the Anglophone world, from William Faulkner's fictions about the US Civil War and its aftermath, which depict Quentin Compson as 'an empty hall echoing with sororous defeated names ... not a being, an entity' but rather 'a commonwealth'; to Salman Rushdie's groundbreaking postcolonial novel, *Midnight's Children* (1981).[31] As the disenfranchised centre of the British Empire-Commonwealth for the first half of the twentieth century, and the world's largest federal state after 1947, India exemplifies the doubly complicated status of federation as an imperial-turned-postcolonial form of government. The arrival of independence in 1947 inverted the question of how India might be integrated into the Empire-Commonwealth, as federal form went from being an external political container imposed on the subcontinent to being the region's internal organising (or disorganising) principle. This process of inversion galvanises the formal and stylistic innovations in Rushdie's *Midnight's Children*, even as the occluded relationship between imperial and postcolonial constitutions presses the rhetoric of federation into the story's margins. Although Rushdie's later work embraces federal language and metaphors as part of his notion of cultural hybridity, this novel identifies the deep-seated, indeed constitutional violence that simultaneously undergirds and undermines postcolonial federalism.

Known for its narrator's distinctive self-declarations, such as 'Please believe me that I am falling apart ... I am not speaking metaphorically', Rushdie's narrative conveys the material and psychic effects of the fact that federal governance inverted and internalised, rather than resolved, the violent contradictions of India's colonial constitution.[32] Rushdie's narrator-protagonist, Saleem Sinai, wonders whether the 'spirits' of earlier proponents of federalism had 'leaked into me, imbuing me with the notion of loose federalism and making me vulnerable to knives'.[33] Such self-conscious anxiety differs markedly from the attitude of Saleem's literary precursor, the ostentatious narrator of G. V. Desani's *All About H. Hatterr* (1948), who breathlessly designates himself honorary treasurer of the 'U.S. of India'.[34] Saleem's inability to accurately recognise these spirits over more than 500 pages of narrative makes *Midnight's Children* not only a distinctively original national allegory but a sophisticated reflection on the conditions of postcolonial statehood. Specifically, Rushdie reanimates federalism as a postcolonial concern by calling attention to the gap between India's disruptive colonial history and the rhetorical conceits of nationalist autobiography, which is meant to depict 'not merely the quest of one individual for freedom, but . . . the making of the mind of new India', and thus to demonstrate how the individual becomes 'merged, to a large extent, in the larger movement and therefore represents, in a large measure, the feelings of many others'.[35]

Federalism's contradictions as a constitutional form for India are represented in Saleem's telepathic relationship with his Midnight's Children Conference, an ironic mutation of the dignified 'conference of Oriental statesman' envisioned by Dr Aziz at the close of E. M. Forster's *A Passage to India* (1926).[36] However, when this latter-day Conference dissolves into cacophony, Saleem misidentifies the source of his federal aspirations, which ultimately derived not from an 'optimism epidemic' among Indian nationalists but from the colonial constitution imposed on the region by the British Parliament in 1935, based on the recommendations of the all-white 1928 Simon Commission.[37] This 'paper federation' was designed to fail, but nonetheless served as the basis for India's government after formal independence, providing approximately two-thirds of the articles in its constitution.[38] The colonial origin of Saleem's contradictory character – simultaneously self-centred and tending towards disintegration – is underscored by the eventual revelation of his true paternity. Descended from an English colonial official (William Methwold), rather than his Forsterian-inspired adoptive grandfather (Dr Ahmed Aziz), Saleem embodies the 'Anglo-Indian' character of India's constitutional origins.[39]

By narrating and yet misdiagnosing federation's instability as a constitutional form for the subcontinent, Rushdie makes the political and epistemic uncertainties of decolonisation spectacularly palpable for his global audience and newly cognisable for his Indian readers. Rather than 'glossing over all earlier contradictions, divergences[,] and differences and incorporating within the body of a unified discourse every aspect and stage in the history of [the nation's] formation', *Midnight's Children* conveys the story in fits and starts, repeatedly inhabiting past confusions and asserting itself through them.[40] The book's hodgepodge assortment of sections, chapters, and subplots intersperse life story with national history, annotating and footnoting (and, at times, conspicuously attempting to erase) the relationship between a postcolonial present and its imperial past. Saleem's narrative prevaricates, hedges, contradicts, rearranges, and ultimately dissolves itself in the face of the postcolony's occluded origin stories and the (necessary?) illusion of its absolute self-determination: 'lies being spoken ... anything you want to be you kin be, the greatest lie of all'.[41] Through these manoeuvres, it wrestles loudly with the 'ambiguities and contradictions in the doctrine of nationalism' – notably, the paradox of postcolonial sovereignty – and attempts to repurpose federalism from a tool of subjection to a resource for subjectivity.[42] Rushdie's success in *Midnight's Children* was not only to 'write back', as he later described it, to imperial assumptions and judgements, but to contend with a pressing rhetorical and epistemic problem: how to write the 'life-history' of the postcolonial nation without recourse to a 'single, consistent, unambiguous voice'.[43]

While federation might seem to offer a viable alternative to the nation state's consolidated voice, *Midnight's Children* confronts the difficulty of balancing unity and difference within conceptual-institutional forms derived from colonial division and imposition. Saleem himself fails to develop a fully reflexive or sustainable model of postcolonial subjectivity. In place of both unitary coercion and federal optimism, what Rushdie develops is an amplified rhetorical style capable of conveying colonial constitutional history's mixed-up influence on life after independence: from the partition of India and Pakistan (1947), to the civil war between Pakistan and what is now Bangladesh (1971), and then Indira Gandhi's declaration of emergency powers (1975–7). Saleem's consistently unsettled voice and identity confront readers with the uncertainty of navigating postcolonial statehood and of pursuing federal democracy in the wake of colonial subordination and disseverment.

At two key points in Rushdie's narrative, Saleem Sinai identifies 'loose federalism' as the ill-fated political ideal that has contributed to his own subjective crises in identity. Early on, in the chapter that opens with him insisting that 'I am falling apart ... I am not speaking metaphorically', Saleem recounts the emergence of federal ideas as part of the 'optimism epidemic' that swept through India in the decades preceding formal inde-pendence. His own non-biological father (Ahmed Sinai) picks up federal ideas from a charismatic street magician turned political leader and 'unifier', Mian Abdullah, whose plans are cut short when he is brutally dismembered by dogs and knife-wielding assassins.[44] In this first pass of narration, Saleem states in no uncertain terms that interest in Abdullah's 'loosely federated alternative' came to an end with the magician's death: 'That was the end of the optimism epidemic.'[45] However, Saleem continues to encounter the difficult contradictions of federal unity-in-diversity: the breakdown of his telepathic negotiations with the Midnight's Children Conference; the civil war between East and West Pakistan; and, finally, Indira Gandhi's declaration of national emergency, which activated a British-authored constitutional Article to temporarily reconstitute federal India as a unitary state. It is only 200 pages later that Saleem recognises in himself the ambiguously persistent influence of Abdullah's federal aspirations: '[W]hether the spirits of Mian Abdullah, whom knives killed years before, had leaked into me, imbuing me with the notion of loose federalism and making me vulnerable to knives, I cannot say.'[46]

With Saleem's recognition of his own uncertainty, *Midnight's Children* presents federalism as a problematic legacy of colonisation and a precarious technology for organising postcolonial experience. As a conceptual and institutional form, federalism is central to what Rushdie has called 'the riddle of midnight', that is, the question of India's origins and organisation as 'a political entity'.[47] Compared to the cultural pluralist ideal of 'cultural federation', in which differences are held together within a common framework of information, interests, and aspirations, this question of political federation has the added dimension of assigning such differences to particular territorial regions – of aligning demographics with borders and boundaries. Yet the centralisation of the colonial state prior to independence proceeded not just blind to demographic divisions but specifically by manipulating and exacerbating them. British sovereignty was consolidated through the opportunistic division and decentring of prior local sovereignties, with the princely states dependent on the directly administered territories with which they were intertwined, and both categories of state economically and politically subjected to the United Kingdom.

Given this imposed dependence, it is not surprising that Saleem's account of federalism's origins is 'unreliable', to use Rushdie's term for him. Saleem offers a tellingly incomplete version of federation's history, for his story 'is not history, but it plays with historical shapes . . . The reading of Saleem's unreliable narration might be . . . a useful analogy for the way in which we all, every day, attempt to "read the world".'[48] With this understanding of unreliability, Rushdie offers more than a statement of postmodern scepticism or postcolonial pessimism. Rather, Saleem's 'distortions' and the novel's failure to provide 'an authoritative guide to the history of post-independence India' speak to the central epistemological predicament of postcolonial historiography: the understanding that it is not only the content of historical narratives but their assumptions, categories, and concepts that were altered by colonisation.[49] The transition of power surrounding independence required simultaneous acts of translation, disavowal, and reinvention, as political leaders attempted to stabilise the subcontinent using a federal prototype designed to destabilise the region. Locating the origins of 'loose federalism' in the miraculous figure of Mian Abdullah, Rushdie's narrator attempts to claim it as an autochthonous model of Indian nationalism. Like other stories or histories that take 'the south' as their subject, this unreliable genealogy of Indian federalism might be a necessary and even a generative fiction, given the task of realising independence from conditions that are anything but independent. As Saleem concludes about the story of Mian Abdullah's death: 'Sometimes legends *make* reality, and become more useful than the facts.'⁵⁰

Notes

1 Pierre-Joseph Proudhon, *The Principle of Federation and the Need to Reconstitute the Party of Revolution* [1863], trans. Richard Vernon (Toronto: University of Toronto Press, 1979), pp. 68–69.

2 Vladimir Lenin, 'The National Question in Our Programme', *Iskra* 44 (15 June 1903), in *Collected Works*, Vol. 6, 4th English edition (Moscow: Progress Publishers, 1965), pp. 454–63 (p. 458); and 'On the National Pride of the Great Russians', *Sotsial-Demokrat* 35 (12 December 1914), in *Collected Works*, Vol. 24, ibid., pp. 102–6 (p. 102).

3 Raoul Blindenbacher and Ronald L. Watts, 'Federalism in a Changing World', in *Federalism in a Changing World: Learning from Each Other*, ed. Blindenbacher and Arnold Koller (Montreal, QC: McGill-Queen's University Press, 2003), pp. 7–25 (p. 9).

4 Proudhon, *The Principle of Federation*, p. 7.

5 Sigmund Freud, 'Further Remarks on the Neuro-Psychoses of Defence' [1896], *Early Psycho-Analytic Publications*, trans. James Strachey (London: Hogarth Press, 1962), pp. 157–85 (p. 170).

6 George Orwell, 'Not Counting Niggers', Review of Clarence Streit's *Union Now, Adelphi* (July 1939), in *The Collected Essays, Journalism and Letters of George Orwell*, Vol. 1: *An Age Like This, 1920–1940*, ed. Sonia Orwell and Ian Angus (New York: Harcourt Brace, 1968), pp. 394–8 (p. 394).

7 Leslie Stephen, *The Science of Ethics* (New York: G. P. Putnam's Sons, 1882), pp. 68–9 (emphasis added).

8 Susan Manning, *Fragments of Union: Making Connections in Scottish and American Writing* (New York: Palgrave, 2002), p. 2.

9 Joseph Keith, *Unbecoming Americans: Writing Race and Nation from the Shadows of Citizenship, 1945–1960* (New Brunswick, NJ: Rutgers University Press, 2013), pp. 160, 161.

10 William James, *A Pluralistic Universe: Hibbert Lectures at Manchester College* [1909] (London, Bombay, and Calcutta: Longmans, Green, & Co., 1920), pp. 321–2.

11 Sobei Mogi, *The Problem of Federalism: A Study in the History of Political Theory*, Preface by Harold Laski, 2 vols. (New York: Macmillan, 1931), Vol. 1, p. 9.

12 Ibid., Vol. 2, p. 1063.

13 Gertrude Stein, 'The Gradual Making of *The Making of Americans*', *Lectures in America* (New York: Random House, 1935), pp. 136–61 (p. 159).

14 Gertrude Stein, 'What Is English Literature', *Lectures*, pp. 11–55 (pp. 42–3, 48–9) (emphasis added).

15 The eight-part series, released over the course of the year, consists of the following titles: William Beveridge, *Peace by Federation?*; Lionel Robbins, *Economic Aspects of Federation*; Norman Bentwich, *The Colonial Problem and the Federal Solution*; K. C. Wheare, *What Federal Government Is*; C. E. M. Joad, *The Philosophy of Federalism*; Barbara Wootton, *Socialism and Federation*; Lord [Frederick] Lugard, *Federation and the Colonies*; George Catlin, *Anglo-American Union as a Nucleus of World Federation*.

16 George Catlin, *One Anglo-American Nation: The Foundation of AngloSaxony as Basis of World Federation; A British Response to Streit* (London: Andrew Dakers, 1941), p. 81.

17 William Selinger, 'The Politics of Arendtian Historiography: European Federation and *The Origins of Totalitarianism*', *Modern Intellectual History* 13.2 (August 2016), pp. 417–66 (p. 420).

18 Evelyn Waugh, 'Fan-Fare', *Life* (April 1946), in *Evelyn Waugh: The Critical Heritage*, ed. Martin Stannard (New York: Routledge, 1984), pp. 248–53 (p. 248).

19 John Marx, *The Modernist Novel and the Decline of Empire* (New York: Cambridge University Press, 2005), p. 199.

20 W. H. Auden, *Collected Longer Poems* [1968] (London: Faber, 2012), pp. 79, 80, 109.

21 Ibid., pp. 125, 112.

22 Linguistic paleontologists associate the root, 'bheidh-' (to trust, confide, persuade), with words including 'federate', 'confederate', 'faith', 'fiduciary', 'fiancé', 'infidel', 'confide', and 'defy'. See Calvert Watkins, ed., *The American Heritage Dictionary of Indo-European Roots*, 3rd edition (Boston, MA: Houghton Mifflin, 2011).

23 Auden, *Collected Longer Poems*, p. 80.

24 Ibid., p. 96.

25 Ibid., p. 127.

26 Ibid., pp. 127, 128.

27 Virginia Woolf, 'A Sketch of the Past' [1939–40], *Moments of Being: A Collection of Autobiographical Writing*, ed. Jeanne Schulkind (San Diego, CA: Harvest, 1985), p. 73.

28 Virginia Woolf, *Between the Acts*, ed. Melba Cuddy-Keane (Orlando, FL: Harcourt, 2008), p. 136.
29 Virginia Woolf, *Orlando: A Biography*, ed. Maria DiBattista (Orlando, FL: Harcourt, 2006), p. 225.
30 Ibid., p. 230.
31 William Faulkner, *Absalom, Absalom!* (New York: Vintage, 1990), p. 7.
32 Salman Rushdie, *Midnight's Children* (New York: Random House, 2006), p. 39.
33 Ibid., p. 253.
34 Ibid., p. 91.
35 Jawaharlal Nehru, *An Autobiography* [1936] (New Delhi: Oxford University Press, 1982), pp. vii, xiii.
36 E. M. Forster, *A Passage to India* (New York: Harcourt, 1952), p. 321.
37 Rushdie, *Midnight's Children*, p. 39.
38 R. J. Moore, 'The Making of India's Paper Federation, 1927–1935', in *The Partition of India: Policies and Perspectives, 1935–1947*, ed. C. H. Philips and Mary Doreen Wainwright (London: George Allen & Unwin, 1970), pp. 54–78 (p. 54). Not formally repealed by Parliament until 1999, the 1935 Government of India Act supplied 250 of the 359 articles adopted in India's 1949 constitution. See Perry Anderson, *The Indian Ideology* (London: Verso, 2012), pp. 106–7.
39 Rushdie, *Midnight's Children*, p. 131.
40 Partha Chatterjee, *Nationalist Thought and the Postcolonial World: A Derivative Discourse?* (Minneapolis, MN: University of Minnesota Press, 1993), p. 51.
41 Rushdie, *Midnight's Children*, p. 533.
42 Chatterjee, *Nationalist Thought*, p. 52.
43 Salman Rushdie, 'The Empire Writes Back With a Vengeance', *The Times*, 3 July 1982; Chatterjee, *Nationalist Thought*, p. 52.
44 Rushdie, *Midnight's Children*, p. 39. Rushdie's character Mian Abdullah corresponds loosely to the historical figure Sheikh Abdullah Mohammed, though the differences between the two are significant. Other analogues include Rabindranath Tagore, considered by some the earliest proponent of Indian federalism.
45 Ibid., pp. 46–7, 53.
46 Ibid., p. 253.
47 Salman Rushdie, *Imaginary Homelands: Essays and Criticism, 1981–1991* (New York: Penguin, 1992), p. 27.
48 Ibid., p. 25.
49 Ibid., pp. 24, 23.
50 Rushdie, *Midnight's Children*, p. 47, emphasis added.

CHAPTER 8

Cold War

Rachel Potter

The political Cold War, spanning the end of the Second World War to the collapse of the Soviet Union in 1991, was also a cultural war fought with unprecedented ferocity and unprecedented government resources. 'The Word', as David Caute puts it, 'was the Helen of this Trojan War.'[1]

The term 'Cold War' was coined in 1945 by George Orwell to describe what he envisaged as the chilling global effects of the atomic bomb. Predicting that the world would be carved up into three giant super-states, the US, the Soviet Union, and East Asia (dominated by China), he foresaw that each would be 'unable to conquer' the other, and would therefore be 'in a permanent state of "cold war" with its neighbours'.[2] The following year, Winston Churchill delivered the 'Sinews of Peace' speech at Fulton Missouri, where he described the 'Iron Curtain' that had 'descended across' Europe, from 'Stettin in the Baltic to Trieste in the Adriatic', a metaphorical curtain that would be concretised in the creation of the Berlin Wall in 1961.[3] The nuclear-induced conflict stasis of the Cold War was, in Orwell's words, a 'horribly stable' US-Soviet battle for global alliances, power, and political ideas. The global proxy wars, civil wars, insurgencies, and interventions in East Asia, South America, and Africa of the period, however, were far from 'cold' or static. As Andrew Hammond puts it, the Cold War viewed in its global dimensions was hot and active, characterised by 'ongoing armed aggression'.[4] While Soviet influence in Europe was dented significantly following its armed invasion of Hungary in 1956, US armed involvement in the Vietnam War (1954–75) sparked a global anti-war movement, particularly after the watershed year of 1967, when a combination of mass casualties in Vietnam and the mounting power of the Civil Rights struggle in the US led to the clear emergence of the American New Left as a mass movement. Within the Soviet Union, Mikhail Gorbachev's initiatives in the 1980s to restructure the Soviet economy towards market-like reforms also entailed a new kind of 'glasnost' (openness) with the West, particularly after the 1986 Chernobyl nuclear disaster exposed the catastrophic problems with Soviet state secrecy. In the immediate aftermath of the collapse of the Soviet Union, many argued that the great twentieth-century ideological struggles between Communist-socialism and liberal democracy had also terminated, concluding what Eric Hobsbawm labelled the ideological 'Age of Extremes'. Francis Fukuyama controversially, and mistakenly, claimed in 1992 that the ending of the Cold War signalled the end of ideological history and the triumph and universalisation of Western liberal democracy.[5]

The Cold War not only spanned the second half of the twentieth century, but also shaped an evolving critical debate about literature's relationship to politics. In the era of Cold War nuclear paranoia, state secrecy, and covert state funding for anti-Communist and anti-American propaganda, writers and literary texts often depicted the political state itself as a totalising and opaque Cold War system against which literature pitched its energies. Post-war and postmodern representations of paranoid fantasies, trauma, and the experience of victimhood, captured the psychological experiences of political alienation. As Jessie Victor, daughter of US presidential hopeful, Harry Victor, puts it in Joan Didion's anti-Vietnam War novel, *Democracy*, 'politics was for assholes'.[6]

This oppositional stance was all the more pronounced because literature, viewed by both the US and the Soviets as a powerful weapon in the propaganda war, was put to work in the service of the Cold War state. Both sides pumped impressive levels of government resources into fighting the word war. The Soviets, who had made socialist realism the official literature of the Communist state from 1934 and censored literature deemed hostile to Communism, directly controlled the mechanisms of literary production, but also fuelled significant funding into the arts in Europe after the Second World War. The US both clamped down on home-grown Communist writers and artists in the early 1950s and also funded and promoted global anti-Communist literature, broadly construed, in the cultural battle for hearts and minds. The longstanding rumours about covert CIA funding, known as 'Washington Gold', for a range of global literary publications and organisations, would be partially revealed after a series of *New York Times* exposés in the mid-1960s.

The post-Second World War global ideological battles between Communist and liberal democratic political philosophies of governance evolved, then, against the sheer power of monolithic Soviet and US state bureaucracies. Many of the Western writer-Communists despised by Orwell in the 1930s and 1940s were activist members of local Communist parties in the 1950s, either refusing to believe reports of Stalin's autocratic rule and the false trials, forced labour, and mass deportations it involved, or defending them, sceptically, as transitional responses in the consolidation of Soviet Communist rule. Yet, this was also a period of transition within the European Communist Left. As Communist Party member Doris Lessing retrospectively put it, in the early to mid-1950s, while many 'stayed communists, long past the time when they should have left', inside the Left, despite the fact that the 'Cold War was still blasting us with bombast and rhetoric', opinions were changing: 'It was that stage in a process where ideas, opinions, fresh opinion – all critical of a predominant cast of thought – are building up behind a dam and will shortly burst it open.'[7] When the dam burst, it cleared space for the rejection of procedural politics and the embrace of the anti-war and anti-nuclear activism of the New Left, producing the Aldermaston Marches (1958–62) in the UK and the anti-Vietnam protests in the US. A number of US writers of this new generation fused literary expression with a political activism of direct action, including Susan Sontag, who was one of nearly 200 Americans to defy government restrictions in order to travel to North Vietnam in 1968, and who wrote about her experiences in 'Trip to Hanoi' (1968); Denise Levertov, whose poems 'Life at War' and 'What Were They Like?' (1966) tackled the Vietnam War; and Robin Morgan in 'Four Visions on Vietnam' (1972).[8]

Many other writers and theorists of the 1950s through to the end of the Cold War, from both sides of the Iron Curtain and from across the political spectrum, recoiled from the idea that literature could or should serve either the political state or party politics. The literary politics of an earlier anarchist, nihilistic, and revolutionary modernism was harnessed and reframed in literary responses both to the Cold War state as a mechanism of control and to the idea that literature could have political use value. Jean-Paul Sartre's influential *What is Literature?* (1948), which argued for a prose literature of explicit and thematic Marxist 'commitment', helped frame this post-war debate. Theodor Adorno's Marxist denunciation of Sartre's argument, in his 1962 essay 'Commitment', insisted that the 'politics of autonomous art' is disconnected from 'the thematic commitment of a work'.[9] In another essay, Adorno argued that, in a 'society in which human beings have been torn from one another and from themselves', the idea that the novel should have 'any message with ideological content' or that the narrator should write as though she was 'directly capable of something' was 'ideological in itself'.[10] Adorno's focus on the incompatibility of meaningful literature and committed political messaging has continued to energise a broader identification of literary politics with withdrawal and negative critique. As Adam Piette puts it in a discussion of Samuel Beckett's *Trilogy* as a series of Cold War novels, 'Beckett's writing implies at least a comic acknowledgement that' withdrawal into introspection 'might itself be an act of engagement'.[11]

The Cold War period, however, was also notable for the cultural prowess of public writer-intellectuals, whose words were amplified, domestically and internationally, not only by Soviet and CIA funding and writers' roles in state-sponsored cultural organisations, but also by the technologies of the radio and an emerging TV platform. The incompatibility of literature and political 'content', or messaging with intention, as Adorno puts it, does not apply neatly to some liberal or Communist Western writers who were also activists for democratic or revolutionary change or who involved themselves in rights-based activism, nor to the authors of the 'hot' anti-colonial Cold War whose political commitments were often foregrounded. Peter Kalliney contends that the anti-fascist struggle of the 1930s 'morphed' into the Cold War in the political commitments of socialist anti-colonial writers. He shows that they 'were relatively free to adjust their aesthetic patterns to fit an evolving geopolitical landscape', distinct from what he eloquently summarises as the US-promoted 'narcissistic modernism of individual autonomy' on the one hand, and the Soviet use of intellectuals as 'instruments of the State' on the other.[12]

This chapter concentrates on what Stephen Whitfield labels the period of the 'First Cold War', which he concludes with Stanley Kubrick's satirical film, *Doctor Strangelove*, in 1964.[13] It considers Cold War literature in its explicit engagement with and questioning of the state-sponsored literary values and forms of the cultural cold war itself, and attends to the figure of the literary dissident, who was at once a prominent propaganda tool, a magnet for forms of non-state-organised literary activism, and a character type in literature of the First Cold War period.

The literary responses to the Cold War are as multiple as the global experiences and shifting responses outlined above. Nevertheless, it spawned a number of new genres in fiction. Cold War thrillers, spy novels, political novels, and science fiction brought to life the polarised world and activities of Soviet and US technological achievements, espionage, psychological warfare, and torture. Richard Condon's *The Manchurian Candidate* (1959) depicted Cold War brainwashing, a term ushered in by the psychological warfare of combatants in the Korean War (1950–3). Graham Greene's *The Third Man* (film 1949; novella 1950) represented a two-sided conflict taking place against the backdrop of a post-war 'smashed' Vienna, while his *The Quiet American* (1955) focused on a catastrophically idealistic American imperialist in Vietnam prior to the arrival of American troops. Robert Heinlein's science fiction novel, *The Puppet Masters* (1951), described Soviet-style invading extraterrestrials, while Polish-born Stanislaw Lem's science fiction novels, including *Solaris* (1961), portrayed new technological inventions and attempts to communicate with extraterrestrial life. John le Carré's *The Spy Who Came in from the Cold* (1963), meanwhile, depicted the covert operations of Eastern and Western governments in the face of the recently erected Berlin Wall.

Neither the Soviets nor the Americans, however, left the culture war to the vagaries of individual writers working in the literary marketplace. During the cultural cold war, literature was both funded and censored as never before.

While the Bolsheviks regulated the circulation of books from 1917, their control of literature became more centralised in 1934, when a range of organisations were amalgamated into the Union of Soviet Writers. The Union ran a publishing house and oversaw periodicals, including *Novy Mir* (New World), and, from 1946, *Soviet Literature Monthly* (later *Soviet Literature*), which translated Soviet literature into most European languages. Membership of the Union was effectively compulsory for writers. Presided over by its first leader, Maxim Gorky, it made socialist realism the official literature of the Soviet state, and condemned experimental, expressionist, and anti-realist literature. As he put it in 1934, 'Books are the most important and powerful weapons in socialist culture.'[14]

After the Second World War, and with strong Communist parties in most European states, the Soviets went all-out to win the psychological battle for European hearts and minds. Under the initial direction of Andrei Zhdanov, they kept tight control over domestic book production and ploughed enormous state subsidies into funding the arts, both within the Soviet Union and in war-ravaged European cities. They styled themselves as champions of high culture in Europe, both preserving Europe's cultural traditions and promoting the greatest achievements in the arts against the threat of what they described as crass American monetised and mass-produced popular culture.

The Americans, lacking the bureaucratic structures that already existed in the Soviet Union, were much slower off the mark. They were, in 1947, as Frances Stonor Saunders puts it, 'virgin[s] in the practice of international *Kulturcampf*.[15] The CIA took control of the international cultural programme from 1947, ploughing significant government funds into the arts (millions of dollars annually) – and particularly into the high cultural forms both the Soviets and the Europeans believed they lacked. These initiatives were spearheaded by a number of CIA personnel with significant literary interests, including the novelist Peter Matthiessen, co-founder of the *Paris Review*, who worked for the CIA in the 1950s; Ezra Pound's friend, James Jesus Angleton, editor of the Yale literary magazine *Furioso*; and Cord Meyer, Jr., who also worked at *Furioso*. As the CIA chief of covert action put it, books are 'the most important weapon of strategic (long-term) propaganda'.[16]

The CIA promoted intellectual exchange programmes through dummy organisations and funded other organisations – sometimes transparently, more often covertly. The most notable conduit for the funding of the word war in Europe was the Congress for Cultural Freedom (CCF), run by Michael Josselson from 1950 to 1967, and with Denis de Rougemont as Director and Nicolas Nabokov (Vladimir Nabokov's cousin) as General Secretary. The CCF was launched at a 1950 Berlin Congress of artists and intellectuals from across the anti-Communist West, including ex-Communist Party members Arthur Koestler and Ignazio Silone. The CCF, based in Paris, would expand to having offices in thirty-five countries. It organised exhibitions and award ceremonies and published over twenty prestige magazines and journals, including international literary journals such as *Partisan Review*, which started as a Trotskyite magazine in the 1930s, but became staunchly anti-Communist from the 1950s until its folding in 2003; the London-based *Encounter* magazine (1953–91) launched by Stephen Spender, a key figure in the international non-Communist Left, and New Yorker Irving Kristol, who later became a political conservative; and *The Paris Review* (1953–present). Other journals included *Preuves* in France (1951), *Cuadernos* in Latin America (1955), and *Tempo Presente* in Italy (1956).

Many of the most significant post-war Anglo-American and European authors wrote for CCF-funded publications, including Albert Camus, Ralph Ellison, Richard Wright, Samuel Beckett, Adrienne Rich, James Baldwin, Saul Bellow, and Susan Sontag, and were thereby unknowingly funded by the US government. Between 1945 and 1967, the CIA also facilitated the translation and worldwide distribution of more than 1,000 books by authors such as John Steinbeck, Ernest Hemingway, James Joyce, Philip Roth, Henry Miller, Vladimir Nabokov, William Faulkner, Truman Capote, and Tennessee Williams. American-funded organisations and publications recast the stylistic abstraction, psychologism, and experimentalism of both early twentieth-century and post-war modernist literature and art as the product and expression of anti-Soviet liberal freedoms. Modernism, as Greg Barnhisel argues, was 'presented as a pro-Western, pro-"freedom", and pro-bourgeois movement, evidence of the superiority of the Western way of life'.[17]

While literary writers were recruited and promoted for their propagandist power, they were nevertheless also feared as powerful subversives. The Soviet and East European dissident writer was a particularly potent product and symbol of the cultural Cold War, controlled and persecuted by the East and, in all her denied rights to freedom of thought and expression, lionised by the West.

The suppression of the Hungarian uprising of October–November 1956 entailed the imprisonment of intellectuals including Hungary's most celebrated writer, Tibor Déry. Along with writers Gyula Háy, Tibor Tardos, and Zoltán Zelk, he was secretly tried and committed to prison in the autumn of 1957. Western writers from across the political spectrum – including Sartre, Albert Camus, François Mauriac, T. S. Eliot, E. M. Forster, and Rebecca West – came together to protest the imprisonment. The English writers channelled their activism through the nongovernmental writers' organisation English PEN, with a collectively signed letter to *The Times* defending the 'right of the individual to freedom of expression' and 'basic human rights'.[18]

In the same year, when the Soviets tried to prevent publication of Boris Pasternak's *Doctor Zhivago*, the anti-Soviet rhetoric of humanism and rights was mobilised again. Viewed as hostile to the Russian Revolution, its publication was blocked in the Soviet Union and Pasternak sought publication elsewhere. Alexey Surkov, head of the Union of Soviet Writers from 1953–7, when aggressively trying to prevent the Italian publication of the book, stated: 'The Cold War is beginning to involve literature . . . . If this is freedom seen through Western eyes, well, I must say we have a different view of it.'[19] The CIA, regarding the Soviet suppression of the novel as an opportunity, endeavoured covertly to publish and publicise it. John Maury, head of the agency's Soviet Russia Division, insisted that Pasternak's novel was not directly subversive. Rather, its message was more general:

> Pasternak's humanistic message – that every person is entitled to a private life and deserves respect as a human being, irrespective of the extent of his political loyalty or contribution to the state – poses a fundamental challenge to the Soviet ethic of sacrifice of the individual to the Communist system.[20]

When Pasternak was awarded the Nobel Prize in Literature in 1958, the Soviet authorities forced him to renounce it, insisting that the accolade was a Western anti-Soviet weaponisation of the prize.

Dissident writers and scientists continued to be both targeted by the authorities and to be a focus point for free speech activism. In 1968, the Russian scientist Pavel Litvinov protested the draconian seven-year sentences handed out to the writers Yuri Galanskov and Alexander Ginzburg. Fearing for Litvinov's safety, Stephen and Natasha Spender organised a telegram of support, with signatories including W. H. Auden, Julian Huxley, Mary McCarthy, Henry Moore, and Bertrand Russell. Litvinov's grateful reply included a suggestion that the Spenders create an organisation that would concern itself 'with making known the fate of victims of persecution and censorship'.[21] The idea for *Index on Censorship*, which would be created four years later, in 1972, had been born. Aleksandr Solzhenitsyn, meanwhile, spent eight years in a Soviet labour camp for criticising Stalin in a private letter. He was awarded the Nobel Prize in Literature in 1970 for works including *One Day in the Life of Ivan Denisovich* (1962) and *Cancer Ward* (1968), and was deported to West Germany in 1974 for his criticisms of the Soviet state in novels including *The Gulag Archipelago* (1973).

These disputes exposed the interconnections of political ideology and *realpolitik* in the battles over books and authors, revealing what Lessing referred to as 'the snarling, hating atmosphere of the Cold War'.[22] Surkov and Maury's covert state-sponsored operations in the Pasternak case activated opposed political understandings of freedom, humanism, and privacy. These political bureaucrats enforced, at a governmental level, the Cold War literary-political distinctions between Soviet socially engaged realist literature and Western aesthetic modernism or experimentation, and between narratives of historical or social determinism and liberal doctrines of autonomous individuality.

While the political commitments of literary authors engaging explicitly with the Cold War ranged across the political spectrum, there were some notable intellectual strands. As Matthew Taunton documents in Chapter 2 of this volume, 'conversion' narratives staged a protagonist's coming to political consciousness, particularly in the Communist affiliations that formed part of the fight against colonial rule. Reversing this plot structure, the story of Communist disillusionment, what Matthiessen dramatically described as the 'scream of disenchantment', became a recognisable theme within Anglo-American liberal 1950s Cold War novels, functioning either as an organising narrative thread or as a key parallel narrative shaping the political dilemmas of naive or liberal protagonists, as in Lionel Trilling's *The Middle of the Journey* (1947) and Matthiessen's *Partisans* (1955).[23] The cynicism, complexity, violence, and amoralism of a political pragmatism tied to East-West state or party machinations was pitched against the political idealism of ideology and belief.

A significant literary strand of this liberal formation was produced by anti-Soviet ex-Communists. The 1949 collection of essays, *The God That Failed*, with contributions by one-time Communists Arthur Koestler, Ignazio Silone, Richard Wright, André Gide, Louis Fischer, and Stephen Spender, brought together key figures in this formation. It was, as David C. Engerman aptly put it, 'the collective autobiography of a generation', which outlined a 'new paradigm for Western intellectual life in the Cold War: American-centred, closely tied to political power, and staunchly anti-Soviet'.[24] The essays documented the phases of revolutionary faith and commitment, what Trilling described as an 'impassioned longing to believe', the clash between faith and intellectual independence, and disillusionment.[25] Disillusionment, for instance, with the Communist narratives of historical progression and the logic that the 'ends justify the means' resulting from Stalinist policies; or with the clashes between the authoritarian structures of local Communist Parties taking directions from Moscow and intellectual freedom. Richard Wright's essay dramatises the conflict between his aspiration to write a novel about the experience of racial oppression in the US, and the Soviet-led dictates of the Chicago Communist Party. As Wright put it: 'I had spent a third of my life traveling from the place of my birth to the North just to talk freely, to escape the pressure of fear. And now I was facing it again.'[26]

Spender was a prominent public intellectual in this liberal formation. His 1958 satirical novel, *Engaged in Writing*, counts the costs for writers of assuming the mantle of public intellectual life, what Engerman summarises as being tied 'to political power'. Dedicated to Nicolas Nabokov, General Secretary of the CCF, whom as editor of *Encounter* Spender knew well, the novel unfolds in the milieu of state-sponsored cultural politics, what Koestler derided as the 'international academic call-girl circuit' of post-war intellectual conferences and symposia.[27] Labelled by Walter Allen in the *New Statesman* as a novel in which Spender's 'disillusion finally crystallizes', it tells the story of Olim Asphalt, who travels to Venice as the representative of a fictional organisation, LITUNO, to attend a week-long East-West Conference of European intellectuals.[28] This novel of ideas weaves together fictional and real events, organisations, people, and debates. The fictional conference was based on the 1956 Venice meeting of the European Cultural Association, the first meeting between Soviet and Western European intellectuals since Stalin's death. With Spender as a British representative, other conference participants included Sartre, Maurice Merleau-Ponty, and Carlo Levi, as well as Soviet representative Konstantin Fedin, whom Spender described as 'feeble and ineffective', and who was to be Chair of the Union of Soviet Writers from 1959 until his death in 1977.[29]

Along with fictional characters Serrat (anagram for Sartre) and Marteau (Merleau-Ponty), the fictional LITUNO is a literary subsection of the real UNESCO Spender briefly helped to run. The novel describes the cultural politics of international intellectual conferences, as well as the formation of a professional class of literary bureaucrats – a class to which Spender himself belonged. It satirically exposes the intellectual nihilism of state-funded cultural politics, in which intellectual meetings express 'nothing' except themselves: the conference organiser's 'whole philosophy', we are told, is based on 'the idea of meeting, until the meeting itself is supposed to express and represent nothing else except the idea of meeting, in a vacuum'.[30]

On the train journey to Venice, Asphalt reads Khrushchev's speech to the Twentieth Party Congress in February 1956. Denouncing Stalin's cult of personality as contrary to the spirit of Marxist Leninism, Khrushchev insisted that Stalin's attempt to make himself into a superman conflicted with Marx's anti-individualism and Lenin's insistence that the people, not the individual, were the creators of history. Delivered a 'few days' before the conference, the intellectuals discuss the cultural significance, for East and West, of Khrushchev's speech. The European landscape over which Asphalt travels is 'jigged over by near-skeletons', the product of 'thirty years of modern tyranny'.[31] Asphalt sniggers at the idea of pitting the feebleness of a 'private life' lauded by American Cold War warriors against the inescapable force of this history, whose violence and terror is 'too vastly real to contemplate'.[32]

Serrat's Marxist arguments, which involve treating murder as an 'abstraction', are put into dialogue with the experiences of the Hungarian writer Botor, who is President of the Hungarian Writers Academy. Botor is haunted by his public role in condemning his fellow writer and friend Premontvian to imprisonment and death at Recsk (the notorious real Hungarian forced labour camp in which over 1,500 political prisoners were interned between 1950 and 1953) because of his anti-Communist poems.[33] Within this retrospective narration we are also told that a few days later, two other Hungarian writers in Botor's circle are sent to Recsk: Falus, who is imprisoned there, and the Communist poet Heves, who is tortured to death.[34]

Spender's fictional Falus is based on the Hungarian writer György
Faludy, whose autobiographical novel, *My Happy Days in Hell* (1962),
would subsequently reveal what life was like at Recsk. In Spender's
novel, Botor is haunted by the role he has been forced to assume as
a Hungarian public intellectual in the imprisonment of his fellow writers:
he had 'touched a zero of behaviour where no human feeling could reach
and forgive. A climate in which nothing grows. Zero.'[35] The reference to
a 'Zero' climate and behaviour resurrects the imagery of Spender's impressions of the physical and existential blankness of a war-ravaged Paris as
starting at 'year zero' when he visited in 1945 – he was reading Camus's
L'Étranger at the time.

Botor's zero is the ground from which he attacks Serrat's arguments:
'You are wrong, utterly wrong.' He states:

> How can I explain that reality is that which, in being lived, cannot be
> described or explained? You talk of Social realism – but things that happen
> to you can be so real that you can't call them realism – because – and this is
> what I am trying to say – 'reality' is in itself an abstraction.[36]

Botor's distinction between a lived reality and an explained reality shapes
the novel's engagement with the cultural cold war; it questions both the
Marxist belief in a realist totality and the capacity of literary realism to
represent it.

Spender recalled how at the real conference of 1956, Sartre and Merleau-
Ponty had participated in a keynote debate about 'the idea of Literature
Engagée', with Sartre arguing that the discussion was meaningless because
the Russians and those in the West were inhabitants of incommunicable
ideological worlds.[37] Sartre reiterated his argument from *What is
Literature?* that the '"committed" writer knows that words are action'
and should therefore direct their words towards political goals.[38] Spender
remembered his suggestion to Sartre that 'the only good cause' is that 'of
one person unjustly imprisoned', and Sartre's reply that 'perhaps we live in
a situation in which the injustice against one person no longer seems to
apply'.[39] Spender describes Botor's fictional responsibility for Falu's torture as reducible neither to Serrat's historical and political explanation that
'murder is an abstraction', nor to a faith in individual autonomy. The novel
voices the conflict between abstract political ideals – the abolition of
poverty through socialism, murder is an abstraction – and the lived reality
of experiences that are either 'so real', as Botor puts it, or in Asphalt's
words, 'too real', that they are 'Zero': resistant to existing political and
cultural representation.

Other novelists experimented with literary form to capture the psychological responses of paranoia, disintegration, and terror in the face of nuclear conflict and war, such as Doris Lessing in *The Golden Notebook* (1962). Lessing was a member of both the Southern Rhodesia Communist Party and, after her arrival in London in 1949, the British Communist Party, even though, as she described it, they considered writing novels a 'bourgeois' indulgence.[40] In 1952, she went to the Soviet Union with Naomi Mitchison and Alex Comfort's 'Authors' World Peace Appeal', and was hosted by the head of the Union of Soviet Writers, Alexey Surkov. As she put in her autobiography, 'politics permeated everything then; the Cold War was a poisonous miasma'.[41] Lessing's early novels and stories were often overtly Communist, particularly the Martha Quest novel series, *Children of Violence* (1952–69). On her visit to the Soviet Union, meanwhile, she wrote the story 'Hunger', as she put it, 'according to the communist formula'. Her later novels, particularly *The Golden Notebook*, were more formally experimental.[42]

The Cold War and what the narrator, Anna, describes as the 'terrible dry anguish' of memories of being 'in or near "The Party"', are a backdrop to the action and dialogues of *The Golden Notebook*.[43] The novel portrays the disillusionments and aspirations of the progressive Left, detailing, among other things, the Twentieth Soviet Congress and the suppression of the Hungarian uprising, the refugee experience (both Willi Rodde of the Black Notebook and Michael of the Blue Notebook are refugees), and Anna's editorial job for the London Communist Party. The novel also stages debates about the impact of Cold War cultural politics on literary form. The socialist realist novels Anna is encouraged to endorse in her editorial role are, as she puts it, 'essentially impersonal . . . [Their] . . . banality is that of impersonality.' She concludes that, despite accusations that she is a bourgeois individualist, she believes that 'the flashes of genuine art are all out of deep, suddenly stark, undisguisable private emotion'.[44] These political debates about the proper parameters of the novel form both frame and explain the formal experimentation of Lessing's novel. As Amanda Anderson puts it, the novel is 'as much about a crisis of realism and what it stands for as about a crisis of political commitment'.[45]

Rather than a withdrawal from politics, however, political and literary crisis fuels the novel's palimpsestic writing of 'private emotion'. It registers both conscious responses to the Cold War as history – 'I had a vision of the world with nations, systems, economic blocks, hardening and consolidating' – and unconscious responses – 'it wasn't words, ideas, but something I felt, in the substance of my flesh and nerves, as true'.[46] The Cold War as historical and psychic 'substance' is expressed forcefully in the tortuous and repetitive final sections of the novel, where Anna and Saul disintegrate into each other: as Anna states of Saul, 'I'd gone (*18) right inside his craziness'.[47] The writing of psychic disintegration layers together both politics and psychology, and the languages of knowledge and feeling. Take the following extraordinary passage:

> [there] was a kind of shifting of the balances of my brain, of the way I had been thinking, the same kind of realignment as when, a few days before, words like democracy, liberty, freedom, had faded under pressure of a new sort of understanding of the real movement of the world towards dark, hardening power. I *knew*, but of course the word, written, cannot convey the quality of this knowing, that whatever already is has its logic and its force, that the great armouries of the world have their inner force, and that my terror, the real nerve-terror of the nightmare, was part of the force. I felt this, like a vision, in a new kind of knowing. And I knew that the cruelty and the spite and the I, I, I, I, of Saul and of Anna were part of the logic of war [...][48]

This extract brings together the languages of brutal state violence and interpersonal conflict. The 'inner force' of the world's armies *is* also the force of Anna's 'nerve-terror', a conflation that collapses the Cold War opposition of historical determinism and autonomous individuality. The layering of knowledge and feeling, and the brain's realignment, shadows a political rebalancing in which political philosophies – the words 'democracy, liberty, freedom' – transmute into sheer power. The final 'Golden Notebook' chapter is replete with such conflations. In Anna's dream scene, for instance, memories of the Mashopi hotel covered in butterflies shift from looking like a 'white flower opening slowly' to looking like 'the explosion of a hydrogen bomb'. One image superimposes on the other because of the temporal ebb and flow of collective, rather than individual, affect: 'Then', we are told, 'a feeling of menace came into us, and we knew we had suffered a trick of light.'[49]

In both *Engaged in Writing* and *The Golden Notebook*, dialogues between situated characters dramatise Communist-liberal debates about politics, individualism, psychology, and literary form. Both Spender and Lessing, at intermittent periods of their lives, channelled their political commitments, in Sartre's sense of the word, into their novels. They came from opposed political positions, with Spender a liberal public intellectual at the heart of London cultural power, and Lessing involved in the London-based progressive Left. In both novels, however, the politics of ideology and belief recedes before the state-sponsored cultural *realpolitik* or the 'hardening' power of opposed nuclear powers. Meanwhile, both novels depict and move beyond the political policing of the parameters of literary form. The nihilistic worldview breaks down when characters sacrifice their 'cold' – and Cold War – cynicism in order to recognise the lived reality of individual persecution or write of the psychological substance of 'terror'.

In the 1960s, the sheer power of the Soviet and US Cold War state mechanisms prompted the disillusioned relinquishment of a faith in the procedural politics of the state or party politics and the turn to the grass-roots direct activism of the New Left and the Civil Rights movement, or rights-based – and particularly free speech – activism in defence of imprisoned or dissident writers. Lessing's writing of the 'shifting' psychological balancing of the brain and literary form also points towards this historical 'turn' to direct action – what she had described as the transitional building up of new political ideas behind a 'dam' in her autobiography. The literary attempts to acknowledge both the reality of persecution and psychological 'nerve-terror' provide a vantage point from which to view the cynicism of Cold War cultural activities and the limits of the state.

Notes

1 David Caute, *The Dancer Defects: The Struggle for Cultural Supremacy During the Cold War* (Oxford: Oxford University Press, 2003), p. 7.
2 George Orwell, 'You and the Atomic Bomb', in *The Complete Works of George Orwell*, Vol. 17: *I Belong to the Left, 1945*, ed. Peter Davison, Ian Angus, and Sheila Davison (London: Secker and Warburg, 1997).
3 Winston Churchill, 'The Sinews of Peace' [The Iron Curtain Speech], 5 March 1946, *The Sinews of Peace: Post-War Speeches by Winston S. Churchill*, ed. Randolph S. Churchill (London: Cassell, 1948), p. 103.
4 Andrew Hammond, 'From Rhetoric to Rollback: Introductory Thoughts on Cold War Writing', in *Cold War Literature: Writing the Global Conflict*, ed. Hammond (London: Routledge, 2006), pp. 1–14 (p. 1).
5 Eric Hobsbawm, *The Age of Extremes: The Short Twentieth Century, 1914–1991* (London: Michael Joseph, 1994); Francis Fukuyama, *The End of History and the Last Man* (London: Penguin, 1992).
6 Joan Didion, *Democracy* (New York: Simon & Schuster, 1984), p. 176.
7 Doris Lessing, *Walking in the Shade: Volume Two of My Autobiography, 1949–1962* (London: Fourth Estate, 2013), pp. 107, 166.
8 Susan Sontag, 'Trip to Hanoi', *Esquire* 70.6 (December 1968), pp. 131–290; Denise Levertov, 'Life at War', *Poetry* 108.3 (1966), pp. 149–51 and 'What Were They Like?', *Nation* 202.26 (1966), p. 781; Robin Morgan, 'Four Visions on Vietnam', *Off Our Backs: A Women's Newsjournal* 2.10 (1972), p. 4.

9 Jean-Paul Sartre, *What is Literature?*, trans. Bernard Frechtman, with an introduction by David Caute (Abingdon: Routledge, 2001); Theodor Adorno, 'Commitment', in Ernst Bloch, Georg Lukács, Bertolt Brecht, Walter Benjamin, Theodor Adorno, *Aesthetics and Politics*, trans. and ed. Ronald Taylor (London: Verso, 1988), p. 190.

10 Theodor Adorno, 'The Position of the Narrator in the Contemporary Novel', *Notes to Literature*, Vol. 1, trans. Shierry Weber Nicholsen (New York: Columbia University Press, 1991), pp. 30–6 (pp. 32, 31).

11 Adam Piette, 'Lobotomies and Botulism Bombs: Beckett's *Trilogy* and the Cold War', *Journal of Medical Humanities* 37.2 (2016), pp. 161–9 (p. 162).

12 Peter Kalliney, 'Colonial Intellectuals and the Aesthetic Cold War', in *A History of 1930s British Literature*, ed. Bejamin Kohlmann and Matthew Taunton (Cambridge: Cambridge University Press, 2019), pp. 376–90 (pp. 377, 388).

13 Stephen J. Whitfield, *The Culture of the Cold War* (Baltimore, MD: Johns Hopkins University Press, 1991).

14 Maxim Gorky, 'Statement', First Congress of Soviet Writers' (1934); quoted in Peter Finn and Petra Couvée, eds., *The Zhivago Affair: The Kremlin, the CIA, and the Battle Over a Forbidden Book* (London: Vintage, 2015), p. 127.

15 Frances Stonor Saunders, *Who Paid the Piper? The CIA and the Cultural Cold War* (London: Granta, 1999), p. 17.

16 Quoted in Finn and Couvée, *The Zhivago Affair*, p. 127.

17 Greg Barnhisel, *Cold War Modernists: Art, Literature, and American Cultural Diplomacy* (New York: Columbia University Press, 2015), p. 2.

18 'To the Editor of *The Times*: Hungarian Writers on Trial', *The Times*, 29 October 1957, p. 11.

19 Quoted in Finn and Couvée, *The Zhivago Affair*, p. 112.

20 Ibid., p. 115.

21 Quoted in John Sutherland, *Stephen Spender: The Authorized Biography* (London: Penguin, 2005), p. 458.

22 Lessing, *Walking in the Shade*, p. 80.

23 Peter Matthiessen, *Partisans* (London: Harper Collins, 1983), p. 106.

24 David C. Engerman, 'Foreword', in *The God that Failed*, ed. Richard Crossman (New York: Columbia University Press, 2001), p. vii.

25 Lionel Trilling, 'Introduction to the 1975 Edition', *The Middle of the Journey* (New York: New York Review of Books, 2002), p. xxviii.

26 Crossman, ed., *The God that Failed*, p. 137.

27 Arthur Koestler, quoted in Stonor Saunders, *Who Paid the Piper?*, p. 5.

28 Walter Allen, *New Statesman*; quoted in Sutherland, *Authorized Biography*, p. 398.

29 Lara Feigel and John Sutherland, eds., with Natasha Spender, *Stephen Spender: New Selected Journals, 1939–1995* (London: Faber, 2012), p. 214.

30 Stephen Spender, *Engaged in Writing and The Fool and the Princess* (London: Hamish Hamilton, 1958), p. 141.

31 Ibid., p. 10.

32 Ibid., pp. 10, 11.
33 Ibid., p. 89.
34 Ibid, p. 91.
35 Ibid.
36 Ibid., p. 86.
37 Stephen Spender, 26 March 1956, Venice, in *New Selected Journals, 1939–1995*, ed. Feigel and Sutherland, with Natasha Spender, p. 215.
38 Sartre, *What is Literature?*, p. 14.
39 Spender, *New Selected Journals*, p. 220.
40 Lessing, *Walking in the Shade*, p. 23.
41 Ibid., p. 53.
42 Ibid., p. 70.
43 Doris Lessing, *The Golden Notebook* (London: Fourth Estate, 2014), p. 99.
44 Ibid., p. 311.
45 Amanda Anderson, *Bleak Liberalism* (Chicago, IL: University of Chicago Press, 2016), p. 130.
46 Lessing, *The Golden Notebook*, p. 496.
47 Ibid., p. 512.
48 Ibid., pp. 513–14.
49 Ibid., p. 536.

CHAPTER 9

Irish Nationalism

Emer Nolan

Modern Irish separatist republicanism emerged in the wake of the French Revolution. Wolfe Tone is the most important political thinker of the radical Society of United Irishmen, founded in Belfast in 1791. He declared that his aims were 'To subvert the tyranny of our execrable government, to break the connection with England, the never-failing source of all our political evils, and to assert the independence of my country.'[1] During the rebellion of 1798 in Ireland, the leaders of the United Irishmen, mainly middle-class Protestants, hoped to make common cause with the mass of Irish Catholics. The latter had been dispossessed of their land, particularly during the catastrophic seventeenth and eighteenth centuries, as part of the specifically Protestant British colonisation of Ireland, and excluded from public life by the Penal Code which outlawed the practice of their religion.

After the bloody suppression of the failed United Irish rebellion, the Act of Union of 1800 abolished the Irish parliament in Dublin. Promised relief for Catholic grievances was abandoned in the process of political coercion that followed. Daniel O'Connell led a successful campaign for Catholic Emancipation, finally conceded by Westminster in 1829. He organised the large-scale non-violent mobilisation of lower-class Catholics for the first time. But O'Connell's politics were inescapably denominational in a Protestant polity and therefore at odds with the United Irish ideal of non-sectarianism which had roused such official alarm and fury. Although himself an Irish speaker from Kerry, where elements of Gaelic culture had survived, O'Connell wanted to create an English-speaking Catholic nation. The rival Young Ireland movement, modelled on Johann Gottfried Herder and Johann Gottlieb Fichte's German Romanticism, called for a national cultural regeneration and self-definition. Armed insurrection was a vital dimension of their programme for the recovery of the ancient spirit of the nation. But this was all swept away by the Great Famine of the 1840s, during which a million people died and several million more fled to Britain or the United States.

Each of these strands of Irish political resistance – militant republican-ism, constitutional agitation, and cultural revivalism – remained influen-tial in Ireland to varying degrees during the later nineteenth and twentieth centuries. Most Irish Protestants, whether Anglicans or Presbyterians, remained loyal to the Union with Britain and opposition among Protestants in the north of the country to any measure of 'Home Rule' was especially fierce.

Charles Stewart Parnell led the Irish Parliamentary Party at Westminster during the 1880s with considerable strategic skill. He seemed to some hostile British observers himself to be an avatar of 'Fenianism' (from the alternative name for the underground Irish Revolutionary Brotherhood, or IRB), which had emerged in Ireland and among the Irish-American diaspora in the decades after the Famine. Parnell was in fact the only Irish political figure who had the capacity and personality to forge an alliance between the constitutional and militant elements in Ireland in support of his party, which held the balance of power in the Westminster parliament. But in 1890, Parnell became the first of three prominent Irish victims of sexual/political scandal in England, when his affair with Katharine O'Shea, the wife of one of his fellow MPs, was exposed (the others were Oscar Wilde, imprisoned in 1895, and Roger Casement, executed in 1916). His party split between his opponents and supporters; the subsequent epic battle for the leadership in effect killed him in 1891, just a year after his disgrace. These three became resonant figures in Irish literature and in the country's political imagination thereafter. James Joyce's largely autobiographical *A Portrait of the Artist as a Young Man* (1916) registers the decisive impact of the Parnell episode on Joyce himself and on Ireland. Political and sexual betrayal, symptoms of an internal fear of independence, become enduring themes throughout Joyce's work, and are still prominent in his final novel, *Finnegans Wake* (1939).

William Butler Yeats was twenty-six years old when Parnell died. He later suggested that Ireland after Parnell was like 'soft wax' – open to being moulded in new ways.[2] He hoped that the passion for politics would migrate into a passion for cultural recovery, replacing sectarian and party allegiances. Yeats was the leading writer, theorist, and organiser of the Irish Literary Revival between the 1890s and the First World War. The Revival would break with stereotypes of the 'stage Irishman'; Yeats and his collab-orator, Augusta Gregory, declared in their prospectus for an Irish Literary Theatre that Ireland was not 'the home of buffoonery and easy sentiment, as it had been represented, but the home of an ancient idealism'.[3] Yeats gave the national movement for artistic and spiritual renewal a specifically

'Celtic' inflection that would distinguish it as an ancient, reconstituted alternative to what he regarded as the soulless materialism of Britain and later, in the aftermath of the Great War, as an antidote to a monstrous mass society. In the meantime, what remained of the Irish Parliamentary Party carried on its pursuit of parliamentary independence in London. When a Home Rule Bill was finally passed in 1914, the Ulster Volunteers mobilised to oppose its implementation by violence (this was postponed, in any case, due to the outbreak of the war). Clandestine preparations among republican organisations for a military confrontation with British forces also continued. In April 1916, Patrick Pearse on behalf of the IRB read the Proclamation of the Irish Republic from the steps of the General Post Office in Dublin. The Easter Rebellion, during which the rebels in Dublin held out against the British forces for six days, was followed by the War of Independence, mostly conducted through a guerrilla-style campaign in the countryside. This conflict was concluded by the Anglo-Irish Treaty of 1921, which instituted the partition of the country into the Irish Free State in the south and the six-county territory of Northern Ireland in Ulster.

It could be argued that the state which emerged in the south (following a civil war between those who accepted and those who opposed the Treaty) owed more to O'Connell than to more radical traditions. Eamon de Valera was Taoiseach (Prime Minister) at the outbreak of the Second World War. Formerly the leader of the anti-Treatyite republican forces in the civil war, De Valera had entered the Free State parliament in 1927. During several lengthy periods in office, he came in the eyes of many to embody a conservative, Catholic-influenced nationalism; in this Ireland, social stability and conformity were the key priorities. Contraception and divorce were illegal. In 1929, the Censorship of Publications Act was passed to protect the country from 'indecent' literature; the works of many Irish and international writers were banned.

De Valera was determined to preserve the neutrality of the Free State during the global conflict that was known in Ireland as the 'Emergency'. Samuel Beckett, the most important literary legatee of Irish revivalism and of the exuberant modernist aesthetic experimentation that had accompanied it, was appalled by what he saw as this evidence of Ireland's moral withdrawal from Europe. Beckett was at this time an expatriate in Paris, where he had assisted Joyce with his work on *Finnegans Wake*. He wrote to his mother that he preferred 'France at war to Ireland at peace'.[4]

Ireland is sometimes described as both the first colony of the British Empire and its first ex-colony.[5] However, having largely escaped the devastation of the Second World War, Ireland also missed out on the

Marshall Aid that fuelled the enormous economic expansion of the 1950s in a Europe that was now an economic fiefdom of the US. It was not until the mid-1960s that this long wave of capitalist development reached Irish shores. Nevertheless, the Irish Free State declared itself to be the long dreamed of 'Irish Republic' in 1949, content to let the question of partition and the fate of the minority Catholic community in Northern Ireland rest with merely a constitutional assertion of sovereignty over the whole island. Along with the United Kingdom, the country joined the European Economic Community (now the European Union) in 1973.

The conquest of Ireland and Irish resistance to this had been a recurrent but subordinate theme in English political and literary works since the late sixteenth century. Edmund Spenser's pamphlet of 1596, *A View of the Present State of Ireland*, in support of the policy of extinction of the native Irish, is a minatory reminder of the asymmetric power relations between the islands. After the political settlement of the Glorious Revolution of 1689–90, Ireland increasingly became a source – not merely a subject – of political and literary commentary. There was an Irish variant of British Protestantism that began to question some of the assumptions and practices of the feral colonial conditions of the time. Most notable of these in the long eighteenth century were works by Jonathan Swift and Edmund Burke. Swift, the Anglican Dean of St Patrick's Cathedral in Dublin, and Burke, whose family was from Cork, were both sceptical of the benefits of a 'civility' or 'modernity' conferred on an entire population by war and conquest. This perhaps underlies Swift's account of his absurd protagonist in *Gulliver's Travels* (1726), who displays by turns the mentality of a colonising and a colonised subject, although it is his 'Irish' pamphlet *A Modest Proposal* (1729) that brings into satiric view the possibility of civilisational collapse as a consequence of colonial misrule. This prospect, now taken to be a tragic reality rather than a satiric extreme, informs Burke's *Reflections on the Revolution in France* (1790), one of the most influential of all political pamphlets; in later writings such as *Letter to Sir Hercules Langrishe* (1792) and *Thoughts on the Prospect of a Regicide Peace* (1795–6), Burke would defend 'traditional' societies (including Catholic Ireland) against modern notions of enlightenment and revolution.

The comedy or irony of some later works by Irish Protestants, such as Wilde's *The Importance of Being Earnest* (1895) or Elizabeth Bowen's *The Last September* (1929), can be traced in part to a sense of creative estrangement from both English and indigenous Irish identities. The threat posed by the Catholic peasantry to the colonial land settlement and fears about the degeneration of the Anglo-Irish 'Big House' are explored – directly or indirectly – in a sequence of Gothic novels mainly by Protestant authors, from Charles Maturin to Bram Stoker. Anglo-Irish alienation also informs a specific kind of modernist sensibility in some later Irish writing, reaching its apotheosis in Beckett's post-war works, most famously in the plays *Waiting for Godot* (1953) and *Endgame* (1957), and the novels that comprise the *Trilogy* (1947–50). Beckett wrote many of his works first in French, thus distancing himself from the poetic versions of Hiberno-English essayed by his Irish predecessors, especially Yeats, Joyce, and the playwright J. M. Synge (Yeats's protégé at the Abbey Theatre, which Yeats had co-founded with Gregory in 1904). In Beckett's works, characters become progressively untethered from any recognisable settings or histories. Theodor Adorno hailed him as a heroic artist who had confronted modern atrocity in the aftermath of the Holocaust.[6] But while events in Europe are most immediately relevant to Beckett's drama and fiction, his works are also pervaded by a sense of catastrophe that is deeply rooted in Irish history, and especially in the twentieth-century southern Irish Protestant experience of dispossession.

A handful of Irish republicans wrote memoirs or political works of literary distinction, including Tone's *Life of Theobald Wolfe Tone* (1826), the Young Irelander John Mitchel's *Jail Journal* (1854), and Ernie O'Malley's memoir of the revolutionary period, *On Another Man's Wound* (1936). But little of Ireland's remarkable twentieth-century literature in English was produced by authors who could be described as 'nationalist' in any straightforward sense.

Yeats is a partial exception. For example, in the early poem 'To Ireland in the Coming Times' (1893), he placed himself in the nineteenth-century tradition of patriotic poetry (much of it written or inspired by the Young Irelanders): 'Know, that I would accounted be / True brother of a company / That sang, to sweeten Ireland's wrong, / Ballad and story, rann and song'. But he suggests too that his 'rhymes more than their rhyming tell / Of things discovered in the deep'.[7] In announcing these 'discoveries', Yeats also sets out his modernist ambition to facilitate a new imaginative encounter with the symbols and myths that underlie Western culture, which is now taken to be in a period of deep crisis. Ireland, as a place where the 'ancient' can still be apprehended, especially among the people of the western Atlantic regions, had a special status in this project. Yeats still wanted to be numbered among the poets that he hails here as his compatriots. But from the earliest days of the Abbey Theatre, Yeats encountered hostile Catholic nationalist audiences. In 'Easter, 1916' and other poems from the 1921 collection, *Michael Robartes and the Dancer*, he confesses his concern about the 'terrible beauty' of the Rebellion. Later, in the 1924 'Meditations in Time of Civil War', he despaired of the ongoing violence: 'We had fed the heart on fantasises, / The heart's grown brutal from the fare'.[8]

Joyce was intimately familiar with the rising Catholic middle class that was to become dominant in the independent Irish state. He attended school and university in Dublin during the high point of revivalism and was exposed to its more popular manifestations, concerned with sport, music, and the Irish language, as well as to its more elite Yeatsian forms. In his works Joyce anatomised the economic and psychological condition of people from backgrounds like his own; it seemed to him unlikely that their efforts would deliver any utopian outcome. In *Ulysses*, published in 1922 but set in 1904, Joyce avoided direct reference to the 1916 Rebellion and the events that followed it. But in this radically experimental account of Irish middle-class daily life and consciousness, and even more so in the dream-like *Finnegans Wake*, various phases of Irish and world history coexist or blend into each other. Joyce believed that Ireland had been a cosmopolitan, European nation during its medieval Christian Golden Age. While the recent history of the Irish had been one of failure and self-betrayal, it remained nevertheless for him the most compelling microcosmic exemplar of human destiny in general.

The problem for later Irish artists was finding a way to come to terms with the successes and global reputations of Yeats and Joyce. In the mid-century period, only Beckett was a major innovator and contributed decisively to broader developments in European literature. In general, other writers shared the disappointment of the immediate post-revolutionary period at the outcome of the struggle. But for Yeats and Joyce these had nevertheless been events of world-historical importance. Later writers in the Free State and Irish Republic were sometimes thoroughly dismissive both of the aspirations of the rebels and of what had actually been achieved. While rarely lamenting the separation from Britain, some now saw any attachment to an idea of Irish distinctiveness or exceptionalism as a barrier to participation in post-war European modernity. Others were self-consciously 'local', embracing or even relishing their 'provincial' status in an Ireland which was no longer capable of entertaining grand notions of its own importance. Stereotypes of Irish drunkenness, backwardness, practical incompetence, poverty, and humour, became once again as prominent as they had been in the mid-nineteenth century. As ever, these could be commodified for international consumption. 'Celtic' spirituality was occasionally invoked in ways that harked back to the Revival, but it would have seemed absurd to think of it as presenting any kind of political challenge to secular modernity. The critic and novelist Seán Ó Faoláin is a key figure linking the earlier generation of republican combatants (he fought in the War of Independence and with the anti-Treaty forces in the civil war) with a later liberal-modernising critique of independent Ireland. In *The Bell* (1940–54), the literary magazine he founded, Ó Faoláin took a stand against censorship and what he took to be the forces of philistinism in independent Ireland. However, his own fiction shows little trace of influence from those he would have understood as dissident Irish cosmopolitans, such as Joyce; indeed, Ó Faoláin excused the conventional nature of his work by suggesting that he was inevitably hampered as an artist by living in such an autarkic and repressive society.[9]

The careers of three much-mythologised mid-century writers were cut short by heavy drinking: Brian O'Nolan (*aka* Flann O'Brien/ Myles na gCopaleen), Brendan Behan, and Patrick Kavanagh. The first two of these published in both Irish and English, exhibiting an ease in both languages that had eluded many enthusiasts for the revival of Irish earlier in the century. But they were generally suspicious of revivalism and modernism. They did not take the Joycean or Beckettian route into exile. In his newspaper columns for *The Irish Times* and his comic novels, especially *At Swim-Two-Birds* (1939) and *The Third Policeman* (1967), O'Nolan developed aspects of Joyce's parodies of translations of early Irish literature and of his humour, rooted in Dublin vernacular idioms. But he lacked Joyce's interest in sexuality and the unconscious and his precursor's enormous ambition to create a narrative that would encompass the whole of national history while extending the boundaries of literature itself. Behan, son of a well-known republican working-class family in Dublin, was active in the Irish Republican Army (IRA) as a young man in the 1940s. He was convicted of plotting an explosion in Liverpool and spent time in an English prison. His autobiographical novel about this experience, *Borstal Boy* (1958), combines aspects of the republican prison memoir – classic examples include those by Tone and Mitchel – with a celebration of homoerotic working-class solidarity.[10] Behan's works for the stage in London and New York won him considerable celebrity and he spent a good deal of time abroad. In some regards, his early career contrasts with the sense of frustrated under-achievement of contemporaries such as O'Nolan, and he is a forerunner of the 'hell-raising' Irish male star in Hollywood and in Anglophone popular culture generally. The poet

Kavanagh was also a famous personality in the pubs of Dublin, but was originally from a small farm in Monaghan in the rural midlands and a celebrant of the 'ordinary', writing about, for example, 'the spirit-shocking / Wonder in a black slanting Ulster hill / . . . the whins / And the bog-holes, cart-tracks, old stables where Time begins' ('Advent', 1947).[11] He charted an alternative in Irish poetry to what in this era appeared to many Irish writers to have been Yeats's grandiose ideological speculations. Seamus Heaney, who in 1995 became the first Irish Nobel Prize laureate for literature since Beckett in 1969, regularly acknowledged Kavanagh as an enabling influence.[12]

Since Joyce's *Portrait*, the *Bildungsroman* had been the genre of choice for Catholic realist novelists. Then, in the early 1960s, two new writers added to it a new function as an early warning system for the transformations to come in the Republic in the following decades. Edna O'Brien's debut work, *The Country Girls* (1960), and John McGahern's second novel, *The Dark* (1965), were both initially banned in Ireland. O'Brien's story about young women struggling to escape the poverty and sexual brutality of rural Ireland anticipated some of the key preoccupations of Irish second-wave feminists. However, O'Brien saluted Irish male authors, Joyce and Beckett especially, as her chief inspiration, and also remained atypical in her engagement with the Northern Irish conflict in such works as *House of Splendid Isolation* (1994). By contrast, Irish feminist literary critics mainly celebrated women writers who had been sidelined by the heavily male-dominated canon of Great Irish Authors; such critics were also generally uninterested in the 'national question', aside from critiquing the sexism of traditional conceptions of 'Mother Ireland' that sometimes subtended it. So although O'Brien is not a natural ally of this project in some regards, her novels – widely read for many decades in Britain and the US as well as in Ireland – have been important in the work of feminist revision. The poet Eavan Boland was among the earliest Irish writers self-consciously to align her own work with second-wave feminism; in this, Boland was influenced especially by the American writer and critic Adrienne Rich.[13] She was followed by several others, including the Irish-language poet Nuala Ní Dhomhnaill, playwright Marina Carr, and novelists Éilís Ní Dhuibhne and Anne Enright.

McGahern's grim narratives, concerned with psychological and sexual dysfunction in the Irish rural family, can also be recruited for an ameliorist reading of developments in late twentieth-century Ireland, as Catholic hegemony eventually faltered (in part due to a wave of revelations about the historic mistreatment of women and children in Catholic-run institutions and about child sexual abuse by priests). His novel *Amongst Women* (1990), describing the reign of terror and eventual demise of the central character, Michael Moran – a violent and narcissistic domestic tyrant, was seen by many at the time of its publication as marking the end, or the beginning of the end, of the dark era of clerical-authoritarian patriarchy in Ireland. Indeed, in the same year campaigning feminist lawyer Mary Robinson was elected as the first female President of the Republic.

Yet McGahern's own attitudes towards a changing Ireland were complex. He dismissed the 'Troubles' of his own day (he was from the border county of Leitrim) as a sectarian quarrel internal to Northern Ireland. He was also apparently critical of the legacies of earlier conflicts (McGahern's own father, the model for all the paternal figures in his fiction, was a disillusioned veteran of the war of independence). This would all have been in tune with mainstream southern opinion. But *Amongst Women* and McGahern's other works also encompass numinous depictions of Irish Catholic ritual and of lives spent labouring in the small fields of the Irish midlands (McGahern himself chose to live most of his life close to his own place of birth). The qualified optimism of the early Edna O'Brien about the bright lights of Dublin or London still allows that the entry into modernity may be a worthwhile adventure. But McGahern offers no such comfort. Moran's children also notably lack the capacity to be rebels. His sons damage themselves in the attempt to resist his charismatic authority; his daughters, who care for Moran with great devotion, merely frustrate him by occasional stratagems and then outlive him. At his funeral, it is clear that his daughters' 'first love and allegiance had been pledged uncompromisingly to this one house and man and that they knew that he had always been at the very living centre of all parts of their lives'.[14] In any event, *Amongst Women* is certainly among the most accomplished of recent Irish novels, and McGahern is regarded by many later Irish realist writers – including Colm Tóibín, Joseph O'Connor, Belinda McKeon, and Donal Ryan – as the exemplary writer of independent Ireland, who demonstrated unwavering confidence in the value of memorialising his own 'regional' experience.

By the late 1960s and early 1970s, the situation in Northern Ireland had radically changed. Many of the writers who emerged around this time were among the first generation in the North to benefit from free secondary education – a measure that had been introduced, despite protest from the Northern Irish administration in Stormont, by the post-war UK Labour government. In 1968–9, non-violent protest marches against sectarian discrimination in housing and local government were set upon by organ-ised Protestant mobs and by the police. In 1969, in response to widespread disorder in Belfast and Derry, the British army was sent into Northern Ireland. Three years later, on 'Bloody Sunday', thirteen unarmed Catholics at a protest in Derry were shot dead by soldiers from the Parachute Regiment. A reorganised 'Provisional IRA' now emerged more emphatic-ally with the initial priority of defending Catholic areas from attack.

The Troubles lasted for thirty years and cost more than three thousand lives. In 1981, in the face of Prime Minister Margaret Thatcher's refusal to negotiate, ten IRA members died on hunger strike in prison for the right to be treated as political prisoners. However, Sinn Féin, the political wing of the IRA, converted public sympathy for the hunger strikers into electoral victories in Northern Ireland and in the Republic. This eventually helped to enable an IRA ceasefire in 1994; the 'Peace Process', involving the British and Irish governments, had begun.

There had been no late century equivalent to the Irish Literary Revival in Ireland before the Troubles. In 1972, the Dublin poet Thomas Kinsella protested against the official cover-up of Bloody Sunday by the notorious Widgery Tribunal in the pamphlet-poem, 'Butcher's Dozen: A Lesson for the Octave of Widgery', but such a statement was unusual. Yet the early years of the violence coincided with what was sometimes described as a Northern Irish literary 'renaissance', and there was some notable new work, especially (as with the earlier revival) in poetry and drama. In the Republic, academic historians proclaimed their commitment to 'demyth-ologising' popular history; in particular, they rejected any view of a 'Manichaean' struggle between British imperialism and Irish national-ism. In step with this project of historical revisionism, the politician, historian, and critic Conor Cruise O'Brien condemned – in what became a famous phrase – the 'unhealthy intersection' between art and politics in Irish nationalist culture.[15] Most Irish writers were in any case eager to avoid any such hazardous crossroads.

But even in the unpromising conditions of the late 1970s and early 1980s, marked by polarisation and stalemate, some new cultural initiatives were launched. In the Republic, a group associated with the journal *The Crane Bag* (1977–85), including the philosopher Richard Kearney, sought to revitalise intellectual debate about 'Irishness'. Kearney's then colleague at University College Dublin, Declan Kiberd, offered sympathetic re-readings of a range of revivalist writers including Yeats, Synge, and Douglas Hyde (who founded Conradh na Gaeilge [The Gaelic League] in 1893). In his later bestselling *Inventing Ireland* (1995), Kiberd drew parallels between the optimism of the early twentieth-century period and developments in the 1990s – chiefly the 'Celtic Tiger' economic boom in the Republic and the Peace Process.

The Field Day Theatre Company was founded in Derry by playwright Brian Friel and actor Stephen Rea in 1980. Field Day's first theatrical production was Friel's *Translations* (1980), an exploration of language and colonialism in Ireland. *Translations* is set in a nineteenth-century pre-Famine hedge school in Donegal, where the schoolmaster teaches Greek and Latin literature to the Irish-speaking young people of the village of Ballybeg. The first Ordnance Survey map of Ireland is being drawn up. Officials and soldiers travel the country to facilitate the 'translation' of local place names into approximate English equivalents for the purposes of cartography and more efficient administration. Ballybeg comes to recognise that it is on the brink of a sweeping transformation. Like later plays produced by the company, *Translations* toured small venues throughout Ireland as well as being staged in Dublin, London, and New York. Field Day also produced several series of pamphlets on literature, law, politics, and history.[16] In 1991, Seamus Deane, one of the members of the Field Day board of directors, edited the three-volume *Field Day Anthology of Irish Writing*, the most comprehensive such anthology yet to be produced; in response to criticism from feminists, a further two volumes, dedicated to Irish women's writing and edited by a team of women scholars, appeared in 2002.

The Field Day enterprise, rooted in an analysis of the Northern Irish conflict as an episode in the aftermath of colonialism in Ireland, aspired to expand public debate about identity and culture. In essays on Yeats, Synge, and Irish modernism in *Celtic Revivals* (1985), and in pamphlets such as 'Heroic Styles: The Tradition of an Idea' (1984), Deane tracked the emergence of still-potent stereotypes of 'Englishness' during the period of reaction in Britain against the French Revolution. The notion of a 'pragmatic' English national character evolved in opposition to the supposed radical abstraction of French 'theory'. The romantic, practically incompetent Celt – as defined by Matthew Arnold and others and adapted by Yeats – was another antithetical counterpart to the sturdy Anglo-Saxon. But Deane was less convinced than Kiberd and some other Irish critics of the possibility of Joycean modernism offering a liberating alternative to Yeatsian discourses of racial or national essences. The polyvocal style of the later episodes of *Ulysses* and of *Finnegans Wake*, Deane argued, in fact reflects the marketplace logic of consumer capitalism. Joyce achieved a levelling 'harmony of indifference' where 'everything is a version of something else ... [and] contradiction is finally and disquietingly written out'. Deane concluded that the polarised 'hot' and 'cool' rhetorics of Yeats and Joyce respectively were not 'extravagant examples of Irish linguistic energy in a world foreign to every onlooker'; rather, they belonged to 'the highly recognisable world of modern colonialism'.[17] And so, fantasies about the quaint or exotic Irish could only hinder political analysis of the Northern crisis.

There were some hostile responses to Field Day's colonial or postcolonial reading of Irish culture.[18] But it helped to energise work by critics of Irish literature internationally, and the late 1980s and early 1990s saw a considerable expansion of 'Irish studies' as an interdisciplinary academic field both in the UK and in the US.[19] One prominent figure was the poet and critic Tom Paulin, another Field Day board member and a well-known public intellectual in the UK. Paulin investigated some of the occluded political and artistic traditions of Ulster Protestant republicanism and of English radicalism; he also attacked what he saw as contemporary American imperialism.[20] Irish critics' accounts of Joyce and of Irish modernism led to a so-called 'postcolonial turn' in Joyce studies.[21] An enhanced appreciation of Ireland's uneven and traumatic experience of modernisation inspired innovative explorations of parallels between Irish and other postcolonial literatures.[22] In 1988, Terry Eagleton, Fredric Jameson, and Edward Said contributed pamphlets to a Field Day series on 'Nationalism, Colonialism and Literature'; Said's reading of Yeats as a 'poet of decolonization' was included in his later *Culture and Imperialism* (1993), thus according modern Irish literature a central place in this major work of postcolonial scholarship.[23]

Seamus Heaney, the best-known late twentieth-century Irish writer, was a board member of Field Day from 1980 until 1996. In 1990, the company staged *The Cure at Troy*, his version of Sophocles' *Philoctetes*. Lines from the conclusion of this play were quoted by Mary Robinson, US President Bill Clinton, the singer Bono, and many others, eventually becoming more famous than any of Heaney's poems: 'History says, *Don't hope,* / *On this side of the grave* ... / But then, once in a lifetime / The longed-for tidal wave / Of justice can rise up, / And hope and history rhyme.'[24] These words are spoken by the chorus as the wounded Philoctetes leaves the island of Lemnos where he has spent years in lonely anguish. Now the previously abandoned hero is cajoled to join his Greek comrades for the final stage of the siege of Troy. Although the central conversion in the play is the decision to go to war, the idea of hope and history 'rhyming' was nevertheless widely seized upon as a headline harbinger of the Peace

Process – a 'miracle' that sprang from a longing for reconciliation, 'a great sea-change / On the far side of revenge'.[25] This moment also coincided with such promising international developments as the fall of the Berlin Wall and the dismantling of apartheid in South Africa. In 2004, Heaney delivered a poem in celebration of the enlargement of the EU at a ceremony in Dublin's Phoenix Park, and in 2011 he dined with Queen Elizabeth II on the occasion of her first official visit to Ireland.

No earlier Irish writer could conceivably have been asked to lend, nor have been as ready to give, their prestige to official state policy. As Joe Cleary argues: 'Neither as esoteric as Joyce or Beckett nor as politically extreme to the right as Yeats or to the left as Shaw or O'Casey, Heaney's achievements have been absorbed into the national and Anglo-American mainstream much faster than were those of the earlier major twentieth-century figures.'[26] The accommodatory pose in contemporary Irish writing since Heaney has become as routine as the antagonistic pose once had been. This has generally been taken to indicate a new 'maturity' in Irish society and writing, an analgesic for the old Philoctetan agonies. Cleary instead suggests that this phenomenon is linked to a more general loss of purpose in the arts in the wake of modernism's travails and the placatory extension of consumer society.[27]

In his collection *North* (1975), written in the early years of the Troubles and arguably the most powerful literary work inspired by that conflict, Heaney explores colonial, sectarian, and (especially) intra-communal violence in relation to myths and rituals of Iron Age Ireland. Heaney, a constitutional nationalist, also records the considerable pressure he experienced to articulate a sterner critique of British policy in Ireland. But in escaping war, the poet wonders in the last lines of *North* if he has also missed a historic opportunity: 'The once-in-a-lifetime portent, / The comet's pulsing rose'.[28] In a poem from 1984, Heaney is reassured by the ghost of Joyce – no less – who tells him that his artistic vocation need not involve any sense of commitment to an oppressed community: 'that subject people stuff is a cod's game'.[29] Still, by the 1990s, 'History', in all its inconvenient difficulty, may have seemed to him – as to many others at that time – to be 'ending', both in Ireland and globally.[30] Yet even the most Westernised version of history since the 1990s has to include, at the very least, 9/11, the catastrophic invasions of Iraq and Afghanistan, the financial crash of 2008; and even since that, in the midst of the climate emergency, Brexit and the coronavirus pandemic. The Irish literary response to that twenty-first-century world has scarcely yet emerged. Hope and history have definitively ceased to rhyme, if they ever did.

Notes

1 Theobald Wolfe Tone, *Life of Theobald Wolfe Tone*, 2 vols. (Washington: Gales & Seaton, 1826), Vol. 1, p. 51.
2 W. B. Yeats, *Autobiographies* (London: Macmillan, 1955), p. 101.
3 Quoted in R. F. Foster, *W. B. Yeats: A Life*, Vol. 1: *The Apprentice Mage, 1865–1914* (Oxford: Oxford University Press, 1997), p. 184.
4 Quoted in Anthony Cronin, *Samuel Beckett: The Last Modernist* (London: Harper Collins, 1996), p. 310.
5 For an overview of historiographical debates about Ireland's colonial status, see Joe Cleary, *Outrageous Fortune: Capital and Culture in Modern Ireland* (Dublin: Field Day, 2006), pp. 11–35.
6 See Theodor Adorno, 'Trying to Understand *Endgame*', in *The Adorno Reader*, ed. Brian O'Connor (Oxford: Blackwell, 2000), pp. 319–52.
7 W. B. Yeats, *Collected Poems* (London: Macmillan, 1982), pp.56–7.
8 Ibid., pp. 202–5, 230.
9 See Enda Duffy, 'Critical Receptions of Literary Modernism', in *The Cambridge Companion to Irish Modernism*, ed. Joe Cleary (Cambridge: Cambridge University Press, 2014), pp. 195–205 (pp. 201–2).
10 See Michael G. Cronin, 'Eros and Liberation: The Homoerotic Body in *Borstal Boy*', in *Reading Brendan Behan*, ed. John McCourt (Cork: Cork University Press, 2019), pp. 81–92.
11 Patrick Kavanagh, *Collected Poems* (London: Martin Brian & O'Keeffe, 1972), p. 70.
12 For example, see Dennis O'Driscoll, *Stepping Stones: Interviews with Seamus Heaney* (London: Faber, 2008), p. 332.
13 See Eavan Boland, *Object Lessons: The Life of the Woman and the Poet in our Time* (London: Vintage, 1996).
14 John McGahern, *Amongst Women* (London: Faber, 1990), p. 183.
15 See Conor Cruise O'Brien, 'An Unhealthy Intersection', *New Review* 2.16 (July 1975), pp. 3–8.
16 Some of these are collected in Seamus Deane, ed., *Ireland's Field Day* (London: Hutchinson, 1985).
17 Seamus Deane, 'Heroic Styles: The Tradition of an Idea', in *Ireland's Field Day*, ed. Deane, pp. 56, 58.
18 See Edna Longley, *Poetry in the Wars* (Newcastle: Bloodaxe, 1986).
19 See the influential study by UK academics David Cairns and Shaun Richards, *Writing Ireland: Colonialism, Nationalism and Culture* (Manchester: Manchester University Press, 1988). The Keough Chair of Irish Studies at the University of Notre Dame, first occupied by Seamus Deane, was founded in 1992.
20 See, for example, Tom Paulin, *Ireland and the English Crisis* (Newcastle: Bloodaxe, 1984).
21 See Derek Attridge and Marjorie Howes, eds., *Semicolonial Joyce* (Cambridge: Cambridge University Press, 2000).

22 For example, Pascale Casanova, *The World Republic of Letters* (Cambridge, MA: Harvard University Press, 2004), draws on Kiberd for its account of the 'Irish paradigm' in the history of world literature.

23 Later republished as Terry Eagleton, et al., *Nationalism, Colonialism, and Literature* (Minneapolis, MN: Minnesota University Press, 1990). Eagleton went on to write three books about Irish culture, beginning with *Heathcliff and the Great Hunger: Studies in Irish Culture* (London: Verso, 1996).

24 Seamus Heaney, *The Cure at Troy* (Derry: Field Day, 1990), p. 77.

25 Ibid., p. 77.

26 Cleary, *Outrageous Fortune*, p. 79.

27 Ibid.

28 Seamus Heaney, 'Exposure', *New Selected Poems, 1966–1987* (London: Faber, 1990), p. 91.

29 Seamus Heaney, 'Station Island', *Station Island* (London: Faber, 1984), p. 93.

30 The phrase 'the end of history' was popularised by its use in the title of a 1992 book by Francis Fukuyama.

CHAPTER 10

Black Nationalism

GerShun Avilez

'In America, black is a country'

LeRoi Jones (1966)

Black nationalism has featured prominently in twentieth-century African American social and political thought. Black nationalism refers to a set of ideologies that concern the relationship of people of African descent to the US nation state, ideologies which have historically encouraged differing strategies of community building and collective betterment in the context of anti-Black racism and structural oppressions. The emphasis on community formation and collective identity in the face of racism has looked different over time. During the nineteenth century, articulations of nationalism emphasised the creation of a sovereign Black state as well as the ideal of cultural uplift of Black communities to counter the social realities of enslavement.[1] The end of enslavement and subsequent shifts in policies led to reconfigurations of the political philosophy of racial collectivity that undergirded nationalist thought, as opposed to leading to a rejection of that philosophy. Instead of endorsing a sovereign Black state, twentieth-century nationalists generally championed collectivity; in addition, they emphasised the significance of mass culture – reflecting the influence of Marxist traditions on Black political activism – and advocated radical political action.[2] As the shift from advocating a sovereign Black nation to cultivating a collective identity suggests, Black nationalism, as Wahneema Lubiano has argued, has transformed from being primarily a political philosophy to becoming a social logic for Black communities.[3]

Even though nationalism maintained a social presence in the twentieth century, especially because of the ongoing impact of the organising and writing of Marcus Garvey in the 1920s, it was the 1960s that was a key turning point in the history and development of Black nationalist political thought in the United States. Following the extraordinary activism of the Civil Rights movement, which fought against segregation and resulted in

165

the passage of the Civil Rights Act in 1964, there was an expectation that African Americans would be better integrated into society, would face less violence in the social world, and would have better employment possibilities. Unfortunately, Black communities found none of these goals substantively achieved. On top of such disappointments, the assassinations of Malcolm X in 1965 and Martin Luther King Jr. in 1968 convinced many people that it was time for new methods and approaches to working against the systematic undermining of Black citizenship. Artist and activist LeRoi Jones (later renamed Amiri Baraka) insisted that, after Malcolm's death, Black people needed to become 'nationalists' as a response to the ubiquity of violence and if they were to effect any real social change.[4] What happened in the 1960s was the transition from Civil Rights activism to Black Power nationalism, as a result of a barrage of disappointments and setbacks. Responding to these social realities, modern Black nationalism envisages creating a radically different relationship to the state and to the self.

Stokely Carmichael and Charles V. Hamilton's volume *Black Power* (1967), is a key text for understanding the 1960s articulation of Black nationalism.[5] Black Power as an expression seeks to encapsulate *modern* Black nationalism. The authors define Black Power nationalism primarily in terms of a new consciousness rooted in 'a sense of peoplehood': 'pride, rather than shame in blackness, and an attitude of brotherly, communal responsibility among all black people for one another'.[6] The authors assert repeatedly that this consciousness, rooted in collectivity, depends upon acts of redefinition. To be full political actors and achieve social change first requires this redefinition:

> we must first redefine ourselves. Our basic need to reclaim our history and our identity from what must be called cultural terrorism, from the depredation of self-justifying white guilt. We shall have to struggle for the right to create our own terms through which to define ourselves and our relationship to the society, and to have those terms recognized.[7]

For these writers, political change necessitates a reorientation of one's way of seeing the world and of understanding the self. Because Carmichael and Hamilton are taking inspiration from the struggles for national independence around the globe, one way of understanding what they are calling for is through the process of 'decolonizing the mind', part of a larger project of deconstructing racialised colonial power.[8]

Although this project has much to do with the reappraisal of racial identity, there is also an accompanying assessment of gender identity that is part and parcel of the nationalist redefinition. In fact, there are intense gender implications to the new nationalist imperatives surrounding Black Power. In this essay, I focus on this terrain, illustrating how Black nationalism is a discourse concerned with redefining both racial *and* gender identity. Specifically, I demonstrate that the interface of literature and politics under the aegis of Black nationalism becomes a space for exploring and disrupting gender ideologies, paying particular attention to the work of Black women writers. Critiques of the state become explorations of embodied power differentials and the social construction of masculinity and femininity around such differentials. I begin the essay by offering a conceptual framework that characterises how artists engage nationalist discourse. From there, I develop the contention that gender politics provides a foundation for some articulations of Black nationalism through the hierarchical rhetoric of the 'promise of protection', in which women ostensibly trade safety for social power and agency. I then turn to an extended assessment of literature from the period, paying particular attention to Alice Walker's short story collection, *In Love and Trouble: Stories of Black Women* (1973), which exemplifies the artistic engagement of nationalist thought and showcases the danger and falseness of the promise of protection. Walker's fiction makes clear both the potential and the limits of the influential social logic of nationalism.

The concept that provides the substance and framework for Black Power-era nationalist theorising and artistic production is 'Blackness'. This ambiguous term of racial identity is seemingly ubiquitous in much of African American artistic and political culture during the 1960s: it comes to describe a kind of revolutionary politics ('Black Power!'); it marks a shift in the social valuation of the racialised body ('Black is Beautiful!'); and in anthologies such as *Black Fire!!* (1968), *Black Expression* (1969), and *The Black Aesthetic* (1971), and in journals such as *Black Dialogue* (1965–70) and *Black World* (1970–6), it provides editorial parameters for artistic production. A premium is placed on the term, but it is not always clear what 'Blackness' means or if artists employ it in the same manner.

This 'Blackness' should not be read as a concrete concept that articulates racial identity in the context of artistic works and publications. Calls for and expressions of Blackness are rhetorical strategies having to do with positionality and citation. During this period, to declare or write about Blackness is to situate oneself in relation to nationalist thought. 'Blackness' is a citation of nationalism. In making this point, I build on Judith Butler's use of 'citation' in their discussion of performativity and gender identity.[9] Though I am not using their theory itself as a hermeneutic for the history of nationalism or artistic texts I examine, I find the way that 'citation' functions as a sign of affiliation between a subject and a discourse an apt way to describe the relationship I track between the artistic production of the 1960s and political discussions about Blackness. Ruminations on and evocations of 'Blackness' represent artistic means of referencing nationalist political ideologies: platforms that demand autonomy for and solidarity among people of African descent and emphases on radically reimagining the social sphere and the place(s) that these racialised bodies occupy within this space. These areas map out the precise terrain of Black nationalism. The call for 'Blackness' in the Black Power slogan so readily attributed to activists such as Stokely Carmichael is about reimagining the relationship of African Americans to the state and to themselves. The goal is to move away from an out-of-date 'Negro' subject position, as well as the political strategies associated with Civil Rights organising, and towards something new. Blackness becomes a metaphor for this newness. It is a call for a new social orientation; artists cite this politically charged call for new strategies and identities in their cultural declarations of Blackness.

Black Arts poet Sonia Sanchez's impressive literary output illustrates the methodology of political citation and sheds light on the literary engagement of nationalist discourse, especially in her 1970 volume, *We a BaddDDD People*.[10] This referencing of the political is particularly apparent in the speaker's aesthetic call for activism in the poem 'blk rhetoric', which opens with the significant question, 'who's gonna make all / that beautiful blk / rhetoric / mean something'.[11] Following this provocative rhetorical question, Sanchez offers a highly experimental poem in which she plays with spelling, challenges typographical practices, and flouts conventions for writing poetry. Sanchez's syntactical and orthographical practices in the poem – and throughout the collection – represent an attempt to question accepted grammatical rules and principles and the reader's expectations of what a poem should look like. Sanchez finds no use for capitalisation. Ellipses, parentheses, and slash marks are not employed in conventional ways. The visual spacing on the page seems to have no discernible logic. The unusual spacing calls attention to the placement of the words and makes readers aware of the fact that they are reading (or attempting to do so). Much of this textual construction likely has to do with Sanchez's attempt to infuse her engaging performance of her poems onto the page. However, to read this textual manipulation simply as a 'writing' of the performance risks overlooking an important element in Sanchez's poetic project. In reimagining the construction of a poem and the actual writing of words, Sanchez transports revolutionary calls for altering the arrangement of the social sphere into her aesthetic practice. The graphic presentation of the poem is an extended citation of the radical political rhetoric grounding social activism. She emblematises through poetry the search for new forms discussed at length in the volume *Black Power*.

Ironically, the poem's content evinces an anxiety about the exact political ideals that shape the orthography: 'who's gonna make all / that beautiful blk / rhetoric / mean something.' Through this implied question, Sanchez foregrounds a sceptical attitude about the widespread engagement of the political, artfully employing political ideals to transform her poetics. Although the poet finds value in engaging the radical reordering that 'Blackness' demands – the call for 'new forms' that Carmichael and Hamilton describe – she offers a critique of those who devote themselves blindly to the rhetoric alone. She positions her work in relation to this revolutionary logic, while also locating a critique of that logic itself. In light of Sanchez's work, we can understand 'Blackness' as a method of citing a discourse about the viability and value of a nationalist radicalism. Sanchez's discursive positioning of her work embodies the aesthetic location of Blackness.

This connection to the political is to be expected given the activist motivations of many Black Arts-era artists; however, the political is not the only phenomenon being cited through the framework of Blackness. The citational power of Blackness directs our focus to the Black body and to questions of gender – both of which are alluded to in Sanchez's poem. A sustained attention to Black gender politics accompanies and undergirds this nationalist attention to the body. The activism and consciousness-raising associated with nationalist organising was often articulated through the prism of gender. In fact, the avowal of nationalist ideologies in organisational structures and political rhetoric carried with it serious and sometimes contradictory articulations of gender identity. In her analysis of the history of the Black Panther Party, Tracye A. Matthews explains how 'gender struggle affected the Party's political ideology and positions taken on a variety of issues, relationships with the larger black and progressive political communities, daily working and living arrangements, and the organization's ability to defend itself from state-sponsored disruption'.[12] Gender and gendered discourses permeated political organising of the time so much that talking about nationalism means talking about possibilities of gender expression as well as gender hierarchies. One component of these gender struggles can be understood in terms of what Farah Jasmine Griffin describes as the 'promise of protection': 'women get protection; the man acquires a possession'.[13] Assuming a heteropatriarchal organisation of political, social, and personal life would safeguard the lives of women (and children) and offer to them a kind of social power denied them by racist practices in the US. The promise rests upon a hierarchy of gender roles. To defy such roles risks not only the attaining of one's promised social rewards, but the possibilities of freedom and revolution itself. Griffin points to how some political organisations and social interactions offered a constrained freedom to women: a movement away from racial restriction but a doubling down on patriarchy for the good of the community. Radical social action and community building was expressed in terms of gendered power dynamics.

The gendered promises of protection are tenuous at best, and many Black women writers make this point clear. Literary artists have often revealed the pitfalls of gendered hierarchies, while maintaining a critique of racial hierarchies. Writer and former fieldworker with the Student Nonviolent Coordinating Committee (SNCC), Jean Wheeler Smith, provides in her short story 'That She Would Dance No More' a useful illustration of the investigation of gender politics that I see as integral to artistic engagement of nationalist thought.[14] First published in 1967 in *Negro Digest*, this story later appeared in LeRoi Jones and Larry Neal's pivotal Black Arts anthology, *Black Fire!!*. The collection captures the energy of the time as well as the ongoing attempt to translate nationalist thought into artistic projects.

Smith's story focuses on the life and experiences of Ossie Lee, a Mississippi sharecropper. He is presented as having little control over his life because of his socio-economic situation. Although he is defenceless to his white employer's abuses and manipulations, Ossie finds that he cannot change his life because he is effectively bound to the land by familial and financial obligations. He can do nothing except try to stay alive: 'being able neither to accept nor reject his life, Ossie Lee had constantly to buffer himself against it'.[15] In the midst of detailing this dehumanising situation, Smith has her protagonist develop an attraction for and marry a young girl named Minnie Pearl, who loves to dance to jukebox music in a café with her sister. Ossie Lee and Minnie Pearl first meet in the café, where young Minnie and her sister dance for the older man. Unfortunately, this scene of attraction is later transformed into a scene of violence. Excited about his new romance, which represents to him a new opportunity for happiness as yet unmarred by the stresses of his employment, Ossie asks his 'boss man' for a house to live in with his new wife. His white employer offers him a two-room shack so dilapidated that 'the whole building leaned to one side'. Ossie felt 'slapped again by the circumstances of his life'.[16] When Minnie tries to cheer him up by dancing with her sister, Ossie is astounded that she can muster enjoyment in the face of such unending subjugation. He walks over to Minnie and slaps her to the floor.

Not only are Ossie's hopes dashed by the realities of his new domestic space, but he finds that he can only express his confusion and frustration through violence against Minnie. His anger at his manipulative 'boss man' is redirected towards Minnie's body. In slapping her, Ossie forces Minnie into the subjugated social position he feels he is compelled to occupy within the white-controlled economic matrix. The story creates a destructive constellation among power embodied as whiteness, Black masculine agency, and the (assaulted) Black female body. Matrices of power encroach upon the intimate relationship between Ossie and Minnie, and Ossie's unnecessary aggression undermines the woman-centred intimate space of dancing created by Minnie and her sister. The story is as much about gender-based conflict and the construction of identity as it is about racialised power dynamics to which political critique explicitly calls attention. As Smith's story indicates, the masculine promise of protection was questionable, if not completely false, and depended upon feminine disempowerment. Heteropatriarchy did not and does not secure protection for Black women. In fact, its rhetoric could enable abuse.[17]

A number of male writers also sought to question the promise of protection and the imagining of a stable sense of patriarchy as being at the heart of community building. John A. Williams's novel *The Man Who Cried I Am* (1967), Barry Beckham's novel *Runner Mack* (1972), and John A. Walker's play *The River Niger* (1973), all focus on the possibilities of Black community and highlight attempts by the state to surveil and infiltrate Black families and organisations, sowing an overall distrust of the state.[18] They engage ideas about nationalist organising and community formation. However, each of these writers also takes up the concept of the promise of protection explicitly, and shows how male characters and patriarchs fail to 'protect' Black women in the context of state and racial intrusion. These texts illustrate the failure of this kind of gendered promise. What is even more fascinating about these different works is that they all destabilise the construction of patriarchal masculinity by featuring Black male characters who die, or who are devastated and left bereft, because of their investment in gender hierarchies and patriarchal expectations. These texts are not necessarily aligned with feminist projects, but they do exhibit an anxiety about and an uncertain investment in patriarchal masculinity in the context of Black collectivities. Williams, Beckham, and

Walker remind us that it was not only women writers and thinkers who demonstrated the limits of gendered thinking as they took up nationalist ideology in their artistic projects.

Black feminist writers remain some of the most critical engagers of nationalist thought and do the most to limn the theoretical constraints placed upon gender expression in nationalist discourse. Many feminist activists and thinkers expressed the promise of radical change outside of the promise of protection and delinked radical nationalist activity from gender hierarchies. Angela Davis talks explicitly about the way some Black male activists 'confuse their political activity with an assertion of maleness'.[19] However, she rejected and pushed past those ways of thinking. In her autobiography, Davis emphasises social and collective transformation in place of social activism premised on gender hierarchy. Thinking along these lines, Toni Cade Bambara insists:

> Revolution begins with the self, in the self. The individual, the basic revolutionary unit, must be purged of poison and lies that assault the ego and threaten the heart [. . .] Perhaps we need to face the terrifying and overwhelming possibility that there are no models, that we shall have to create from scratch. Doctrinaire Marxism is basically incompatible with Black nationalism; New Left Politics is incompatible with Black nationalism; doctrinaire socialism is incompatible with Black revolution; capitalism, lord knows, is out [. . .] The job then regarding 'roles' is to submerge all breezy definitions of manhood/womanhood (or reject them out of hand if you're not squeamish about being called 'neuter') until realistic definitions emerge through a commitment to Blackhood.[20]

From Bambara's perspective, the calls for revolution must begin with reorienting the self and one's perspective, freeing one's mind from constrained ways of thinking. Any actual social change must start with the individual, the 'basic revolutionary unit'. Expounding upon ideas expressed in *Black Power*, a reimagining of gender identity and expression is, in Bambara's mind, the basis of effective political organising and social activism. By turning to gender, we can fully achieve the new consciousness about which Carmichael and Hamilton write. Rather than thinking about Black nationalism in terms of organisations and political activities, Bambara challenges us to consider this expression of Black radicalism through the individual and through the lens of gender. It is not just that a gender matrix undergirds nationalism; Black Power nationalism can realise its goals through attending to gender.

In the remainder of this essay, I elaborate on this point by turning to Alice Walker's first short story collection, *In Love and Trouble: Stories of*

Black Women. Walker is one of the staunchest critics of cultural nationalism and the kinds of gender-based oppressions encouraged by some activist
groups. However, she is a brilliant analyst of political radicalism, and she
consistently plumbed the possibilities of radical politics for expressing
personhood in her work. Her stories explicitly and implicitly cite the
ideology and rhetoric of Black nationalism, as she seeks to find a way to
articulate modern Black womanhood in them. The most famous story in
In Love and Trouble is 'Everyday Use', which considers the limits of
consciousness-raising and the challenges of generational conflict through
the cultural object of a quilt. The opening story, 'Roselily', depicts the
difficulties women have in marriage and the gender hierarchies that manifest in some expressions of Islam. The piece is fascinating in the way it
splices in interior monologue between sections of marriage vows to
advance an argument about the false security of the institution for
women. Nonetheless, it is the short story 'Really, *Doesn't* Crime Pay?'
that best illustrates the citation of nationalism's discourse on gender, while
also manifesting Bambara's ideas about revolutionary selfhood, both
through its presentation of Black womanhood and through its narrative
structure.

'Really, *Doesn't* Crime Pay?' consists of the journal entries of an
unnamed married woman who begins a dalliance with Mordecai Rich,
an artistic man who has travelled to the South to seek inspiration. The
protagonist feels unsatisfied with her marriage and is intrigued by this
energetic visiting artist, all the more so because she has a secret desire to be
an artist herself. After sharing her secret ambition along with her writings
with her new lover, he absconds with her work only later to publish a new
book called *The Black Woman's Resistance to Creativity in the Arts*. She is left
with her husband, Ruel, who insists that she get pregnant so that she will
have something to do. The story begins with him having bought a new
house, likely using a Veterans Affairs loan, so that they could 'forget the
past', meaning her infidelity.[21] The 'crime' referenced in the title is the theft
of happiness and freedom and sense of self by both her controlling husband
and her lying, pilfering lover. Mordecai successfully steals her work and
undermines her dream. Ruel attempts to constrain her freedom by impreg-
nating her, but she takes birth control pills. The question of Black women's
freedom and agency in the context of marriage and social expectations
provides the foundation for this innovative narrative.

As these ideas around love and Black women's agency might suggest,
Walker's story is in deep conversation with Zora Neale Hurston's 1937
masterpiece, *Their Eyes were Watching God*; Hurston was in fact one of

Walker's chief inspirations.[22] One can easily read Mordecai as a version of Hurston's Tea Cake, and the unnamed narrator as a version of Hurston's Janie, with Ruel being an amalgamation of Janie's first two husbands. That said, 'Really, *Doesn't* Crime Pay?' is a text that actively engages political discussions of its own time, the 1960s. The narrator's refusal to get pregnant resonates with important conversations around the birth control pill and Black reproduction within nationalist groups at the time. As I have explained elsewhere, there were vociferous disagreements about the social significance of the birth control pill for Black communities during the 1960s and 1970s, especially in light of fears about government abuses against minority communities.[23] Some Black nationalist groups argued strongly against the birth control pill because they saw it as a form of state-supported population control, even racial genocide. Many other groups argued for its importance because of the control it offered Black women over their bodies.[24] It was a hotly debated topic, and Walker uses her story to intervene in the ongoing debate. The sequence of events in the story take place between May 1958 and September 1961, a span signalled by dates on the journal entries. This timing, which occurs several years before the actual writing and publication of the story, is purposeful. The Food and Drug Administration (FDA) approved the use of the pill to 'regulate menstruation' in 1957, and officially approved Enovid, one type of the pill, as an oral contraceptive in 1960. Within five years, 25 per cent of all married women under forty-five had used the pill, and by 1967, it had been used by thirteen million women worldwide.[25] Walker sets her story about a Black women's attempt to gain control over her life at the precise historical moment when the birth control pill became more easily access-ible to women. Instead of situating her reader within contemporaneous debates, she looks backwards. Questioning those nationalist voices who would argue against the pill's availability, she positions the birth control pill as primarily about Black female agency and avoids other connotations by placing the protagonist in the recent past.

Walker summons nationalist debates alongside Bambara's ideas about revolution beginning with the self and undermining gender protocols. The narrator's repudiation of reproduction and her lack of desire to use her body to fulfil her husband's sense of self, gestures towards an idea encap-sulated in artist Kay Lindsey's untitled poem of 1970, which rejects the idea that 'an act of valor, for a woman / Need take place inside her'.[26] Part of Lindsey's point is that thinking about women primarily through the terms of their sexual value – whether sexual pleasure or reproductive potential – is old-fashioned and does not align with the radical rethinking of identity connected with the Black Power era. She dismisses it as being as outdated as using Civil Rights strategies in the current moment, directly challenging nationalist thinkers to make their calls for a new consciousness apply to all sectors of life and identity. Walker's story performs similar work. Her protagonist insists that she is not 'a womb without a brain'.[27] For Walker, as for Lindsey before her, motherhood is not positioned as a site of freedom and identity making; both call for a reimagining of the boundaries of Black womanhood.

In addition to shifting the presentation of motherhood, this story narrativises a gender reversal in terms of stereotypical behaviours. It is Ruel, the husband and patriarch who desperately wants children, who is forced to comply with his spouse's demands and actions. The protagonist is the unfaithful partner and behaves as she wishes, while Ruel tries desperately to please her. He gets aligned with the space of domesticity as he buys a house, whereas she moves through the public world outside of the home to define herself; it is there that she encounters Mordecai. After Mordecai leaves, the protagonist tries to murder Ruel 'with one of his saws', and this act is only interrupted because the noise of the tool awakens him.[28] Of course, she could have kept going, and he is at her mercy every time he goes to sleep. We also discover in the last sentences of the story that she plans to leave him. Although she is heartbroken, the reader finds that this main character is in the symbolic position of protector as she holds his life in her hands. It is she who has the power to give or take away life, not reproductively but through her ability to kill her husband at will. Walker offers the reader a gender reversal as well as a recasting of the nationalist promise of protection to illustrate its conceptual weaknesses and present a new way of writing Black female identity outside of more familiar, constraining scripts.

Walker's story also refuses the idea that sex itself (i.e., intimacy with Mordecai) necessarily leads to self-fulfilment. The protagonist's sense of self-satisfaction comes from the control she exercises over her body; it does not derive from some sexual relationship with men. The only woman figure in the story who has a satisfying sexual relationship is a character whose story Mordecai narrates to the protagonist. In this story-within-the-story, a man finds that he is unable to satisfy his wife sexually. One day he comes home and hears 'joyous cries' and rushes in to find 'his wife in the arms of another woman'.[29] Even though the husband begs her to stay, the wife leaves with her new lover. Sexual satisfaction that does not lead to disappointment is only available in a tale within Walker's story – therefore at a remove from the protagonist herself – and only through same-sex sex acts. In mentioning even briefly the power of woman-centred desire, Walker is setting up a theme she went on to explore at length in her 1982 novel, *The Color Purple*, which is epistolary and resonates structurally with this earlier story made up of journal entries.

The structural organisation of 'Really, *Doesn't* Crime Pay?' is also related to Bambara's point about revolution beginning with a rethinking of the self. The decision to use twenty-three journal or diary entries means that a Black woman's interiority is put in the foreground. The reader is allowed access to and witnesses the value of the Black interior.[30] What is most interesting about the journal entries is that they are not presented in chronological order. The reader begins the story with an entry from page 118 and then goes on to entries from pages 119 and 120, before being redirected to one from page 2. The story then moves chronologically through the entries until ending on ones from pages 218 and 223. The decision to have the reader begin at the end of the story, or to tell the story roughly out of order, is itself a challenge to expectations about the presentation of the character. Walker disorders the presentation of the narrative because her larger goal is to disrupt the social expectations around and representations of Black women. Walker mirrors Sonia Sanchez's methodology in her poem 'blk rhetoric' by challenging expectations. Both seek to disrupt order. It is not just that Walker plays with the chronological presentation; the reader is also not given all the journal entries. There are many pages – meaning days, weeks, and months – that are not presented in the reconstruction of the journal. Walker chooses to omit certain pages from the fictionalised journal in order to keep some things from the reader, and she makes sure to show the reader the page numbers of the entries that are included so that the reader is visually aware that some entries/pages are left out. I read this active showing and hiding as an attempt to accrue a kind of privacy for the protagonist. If women were made instruments of patriarchy and social advancement in some nationalist conversations, women here are presented as out of reach and therefore as unavailable for instrumentalisation. Even as the frame of a journal suggests interiority, Walker assures the reader that they do not have unfettered access to Black women's interiority. It is an act of agency on the part of Walker, and the exercise of agency happens on the level of the construction of the narrative. Both Mordecai and Ruel try to make use of the protagonist – whether by stealing her work or attempting to make use of her body's reproductive potential. Walker denies us full access to her central character to keep her Black female protagonist out of reach. Kay Lindsey's poem indicates that women were understood as being instrumental, valuable because of their sexual potential. Walker interrupts instrumentality by constructing a disjointed narrative of interiority. She provides a narrative translation of what Bambara analyses. This understanding fuels Walker's decision to keep the protagonist nameless. We know *about* her but are not allowed to *know* her.

In a famous meditation on nationalism, LeRoi Jones asserts that 'in America, black *is* a country', epitomising the way of thinking that would characterise the 1960s and 1970s.[31] Jones defines 'Blackness' as a necessary collectivity bounded by a racialised understanding of kinship. What lies at the base of this understanding of Blackness is a sense of cultural belonging necessitated by racialised discrimination. Walker, however, alongside artists such as Jean Wheeler Smith and Sonia Sanchez, challenged the terms upon which such belonging rests. The nationalist insistence that Black is a country is galvanising, but it also stimulates questions about relationality and the possibility of gender hierarchies. What, these writers ponder, are the terms of belonging to this space of racialised collectivity? This kind of questioning reveals the complicated nature of the artistic engagement of nationalist discourse. Jones provides a beautiful and thought-provoking declaration of collectivity. African Americans have had to take refuge within their communities because of passive and active neglect on the part of the state. However, when and for whom is this metaphorical country a space of refuge, and how could we imagine it otherwise so that it might be? This line of inquiry identifies the way that artists cite and interrogate nationalist discourses in hopes of realising delayed, yet still yearned for political, personal, and psychic freedoms.

Notes

1 See Wilson Jeremiah Moses, ed., *Classical Black Nationalism: From the American Revolution to Marcus Garvey* (New York: New York University Press, 1996).
2 See William L. Van Deburg, ed., *Modern Black Nationalism: From Marcus Garvey to Louis Farrakhan* (New York: New York University Press, 1997).
3 See Wahneema Lubiano, 'Black Nationalism and Black Common Sense: Policing Ourselves and Others', in *The House that Race Built*, ed. Lubiano (New York: Vintage, 1998), pp. 232–52, and 'Standing in for the State: Black Nationalism and "Writing" the Black Subject', in *Is it Nation Time? Contemporary Essays on Black Power and Black Nationalism*, ed. Eddie Glaude (Chicago, IL: University of Chicago Press, 2002), pp. 156–64.

4 LeRoi Jones [Amiri Baraka], 'The Legacy of Malcolm X, and the Coming of the Black Nation', in *Home: Social Essays*, ed. Jones (New York: Morrow, 1966), pp. 238–50.

5 Kwame Ture [Stokely Carmichael] and Charles V. Hamilton, *Black Power: The Politics of Liberation in America* [1967] (New York: Vintage, 1992).

6 Ibid., p. xvi.

7 Ibid., pp. 34–5.

8 The first chapter of the book is called 'White Power: The Colonial Situation' (ibid., pp. 2–33). Ngũgĩ Wa Thiong'o would use the language of 'Decolonizing the Mind' in his book on the politics of language, *Decolonising the Mind: The Politics of Language in African Literature* (London: Heinemann, 1986).

9 Butler explores whether or not actions that appears to express individual identity can also be read as 'citing' or reproducing ideological discourses. See Judith Butler, *Bodies that Matter: On the Discursive Limits of 'Sex'* (New York: Routledge, 1993).

10 Sonia Sanchez, *We a BaddDDD People* (Detroit, MI: Broadside, 1970).

11 Ibid., p. 15.

12 Tracye Matthews, '"No One Ever Asks What a Man's Role in the Revolution is": Gender Politics and Leadership in the Black Panther Party, 1966–71', in *Sisters in the Struggle: African American Women in the Black Power-Civil Rights Movement*, ed. Bettye Collier-Thomas and V. P. Franklin (New York: New York University Press, 2001), pp. 230–56 (p. 232).

13 Farah Jasmine Griffin, '"Ironies of the Saint": Malcolm X, Black Women, and the Price of Protection', in *Sisters in the Struggle*, ed. Collier-Thomas and Franklin, pp. 214–29 (p. 216).

14 Jean Wheeler Smith, 'That She Would Dance No More', in *Black Fire!! An Anthology of Afro-American Writing*, ed. LeRoi Jones and Larry Neal (New York: Morrow, 1968).

15 Ibid., p. 493.

16 Ibid., p. 496.

17 The short story also prefigures Alice Walker's free verse poem 'Democratic Order', published in *Once* (New York: Harcourt, 1968).

18 See John A. Williams, *The Man Who Cried I Am* (Boston, MA: Little Brown, 1967); Barry Beckham, *Runner Mack* (New York: Morrow, 1972); and Joseph A. Walker, *The River Niger* (New York: Hill & Wang, 1973). I offer detailed analysis of *The Man Who Cried I Am* in GerShun Avilez, *Radical Aesthetics and Modern Black Nationalism* (Urbana, IL: University of Illinois Press, 2016), and provide an extended discussion of *Runner Mack* in my essay, ' The Black Arts Movement', in *The Cambridge Companion to American Civil Rights Literature*, ed. Julie Armstrong (Cambridge: Cambridge University Press, 2015), pp. 49–64.

19 Angela Davis, *An Autobiography* (New York: Random House, 1974), p. 161.

20 See Toni Cade Bambara, 'On the Issue of Roles', in *The Black Woman: An Anthology*, ed. Bambara (New York: Washington Square Press, 2005), pp. 123–35 (pp. 133–4).

21 Alice Walker, *In Love and Trouble: Stories of Black Women* (New York: Harcourt, 1973), p. 11.
22 See Alice Walker, 'Looking for Zora', *In Search of Our Mothers' Gardens* (New York: Harcourt, 1983), pp. 93–116.
23 See Avilez, *Radical Aesthetics*.
24 See Toni Cade Bambara, 'The Pill: Genocide or Liberation?', in *The Black Woman*, pp. 203–12.
25 See Planned Parenthood, 'The Birth Control Pill', June 2015. Available at w ww.plannedparenthood.org/files/1514/3518/7100/Pill_History_FactSheet.pdf. (accessed September 2021).
26 See Kay Lindsey, 'Poem', in *The Black Woman*, ed. Toni Cade Bambara [1970] (New York: Washington Square Press, 2005), p. 13.
27 Walker, *In Love and Trouble*, p. 18.
28 Ibid., p. 12.
29 Ibid., p. 13.
30 See Elizabeth Alexander, *The Black Interior* (New York: Graywolf, 2004).
31 LeRoi Jones, 'Black is a Country', in *Home: Social Essays*, ed. Jones (New York: Morrow, 1966), pp. 82–6.

Caribbean Nationalisms

Alison Donnell

As the description 'Caribbean nationalisms' captures perfectly, the political struggles and shifts across the Anglophone Caribbean region from the 1920s to the 1960s that delivered the first wave of independent nation states were distinctively plural and interconnected. This essay discusses how literary works operated within, and were regarded as critical to, the political anticipations towards non-colonial sovereignty that took place from the early twentieth century onwards and which have, often retrospectively, been characterised as nationalism. By focusing only on the Anglophone Caribbean, known then as the West Indies, this essay reduces the complexity of the wider region's transition from colonial rule (which was both experienced and determined differently across the Francophone, Hispanophone, and Dutch Caribbeans) to bring into view the already diverse ideologies and affiliations that generated overlapping frameworks of anti-colonial affiliation and self-determination in the West Indies during this period. This essay expands the terrain of literary nationalisms beyond the acclaimed and now canonical fictions of male Windrush novelists who wrote at the mid-century, such as George Lamming, Roger Mais, V. S. Naipaul, and Samuel Selvon. It attends to the nascent nationalism invoked by a number of literary projects at the turn of the century, then moves to consider the crucial role assigned to the writer in the short-lived project of Anglophone regional Federation between 1958 and 1962, which pre-dated the constitution of nation states, and also addresses how Pan-African and Black Atlantic movements shaped the decolonial literary imagination in the early twentieth century. It acknowledges the role that women played in what have often been inscribed as male-centred histories and politically-engaged literary traditions, and recognises their part in the persistent challenge to imagine, craft, and cultivate a national consciousness that did not reinscribe hierarchies of belonging.

As a region profoundly remade by competing European colonial incursions from the seventeenth century onwards, the Caribbean was importantly different from other British colonies. Barely any of the settled peoples, languages, or cultural traditions specific to Caribbean places that pre-existed the colonial era survived it. Colonialism in the Caribbean was violently dislocating in its constitutive hunger for human labour. The waves of translocated populations that arrived in the region by enslavement and otherwise unfree migration – peoples of African and South Asian (and, to a lesser extent, Chinese, Portuguese, and Irish) descent – were subjected to a colonialism that sought to deny not only their freedom but also their linguistic cohesion, their ancestral heritages, and their cultural expressions as it accrued its vast metropolitan-centred capital through their exploitation and deracination on the plantation. Significantly, this pattern of historical formation, characterised as it was by the displacement of peoples, cultural fragmentation, and dispossession, not only informed the character of colonial rule in the Caribbean but also the possibilities for its undoing. People-making projects in the region had to confront and overcome the ways in which plantation slavery, apprenticeship, and indentureship had not just oppressed and exploited its subjects but had also inscribed racialised identities and hostilities that perpetuated discord between different communities, despite a sizeable population with multiple mixed ancestries. Sovereign subjectivity in the Caribbean could not be based on attachments to a precolonial world of now mainly inaccessible ancestral homelands. Unity had to be reimagined through a traumatic shared history of the plantation and the mutual experience of a place in which they had never officially been recognised as fully human. Anglophone Caribbean peoples started to decolonise by resisting the worldview as well as the legal entitlements of British imperialism, and by imagining a recentred West Indies which was no longer the profitable plantation periphery of the motherland, but a place to call their own and on which to build a self-determining future. Writers played a key role in the monumental task of shaping alternative political imaginaries based on collective belonging and mutual entitlement among such diverse and divided peoples.

It has been commonplace for accounts of literary nationalisms in the West Indies to begin with the demonstrable articulations for self-governance that blistered across the region with a wave of strikes and social unrest in the second half of the 1930s. While the strident oppositional writings of this era are a clear fit for the discussion of literature and nationalism within this essay, it remains important to acknowledge that literary works and projects focused on self-determination were not first forged in the fiery late 1930s, even if writers were certainly galvanised by the ideological solidarities expressed and cemented in that moment. In

Nationalism and the Formation of Caribbean Literature (2007), Leah
Rosenberg offers a meticulous account of publication projects and organisations in Jamaica and Trinidad dating back to 1840 which also deserve to
be recognised as part of a tradition of imagining and claiming citizenship –
albeit in a more uneven and complicated configuration in which 'neither
literature nor politics in the Caribbean moved in a direct fashion towards
black working-class power'.[1] Leaving aside the significant body of writing
from this period that we can now acknowledge in genres such as slave
testimony, correspondence, travel writing, and romance, there were also
significant prose narratives, with an array of local newspapers catering for
a range of audiences defined by social class and ancestry that offered
important print venues for traversing political and literary concerns.

     Yet, while newspapers served and shaped the particular political prefer-
ences of the planter elites, mixed middle classes, Indian-Caribbean communities, and Black working classes, the literary imagination was less easily
contained by partisan politics. An interesting example is E. L. Joseph, the
English-Jewish Trinidadian, who was removed from his role as editor of
the *Port of Spain Gazette* after the publication of his 1838 novel, *Warner
Arundell*, which rendered an ambitious 'vision of the new world as
a modern utopia of independent democracies, religious tolerance, and
free trade', and which was less than laudatory in its depictions of the
planter class who formed the newspaper's readership.[2] A happier early
match between newspapers and the home-grown novel was made by
Thomas MacDermot, a Jamaican White who used his literary interests
and talents to shape the cultural nationalism of the *Jamaica Times*, which
he edited from 1900 to 1920. Founding the All Jamaica Library in 1903,
with sponsorship from the *Jamaica Times*, MacDermot's attention was on
cheap editions 'dealing directly with Jamaica and Jamaicans, and written
by Jamaicans'.[3] In seeking to offer a literary unity of place and to cultivate
both local writers and readers, MacDermot's literary nationalism directly
prefigures the little magazines of later decades which have been so
celebrated within anti-colonial literary histories. Indeed, there is direct
continuity between MacDermot's approach and the cultural nationalism
of Una Marson. In her 1937 article in the political weekly *Public Opinion*,
'Wanted: Writers and Publishers', Marson, a Jamaican writer and journalist whose significant contributions have only been fully recognised this
century, stresses the same link between building a tradition of local writing
and the project of forging a national identity independent from the
colonial inheritance as MacDermot: 'In this new era literature must take
its place. Indeed, the writing and production of books by us about

ourselves and our problems is essential.'[4] As Rosenberg demonstrates, works from the earlier period not only elucidate the fuller and longer shift in political attachments, but they effectively 'constitute a foundation for the development of that [later] anticolonial nationalist vision and literature' that was subsequently obscured.[5]

Recognising these earlier literary activities with a clear focus on connections between West Indian place, culture, language, and peoples also complicates the retrospective characterisation of the literary transition from colony to nation as a 1950s movement that emerged in, and was energised by, the independence era. As I have argued elsewhere, in the anthologies and critical studies that were published during the 1960s and 1970s, the scarce attention given to writing before 1950 is directly related to the need to narrate an emergent nationalist tradition with West Indian literature at a critical moment of academic and political consolidation.[6] Moreover, in the politically urgent task of promoting a postcolonial sensibility and language, earlier writings with less defined decolonial credentials slipped into illegitimacy and invisibility – both of which can be read in C. L. R. James's claim that he did not 'know much about West Indian Literature in the 1930s – there wasn't much to know'.[7] From today's perspective, there is a lot to know, as researchers have unearthed a rich field of literary publications and ventures that demonstrate a lineage of decolonial and pan-African sensibilities stretching back into the nineteenth century.[8] It is, however, likely that the changed political horizons of the West Indian world following shifts in the political landscape by 1970 mandated a break from the early century and a forward-looking gaze.

During the 1930s, political and labour leaders, increasingly discontented with the dire social and economic conditions across the region and exasperated with the lack of opportunity to participate in governance structures, began to mobilise. The wave of social unrest, strikes, and political demonstrations against colonial rule that rippled across the region generated a more structured anti-colonial political vision. Commissions were appointed by the British government to investigate these disturbances, most notably the West Indian Royal Commission of 1938 (also known as the Moyne Commission). Whilst most recommendations related to improved working conditions, such as the regulation of working hours, trade union legislation, and social welfare schemes, the proposal to extend adult suffrage was also made and finally adopted after the Second World War. During this period, fostering cultural sovereignty was integral to cultivating a decolonial West Indian identity, which was, in turn, foundational for articulating and mobilising the political struggles towards self-governance. The alliances between literary and political organisations became stronger and the frameworks for imagining self-determination multiplied. Alongside the growth of political parties in individual territories (which represented broadly middle-class or labouring-class interests), political solidarities across the region and into the diaspora were built around Pan-Africanism and around both top-down and bottom-up discussions of Federation as an inclusive West Indian framework for self-rule.

As Kenneth Ramchand notes in his landmark study, *The West Indian Novel and Its Background* (1970), nationalism emerged at the convergence of social crisis, educational and constitutional reform, and Black Atlantic ideologies:

> The popular discontents that swept the West Indian islands between 1934 and 1938 mark the beginnings of modern West Indian nationalisms. The discontents owed their immediate origins to the economic depression of the 1930s but they cannot be separated from the Pan-African and Pan-Negro movements of the twentieth century; nor would they have become so articulate had the effects of popular education in the West Indies not begun to be operative. The nationalist ferment was intensified by the achievement of universal adult suffrage, and improved political constitutions in most of the territories.[9]

Indeed, while the terms 'nation' and 'nationalism' were used extensively during the early twentieth century to signal the primary political objective of self-determination, these terms equally referenced the more lateral identities and ideologies of the time that contributed momentum to the drive towards sovereignty, and which both shaped and were shaped by literary imaginations of this period.

In this regard, it is important to recognise how at this time West Indian 'imagined communities' (to invoke Benedict Anderson's term) had fluid and plural parameters. As Curdella Forbes points out, during the period from the 1930s to the 1950s, '"Nation" meant the distinctive political and cultural identity both of the individual territories and of the region as a whole.'[10] Indeed, although 'nation' was a term incapable of elucidating the striking ethnic, racial, religious, and linguistic pluralism both within and across individual territories, it was a legible symbol within political discourses and debates of the time. As Forbes explains, 'We knew we were "different", requiring different modes of self-analysis and self-identification, yet in the vulnerability of our situation, finding ourselves adrift and called to name ourselves in the midst of Western modernity, we embraced the Western category of nationhood, with all its attendant and singularizing paraphernalia.'[11] To understand Caribbean nationalisms, it is vital to appreciate how these frameworks multiplied rather than divided political sensibilities, and how nationalism was imagined through possibilities for what we would now refer to as transnationalism – in this instance before the nation and not subsequent to it.

The proximity between West Indian political and literary concerns at this time can also be noted in the crossover between writers and active anti-colonialists, including most obviously Albert Gomes in Trinidad, Roger Mais and Edna Manley (married to Norman) in Jamaica, and Phyllis Shand Allfrey and Elma Napier in Dominica (both of whom held political office). Literary nationalism developing in the region can also be productively traced to clusters of little magazines and their associated groups. Both *The Beacon* in Trinidad and *Focus* in Jamaica were important for knitting literary expression to social solidarity and cultural sovereignty. They advocated writings that were not only localised in their sensibilities but that also affirmed the lives of working-class West Indians, although concerns about the downward gaze of the middle-class writer were often expressed. In their editorial roles for these little magazines, writers such as Frank Collymore (*Bim*), Alfred Mendes (*Trinidad* and *The Beacon*), and A. J. Seymour (*Kyk-Over-Al*) deployed a variety of strategies – manifestos, editorials, and competitions – in order to foster a transition in literary subject and style towards local lives and voices.

These little magazines, and very many others, became a vital venue for the discussion and development of a West Indian aesthetics that had begun to surface within print projects in the early twentieth century.[12] Esther Chapman's Jamaica-based *West Indian Review*, first published in 1934, was an early example of looking beyond its home territory towards regional inclusivity. The review published many of the writers whom we still associate with canonical West Indian literature today, gathering work across territories and linguistic boundaries. Other little magazines of the 1940s began with a clear mission to cultivate and recognise highly localised writings, based on subjects and voices with which the writers shared literal ground. As editor of *Kyk-Over-Al*, published in British Guyana from 1945, A. J. Seymour explicitly dedicated his little magazine to fostering national culture: it was to be 'an instrument to help forge a Guianese people, and to make them conscious of their intellectual and spiritual possibilities'.[13] Yet while *Focus*, published irregularly from 1943, did retain its focus on the voices of a new Jamaica, both *Bim*, edited in Barbados from 1941, and *Kyk-Over-Al* shifted towards a regional scope aligned with the larger West Indian nation that was being imagined in political projects of this time. This was mainly a curatorial emphasis, with individual literary works that may have been written from, for, and about a national context being gathered together as part of a more expansive imaginary into which West Indian peoples read themselves as part of a regional community with shared struggles and concerns. As Barbadian writer and radical George Lamming remembers, these ventures were responding to 'the gravitational pull of what was happening in the region at the time':

> It is the time after the War, when the region, that is the English-speaking Caribbean, is being called upon to think in terms of the Federation and the unity of the region . . . That regionalizing of politics of the particular islands coincides with the emergence of these various journals and creates a curious marriage, you might say, of politics and culture.[14]

Indeed, it is also in this context of a move towards Federation that the literary becomes most demonstrably a privileged domain for the people-making projects of a sovereign West Indies.

The political vision of West Indian peoples attaining self-governance through a federal framework had first been advanced in 1932 at the West Indian Conference in Dominica – ahead of the unrest of the late 1930s. Given the substantial role played by the colonial governance in these negotiations, it was not until after the war that planning began, most clearly in 1947 in Jamaica where the Secretary of State for the Colonies was joined by political representatives from all West Indian territories. Almost a decade later, in 1956, the legal framework was adopted by the majority, but, despite its long gestation, Federation lasted just four years from 1958 before its political structure collapsed in a shift towards nation states in 1962, the year when Jamaica and Trinidad and Tobago declared independence. Although the first half of the twentieth century is seldom viewed as a single chapter in the region's decolonising story now, there were consistent moves across these decades towards sovereignty and unity – in terms of both political and literary expression. These moves arguably comprised an extended and complicated nationalist phase, during which achieving freedom from colonialism and crafting a meaningful co-belonging among Caribbean peoples and places remained the prevailing ideals.

It is perhaps the Trinidadian writer Samuel Selvon, now best known for his 1956 novel of migrant life, *The Lonely Londoners*, who most directly addresses the challenge of preserving the region's inherent pluralism whilst building common political purpose. Although based in London from 1950, Selvon's writings consistently grapple with the possibilities for building solidarity and community from the ethnic and cultural multiplicity that comprised West Indian societies, both at home and in the diaspora. In his first novel, *A Brighter Sun* (1952), set in rural Trinidad during the Second World War, Selvon models interethnic co-belonging at the level of friend and neighbour. He does so in the rapport established between the Indian-Trinidadian protagonist, Tiger, and the African-Trinidadian Joe. Alongside the house-building trope of decolonial social accommodation that also structures V. S. Naipaul's classic *A House for Mr Biswas* (1961), the amity between the two men and their wives imagines conditions for a transracial self-governed island. However, Selvon does not romanticise the national struggle, and while Tiger ventures his pluralistic vision ('think of all of we as a whole, living in one country, fighting for we rights'), Joe enunciates the particular struggle of Caribbean nationalisms to unite as they decolonise: 'Dat is wat we fighting for now, but yuh yuhself know how dis place have so much different people, it go be ah big fight.'[15] In Selvon's 1955 novel, *An Island is a World*, this same challenge to establish solidarity and community across different peoples is voiced by Andrews. Now it is in relation to an incipient Federation and its aspirations for common purpose: 'Ah, with all the differences in these islands it will be one hell of a job to unify and have a common loyalty.'[16] Yet, while Selvon draws attention to the scale of the task involved both in resisting colonialism and in integrating the nation, his literary works tenaciously write towards a social imaginary of mutual recognition and common cause between West Indians of different ethnic groups.

Indeed, many of the writers of this period were passionate advocates of Federation and the possibilities it offered for building connected communities and resilience through collaboration. The St Lucian poet Derek Walcott was commissioned by the University College of the West Indies to write and direct a play for Federation's inauguration event. The resulting epic historical saga, *Drums and Colours*, staged in 1958, samples 600 years of an interlaced historical fabric underpinning the region's anticipated entwined future. While Walcott's creative vision of the West Indies has arguably become its most celebrated one, Tobagonian Eric Roach's self-styling as the poet of Federation seems to have fated his literary legacy, with his considerable talent and significant body of work slipping out of view for decades after the demise of Federation.[17]

Given that Federation had to conjure into imagination a regional consciousness to which West Indian peoples – already fragmented by different ethnic, class, and territorial allegiances – needed to assent, it is perhaps not surprising that politicians and political commentators promoting this project invested heavily in writers to imagine the radical shift in belonging that was needed to underpin regional sovereignty.[18] At the end of his 1958 speech on Federation, in which he sets out the political and economic benefits of regional reorganisation across the decolonising Anglophone Caribbean, C. L. R. James, the acclaimed Trinidadian writer, Marxist theorist, and anti-colonialist, turns to the work of Selvon and Naipaul and to the privileged power of the literary to reimagine West Indian identities and lives:

> Writers, and artists of all kinds, are of particular importance at this transitional stage of our development. They interpret us to ourselves and interpret us to the world abroad which is anxious to know about us. These highly gifted people are able in a few thousand words to illuminate aspects of our social and personal lives which otherwise would have taken us years and great pain and trouble to find out.[19]

As was proven, the literary and political imaginaries underpinning Federation's vision and its motto of 'dwell[ing] together in unity' could not ultimately overcome the tensions between commitments to national, regional, and ancestral interests, as imbalances in resource and scale fractured its lateral foundations. Although in 1969 Eric Williams, the first Prime Minister of Trinidad and Tobago and author of the 1944 monumental alternate history of the Caribbean, *Capitalism and Slavery*, spoke about Federation as 'doomed from the start', given its 'ridiculous structure of old-fashioned crown colony government', this political vision had clearly garnered considerable support from radicals and writers at the time, who hoped for a more thoroughgoing transition from colonial power than offered by bourgeois nationalism.[20]

Yet, while the political structure of Federation did not prevail, a West Indian regional imagination and literary sensibility was sustained. Indeed, Ramchand argued that the idea of the West Indies 'remained to signal a reality stronger than any political institution', because West Indian literature – along with 'the University of the West Indies, [and] the all-conquering West Indian cricket team' – kept the ideal of regional identity alive.[21] Certainly, the idea of the West Indies as a unit of cultural and literary definition has remained strong, although a growing emphasis on the larger multilingual Caribbean now provides a more expansive portal still. Importantly, though, Federation was not the only political movement of this period to be actively fostering a consciousness of shared cause and belonging. Pan-Africanism was a hugely influential people-making project involving West Indians which overlapped with Federation. It also similarly aspired to imagine a community of citizens whose sense of place and commitment to each other provided a promise of belonging and self-determination wilfully denied by colonialism and lost in ruptured ties to historical and ancestral elsewheres. The key differences are that the community of identity imagined into being by Pan-Africanism was issued by a global call to those of African ancestry, and that it was a movement developed in the diaspora.

The central role played by West Indians in the formation of Pan-Africanism dates back to Henry Sylvester Williams, the Trinidadian lawyer who organised the first Pan-African Conference in 1900 in Westminster Town Hall. Better known than Williams is the central role played by Pan-Africanists and Trinidadians C. L. R. James and George Padmore in the anti-imperialist networks of the metropole through the first half of the twentieth century. Along another vector, the recognition of Africa as integral to the West Indian world had gained widespread representation in Jamaica from at least 1914 onwards with Marcus Garvey's founding of the Universal Negro Improvement Association. These two movements advocating political solidarity and a forceful conceptualisation of Pan-African unity and Black Internationalism as a platform for advancing the principles of racial justice, cultural sovereignty, and independent governance, overlapped in 1930s London, a hot-bed of anti-colonialism. Padmore met Kwame Nkrumah, the then Ghanaian revolutionary and later first Prime Minister and President of Ghana, at the station when he arrived at the capital, and it was also in London that Garvey met Dusé Mohamed Ali, the Sudanese-Egyptian political activist who became an important figure in Garvey's African education.

Given that undoing colonialism's culture in the West Indies involved coming to terms with ruptures and dispossessions, it made sense that Africa would hold a crucial place in the political imagination of Caribbean writers. In *Race and Colour in Caribbean Literature* (1962), G. R. Coulthard pointed out that Jamaicans Claude McKay and George Campbell 'were in the vanguard of the revaluation of African culture long before the nationalist awakening in Africa and before the concept of négritude was developed in the Caribbean'.[22] What Coulthard is referencing here is precisely the longer processes of forging an anti-colonial nationalist consciousness which evolved from the opening decades of the twentieth century. For Campbell, looking to Africa was a crucial step in building a Jamaican nationalist consciousness, just as it was for Vera Bell, a lesser-known Jamaican writer and dramatist, whose poem 'Ancestor on the Auction Block', originally published in *Focus* in 1948, has remained emblematic of the need to commemorate the devastating experience of

African enslavement on which West Indian colonial societies were built. Quoted by the Jamaican Prime Minister Portia Simpson Miller in her 2014 Emancipation Day Message, Bell's poem articulates the humanising call of ancestral memory and the significance of preserving a historical consciousness of slavery and a sensibility of Africa in the Caribbean: 'Across the years your eyes seek mine / Compelling me to look.'[23]

James and Marson were both in the UK in the 1930s, and were both firmly associated with Pan-Africanism as this took shape in the colonial capital. For Marson, it was a fuller understanding of the present of Africa's colonial situation that was transformative. In 1934, Marson was assigned as the representative of the League of Coloured People (LCP) to Sir Nana Ofori Atta Omanhene, a king from northern Ghana, on his visit to England. She shared a platform with him at the LCP conference that year on the subject of 'The Negro in the World Today', alongside Jomo Kenyatta. Her friendship with Ofori Atta and deepening understanding of colonial Africa's history and politics informed her second play, *London Calling*, which premiered in Kingston after she returned to Jamaica in 1937.[24] In this play, which dramatises the experiences of Black international students in England, Marson not only satirises the ignorance of the British about Caribbean peoples, but also the necessary performativity of Black identity for Caribbean subjects who have lost connection with their African heritage. When in 1935 Marson was the first Black woman invited to attend the League of Nations at Geneva, she met with Dr Charles Martin, Ethiopia's Minister to the UK, and, outraged by Mussolini's invasion of Abyssinia, offered to assist the delegation by carrying out secretarial work for Haile Selassie.

The affirmative Blackness and the declarative anti-colonial sentiment of *The Moth and the Star*, Marson's third volume of poetry, published in 1937, might reasonably be attributed to the Pan-African sensibility she developed, alongside, of course, her experience of the racist metropole. In 'To Joe and Ben', who we are told in parenthesis were 'Brutally murdered in April 1937 at Addis Ababa by the Italians', Marson memorialises Joseph and Benjamin Martin, the two sons of Dr Martin, executed by the Italians after their capture in Wollega.[25] This elegy to specific African lives is both intensely personal and passionately political, as it brings to the attention of a Jamaican readership the idea of Pan-African resistance against ongoing colonial violence, as well as the bonds that West Indians have to Africa through common political struggle as well as a shared ancestor.

The supranationalism of Pan-Africanism that infused Caribbean nationalisms generated a foundational principle of racial non-domination within anti-colonial ideologies, and presented a model of co-belonging that operated beyond, as well as within, the nation. As Adom Getachew has recently argued in *Worldmaking after Empire* (2019), these supranational politics played a vital role in the history of anti-colonialism and highlight how the political ambitions and stakes of Black international movements towards non-domination not only contested colonialism, but also sought to resist the innately imperial character of global economic systems and to challenge and dismantle them.[26] Yet while both Pan-Africanism and Federation created an alternative and more expansive 'nation' for West Indians to belong in, they were also troubled by and criticised for exclusions of their own. The entrenched racialisation of colonialism meant that those seeking to empower and liberate Black populations were often unable to recognise any shared ground with those who inherited white privilege, and solidarities of the oppressed were also fragile due to ongoing tensions between communities of African and Indian descent.

[Edward] Kamau Brathwaite's 1974 claim that Jean Rhys's 1966 novel, *Wide Sargasso Sea*, speaks to a racialised history separated from the experience of Black West Indians, and cannot, 'given the present structure, meaningfully identify or be identified, with the spiritual world on this side of the Sargasso Sea', has attracted enormous critical attention and been widely contested.[27] Less notice has been given to his estimation of Phyllis Shand Allfrey's 1953 *The Orchid House*, a novel that explores the fraying ends of the colonial era through a family of three white Dominican sisters, narrated mainly through the eyes of Lally, their ageing Black nurse, and which Brathwaite found 'a brilliant but irrelevant novel within the West Indian context'.[28] In both statements, Brathwaite conceptualises West Indian realities as concentrically formed through the experiences of ancestrally different peoples that do not always overlap meaningfully in proximity, as they do not share the same history of struggle. Indeed, despite Allfrey's co-founding of the island's first political party, the Dominica Labour Party, with Dominican trade unionist E. C. Loblack, she eventually stepped out of politics on account of her whiteness and the history it manifested – despite her unquestionable commitment to West Indian decolonisation.

While Pan-Africanism explicitly called for the mutual liberation and solidarity of peoples of African descent, Federation claimed to offer a framework for equal representation whilst also recognising the plurality of the region's peoples. According to Eric Williams, 'differences of race, religion, language or nationality, far from encouraging hostility to federation, strengthen the sentiment for it', but this inclusive sentiment alone was not enough to reassure minorities.[29] Guyana never joined the Federation because its Indian-descent community did not feel sufficiently acknowledged within its plans, and the requirement and obligation to offer a generative idea of co-belonging and right of place to such a diverse people remained a significant challenge even after Independence. One novel that stands out as representing the social complexity of West Indian society, alongside narrating the development of Black political consciousness, is Trinidadian Ralph de Boissière's *Crown Jewel* (1956), a novel about Trinidadian society in the turbulent 1930s. Depicting the simultaneously stratified and creolised world of Trinidad, *Crown Jewel* notices the ways in which race and class intersect to inform the relations between different communities and families and their distinctive voicings of their place – also reminding us that the Venezuelan immigrant is not a recent figure in the island's history. De Boissière, descended from French Creoles, had been part of the radical *Beacon* group in the 1930s but emigrated to Australia in 1948, where he joined the Communist Party of Australia. It was not until 1981 that an edition of the novel was published for the West Indies and UK readership.

The gulf between the history, experience, and political imagination of those whose ancestors benefited from colonialism and those who were exploited and injured by it would take generations to address productively. What Walcott draws attention to in his 1979 collection, *The Star-Apple Kingdom*, is the unanswered problem in an ancestrally conceptualised West Indies – the Creole citizen whose ancestry is mixed and whose history cannot be read off his body: 'I have no nation now but the imagination. / After the white man, the niggers didn't want me / when the power swing to their side. / The first chain my hands and apologize, "History" / the next said I wasn't black enough for their pride.'[30] By the 1970s, disillusionment with the concessions and exclusions involved in the imagined and now politically functional nation led to a new phase in the rights-bearing history of West Indian literature, with still marginalised and voiceless elements of society – Black women, Chinese Caribbeans, the urban poor, queer subjects – speaking out to legitimate their place in the national community in their own voices.

As this account of the political and literary ecologies operating in the West Indies in the first half of the twentieth century shows, the imagined nation in and for this region had to achieve something much greater than constitutional decolonisation. West Indian literature contributed very significantly to the progressive people-making projects that emerged during this period and was crucial to establishing the legitimacy of its plural and creolised populations, alongside a literacy of the West Indian world in its unrivalled cultural multiplicity and social complexity. In this way, West Indian literature both represented and advanced the possibilities for meaningful self-determination and an imagination of co-belonging without domination that represented national consciousness at its best.

Notes

1 Leah Rosenberg, *Nationalism and the Formation of Caribbean Literature* (London and New York: Palgrave Macmillan, 2007), p. 9.
2 Ibid., pp. 15–16.
3 For further information, see Mervyn Morris, 'The All Jamaica Library', *Jamaica Journal* 6.1 (1972), pp. 47–9.
4 Una Marson, 'Wanted: Writers and Publishers', *Public Opinion*, 12 June 1937, p. 6.
5 Rosenberg, *Nationalism and the Formation of Caribbean Literature*, p. 32.
6 Alison Donnell, *Twentieth-Century Caribbean Literature: Critical Moments in Anglophone Literary History* (London: Routledge, 2006), p. 42.
7 C. L. R. James, 'Discovering Literature in Trinidad: The 1930s', *Spheres of Existence: Selected Writings* (London: Allison & Busby, 1980), pp. 237–44 (p. 237).
8 For a full account of this period, see Evelyn O'Callaghan and Tim Watson, eds., *Caribbean Literature in Transition, 1800–1920* (Cambridge: Cambridge University Press, 2020).
9 Kenneth Ramchand, *The West Indian Novel and its Background* (London: Faber, 1970), p. 71.
10 Curdella Forbes, *From Nation to Diaspora: Samuel Selvon, George Lamming and the Cultural Performance of Gender* (Kingston, Jamaica: University of the West Indies Press, 2005), p. 4.
11 Ibid., p. 6.
12 For a comprehensive account of little magazines, see Clare Irving, 'Printing the West Indies: Literary Magazines and the Anglophone Caribbean, 1920s–1950s', unpublished PhD thesis, Newcastle University, 2015.
13 A. J. Seymour, 'Editorial Notes', *Kyk-Over-Al* 1 (December 1945), p. 27.
14 Erika J. Waters, 'Music of Language: An Interview with George Lamming', *The Caribbean Writer* 13 (1999), pp. 190–201 (p. 193).
15 Samuel Selvon, *A Brighter Sun* (London: Longmans, 1952), pp. 195, 196.
16 Samuel Selvon, *An Island is a World* (London: Allan Wingate, 1955), p. 212.
17 See E. M. Roach, *The Flowering Rock: Collected Poems, 1938–1974* (Leeds: Peepal Tree, 2012).
18 For a fuller exploration, see Alison Donnell, 'West Indian Literature and Federation: Imaginative Accord and Uneven Realities', *Small Axe* 24.1 (61) (2020), pp. 78–86.

19 C. L. R. James, 'On Federation (1958–9)', *At the Rendezvous of Victory: Selected Writings* (London: Allison & Busby, 1984), pp. 85–128 (p. 105).

20 Eric Williams, *Britain and the West Indies*, The 5th Noel Buxton Lecture of the University of Essex (London: Longmans, 1969), p. 19.

21 Kenneth Ramchand, 'West Indian Literary History: Literariness, Orality and Periodization', *Callaloo* 34 (Winter 1988), pp. 95–110 (p. 95).

22 G. R. Coulthard, *Race and Colour in Caribbean Literature* (London: Oxford University Press, 1962), p. 117.

23 Vera Bell, 'Ancestor on the Auction Block', *Focus* (1948), p. 187.

24 Una Marson, *Pocomania and London Calling* (Kingston, Jamaica: Blouse & Skirt Books, 2016).

25 Una Marson, *The Moth and the Star* (Kingston, Jamaica: Published by the Author, 1937), pp. 81–3.

26 Adom Getachew, *Worldmaking after Empire: The Rise and Fall of Self-Determination* (Princeton, NJ: Princeton University Press, 2019).

27 [Edward] Kamau Brathwaite, *Contradictory Omens: Cultural Diversity and Integration in the Caribbean* (Kingston, Jamaica: Savacou, 1974), p. 38. See Kamau Brathwaite, 'A Post-Cautionary Tale of the Helen of Our Wars', *Wasafiri* 11.22 (1995), pp. 69–78, and responses to this piece published in *Wasafiri* 14.28 (1998).

28 Kamau Brathwaite, 'Roots', *Roots* (Ann Arbor, MI: University of Michigan Press, 1993), pp. 28–54 (p. 51).

29 Eric Williams, 'Federation in the World of Today: Lecture at the Extra-mural Department in Trinidad and Tobago of the University College of the West Indies', 25 February 1955, Eric Williams Memorial Collection, Box 813, University of West Indies-St Augustine; quoted in Getachew, *Worldmaking after Empire*, p. 210.

30 Derek Walcott, *The Star-Apple Kingdom* (London: Cape, 1979), p. 8.

CHAPTER 12

African Nationalisms

Donna V. Jones

On Nationalism

Perhaps there is no more vexing question than 'what is a nation?' Current political theory and cultural studies have agreed that the nation state is modern, a state formation that emerged to address and accommodate the political and economic contingencies of nineteenth-century Europe. Yet, while the nation state is the political designation that most defines and determines the outcome of individual lives (one's health and life expectancy will vary considerably depending on the country in which one was born: what Amartya Sen would refer to as the 'birthright lottery'), a scientific definition of what constitutes a nation continues to elude us.[1] Two rough forms of the nation emerged in the nineteenth century, one defined by abstract citizenship and the other by culture, language, and origin. Ernst Renan, musing on what binds the linguistic and regional threads of hexagonal France, imagined the nation as a 'shared project'; this suited the established vision of republicanism. By contrast, German nationalism, from Herder to Bismarck, imagined the nation as a collective bound by blood and language. Drawing from Robert William Seton-Watson's description of the nation as emerging when 'a significant number of people consider themselves' as part of one, Benedict Anderson famously declared the nation an 'imagined political community'.[2] Nations for Anderson are 'cultural artifacts', made and maintained through myth, popular culture, iconography, common practices, and institutions. Anderson's work illuminates that the general consensus that Seton-Watson references, by which a majority understand themselves as belonging to a given nation, develops over time with the establishment of quotidian cultural rituals, with reading the national newspaper, for example, or singing a national anthem or declaring a national oath. Nations and the sentiment of national belonging,

which is at the foundation of nationalism, are not an eternal or immutable facet of political life.

Remarking on the development of French national identity, the
historian Theodore Zeldin tells the story of a school inspector sent to
a rural provincial village in 1864. The inspector asked the students: 'Are
you French or Russian?' The response was: 'They could not say.'³ As
Zeldin and other historians would observe, it would take near a century
before the vast heterogeneous populations of the provinces would come
to understand themselves at best, and in a qualified manner only, as
citizens of the French Republic. Nations are, indeed, vast organisational
projects, frequently the brainchild of an elite, as Joseph Conrad's
Nostromo (1904) suggests in the tragic origin story of 'Costaguano',
a fictional South American nation born from the silver lust of a ruling
family and justified through the poetry of an idealist journalist.
However, the true work of a nation comes in the formation of national
identity. And so *Nostromo* deftly stages how elites and common people
harbour distinct investments in the project of nation-building. For the
Goulds (the mining family), and for Costaguano's elite, the material and
social benefits that would come as a result of independence justified their
fidelity to the concept of nation. Providing material support to the
young journalist, the Goulds hide behind the poetry of nationhood to
obscure their material motivations. Yet, it is in the poetry that the most
difficult task of the national project comes: that is, in how to enlist the
common people, those who, by the contingencies of history, find themselves as members of a new nation. In the end, nation-work constructs
the shared myths, cultures, and histories that bind ethnicities, regions,
social classes, and, in the rare modern instances, races. And such work
operates as much in nations newly formed as in nations that claim
antiquity: as Anderson notes, the nation is at once modern and eternal.
One might assert that the contrivance of national identity is that one
feels it as at once eternal and ephemeral – that the shared sense of what it
means to be 'French' enlists qualities that pre-exist the formation of
France as a national entity.

The Nation as Palimpsest: The Berlin-Congo Conference of 1884–1885

'my map of Africa lies in Europe. Here lies Russia and here . . . lies
France, and we are in the middle – that is my map of Africa'

Otto von Bismarck⁴

'Writers are not only writers, they are citizens'

Chinua Achebe[5]

In his 2003 piece, 'The Scramble for Africa', the installation artist Yinka Shonibare interprets the Berlin–Congo conference of 1884–5 as a collection of headless mannequins around a table designed with a lacquered map of Africa (Fig. 12.1). The figures, adorned in jackets made of elaborate West African waxed-cotton patterns, gesticulate with a rhetorical flourish while their bodies convey a performative authority. As Shonibare's lacquered map suggests, known and unknown Africa would serve as a surface upon which Europe's imperial designs would be superimposed. For the Europeans dividing the continent, what lies beneath this new map, the frontiers and boundaries Africans had themselves designed, held little interest. Thus, the focus of the installation draws our attention to the mannequins convened around the map, inviting us to interpret both their

Fig. 12.1 Yinka Shonibare, 'The Scramble for Africa' (2003) © Yinka Shonibare CBE. All Rights Reserved, DACS/Artimage 2021. Image courtesy Stephen Friedman Gallery, London and James Cohan Gallery, New York. Commissioned by the Museum for African Art, Long Island City, NY.

gestures and, more importantly, the intricate patterns of their dress coats. In their gestures, we witness grand yet mindless deliberations: in an interview, Shonibare remarked: 'I imagined this group of brainless men sitting around a table ... deciding the fate of Africa.'[6] Shonibare's piece suggests that we reckon with a history which presents the division of the continent as simultaneously 'the model of peaceful solidarity' and 'cooperation' of European nations, and an occasion to placate the avarice of the king of a small nation with territory seventy-seven times its size.[7]

The very concept of the nation state, and its political expression, nationalism, emerged alongside imperialism. For Africa, the Berlin–Congo Conference marks the conjunction of empire and nation; indeed, nation and nationalism were introduced through empire, and the two political concepts are inextricably bound. Initiated and organised by the German statesman Otto von Bismarck, the Berlin Conference served to further solidify Germany's national unification and grant them the sought-after status of an imperial nation. Rather than quelling the simmering rivalry between the new nations – Germany and Belgium – the conference set in motion between them a rapacious competition for African territory and resources: the route to true nation-state status, to a national status equal to France or Britain, ran through Africa.

The Berlin Conference displayed the contradiction inherent in nineteenth-century nationalism. While among the European nations, 'the rapid success of colonization' gave rise to 'chaos and conflict', wars of pacification, diplomatic impasses, and political scepticism at home, Bismarck presented the Conference as a means to neutral arbitration. Reflecting on the legacy of the Berlin Conference at its centennial, African scholars recognised the irony that the shared organisational project of African colonisation provided a short-lived moment of European unity.[8] Again, Shonibare's headless figures, frozen in fervent deliberation, perfectly capture the fragility of European unity, and reveal the avarice beneath the European representatives' careful excogitation.

Europe had centuries to adapt to the centrifugal processes of nation formation; institutions and traditions that appear timeless and immutable developed within a timeframe set by the frequently conflicting interests of elites and the common people. In many ways, the nation itself is an atemporal marker for this long and arduous and continuous process of organisation. However, Africa had no such luxury of time, nor the conceit of participation in the consolidation and establishment of a shared national project; borders and frontiers were hastily drawn, thus making the work of nationhood a shock imposition. Excluded from the foundational efforts of modern nation-building, Africans experienced the very concept of nation as a mode of disorganisation, rather than a concept introducing the methods by which the vast heterogeneity of its people might find shared membership. By 1885, Europe had divided and apportioned Africa among themselves; the new map appeared as the top layer of a palimpsest, a surface that conveys the will of the new artist and conceals and reorganises the interpretive framework of what lay beneath.

With independence, African writers produced a flurry of novels oriented towards a global readership. In the Francophone world, the Martinican author René Maran's Africa-themed novel, *Batouala: A True Black Novel,* won the Prix Goncourt in 1921. French critics lauded this work for its portrayal of an exoticised African, an image of the continent that sat easily with the interwar colonial imagination that positioned Africa as a source from which Europe might draw revitalising aesthetic methods and energy. It was not until the publication of Chinua Achebe's *Things Fall Apart* in 1958 that a work centred on the torment and tragedy of the colonised subject received wide and universal critical praise and circulation; in effect, *Things Fall Apart* became the novel that would enact the promise of *Weltliteratur* for African literature, transmuting the particular tragedy of the Igbo everyman Okonkwo to the universal struggle with one's own limitations and desires for self-definition. In addition to his own creative works and through his editorial efforts, Achebe would shape the course of the postcolonial African novel. In 1962, he became editorial advisor of the Heinemann African Writers Series, publishing new literary works from primarily Anglophone West Africa for mass consumption on the continent and abroad. The publication and circulation of literature for Africans by Africans, through an African editorial series, was unprecedented. Alan Hill, the managing director of Heinemann UK, linked the publication project to a programme of social development. Describing Ghana, he remarked that the bookstores stocked exclusively technical works; part of the education of an independent nation, Hill reasoned, should include the cultivation of a national literature.[9] Out of this series a canon was born; by the 1980s, the press would publish the works of formidable writers – Bessie Head, Alex La Guma, Ayi Kwei Armah, Ngũgĩ wa Thiong'o, Hamidou Kane, and Ousmane Sembène. What I earlier described as a palimpsest is once more at work here. Beneath the surface of the global novel was a thriving indigenous popular literary tradition. As Wendy Griswold details in her literary history of popular writing in pre- and post-independence Nigeria, penny press works, romance stories, and pamphlets circulated widely throughout Anglophone Africa; written in either pidgin or transliterated into the myriad languages of Nigeria's numerous ethnic groups, these works formed the foundation of national reading practices that focused inwards and catered to the heterogeneity of the nation.[10] Some of these works travelled across ethnic and regional divides; romance stories written by Hausa women writers were a cottage industry and were read by women throughout the North, while other works reinforced them; and, as with so many ethnic conflicts, pamphleteers played a significant part in the Nigerian civil war.

Some critics would voice concern that the post-independence African novel would align with the pedagogical mission of neocolonialism and global capitalism; in other words, that the postcolonial novel introduced a critical framework that emphasised individual struggles over collective movements, while characterising socio-economic problems – such as poverty or land dispossession – in terms of either individualised struggle or as part of larger, intractable problems like corruption. Gareth Griffiths is one such critic. In his 1997 essay, 'Documentation and Communication in Postcolonial Societies: Politics of Control', Griffiths warns that 'when the postcolonial world wants to employ the resources and technology of the metropolitan to speak, it had better learn to do so in the voices and accents (for these read formats and structures) which people in the West want to hear'. Griffiths cautions that we be aware of the motivations of 'Western publishers and media barons'.[11] They are gatekeepers, he argues, marking the limits of what is critically permissible, rather than midwives assisting the birth of emergent and authentic African voices. While Griffiths's criticism reveals the asymmetrical power dynamics of Africa and Europe, it is nonetheless impossible to ignore the complexity and critical variety of the storytelling of the novels selected to serve the project of cultural development. Many of the novels in the Heinemann series featured an individual subject that guided the reader through the vicissitudes of colonisation; however, fragmentation, disruption, and the eventual dissociation from the project of both national and individual psychological development prevailed. Rather than project a model for an idealised individual psyche attuned to the persisting economic demands of neocolonialism, these novels portray psyches deformed by their efforts to conform to the demands of both national and colonial subjecthood.

The personality type that precedes the establishment of nationhood is one traumatised and fragmented by the experiences of colonial and postcolonial subjection. Indeed, one may argue that, in order for the modern African novel form to reflect the project of liberation, it should abandon the myopic individualism that is frequently featured in the post-war European novel, and aim instead for narratives structured around a palaver of voices that make up the collective struggles for independence and self-determination. Brilliant works such as Ousmane Sembène's 1960 *Les bouts de bois de Dieu* (*God's Bits of Wood*, 1962) provide such a polyvocal representation of resistance. Recounting the 1940s nationwide railroad strike in what was French West Africa, the novel shifts narrative perspective and location, moving from the colonial capital, Dakar, to the waystations of the country's interior, Thiès and Bamako, shifting all along from the union organisers to a French colonialist to the strikers, and, in the end, to the women, whose willpower to endure the deprivations of hunger and humiliation sustains the strike. While this novel and others like it depict the political potential and might of the colonised in and through collective action, I must nonetheless stress the importance of African writers' turn to the interior. For these intimate depictions of the profound mental and emotional toll on an individual life under colonialism provide the requisite work towards decolonisation as well.

The psychological theories of Lucien Lévy-Bruhl (*La mentalité primitive*, 1922) or of C. R. Aldrich (*The Primitive Mind and Modern Civilization*, 1931), born of empire as they were, reduced the inner world of the colonised to a vestigial and pre-rational state of consciousness incapable of individual differentiation, and thus not possessing the personality type necessary for modern nationhood. The novel form, however, provides the space in which the complex dialectic engagement between the individual psyche and the world can be staged and reimagined. Achebe reached for such potential in his African realism. *Things Fall Apart* embraces the polyvocality and dialogic of village life, but concludes with a bold attempt to salvage the individual psyche of the novel's tragic hero by depicting the British colonial administrators' efforts to reduce Okonkwo's rich and turbulent life, his explosive interior, to a mere footnote in a second-rate ethnography detailing 'the pacification of the primitive tribes of the Lower Niger'.[12] The haunting indignity lingers all the more, because we, as readers, have read the *Sturm und Drang* of his personal struggle with a world in transformation. Achebe was quite attuned to the promise of the novel form to resist the erasure of African minds and interiors. In his denunciation of Joseph Conrad's 1899 *Heart of Darkness* as racist, it is clear that Achebe's principal objection was not the 'negative' portrayal of Africa, but Conrad's inability to indicate or attribute any feature other than silent impassivity to his African characters. 'Kurtz – he dead' for Achebe was the synecdoche of the pervasive and persistent features of imperial racism: the

reduction of African peoples to an undifferentiated mass, mute and insens-
ate, possessing the amoral indifference of nature itself.

The psychological novels of post-independence are vibrant and experimental; they defy and exceed the individualist and sometimes solipsistic
torpor that grips their bourgeois counterparts. Moreover, African works of
this period declare resolutely that work on the psyche is inextricably linked
with the collective processes of decolonisation; thus, they reject Georg
Lukács's, and by extension the Left's, assessment of interiority as an
abandonment of political engagement. One must work through the psychological toll of colonialism; this ongoing process of decolonisation was
the precondition for the establishment of national culture. Ngũgĩ wa
Thiong'o writes: 'Colonial alienation is like separating the mind from
the body so that they are occupying two unrelated linguistic spheres in
the same person. On a larger scale, it is like producing a society of bodiless
heads and headless bodies.'[13] For Ngũgĩ, the return to and cultivation of
indigenous languages was foremost: 'language carries culture . . . the entire
body of values by which we come to perceive ourselves and our place in the
world'. In 1977, Ngũgĩ published his last novel in English, *Petals of Blood*,
a realist narrative tracing four lives entangled in the Mau Mau rebellion; his
next novel, *Devil on the Cross* (*Caitaani mutharaba-ini*) of 1980, written in
Gikuyu, reads like an act of liberation, a tempestuous and hallucinatory
tale of the poor and pregnant Jacinta Wariinga, who must match wits with
her own ambitions and the pantheon of venal and corrupt adversaries that
lurk in her every encounter in post-independence Kenya. While writing in
Gikuyu is indispensable to unifying an alienated consciousness, ironically
it is the language of the unified mind that is best suited to convey the
processes by which the colonised subject is broken, and the mental anguish
that comes as a result. Delusional visions torment Jacinta; auditory and
visual hallucinations and inner jeremiads conjure a physical world distorted and exaggerated. Jacinta cannot align her simple desire to study to
become an architect with a world which requires one to adopt a self-
destructive and maddening moral framework to obtain basic subsistence –
and so her ambition is gradually reduced to a hardscrabble effort to feed
and house herself.

On the Epic: To Draw Our Poetry from the Struggle, Here and Now; or to Recuperate the Past

A national culture is not folklore nor an abstract populism that
believes it can discover the people's true nature . . . A national culture

is the whole body of efforts made by people in the sphere of thought to describe, justify, and praise the action through which that people have created itself and keeps itself in existence. A national culture in under-developed countries should, therefore, take its place at the very heart of the struggle for freedom which these countries are carrying on.

Frantz Fanon[14]

For African writers, the epic form is as vexed as the nation. Among all literary forms, the epic is the most closely aligned with the establishment of national identity. The novel assures the inception of a national culture. For example, one might compare the function of the novel with Benedict Anderson's description of the national newspaper: both novel and newspaper are artefacts whose consumption serves as a form of civic education. Citizens read the national news to be well-informed, whereas the novel is the unit of the national canon; familiarity with the canon is one measure of being well-cultured. The epic, by contrast, performs a function above and beyond cultural literacy. The epic narrates the prehistory of the nation.

The African epic became a form overburdened by the expectations of an intellectual class tasked with the responsibility to undo cultural suppression and distortion of the colonial period. Perhaps no other intellectual illuminates this problematic better than Frantz Fanon. In his 1961 essay, 'On National Culture', Fanon, while recognising the pull of the past for African intellectuals, argued for a national culture drawn from the 'very heart of the struggle for freedom', a national culture, that is, not structured on the antiquarian efforts of an intellectual class to reassemble the fragments of precolonial traditions ruptured by the epistemic violence of colonial rule, but around the shared project of national liberation. In Fanon's words:

> While the politicians situate their action in actual present-day events, men of culture take their stand in the field of history. . . . The passion with which native intellectuals defend the existence of their national culture may be a source of amazement, but those who condemn this exaggerated passion are strangely apt to forget that their own psyche and their own selves are conveniently sheltered behind a French or German culture which has given full proof of its existence and which is uncontested.[15]

Rather than simply 'hide' or erase the precolonial past, Fanon contends that colonialism 'distorts, disfigures and destroys it'.[16] European anthropologists limited the African epic to the status of folklore, and the heroic epic, which prefigured the stage prior to the nation, would be forever beyond them. Not even the Mande heroic epic the *Sunjata*, the story of the establishment of the medieval (between 1200 and 1235) Mali empire, which stretched from Bamako to Ghana, by the warrior-king Sundiata Keita, qualified.[17] The French anthropologist Maurice Delafosse attributed the *Sunjata* to Arab traders, although Sundiata Keita established enduring political and social codes, castes, and fraternal orders which endure and structure much of Mande life to this day. The *Sunjata* is an exclusively oral tale, and it could therefore not prefigure the nation.

Indeed, the recovery of African cultural artefacts and practices is necessary beyond the psychological equilibrium it provides a peoples in their quest for self-determination. Yet Fanon encouraged African intellectuals to retain a resolutely presentist engagement with their past. If adopted, the epic, along with the vast folk traditions of the colonised, should be mobilised critically and on behalf of the struggle for the establishment of a new culture. One might say that, in the years of independence, we witnessed the simultaneous invention of Fanon's presentism in the manner in which the African epic was mobilised in forms of literary experimentation.

Throughout the continent, the kaleidoscope of epic tales provided the narrative structure of novels depicting the historical turmoil and psychological torment of empire, as well as the surreal and frantic energies of the struggle for independence. In Amos Tutuola's *My Life in the Bush of Ghosts* (1954), a novel written in the spoken vernacular of Nigerian Pidgin and detailing the misfortunes of a young boy taken captive by capricious spirits of the underworld, we see the underlying structure of the Bantu myth *Mwindo*, the story of a youth estranged from his family who must journey to the underworld to avenge the father who betrayed him. *My Life in the Bush of Ghosts* is frequently read as a model of naive fiction, wherein the oral cadence of the writing, fantastic milieu, and temporally disjointed plotline bear evidence of a proto-novel, an artefact of consciousness not fully individuated as is necessary for a modern work. However, the political philosopher Achille Mbembe wrests from the story the quintessentially modern and experimental workings of Tutuola's surreal tale of abandonment. Rather than face a conceptually unified danger in the wood, a witch set on punishing transgressive children – as is the case in many a Grimm's tale – Tutuola's anonymous youth is cast into a world governed by volatile ghosts who are grotesquely carnal in their motivations, and maddeningly unpredictable in their actions and reactions. One moment the ghosts adore the foundling, and next, just as quickly, they threaten him with violence.

Building on Fanon's observation – the colonised experience, the pragmatism and rationality of the civilising mission as caprice and irrationality –

Mbembe argues that the mirror world of the ghosts 'allows us to envision ghostly power and sovereignty as aspects of the real integral to a world of life and terror'.[18] The violent enchantment of the bush of ghosts provides a simulacrum through which the reader witnesses the workings of colonial power from the position of the precarious subject, who does not experience power as clarifying or defining, but as terrifying and disorganising. The quartet of ghosts have created an elaborate and incomprehensible hierarchy that the reader is invited to interpret as mere anarchy. Oddly, however, there is order to this anarchy, the domain of the ghosts is structured on each ghost's capricious desire for dominion over the foundling. The foundling is caught in endless negotiations and transactions that lead nowhere and produce nothing, certainly not liberty or safe being. In Grimm's tales, the violence of the witch functions as a behavioural caution, a social warning: this is what becomes of children who do not do what they are told, who fall out of the structures of social organisation, and who journey into the chaos of the wilderness. In this respect, this type of folklore marks the prehistory of the *Entwicklungsroman*, the novel of development, demonstrating through transgression acceptable social norms necessary for the emergence of a modern citizen. In this way, the epic is structured dialectically – the form of developmentalist narratives beloved by historians, social theorists, and moral philosophers.

The *Mwindo*, in its original form, functions similarly. It tells the story of the triumph of moral legitimacy; the *Mwindo* is, after all, an epic which encourages a people to look to the qualities of moral leadership over birthright when choosing a king. In many versions of the epic, the youth emerges from the underworld to take the throne, ruling alongside his morally suspect father, who sits to the left of him, not ostracised but positioned publicly in a place of diminished status. In most myths that involve a journey to the underworld, a cost to the hero is extracted in the form of loss, yet there is, in the end, something gained and something learned: but this is not the case in Tutuola's work. There is a cyclical repetitive quality to the storytelling itself. This denies the sense of forward motion of diachronic narrative – one act building on another. The fantastic and surreal are hardly the expressions of a naive attempt to mimic the epic stories of the West; it is not an expression of miscomprehension. Tutuola's depiction of the frenetic and absurd governance of the kingdom of ghosts is a sage rendition of the terrors of being ruled. What is earned in the end? What is the moral of the story? Even Demeter in her negotiation with Hades emerges with a conditional win, the shared custody of Persephone's affection. In *My Life in the Bush of Ghosts*, our hero emerges from this world of torment having learned that 'This is what hatred did.'[19] He emerges, that is, with his trauma and nothing else.

Rather than enlist the epic to retroactively confirm the modern formation of a nation, the African novel employs the epic towards a critical examination of the present; in other words, the framework of the past is only useful insofar as it is plastic, capable of being reformed and repurposed for the demands of present-day struggles. Despite its experimental usage, we should not overlook the frequency with which nationalist leaders, populists, cultural nationalists, and strongmen alike have anointed themselves as the protagonists of the national epic. While a feature of the African epic is its discontinuity, the centuries of colonialism ruptured the momentum that would have had the epic prefigure a transition to the modern nation; nationalist leaders present themselves as the inheritors of an interrupted national culture. This is particularly the case in the political landscape of Malian independence. The Mande epic the *Sunjata* became the focal point around which multiple visions of independence and national culture were considered. The breadth of Sundiata Keita's empire, comprising much of what, at the time of independence, was the entirety of French West Africa, was one of the inspirations behind Senegalese statesman Leopold Senghor's short-lived dream of a West African federation, while, in Mali, the *Sunjata* would establish legitimacy. As Manthia Diawara elaborates, 'the Griots praised Modibo Keita, the country's first president, as the direct descendant of Soundiata Keita, Emperor of Mali. After the coup d'etat in 1960, however, the same Griots hailed the new president, Moussa Traoré, as the savior of the country.'[20]

En attendant le vote des bêtes sauvages of 1998 (*Waiting for the Vote for the Wild Animals*, 2001), by the Côte d'Ivorian author Ahmadou Kourouma, narrates West African postcolonial political realities through a parody of the *donsomana*, the griot praise song meant to tell the stories of the great deeds of rulers of the past and their progeny. The critic Isaac Ndlovu argues that, despite the negative critical reception of the novel (Abiola Irele referred to it as an 'epic of African atrocity'), *Waiting for the Vote* invites us to 'think historically'.[21] In the parody of the *donsomana* form, the novel reveals the political interest of the griot. Much of the ludic and crude segments come prompted by the griot's efforts to narrate the atrocious deeds of the strongman through the laudatory framework of the praise song. Narratives of the nation told from the position of those with a psychic investment in power appear distorted, phantasmagoric. The Guadeloupian writer Maryse Condé explores the libidinal investment associated with the figure of the 'strongman', or 'father of the nation'. In the novel *Hérémakhonon* (1982), a female protagonist from the diaspora travels to West Africa in an undefined search for roots and political affiliation. She becomes romantically involved with the emerging nationalist leader, whom she refers to as 'a n—r with ancestors'; the novel depicts brilliantly the protagonist's struggle to disentangle her own investments in the fantasy of dynasty power and the political realities of the violence the maintenance of such power requires.[22]

The critical epic in African literature not only illuminates the pitfalls, ethical compromises, and individual interests that are at work in claims to power that look to re-establish continuity of rule and authority in the strongman era of postcolonial Africa. These works also focus our attention on the relationship between the epic form and historical writing in the Western tradition. In this manner, Ndlovu asserts that *Waiting for the Vote* takes on a metahistorical perspective; the reader must disaggregate the form of 'historical narration' – praise – from the content: repressive horror.[23] Moreover, the metahistorical also entreats us to reconsider the metonymic historiographic mode of the 'great man' narrative. In other words, the story of the nation can be narrated through the story of its patriarchal founders. This is frequently the default form of nationalist histories in the West, and is as frequently mimicked in the postcolonial world.

Fanon warned African intellectuals of this antiquarian use of the epic: what purpose does the framing of anti-colonial resistance through the epic story of the ancient Songhay empire serve for those disenfranchised Mande in their struggle for liberation and dignity? Indeed, the critical potential of the African epic is its engagement with the fractiousness of the present, and in the years following independence, the 1960s through the 1980s, the African novel drew much of its experimental energy from its engagement with the turbulence and elation of their present.

Whiter the Nation?

The heady questions of nation, nationalism, and national culture preoccupied African intellectuals in the years from colonisation to independence and in the immediate years following. But has the concept of the nation become a quaint anachronism at the current moment? At the end of the twentieth century, the globalised economy lauded the transnational future wherein people, goods, and information would traverse boundaries to accommodate the tastes and desires of a global marketplace. For those in the Global North, this gave way to transnational political and economic coordination in the form of the European Union and NAFTA; in the

Global South, however, transnationalism inaugurated a new stage of precarity for postcolonial people, whereby the local and national became increasingly immiserated, resulting in migration to the megacities of the south and the cities of Europe and North America. It is the cruellest and most tragic irony that, at the moment of a near universal application of globalisation, Europe and much of the Global North have resurrected virulent forms of political and economic nationalism, while the poor of the Global South have experienced globalisation's dispossession as climate refugees, economic refugees, and war refugees.

Contemporary African literature has all but abandoned the nation and nationalism as either an organising or a viable theme. The economic realities of globalisation have so transformed the continent that writing from the location of Africa's elites, expanding middle classes, and the poor no longer focuses on the fraught project that was the establishment of a national cultural identity. The novels situated in the experiences of the African elite and middle classes are no longer focused on extracting and elevating a Ghanaian or Senegalese history, or shared cultural practice from the stifling superimposition of British or French conceptual frameworks. As Chielozona Eze observes, new African writing does not focus on the particularities of region, ethnicity, or language; rather, the novels of Chris Abani, Taiye Selasi, and NoViolet Bulawayo take on an Afropolitan perspective.[24] These authors present protagonists who are not formed in and through the distorting processes of colonisation, but who are rather formed in and through the kaleidoscopic lens of the global racial imaginary. Their journeys are not those of Mustafa Sa'eed, the protagonist of Tayeb Salih's *Season of Migration to the North* (1966), whose life follows the inverse path of Conrad's Marlow: upriver to Oxford, the site of his mental undoing, and downriver to Sudan, the site of his failed reassimilation. Instead, their journeys map the erratic global flow of capital. The Afropolitan is part of a broad diaspora. Following the path of globalised opportunity, these new protagonists travel to the former Metropole – to London, Paris, or Lisbon – but they are just as at home in the Gulf States or North America. The Africa they depict is cosmopolitan; the foreign is made African, the African made foreign. They are not the diaspora born of the internationalism of anti-colonial struggle, but the diaspora formed from the contingencies of race. Eze describes this shared identity as follows: 'They are African or Afrihyphenated, and because their identities are constituted by relation rather than opposition, they present good examples of Johann v. Goethe's concept of "elective affinities" – (*Wahlverwandtschaften*) – contributing in complex ways to a fluid definition of African.'[25] This reader concurs with Eze; critics have pointed out that these new African novels are part of a creative renaissance on the continent, and they contributed to the global revitalisation of the novel form itself. Indeed, far beyond the national aspirations of the Heinemann years, the Afropolitan novel has joined the ranks of *Weltliteratur*.

While Afropolitanism insists on a measure of *sans souci* amidst the turbulence of globalisation, the novels of *migritude* – works centred on the experience of dispossession and precarity that globalisation engenders for the continent's poor – tell us another, yet equally important, story. The critic Jacques Chevrier describes contemporary African literature as defined by *migritude* – a category melding race, identity, and migration.[26] Chevrier extends *migritude* backwards to the long history of the African diaspora, the experiences of wandering, flight, and exile that are central to the literary works of Claude McKay, Richard Wright, and Aimé Césaire. For intellectuals of the diaspora, nationhood and national belonging were foreclosed. Any sense of a collective culture or history would, from necessity, be drawn from the shared Black experience that did not hold nation as a unifying concept – Blackness is transnational. The lessons of diaspora authors collide with Paul Gilroy's assessment of Black culture as an identity born in the turbulent formation of global modernity.[27] To be Black is to be forever homeless, Gilroy declares; and the work of so many Afro-European artists and intellectuals coalesces around this very sensibility: John Akomfrah's *The Nine Muses* (2010) and *Handsworth Songs* (1986), two films that are visual meditations on migration, history, and the experience of uprootedness and belonging for Black Britons of the Windrush generation, come immediately to mind. Contemporary African literature of *migritude* rejects the problematic of nationalism, and instead centres itself on the dislocated, the marginalised, and the peripatetic lives of African migrants. The work of the novelists Fatou Diome (*Le ventre de l'Atlantique*, 2003 [*The Belly of the Atlantic*, 2006]) and Marie N'Diaye (*Trois femmes puissantes*, 2009 [*Three Strong Women*, 2012]), and of the filmmaker Mati Diop (*Atlantiques*, 2009), perform what Christina Sharpe has described as 'wake work'.[28] Sharpe builds the concept of 'wake work' around a polysemic understanding of 'wake', a word that describes at once the mourning ritual and the physical phenomena of the trace disturbances caused by a body moving through water or air. Wakes are 'processes' whereby 'we think about the dead and about our relations to them'.[29]

Migritude is a form of 'wake work' because these narratives trace migrant lives that are formed through grief and loss. Moreover, like Gilroy's diaspora, the 'wake' directs our attention to the sea, to the terrifying yet formative shared experience of Black people and the Atlantic. Indeed, 'the sea is history', to invoke Derek Walcott, and the 'wake' is the figurative location wherein a diasporic identity forged in the tragedy of the Atlantic slave trade converges with the ongoing cycle of migrant deaths at sea.[30] Perhaps it is in this void that the African novel has cast the concept of nation, along with the work of conceptualising 'national culture'.

Notes

1 See the title and the introduction in Amartya Sen, *The Birthright Lottery: Citizenship and Global Inequality* (Cambridge, MA: Harvard University Press, 2009).

2 Benedict Anderson, *Imagined Communities: Reflections on the Origins and Spread of Nationalism* (London: Verso, 1983).

3 Theodore Zeldin, *France, 1848–1945*, Vol. 2: *Intellect, Taste and Anxiety* (Oxford: Oxford University Press, 1977), p. 5.

4 Otto von Bismarck, *Die Gesammelten Werke*, ed. Hermann von Petersdorff, 15 vols. (Berlin: Otto Stolberg, 1924–35), Vol. 8, p. 646.

5 Jerome Brooks, Interview with Chinua Achebe, 'The Art of Fiction, No. 139', *The Paris Review* 133 (Winter 1994). Available at www.theparisreview.org/interviews/1720/the-art-of-fiction-no-139-chinua-achebe (accessed 10 September 2021).

6 Yinka Shonibare, 'Art 21' (2009). Available at https://art21.tumblr.com/post/42934512845/my-figures-dont-have-any-kind-of-facial-features (accessed 10 September 2021).

7 Thea Büttner and Hans-Ulrich Walter, eds., *Colonialism, Neo-colonialism, and the Anti-Imperialist Struggle in Africa: Marxist Studies on the Berlin Conference 1884/85* (Berlin: Akademie-Verlag, 1984), p. 8.

8 'Colloquium on "The Centenary of The Berlin Conference: 1884–1885": Brazzaville: March 30–April 5, 1985: Final Report', *Présence Africaine* NS 133/134 (1985), pp. 280–90 (p. 282).

9 Phaswane Mpe, 'The Role of the Heinemann African Writers Series in the Development and Promotion of African Literature', *African Studies* 58.1 (1999), pp. 105–22 (p. 110).

10 See Wendy Griswold, *Bearing Witness: Readers, Writers, and the Novel in Nigeria* (Princeton, NJ: Princeton University Press, 2000).

11 Gareth Griffiths, 'Documentation and Communication in Postcolonial Societies: The Politics of Control', *Yearbook of English Studies* 27, Special Issue: 'The Politics of Postcolonial Criticism' (1997), pp. 130–6. Quoted in Mpe, 'The Role of the Heinemann African Writers Series', p. 111.

12 Chinua Achebe, *Things Fall Apart* (New York: Random House, 1994), p. 205.

13 Ngũgĩ wa Thiong'o, *Decolonizing the Mind: The Politics of Language in African Literature* (London: James Currey, 1981), p. 28.

14 Frantz Fanon, 'On National Culture', *Wretched of the Earth*, trans. Constance Farrington (New York: Grove Press, 1963), pp. 206–48 (p. 233).

15 Ibid., p. 209.

16 Ibid., p. 210.

17 The *Sunjata* is an exclusively oral tale, performed every seven years during the Kamabolon ceremony in Kangaba, Mali. While it is in parts improvisational, and elements of Dogon myth, genealogy, and the Koran are incorporated, the core element of the performance is the recitation of the *Sunjata* epic.

18 Achille Mbembe, 'Life, Sovereignty, and Terror in the Fiction of Amos Tutuola', *Research in African Literatures* 34.4 (Winter 2004), pp. 1–26 (p. 1).

19 Amos Tutuola, *The Palm-Wine Drinkard and My Life in the Bush of Ghosts* (New York: Grove Press, 1994), p. 174.

20 Manthia Diawara, 'Canonizing Soundiata in Mande Literature: Toward a Sociology of Narrative Elements', *Social Text* 31/32, 'Third World and Post-Colonial Issues' (1992), pp. 154–68 (p. 157).

21 Abiola Irele, cited in Isaac Ndlovu, 'Poverty in Freedom versus Opulence in Chains: Satirical Exposé of the Postcolonial Dictatorships in Kourouma's *Waiting for the Wild Beasts to Vote*', *Theoria: A Journal of Social and Political Theory* 59.130 (2012), pp. 59–86 (p. 67).

22 Maryse Condé, *Hérémakhonon* (Washington, DC: Three Continents Press, 1982), p. 24.

23 Ndlovu, 'Poverty in Freedom versus Opulence in Chains'.

24 Chielozona Eze, 'Rethinking African Culture and Identity: The Afropolitan Model', *Journal of African Cultural Studies* 26.2 (2014), pp. 234–47.

25 Ibid., p. 235.

26 Jacques Chevrier, *Littératures francophones d'Afrique noire* (Aix en Provence: Edisud, 2006).

27 Paul Gilroy, *The Black Atlantic: Modernity and Double-Consciousness* (Cambridge, MA: Harvard University Press, 1993), pp. 112–35.

28 Christina Sharpe, *In the Wake: On Blackness and Being* (Durham, NC: Duke University Press, 2016).

29 Ibid., p. 15.

30 Derek Walcott, 'The Sea Is History', *The Selected Poems of Derek Walcott* (New York: Farrar, Straus & Giroux, 2007), p. 364.

CHAPTER 13

Apartheid

Corinne Sandwith

The April 1950 edition of *The Voice* magazine – a small, mimeographed periodical published from the Johannesburg township of Orlando – featured a piece by regular contributor 'Naledi', penname of Es'kia Mphahlele. The subject was a recent Yehudi Menuhin concert, belatedly arranged for Black audiences after opposition arose to the fact that the renowned violinist would only appear before whites:

> It is all over now – the Menuhin concert. I'm not a music critic and all that. I listened with my native ear, surrendered myself to the effects of the music. I don't know anything about E minor or E major. They mean nothing to my simple untutored mind ... But Bach's concerto in E major and Mendelssohn's in E Minor brought that night 'sensations sweet, felt in the blood and felt along the heart' and 'feelings too of unremembered pleasure,' as Wordsworth says ... So, if on hearing that music I may have seen some maiden 'amid the alien corn,' 'faery lands forlorn,' 'the crystal streams,' a river flowing 'through caverns measureless to man down to a sunless sea,' or 'meandering in a mazy motion,' or 'alone upon a branch that's bare, a trembling leaf left behind' or may have heard the wailing of 'a God in pain,' it is because the height of poetic truth reached by the composer ... struck on the lyrical strings of my being.[1]

In this intervention, Mphahlele undertakes a self-effacing, sardonic protest against the cultural exclusion of Blacks institutionalised by apartheid, via a parody of native ignorance and a flamboyant, excessive assemblage of high romantic reference. Assuming the pose of the exemplary romantic sufferer, Mphahlele makes an emotive appeal, in the mode of W. E. B. Du Bois's *The Souls of Black Folk* (1903), for the right to participate in a humanist culture, and reinforces his claim through the conspicuous, accumulative performance of Western civilisational accomplishment.

In another example of writing during apartheid published in *Staffrider* magazine in 1979, Durban poet Mafika Gwala takes up a defence not of Black rights to a proscribed culture, but, rather, of the recent efflorescence of political poetry by Black writers and the Black Consciousness philosophy which underpinned it:

> People who tamper with Black Consciousness and the Black Experience better watch it from now: the days of paradisal innocence are over. Anyone who has an intellectual or moral quarrel with black terms of reference within the given reality of white baaskap and black depravity is on the other side of the line. And therefore in favour of the status quo ... [I wish] to point out that Black Consciousness does not mean politics disguised as literature. Neither does it mean 'anti-white' writing, as some headshrinkers love to categorise. Black Consciousness helps to fight the bourgeois, and at times, neo-fascist context of white terms of reference within the apartheid reality. Black Consciousness, to us, means the structuring of an alternative context to the apartheid context. As Herbert Marcuse aptly pointed out [. . .]: 'One must revoke the Ninth Symphony not only because it is wrong and false (we cannot and should not sing an ode to joy, not even as promise) but also because it is there and it is true in its own right. It stands in our universe as the justification of the "illusion which is no longer justifiable"'. Apartheid is there; in its own right on terms determined by a selfish minority. We revoke it.[2]

The differences in tone, register, and political purpose could not be more striking. Where Mphahlele deploys the mode of ambivalent, ironic mimicry, Gwala is confrontational, direct, and uncompromising. Where Mphahlele grounds an appeal for inclusion in the performance of civility, Gwala points to a racially polarised political field and draws on the emancipatory possibilities of radical critical theory in order to revoke bourgeois high culture in its entirety and to expose its oppressive political effects. Especially noteworthy is the interpolation of the arguments of Frankfurt School critic Herbert Marcuse within a Black Consciousness problematic; in particular, the reimagining of Marcuse's gesture of cultural repudiation in explicitly racial terms.

Both these interventions arose in response to the iniquities of apartheid, a political-economic system of institutionalised racial discrimination inaugurated under the National Party government in 1948, but which built on, and intensified, an already well-established segregationist regime. The differences in their responses have everything to do with the history that separates them: Gwala's more acerbic engagement takes its cue from the immediate context of the 1970s Black Consciousness movement and the new spirit of militant civic resistance and mass political organisation which was met with a corresponding escalation of state violence and repression. Prior to this, the 1950s saw the entrenchment of an inferior

'Bantu Education', the institution of a plethora of racially discriminatory laws, and a massive project of social-spatial re-engineering. Particularly decisive were the 1960s anti-pass protests in Sharpeville, Langa, and Nyanga townships, which left sixty-nine protesters dead and which culminated in the banning of political organisations and the arrest and imprisonment of their leaders. This was followed, in June 1976, by the Soweto student uprising in which hundreds of school children were gunned down by police, an event which also precipitated country-wide demonstrations against the apartheid regime.[3]

I highlight these cultural interventions not only as an important index of changing historical-political circumstances and the cultural responses they conditioned, but also as a striking exemplification of a long and vital history of dissident cultural debate in South Africa and its broader political significance. What is claimed here, and what these examples amply demonstrate, is that political struggles in apartheid South Africa were frequently articulated in cultural terms and that forms of political critique often took shape as arguments about culture and the reading of texts. This history of cultural radicalism and the oppositional public sphere offers a particularly productive approach to the literature and politics of apartheid.

As suggested, this chapter's contribution to an understanding of the historical relationship between politics and literature is centred on the history of dissident cultural debate. It is principally concerned with the ways in which political claims were refracted in the cultural sphere and the changes and continuities in this discourse over time. As such, it departs from a more conventional history of the celebrated oppositional texts and figures of the anti-apartheid canon, in order to foreground the cultural discussions that circled around and informed them. In this way, it invokes a thicker discursive/intellectual history, elucidating what might be seen as a 'hidden transcript' of political engagement alongside more spectacular, visible examples of literary-cultural resistance and political dissent.[4] This engagement with the relationship between literature and politics – one which also exemplifies their multiple complicities – is oriented towards the wider public sphere of dissident cultural engagement: to the periodicals, discussion groups, and little magazines of an oppositional cultural tradition, the publics they convened, and the debates they staged. These included questions of racial 'advancement', cultural exclusion, precolonial culture, creolisation, the social function of art, Western academic authority, the figure of the artist, the role of the audience, and, crucially, the reading and interpretation of literary-cultural texts. This long history of apartheid cultural radicalism is only available in the present as the traces, ruins, and fragments of a larger and more complex historical unfolding. I approach these traces here with the aim of reconstructing something of their wider historical significance.

Traditions of literary-cultural radicalism do not emerge *sui generis* as an efflorescence of apartheid structural violence, but rather build on earlier dissenting traditions. Among these are the heterodox reading practices associated with the nineteenth-century Ethiopianist church movement, as well as the energetic literary-cultural debates that resonated across nineteenth-century Black print culture. Early twentieth-century traditions developed in close proximity with the Communist Party of South Africa (CPSA), as well as in a number of Trotskyist-linked discussion groups such as the New Era Fellowship (NEF). The late 1930s also saw the emergence of the South African chapter of the Left Book Club and, in 1938, the launch of the *Guardian* newspaper. These, along with *Trek* magazine and *Fighting Talk*, became important sites of left-leaning cultural discussion throughout the 1940s. Various interventions by H. I. E. Dhlomo – appearing across several journals and newspapers – also comprise an important counter-cultural engagement, this time oriented towards an Africanist revisioning of South African literary-cultural history.[5] Centres of radical cultural discussion in the late 1940s include *The Torch*, a publication of the Non-European Unity Movement (NEUM), *The Voice*, the *Guardian*, *The Citizen*, *Spark*, and *Liberation*, along with several left-aligned fellowships and discussion groups.[6] The launch of Nat Nakasa's *The Classic* in 1963 inaugurated a new phase in this history, as post-Sharpeville repression began to take its toll on the lives of writers and the bounds of permissible speech. This was followed in the mid-1970s by Sipho Sepamla's *New Classic*, Jaki Seroke's revived *Classic*, and the launch in 1978 of *Staffrider* magazine, along with a range of community-based theatre and writers' groups.[7]

Many of the literary-cultural interventions of the late 1930s and early 1940s adopted a distinctive mode of satirical deflation. This was in order to expose a key assumption of the liberal political traditions of the early Cape colony in which the 'non-racial' franchise was made contingent on the demonstration of certain property and educational qualifications. Intellectuals associated with the NEF derided this 'spurious cult of respectability', which called for the conspicuous demonstration of civilisational 'advancement', as a 'state of chronic expectation' in which people waited to be declared 'fully human'.[8] The satirical posture was a key rhetorical tactic

of R. R. R. Dhlomo's 'Roamer' column in the *Bantu World* newspaper, as it
was in the political polemics of *Trek* and *The Voice*. In the popular column
'Rabelais and His World' which appeared in *The Voice* from the late 1940s,
Mphahlele satirised Afrikaner nationalism in the figure of 'Baas Pieter' and
the society of 'Rooikop'. This playfully resistant stance is also exemplified in
satirical rewritings of Western canonical texts, such as Milton's *Paradise Lost*
and Byron's 'Vision of Judgement', which are simultaneously honoured and
disfigured as heretical commentaries on Afrikaner nationalism and the
absurdities of apartheid rule. The satirical mode continues into the late
1950s and early 1960s, as evident, for example, in Alex La Guma's *New Age*
column 'Up My Alley', Nakasa's articles in the *Rand Daily Mail*, and Casey
Motsisi's 'On the Beat' column in *Drum*. A closely allied rhetorical strategy –
which was also a distinctive feature of the writing of both R. R. R. Dhlomo
and NEF intellectual Ben Kies – had to do with the English language itself,
undermined from within through various practices of verbal play, stylistic
virtuosity, linguistic and semantic disruption, deformation, and excess. This
strategy was key to the political polemics in *The Torch*, in which a general
stance of questioning and refusal was augmented with the stylistic devices of
hyperbole, malapropism, syntactical and grammatical deviance, and the
provocative rejection of prevailing conventions of polite speech. The above
examples confirm not only the political traction of the ironic and satirical
modes in South African letters, but also the importance of the semiotic arena
itself as a space in which dominant codes are unwritten or 'defaced'. The
oblique tactics of the underdog are replaced in the post-Sharpeville period
with more unequivocal and outspoken, but equally experimental and transgressive, styles.

  As Mphahlele's article indicates, the cultural debates of the 1950s were
dominated by claims to the right to participate in and enjoy Western 'high
culture', a right which was increasingly being denied by the apartheid state:
by 'the little, frightened, selfish, racialistic men who govern our country'
who have decreed that culture is for 'Europeans Only'.[9] Black intellectuals
took issue with disingenuous state rationalisations of apartheid as a means
of defending cultural 'purity' through the repetitive, often ironic, assertion
of a modern, urbanised, cosmopolitan identity. This was evidenced in part
in the performative mode: in the practices of incessant citation, interpolation, and rewriting of Western canonical texts. It was also evident in an
important early theorisation of culture as a transnational and unbounded
space of encounter, one which is inevitably enmeshed with, invigorated,
and contaminated by adjacent cultural-intellectual systems. In extended
discussions in the periodical press, cultural activists emphasised historical,

spatial, and cultural entanglement, drawing on biological tropes of cross-pollination, diversity, and sterility to undermine normative ideas of genea-logical and racial purity. They presented a view of cultural identity as syncretised, layered, complex – as the sum of multiple contributing streams – and opposed an ethno-patrilineal view of cultural inheritance with a model of cultural transmission based on affiliation and adjacency. As Mphahlele's article makes clear, in the hyper-racialised environments of 1950s South Africa, the performance of Western cultural accomplishment constitutes a central oppositional mode; it takes shape not as the spurning of Western culture but, rather, as an assertion of entitlement to a 'world culture'.

Resistant political gestures were also inscribed in the act of reading itself, in the ways in which literature was interpreted and assessed, in various modes of parsing the text and of understanding its place in the world. Central to the reading practices of the 1950s was the question of the relationship between politics and art. Against a hegemonic guild-based insistence on the separation of art and politics, and a corresponding hostility to the arts of political inscription, cultural activists argued for their mutual imbrication and entanglement. This is evident not only in an understanding of literature as inflected in various ways by the broader socio-political context, but also in assumptions about its epistemological value as a means of telling the 'truth' about the social world against the obfuscations and evasions of the colonial-apartheid state. In these contexts, the practice of literary analysis becomes a central means of attacking and exposing dominant apartheid logics.

The relationship between politics and literature was taken up in various ways. In the reading communities of the Stalinist Left, the literary-cultural text was approached as a site of political emancipation and education. Emphasis was placed on a left-wing canon and privilege was granted to the modes of documentary realism and testimony, as well as the literary depiction of social abjection, working-class agency, and heroic resistance. In this way, a dissenting cultural politics took shape in part as the reassign-ment of aesthetic and social value against dominant representational regimes. Black intellectuals in particular placed emphasis on the literary representation of secular Black modernity as part of ongoing polemics against de-urbanisation. They welcomed what they saw as an important shift from the politically evasive 'moral-dealing' stories of the colonial mission tradition, to those depicting 'the slumdom of the gold-mining compounds [and] the fenced, ghetto-reminiscent "Native location"', and anticipated the emergence of a 'faithless, but vigorous literature of frustration, protest, indignation, abusive and iconoclastic rebellion'.[10] Similar calls throughout the 1950s for a socially engaged artistic practice against art of the 'ivory tower' were to be found across a wide range of oppositional forums.

Those drawing more closely on classical Marxist traditions advocated a historicising reading practice that sought to locate literary texts and their authors within their social-material contexts. Jack Cope's 'Art and the People' column in the *Guardian* and its successor paper *New Age*, took up this methodology in order to resurrect a radical, resistant writing tradition against the de-politicisation of literature by mainstream critics. Dora Taylor and other NEUM intellectuals were less interested in the radical text per se as in developing an oppositional critical practice. They sought to draw out the social implications of literary texts – irrespective of their political provenance – as a means of engaging with the contemporary political scene, and advocated a Lukácsian aesthetic that placed emphasis on the rendering of historical process and connection rather than static spectacle. In keeping with their Trotskyist sympathies, they took a much more circumspect view of the idea of art as a 'weapon of struggle' and questioned the value of attempting to 'sjambok' the reader into political enlightenment. These interventions mark the beginnings of an important tension in South African letters between those who advocated the literature of unbridled opposition and those who cautioned against overt didacticism and the literature of spectacle.

A striking early example of these resistant reading traditions is to be found in A. C. Jordan's opening address to the 1946 conference of the Teachers' League of South Africa.[11] Here, Jordan undertakes a radical re-reading of Shakespeare's *The Tempest* as a means of engaging with the repressive function of education and the futility of civilised aspiration in contexts of racial violence. In this unorthodox critical intervention – moving easily between the conventionally polarised modes of critical exegesis and political polemic – a canonical Western text is compelled to speak to the colonial-apartheid scene.

In 1950s debates, the argument that no text is politically neutral is accompanied by an important early theorisation of the role of culture in fostering and augmenting racial hierarchies and exclusions. According to one commentator, culture is 'simply one of the implements with which the Herrenvolk work to keep the Non-Europeans mentally bound'.[12] Cultural activists responded to the problem of mental enslavement with a broad-based 'hermeneutics of suspicion' and a pervasive practice of ideological critique centred on the violence of representation and the politics of the text. Many such interventions were directed towards identifying examples of racist distortion and stereotyping in South African 'white writing'. A particularly resonant example is the response that greeted the publication of a glowing review of Alan Paton's *Cry, the Beloved Country* (1948). The review, published in *The Torch*, elicited a flood of letters pointing to its 'dope-peddling' politics, its reinforcement of re-tribalisation, and its elevation of political quiescence. In the resulting polemical fallout, the hapless reviewer was called upon to explain his 'political creed'.[13]

The reading communities associated with NEUM and *The Voice* are noteworthy for their pervasive practice of questioning and critique, and an interrogative rather than deferential reading practice, in which literary criticism is explicitly refashioned as a mode of political engagement. In this view, literary criticism is 'social criticism': it is 'charged with judgement' and 'rooted in the need for social change'.[14] In these and other forums, literary texts are drawn into wider debates about political complicity, organisational strategy, and the limits of African nationalism. As such, the literary artefact is reimagined as a kind of intellectual commons or public sphere; it is approached not as the privileged object of a revered canon but as just one of the elements in a wider discursive field.

While practices of ideological critique continue into the early 1960s, a far more compelling mode from the 1970s onwards was to be found in the genre of revisionist literary historiography. This includes an explicit emphasis on reversing the distortions of the colonial library as well as on traditional forms and indigenous languages, seen as dynamic sites of adaptation rather than static repositories of conservative values. Key literary mappings in this regard include A. C. Jordan's articles in *Africa South* in the late 1950s, several histories of Black literature published in *Fighting Talk* in 1957, as well as a series of key interventions in *The Classic, New Classic*, and *Staffrider* by Mbulelo Mzamane, Mphahlele, Gwala, Daniel Kunene, Zakes Mda, and Richard Rive.

The art/politics debate only intensified in the cultural discussions of the 1970s and 1980s, with similar, although more disconcerting, implications for the Western critical consensus. Foregrounded in the introductory comments of all three Black-edited literary magazines launched during this period (*The Classic*, 1965; *New Classic*, 1975; and *The Classic*, 1982), it was also central to a number of critical interventions by Gwala, Mzamane, Dikobe Ben Martins, Mda, and Mphahlele, all of whom take up an extended defence of the necessity of political inscription in the arts in the face of growing white/establishment hostility and the ideology of 'art for art's sake'. These arguments derive less from a Marxist understanding of culture than from the experiential knowledge of Black life under apartheid, which, as Nakasa, Mzamane, and many others argued, is inherently political: 'art and politics in South Africa [. . .] have become inseparable for the simple reason that politics pervade all aspects of a black man's existence'. In such a context, a writer is 'unimportant, irrelevant and probably alienated unless he is political'.[15] For Seroke, art as the 'conscience of society' is imbued with the broader cultural aim of contributing to 'the growth of the African people's languages, history and culture', as part of a wider anti-colonial intervention.[16] These and other arguments for political purpose are bolstered by a renewed interest in traditional African understandings of art as socially useful, people-oriented, and community based. These were accompanied by a number of Black-centred literary histories, which set out to restore a suppressed tradition of political resistance in the arts.

As in the radical pre-Sharpeville traditions, literature is not confined to the printed page but is understood as reaching outwards – as judgement, exposé, inspiration, education, and catalyst – to the wider social reality. In this period, there is a continued emphasis on gritty social realism, the valorisation of intemperance and immoderation, and the representation of contemporary Black experience as against a nostalgic return to the past. What distinguishes these debates from those of the pre-Sharpeville era is the impetus of the new Black Consciousness philosophy; in particular, its more pointed and more racialised understanding of the importance of the cultural sphere for a revindication of Blackness against demeaning apartheid designations as a 'necessary precondition to total freedom'.[17] For Steve Biko and other Black Consciousness advocates, culture is understood as playing a crucial role in the 'psychological and physical liberation of black people in South Africa' and in instigating a new emphasis on Black self-definition and agency.[18]

Biko's call for a 'culture of defiance' and the associated assertion, 'Black man you are on your own!' was echoed across the literary-cultural scene.[19] It is evident in an unorthodox refusal of the conventions of polite speech – as in Mongane Wally Serote's 1972 poem, 'What's in this Black "Shit"?' – as well as in the emergence of a new pared-down, colloquial style and the gestures of apocalyptic resistance:[20]

> and they say that that the people
> are a happy people [. . .]
> not knowing that our smiles
> are the masks we wear to cover
> the rage stirred up that will
> jump out and tear white arrogance
> apart [. . .][21]

Central to this aesthetics of resistance, affirmation, and renewal is the preoccupation with the representation of Black experience and Black perspectives. As such, Black Consciousness played a central role in the reframing of the wider epistemological and representational field, in unmaking dominant orders of meaning, and in 'shifting the geography of reasoning'.[22]

As in the earlier tradition, cultural activists asserted an alternative set of cultural claims in direct contention with a powerful institutional consensus and, increasingly, against the 'misleading enemy critic'.[23] As Peter Horn points out, 'this new generation of blacks conceived of the western literary conceptions as an integral part of western imperialism'.[24] This period sees a particular and pointed resistance to Arnoldian and Leavisian conceptions of artistic detachment and disinterestedness, and the related dismissal of Black literature and poetry as 'nothing more than "shrill, hysterical, thinly disguised political propaganda"'.[25] For Mzamane, it is 'ridiculous to expect sweet Handelian music from the oppressed, unless the oppressed acquiesce to sing like the slaves of old, for their master's gratification'.[26] Gwala makes a similar point, alerting readers to the absurdity of transposing nineteenth-century British ideals to the South African apartheid context: 'We cannot and shall never have the free art of "disinterested endeavour after man's perfection" in a society that is rotten to the core.'[27] In a later piece, Gwala reframes the question in the language of rights, arguing that Black writers 'have a human right to claim a sociological imagination that challenges their sociological locale'; in this view, the arts of political resistance are understood as an important mode of survival: you either 'swim out of the muddy and polluted waters of apartheid society or drown'.[28]

What is striking about these interventions – all of which work against a simple polarisation of politicised art and literary craft – is that the valuing of the literature of commitment is also accompanied by persistent anxieties about aesthetic quality. This is evident in Nakasa's insistence that *The Classic* publish only literature of 'merit', and continues in Sepamla's 1975 call for a form of loose literary guardianship rather than overt prescription, in order to defend against a publishing practice made absolutely contingent on political commentary about the 'black man's condition'.[29] For others, like Mzamane and Chris van Wyk, political utility and aesthetic sophistication are seen as mutually reinforcing rather than exclusive.

As already indicated, post-Soweto cultural critique is dominated by a range of engagements which sought to contest and thereby diminish the influence of Western critical models. Critics pointed to a pervasive tendency to view African literature through 'Western spectacles', and the

serious misreadings that could result. On the critical reception of Oswald
Mbuyiseni Mtshali's poetry collection, *Sounds of a Cowhide Drum* (1971),
for example, Mzamane writes: 'I like Mtshali's [work] for reasons completely different from those that have been advanced by whites': 'not
because Mtshali evinces Blake's simplicity and innocence . . . (not because
he's worked as a messenger boy, either) but because he approximates the
pulse of the township'.[30] In similar fashion, Sepamla, writing on the eve of
the 1976 Soweto uprising, urges Black writers not to 'pander to the whims
of white taste' but to foreground a distinctive Black experience,
a preoccupation which he traces to much earlier cultural interventions
such as Mphahlele's *Man Must Live* (1946).[31] Resistance to dominant
aesthetic regimes translated into suspicion of those writers – like Mtshali
and Amos Tutuola – who had been embraced by the white establishment,
and a corresponding sympathy for poets like Serote who had been pigeon-
holed and therefore marginalised as 'radical' and even 'racist'. The debate
reaches a steely apotheosis in Ayi Kwei Armah's critique of US scholar
Charles Larson's *The Emergence of African Fiction* (1972), just one of many
indications of the ways in which local debates intersected with a wider Pan-
Africanist discussion. In this piece, Armah offers a quietly enraged dissec-
tion of some of the key axioms of white supremacist criticism: the denial of
African provenance, the dismissal of African readerships, and the reading
of Black texts as mimicry of 'Western masters'.[32]

Against the universalising claims of the Western literary tradition, Black
Consciousness writers called for the formation of a distinctive Black
aesthetic, based in part on the communal-participatory conventions of
African oral traditions.[33] In the volatile 1980s, critics called for a new Black-
centred scholarship, for Black critics to seize the tools of interpretation and
analysis from the 'monopoly of aliens and outsiders' and to develop
specifically Black standards of judgement.[34] This was seen as an important
practice of self-definition and 're-interpretation'.[35] Mutloatse, for his part,
departs from the language of 'aliens' and 'outsiders' to offer a more
damning charge of moral bankruptcy: 'We are not going to be told how
to relive our feelings by anyone who speaks from the platform of a rickety
culture.'[36]

The refusal of white judgement extended well beyond Mothobi
Mutloatse's oft-cited call to 'donder' literary convention, one which was
rendered in the deliberately provocative, proscribed images of the bodily
grotesque.[37] It was also evident in a wider concern with a pervasive structure of white domination, direction, and control. This 'doctrine of white
proxy' was understood as both material and ideological, evident both in

material practices and the realm of representation.[38] As Sepamla asserts at the launch of *New Classic*: 'we are tired of being spoken for, thought about and wheeled around. This memory of our blackness we want to obliterate. Now is the time to articulate new definitions.'[39] Like others, Sepamla proposes both a demythologising of Blackness and a more profound structural change. The call for Black writers to seize the means of cultural production was accompanied by a shift away from what Fhazel Johennesse and Neil Alwyn Williams describe as speaking 'to the deaf ears of those in power' and towards a new, more defiant act of self-definition orientated towards the Black community itself: instead of '[blaming] ourselves on history', 'we have taken our history [. . .] and repossessed it'.[40]

A striking new emphasis in the cultural debates of the period concerns the politics of the publishing field, evident in Nakasa's remarks on the growing international interest in material from Africa leading to a 'vigorous, almost frantic search for African writing', and also taken up in Lewis Nkosi's probing questions in a series of interviews with contemporary writers and critics which addressed the Western publishing industry itself: its desire for exotica, its framing of African literature as sociological record, and its widespread assumption that African writers modelled their work on Western examples.[41] It continued in ongoing debates in the 1970s about the problems Black writers experienced at the hands of a white-controlled publishing industry, a concern which was answered in part by the formation in 1982 of the African Writers Association.[42]

The emergence of *Staffrider* in 1978 was a powerful and subversive response to this white-dominated cultural context, one which also altered the contemporary literary-cultural scene in profound ways. Positioned in opposition to 'officially sanctioned culture and its concomitant aims of domination', the magazine carved out a democratic, community based, and quotidian space of cultural production away from the institutional gaze, and went out of its way to encourage publication by young and inexperienced writers.[43] An advert for *Staffrider* exhorted readers to 'Tune into the voice of South Africa's people', a claim to community representation facilitated by its close connections with Black Consciousness-inspired township cultural groups. In this way, the magazine reinforced a move towards a more democratic understanding of the writer/audience relationship and a more participatory, reciprocal aesthetic. Central to the project of cultural democratisation was the attempt to wrest editorial control away from powerful institutions and personalities through the adoption of a loose editorial structure and a practice of self-editing, in which decisions about literary merit were handed over to the writers themselves. While some expressed reservations about this practice, others saw its value as a means of widening opportunity and access, thus securing the magazine's primary function as a lively community forum.

Staffrider was also striking for its 'kaleidoscopic and eclectic mix of written and visual materials', a combination which set it apart from the more sober formats of contemporary literary magazines.[44] Innovations in genre are evident in the space it gave to the non-canonical genres of autobiography and oral storytelling as part of a wider attempt to '[prise] history from the death grip of the rulers'.[45] The popular 'Soweto Speaking' feature, based on interviews with working people by Miriam Tlali, 'turned "everyman" into an author' and produced an important public storytelling archive.[46] The project of cultural democratisation was also pursued in the magazine's reviews section and a related 'Reading Revolution' initiative, in which readers were encouraged to write reviews on the basis of regular lists of recommended books in the field of African literature. An open forum in which ordinary people were encouraged to take on the positions of literary critic and cultural adjudicator, it facilitated important debates about the role of art in perpetuating oppression, the work of Western criticism in mitigating literary radicalism, and the definition of an oppositional aesthetic. By including a number of pieces on women's writing, as well as a controversial women's section, the magazine also initiated an important discussion of gender issues.

What binds this resistant cultural history is the defence of political art, the concern with the representation of Black history and experience, the refusal of Western aesthetic and cultural norms, and the promotion of alternative interpretive and evaluative schemes. There are also important discontinuities: a decisive shift from sardonic critique and the partial, ambiguous occupation of a humanist Western culture to a much more deep-rooted and uncompromising refusal of what is understood as an inherently racialised terrain comprising white terms of reference, Western 'bourgeois' artefacts, and white regulation. This is accompanied by a sharpened understanding of the role of Western culture in propping up imperialist schemes, and a much more emphatic turn to Black intellectuals and writers as mediators of their own experience and aesthetic judgements as a step towards the 'repossession of history'. This chapter has approached the literature and politics of apartheid via an exploration of the hidden transcript of cultural-political debate and the dissident public sphere. It thus highlights an interstitial history of popular cultural discussion – as against the more celebrated anti-apartheid canon – as a means of extending our understanding of the intricate and varied ways in which the cultural field is implicated in the political sphere, both in the exercise of oppression and in the articulation of dissent.

Notes

1 'Naledi' [Es'kia Mphahlele], 'Yehudi Menuhin: True Artist, True Man', *The Voice* (April 1950), p. 10.
2 Mafika Gwala, 'Black Writing Today', *Staffrider* (July/August 1979), p. 17.
3 For details, see Saul Dubow, *Apartheid, 1948–1994* (Oxford: Oxford University Press, 2014).
4 James C. Scott, *Domination and the Arts of Resistance: Hidden Transcripts* (New Haven, CT: Yale University Press, 1990), p. xii.
5 See, for example, H. I. E. Dhlomo's essay, 'Zulu Folk Poetry', *New Teachers' Journal* (April 1948), reprinted in Michael Chapman, ed., *Soweto Poetry: Literary Perspectives* (Pietermaritzburg: University of KwaZulu-Natal Press, 2007), pp. 30–5.
6 Corinne Sandwith, *World of Letters: Reading Communities and Cultural Debates in Early Apartheid South Africa* (Pietermaritzburg: University of KwaZulu-Natal Press, 2014), pp. 129–215.
7 Bhekizizwe Peterson, 'Culture, Resistance and Representation', in *The Road to Democracy in South Africa*, Vol. 2: *1970–1980*, ed. South African Democracy Education Trust (Pretoria: UNISA Press, 2006), pp. 161–86.
8 Ben Kies, 'The Revolt of Youth', *Cape Standard*, 7 June 1938, p. 9; Kies, 'Colouredisation – or Citizenship?', *The Educational Journal* (August 1956), pp. 20–4 (p. 20).
9 Es'kia Mphahlele, 'Othello', 'Open Letter to the Old Vic Company', *The Spark* (1952), p. 5.
10 Woodroffe Mbete, 'Non-European Writers', *Trek* (25 January 1946), p. 14.
11 Archibald Campbell Jordan, '. . . That Our Children May Live', reprinted in *The Educational Journal* (August 1946), p. 4.
12 C. Peters, 'Censorship and Immoral Literature', *The Educational Journal* (October 1954), p. 6.
13 Sandwith, *World of Letters*, pp. 164–6.
14 Dora Taylor, 'The Function of Literary Criticism', unpublished lecture to the NEF (1953).
15 Mbulelo V. Mzamane, 'Literature and Politics among Blacks in South Africa', *New Classic* 5 (1978), pp. 42–57 (p. 42).
16 Jaki Seroke, 'Comment', *The Classic* 3.1 (1984), p. 4.
17 Peterson, 'Culture, Resistance and Representation', p. 168.
18 Thengani Ngwenya, 'Black Consciousness Poetry: Writing Against Apartheid', in *The Cambridge History of South African Literature*, ed. David Attwell and Derek Attridge (Cambridge: Cambridge University Press, 2012), pp. 500–522 (p. 519).
19 Steve Biko, *I Write What I Like: A Selection of Writings* (London: Heinemann, 1989), pp. 46, 97.
20 Mongani Wally Serote, *Selected Poems* (Johannesburg: Ad Donker, 1989), p. 42.
21 James Matthews, 'living in our land is a political action', in *Voices of This Land: An Anthology of South African Poetry in English*, ed. Molly Brown et al. (Pretoria: Van Schaik, 2018), p. 55.

22 Walter Mignolo, 'Epistemic Disobedience, Independent Thought and Decolonial Freedom', *Theory, Culture & Society* 26.7/8 (2009), pp. 159–81 (p. 163).
23 Mzamane, 'Literature and Politics', p. 55.
24 Peter Horn, 'Popular Forms and the United Democratic Front', in *The Cambridge History of South African Literature*, ed. David Attwell and Derek Attridge (Cambridge: Cambridge University Press, 2012), pp. 523–44 (p. 523).
25 Mzamane, 'Literature and Politics', p. 42.
26 Ibid., p. 56.
27 Mafika Gwala, 'Letter to Richard Rive', reprinted in Chapman, ed., *Soweto Poetry*, p. 97.
28 Gwala, 'Black Writing Today', p. 19.
29 Nat Nakasa, 'Comment', *The Classic* 1.1 (1963), p. 4; Sipho Sepamla, 'This Venture ...', *New Classic* 1 (1975), p. 2.
30 Mbulelo V. Mzamane 'The 50s and Beyond: An Evaluation', *New Classic* 4 (1977), pp. 23–32 (p. 30).
31 Sipho Sepamla, 'The Black Writer in South Africa Today: Problems and Dilemmas', *New Classic* 3 (1976), reprinted in Chapman, ed., *Soweto Poetry*, pp. 115–23 (p. 118). For a similar argument in relation to H. I. E. Dhlomo, see Peterson, 'Culture, Resistance and Representation', p. 164.
32 Ayi Kwei Armah, 'Larsony, or Fiction as Criticism of Fiction', *New Classic* 4 (1977), pp. 33–45 (p. 41).
33 See Michael Chapman, 'Introduction', pp. 9–26, and David Maughan Brown, 'Black Criticism and Black Aesthetics', pp. 46–56, both in *Soweto Poetry*, ed. Chapman.
34 Mbulelo V. Mzamane, 'Review of *Mind Your Colour* by Vernon February', *New Classic* 3.1 (1984), p. 45.
35 Ibid.
36 Mothobi Mutloatse, 'Introduction', in *Forced Landing: Africa South, Contemporary Writings*, ed. Mutloatse (Johannesburg: Ravan Press, 1980), p. 5.
37 Ibid.
38 Nadine Gordimer, 'Towards a Desk Drawer Literature', *The Classic* 2.4 (1968), pp. 64–74 (p. 69).
39 Sepamla, 'This Venture ...', p. 2.
40 Fhazel Johennesse and Neil Alwyn Williams, 'Statement', reprinted in *Soweto Poetry*, ed. Chapman, p. 126.
41 Nat Nakasa, 'Comment', *The Classic* 1.2 (1963), p. 5; Lewis Nkosi, 'African Writers of Today: Interviews', *The Classic* 1.4 (1963), p. 55.
42 Insert in *The Classic* 2.1 (1983), p. 48.
43 Andries Oliphant and Ivan Vladislavić, eds., 'Preface' to *Ten Years of Staffrider, 1978–1988* (Johannesburg: Ravan Press, 1988), p. i.
44 Peterson, 'Culture, Resistance and Representation', p. 173.
45 Mike Kirkwood, 'Remembering *Staffrider*', in *Ten Years of Staffrider*, ed. Oliphant and Vladislavić, p. 7.
46 *Staffrider* 1 (1978), p. 2.

PART III

1989–2000: Rights and Activisms

CHAPTER 14

Women's Rights

Rachele Dini

'We're already having postfeminism, and I'm in the Dark Ages. I missed the whole damn thing', screams Elaine Weiss, the protagonist of A. M. Homes's novel, *Music for Torching* (1999), who suspects her husband of having an affair.[1] A frustrated white middle-class housewife in her forties who lives in the wealthy New York suburb of Westchester, Elaine embodies the contradictions of both white feminism and the 1990s. This period was characterised by women of colour and queer women writers' efforts to complicate white-centric and heteronormative accounts of female experience, but also by the view, espoused by many mainstream media outlets, that feminism had achieved its aims and was no longer necessary.[2] The term 'postfeminism' came to refer to both these positions. To understand what Homes is saying through this woman who proceeds, out of sheer boredom, to set fire to her house, we need to go back several decades, to the immediate post-war period. Because in keeping with a large swathe of US fiction of the 1990s, *Music for Torching* is about the legacy of mid-century political activism, its co-option by mainstream culture, and the voices that feminism left out.

Seeds of Revolt

This story begins in the immediate aftermath of the Second World War. Having first persuaded thousands of women to take up jobs in armament factories via the iconic image of Rosie the Riveter, US manufacturers, politicians, and policymakers now set to persuading them to return to the home.[3] Female workers' lower wages as compared to men's posed competition to returning veterans, while the success of reconversion (the shift from a wartime economy based on the production and sale of weapons to Allied countries, to a consumer economy based on the

The author wishes to thank Martha Rosler for granting permission to reproduce her work, as well as the editors and Karina Jakubowicz and Benjamin George for feedback on early drafts of this chapter.

production and circulation of goods) relied on a strict delineation of gender roles: male worker and female housewife-consumer. So too did the fight against Communism. The influential US diplomat George F. Kennan argued that, to prevent Soviet expansion, the United States needed to project an image of national cohesion to the world at large. Ordinary Americans could contribute to this effort by adhering to an 'American way of life' premised on patriarchal, heteronormative values.[4] Over the next few decades, the American public was saturated with images of immaculately dressed white housewives smiling in front of refrigerators heaving with newly affordable food items, and jovial husbands running the lawnmower over the vast expanse of their suburban lawns. In this media landscape, white cherub-like little girls baked cakes in Easy-Bake Ovens for dolls that cried and urinated on demand, while assertive little boys played with toy rockets and atomic energy labs that taught them the power of a masculine, all-American science, ready to be enlisted in conquering 'backward' nations that might otherwise fall prey to Communism.[5] In 1959, vice president Richard Nixon went so far as to argue that capitalism was better for women in particular, since its fruits – refrigerators, washing machines, ovens – offered freedom from household drudgery.[6] Cold War rhetoric thus reinforced the desirability of domesticity while positioning the white middle-class housewife as universal. Working-class, immigrant, and Black women were entirely omitted from this narrative – as were the thousands of women who carried on working after the war's end due to economic necessity.[7]

   The influence of the 'all-American' housewife on American culture of the subsequent decades is difficult to overstate. Most notably, she would become the focus of second-wave feminists, who in the 1960s and 1970s set about revealing her fictitiousness. As the narrating protagonist of Sheila Ballantyne's cult classic, *Norma Jean the Termite Queen* (1975), put it:

> Taken in its most literal sense, the term [housewife] arouses the image of a woman dancing with her house, which has just slipped a half-carat diamond ring on her finger. [. . .] Then she straightens its tie, brushes the leaves off its roof, gives it backrubs, and finally copulates with it.[8]

In other words, mid-century ads simultaneously elevated the house to the status of an animated being with agency while reducing the woman inside it to an ancillary object.[9] In skewering the stereotype of the housewife 'going after dust balls with her Electrolux [and] having orgasms in the laundry room while inhaling the whiteness of her wash', Norma Jean drew attention to the ludicrousness of a generation of ads such as Bendix's 1956 ad for the Tumble Agitator Washer, which unsubtly portrayed an ecstatic housewife and her washing machine overlaid against a gushing waterfall, the reference to 'agitation' implicitly referencing the machine's pleasure-endowing vibrations (see Fig. 14.1).[10] The title of Ballantyne's novel in turn

Fig. 14.1 Bendix Tumbler Agitator Washer advertisement (1956). Mid-century ads portrayed appliances as faithful family members, time-liberating helpers, or erotic lovers capable of transforming a housewife's life by liberating her time – and granting her orgasmic pleasure. Photograph - author's own.

dismantled another feminine ideal: 'Norma Jeane' (with an 'e' at the end) was the real name of Marilyn Monroe, post-war America's most famous female celebrity, who died of an overdose at the age of thirty-six. In calling her protagonist the 'queen' of termites – wood-eating insects best known for their capacity to destabilise the structural integrity of a house – and naming her after the blonde sex symbol pre-makeover, Ballantyne punctured the mythos of the all-American beauty who lives to fulfil the fantasies of American men.

Ballantyne's criticism echoed the views expressed by second-wave feminists over the previous two decades. In 1953, the English translation of feminist philosopher Simone de Beauvoir's *The Second Sex* made the New York Times Bestseller list.[11] Here, de Beauvoir argued that 'one is not born, but rather becomes, a woman': femininity was based on social assumptions about women's capabilities rather than any biological reality. Identifying housework as 'women's work' circumscribed women in the home, ensuring they had no time to contemplate other pursuits, since 'the battle against dirt and dust is never won' – they always return!'[12] She further noted that women were socialised from a young age to objectify themselves.[13] In playing with dolls, for example, little girls were both preparing for motherhood and for their own objectification: 'the little girl pampers her doll and dresses her as she dreams of being dressed and pampered; inversely, she thinks of herself as a marvelous doll'.[14] This idea was literalised in mid-century ads such as Kelvinator's for the Foodarama refrigerator, in which a little girl fed her doll with food from the fridge whose open doors resembled a mother's open embrace, and whose slogan, 'Living Dolls Love Foodarama Living', reduced the child to a doll while elevating the refrigerator to the status of a living being (see Fig. 14.2).[15]

The Jewish labour union activist and writer, Betty Friedan, took up these ideas a decade later. Friedan had worked for the United Electrical Workers' publication, *UE News*, from 1946 to 1952, when she was fired for being pregnant. In *The Feminine Mystique* (1963), however, Friedan made no mention of her union activism, Jewish identity, socialist leanings, or writing career. Instead, to appeal to a broad audience, she positioned herself as one of the many educated white, middle-class, American housewives suffering from what she called 'the problem that has no name'.[16] Citing statistics showing a surge in the psychiatric treatment of this demographic for anxiety, Friedan argued that the post-war economic boom and university education laid bare *other* unmet needs: the need for personal fulfilment.

Fig. 14.2 Kelvinator Foodarama refrigerator advertisement (1961). Mid-century ads like this one explicitly reduced female children to 'living dolls' in a manner that illustrated de Beauvoir's theory of female self-objectification. Photograph - author's own.

While queer and Black feminists argued that Friedan's universalisation of the experiences of white heterosexual middle-class women was as problematic as the advertising landscape that she critiqued (about which more later), the book's effect on mainstream American culture, and white America in particular, is undisputed. The frustrated housewife became a topic of national concern as well as the impetus for grassroots activism. In 1966, Friedan co-founded the National Organization for Women (NOW) to lobby for equal opportunities in the workplace, affordable childcare, access to safe birth control, the redistribution of domestic labour, more stringent laws against sexual violence, better legal rights for women seeking divorce, and sexual health education. These efforts were galvanised by the approval by the Food and Drug Administration (FDA) of the birth control pill in 1957, and the rolling back, in 1965, of laws outlawing the use of contraception by married couples. NOW would go on to campaign for the legalisation of abortion, which they finally obtained in 1973 via the landmark case *Roe v. Wade*, and for nuclear disarmament, civil rights, and the end of the Vietnam War, understanding these projects to be inextricably connected to one another. Indeed, Carol Hanisch, who in 1968 coined the now-famous expression, 'The Personal Is Political', was known as much for her efforts in these movements as for her feminism. The 1970s also saw the emergence of Women's Studies as an academic discipline, buoyed by publications including Mary Ellmann's *Thinking About Women* (1968), which traced the evolution of literary representations of femininity in British and American literature; Kate Millett's *Sexual Politics* (1970), which challenged the male-centrism of both literature and literary studies; and the British academic Ann Oakley's *Housewife* (1974), which made the case for the need for a sociology of housework.

In 1979, the US media pronounced Women's Lib to be 'over' following Congress's failure to pass the Equal Rights Amendment (ERA). This defeat was attributed to the campaigning efforts of a coalition of conservative, Christian fundamentalist, and white supremacist women, led by the anti-feminist activist Phyllis Schlafly, who argued that the ERA would remove access to alimony and a mother's right to child custody, force women to join the military, and deny women the 'right' to be housewives. Women's Studies, however, continued growing. There emerged, too, a body of work by Black and queer women activists, writers, and academics that built on the Combahee River Collective's incitement, in 1974, for attention to the 'manifold and simultaneous oppressions that all women of color face', and on Adrienne Rich's *Of Woman Born: Motherhood as Experience and Institution* (1976) and her 1980 essay, 'Compulsory Heterosexuality and Lesbian Existence'.[17] Countering Friedan's description of lesbians as a 'lavender menace' infecting the movement, Rich argued that heterosexuality was not a natural state, but an oppressive institution imposed by society, one effect of which was the subordination of women.[18] Angela Davis's *Women, Race, and Class* (1981), bell hooks's *Ain't I a Woman? Black Women and Feminism* (1981), and Audre Lorde's *Sister Outsider: Essays and Speeches* (1984) likewise challenged feminism's historical erasure or outright exclusion of Black women, which hooks argued derived from the historical exclusion of Black women from the category of 'woman'. In contrast to white middle-class housewives, Davis noted, Black, working-class, and immigrant women had long had to work outside the home. Receiving 'wages for housework' (the name of a campaign launched in 1972 for housewives to be paid) had not granted domestic servants much more dignity than their enslaved and sharecropping grandmothers. hooks argued that white women's emancipation was attained on the backs of Black women. And Lorde argued that the omission of writing by Black women in the vast majority of Women's Studies courses replicated the very exclusionary practices that the field had set out to challenge. Law professor Kimberlé Crenshaw's coining of the term 'intersectionality' to articulate the dual effects of racism and misogyny on Black women in the legal system helped popularise these ideas beyond Women's Studies.[19]

The Second-Wave Feminist Novel

Feminist fiction published in the 1970s and 1980s includes fictionalised, autobiographical, and semi-autobiographical accounts of feminist and sexual awakening, activism, and failed attempts at liberation. These include Toni Morrison's *The Bluest Eye* (1970), *Sula* (1973), and *Beloved* (1987); Rita Mae Brown's *Rubyfruit Jungle* (1973); Maxine Hong Kingston's *The Woman Warrior* (1976); Marilyn French's *The Women's Room* (1977); Octavia Butler's *Kindred* (1979); Marge Piercy's *Woman on the Edge of Time* (1976) and *Braided Lives* (1982); Joanna Russ's *The Female Man* (1975); Marilynne Robinson's *Housekeeping* (1980); Audre Lorde's *Zami: A New Spelling of My Name* (1982); Margaret Atwood's *The Handmaid's Tale* (1985); and Amy Tan's *The Joy Luck Club* (1989). In tracing the mutual constitution of individual and collective memory, the circuitous path to attaining civil liberties, and the speed with which they might be taken away, these texts challenged linear accounts of historical progress. They also challenged the nostalgic overtones of the period's popular media, fashion, and interior design, revealing America's past to be a site of oppression and struggle.

Part memoir, part political screed, part speculative fiction, and part naturalist novel in the grand tradition of Émile Zola, Frank Norris, or Edith Wharton, the second-wave feminist novel comprised shopping lists, diary entries, poetry extracts, quotes from parenting manuals, newspaper headlines, and ads, and, too, graphic accounts of taboo topics such as menstruation, abortion, sexual violence, and sexual pleasure. In doing so, it reflected the movement's symbiotic relationship with popular media. The use of montage, the 'braiding' together (to invoke the title of Piercy's novel) of multiple narrative arcs, and the movement between time periods in the feminist novel challenged universalist accounts of history, while disclosing the patriarchal imperialist impetus underlying the very concept of a 'master narrative'. It is thus curious (to put it mildly) that accounts of American literature have, until very recently, treated feminist fiction as a genre apart from the postmodernist experimental fiction by white male writers that emerged in the same period, and that adopted so many of the same narrative strategies. Such a distinction between the concerns of feminist writers and those of authors such as Robert Coover, Norman Mailer, Kurt Vonnegut, Thomas Pynchon, and Don DeLillo, who are more generally recognised as 'political writers', has had the dual effect of diminishing the radical aesthetic and political significance of feminist writing and of obscuring the feminist dimension of post-1960s fiction by male writers – not to mention feminist fiction's influence on the latter. Recent scholarship by critics including Mary Foltz and Sarah Wasserman has sought to challenge this distinction.[20]

Feminist fiction also laid bare tensions between feminists and conservative women. In Alison Lurie's *The War Between the Tates* (published in 1974, but set in 1969), housewife Erica Tate, whose husband, a history professor, has just impregnated one of his students, wails: 'Everything's changed, and I'm too tired to learn the new rules [. . .] I don't care about rock festivals or black power or student revolutions [. . .] I feel like an exhausted time traveller.'[21] Like Homes's protagonist, this white middle-class housewife conflates her husband's infidelity with an alienating zeitgeist: in this case, the Woodstock music festival held in August 1969 to protest the Vietnam War; the Black Power movement, which sought to reverse centuries of racial oppression; and student protests that took place on campuses across the nation to denounce gender inequality, racism, imperialism, and environmental degradation. Erica's comparison of these movements to the events in one of her son's science fiction novels displays an understanding of historical change as entertainment one can opt out of viewing, rather than as embodied struggle with vital material consequences. Lurie indicates the short-sightedness of this perspective both in Erica's own trajectory and in that of her neighbour, Danielle: Erica ends up back with her husband despite his affair and his denouncement by campus feminists for sexism, and Danielle ends up with the man who raped her – a veterinarian who performs abortions on dogs while championing the importance of denying women access to the procedure. Both endings highlight the paucity of options available to women in this period that Erica sees as so radical.

By contrast, Anne Richardson Roiphe's *Up the Sandbox!* (1970) uncritically reproduces the view of historical change as a passing fad. Here, a white middle-class housewife's desire to escape domestic drudgery engenders a series of fantasies, in which she takes on the personae of a martyred nun protesting the Vietnam War, an undercover agent who has sex with Fidel Castro (who turns out to be a woman), and the lover of a Black terrorist organisation's leader. In positioning these fantasies as the desperate expression of a woman who longs to join a history that is passing her by, the novel exoticises the peace movement, socialism, lesbianism, transgenderism, and the Black Power movement, reducing them to vehicles of escapism for a white heterosexual woman with no actual skin in the game. In so doing, *Up the Sandbox!* inadvertently stages the speed with which awareness of one's complicity with a regime from which one benefits could turn into either navel-gazing or circumscribed activism focused solely on the needs of one's own demographic. The ending of *Music for Torching*, which sees Elaine's son shot to death by the son of her husband's lover, provides a scathing rejoinder both to Elaine's boredom and the concerns of this genre of 1970s white feminist fiction, which Imelda Whelehan has dubbed the 'mad housewife' novel.[22]

Such rejoinders form a crucial strand of feminist fiction of the 1990s that looks back on the developments of the previous century. Influenced in part by Judith Butler's now canonical *Gender Trouble* (1990), these texts invite the reader to look at women's history through the eyes not of the white middle-class housewife, but of Asian American, Latina, Black, working-class, and queer women, and those who don't identify as women at all. While the Senate nominated Clarence Thomas to the Supreme Court in 1991 despite Anita Hill's testimony that he had sexually harassed her; while Christian conservative groups such as Operation Rescue lobbied to advocate for individual states' right to restrict abortion, so overruling the Supreme Court's ruling in *Planned Parenthood v. Casey* (1992); while marital rape remained a contested term even after its criminalisation in 1993; while prominent white feminists such as Gloria

Steinem and Anne Roiphe's more conservative daughter, Katie Roiphe, vilified White House intern Monica Lewinski after the exposure of Lewinski's affair with the 42nd president, Bill Clinton; and while Francis Fukuyama's *The End of History and the Last Man* (1992) argued that humanity had, following the dissolution of the Soviet Union and the end of the Cold War, reached 'the end point of mankind's ideological evolution'; a growing number of feminist writers in this decade sought to redress gender inequality, universalist narratives such as Fukuyama's, and the homogeneity of feminist fiction to date.[23]

Notable texts of the decade include Sarah Schulman's novel about AIDS activism, *People in Trouble* (1990); Dorothy Allison's arresting account of sexual abuse, *Bastard Out of Carolina* (1992), which also served as a scathing indictment of the classism and racism that limited the prospects of working-class American women; and Leslie Feinberg's *Stone Butch Blues* (1993). The latter drew inspiration from 1930s working-class fiction to record the experiences of working-class gen-derqueer people, butch and femme lesbians, trans men, and trans women – groups marginalised by both mainstream culture and main-stream feminism. They also include Bernadette Meyer's experimental prose poem-qua-memoir of motherhood, *The Desires of Mothers to Please Others in Letters* (1994), and Marya Hornbacher's *Wasted: A Memoir of Anorexia and Bulimia* (1998). And they include accounts of POC experience such as Amy Tan's *The Kitchen God's Wife* (1991); Ana Castillo's magical realist novel-qua-environmental treatise, *So Far from God* (1993); Ruth Ozeki's exposure, in *My Year of Meats* (1998), of the links between globalisation, America's continued veneration of white housewives, and its multi-billion pound meat industry; and Toni Morrison's alternative history of the post-war era, *Paradise* (1997), which imagines the establishment, blossoming, and disintegra-tion of an all-Black community that is eventually destroyed by its members' colourism and misogyny.

These novels not only challenged the implicitly classist white hetero-femininity championed by figures such as 1990s entrepreneur-turned-celebrity housewife, Martha Stewart, who promoted housewifery as a lifestyle choice for a generation of middle-class women who could 'have it all' (career, husband, children, and a beautiful home). They also altered the form of the novel itself, and challenged universalist theories of history by focusing on female characters who championed the importance of subjects that both mainstream culture and the academic establishment deemed worthless. Indeed, the sheer number of novels in this period featuring women who have dropped out of graduate school after their proposed PhD theses were dismissed as trivial by their (white male) supervisors, makes it tempting to read 1990s feminist fiction as a repository for the rejectamenta of a white male-dominated academy. The novels themselves might be read as both alt-theses that attest to the importance of the subjects the academy has rejected, and as evidence of feminism's role in shaping fields and approaches that postmillennial scholars now take for granted – from domestic space studies and the sociology of housework to oral and community-focused histories.

'Despite the Recent Protests for Women's Rights': Whitney Otto's *How to Make an American Quilt*

Whitney Otto's *How to Make an American Quilt* (1991) weaves together the stories of eight elderly women in a quilting circle in Grasse, California. Each woman's narrative is introduced by a set of quilting instructions-qua-parables that foreshadows her trajectory. The narration of these sections in the second person collapses the distinction between protagonist and reader, while the language's coded nature is a reminder that the intricate narrative forms whose beauty we admire are often born of necessity: to hide their radicalism. The novel's prologue and epilogue are narrated by Finn, the granddaughter of one of the women – a twenty-six-year-old former PhD student who bounced between PhD programmes in art history and English literature before dropping out of graduate school altogether, alienated by what she calls the 'intellectualism for its own sake' of critical theory, and by academic historians' valuation of History with a capital H above 'the small, odd details [of] the past'.[24] In celebrating the way quilting 'utilizes that which would normally be thrown out, "waste," and [...] out of that which is left comes a new, useful object', Finn suggests how one ought to approach both this novel and the reading and writing of fiction and history as a whole – how to listen, how to trace patterns, and how to articulate one's own story.[25]

Finn's approach brings to mind Miriam Schapiro and Melissa Meyer's essay, 'Waste Not, Want Not: An Inquiry into What Women Saved and Assembled' (1978).[26] In this essay, Shapiro and Meyer challenged art historians' attribution of the origins of collage to the Cubist artists Pablo Picasso and Georges Braque, noting the latters' debt to long-trivialised domestic practices such as scrapbooking and quilting. Shapiro and Meyer's concept of 'femmage', or 'feminist collage', corrected this erasure, providing a framework for recognising the aesthetic and political value of domestic arts. To qualify as femmage, a work must meet at least seven of the following criteria: be made by a woman; involve the activities of saving/collecting; feature recycled scraps, a pattern, 'elements of covert imagery', handwriting or drawing, and/or photographs or other printed matter; have a 'woman-life context'; address itself 'to an audience of intimates'; 'celebrat[e] a private or public event'; reflect 'a diarist's point of view'; contain 'silhouetted images which are fixed on other material'; and have 'a functional as well as an aesthetic life'.[27]

Otto's novel takes up these same ideas, often explicitly. Consider the penultimate chapter, which narrates the story of Anna, a mixed-race woman who came to Grasse in 1935 as an unwed teenager, and begins with the statement:

> To know my story [. . .] is to understand my superimposition on the world, to see that I am in the world as shadow [. . .] All underneath my image are people [. . .] all of one color. I am placed upon them as an architect uses an overlay sheet to illustrate the details of the structure he will build – and just as quickly, the overlay sheet can be again lifted, removing all traces of detail, leaving the bare structure.[28]

One of Shapiro and Meyer's 'silhouetted images which are fixed on other material' is revealed here to be the Black woman whose hidden labour allows for the smooth functioning of the white American home. Anna's trajectory over the subsequent pages discloses just how many structures this woman has upheld – including that of the novel of which she is a part. Raised in the white household where her great-aunt Pauline worked as a domestic servant, Anna fled home at sixteen with her great-great grandmother's quilt, which Pauline had sold to her white employer under duress. After taking a job as a domestic servant in another white household and falling pregnant by her new employers' son, she moved to Grasse, where she was taken in as a domestic servant by Finn's great-grandmother – the mother of Gladys Joe and Hy Rubens, the two women whose story forms the novel's first chapter. Anna's presence in the Rubens's home, she realises, 'completes the picture of American family perfection by being the charity, the evidence of the goodness of spirit that lives in this house, in this rural town, in the mid-1930s'.[29] This description evokes James Baldwin's famous assertion, in 'Notes for a Hypothetical Novel' (1960), that '[t]he fact of colour [. . .] fulfils something in the

American personality [. . .] the Americans in some peculiar way believe or think they need it'.[30] Otto's text discloses the reliance of the myth of the 'all-American' family, understood here to be a *white* family, on the myths of white saviourism and Christian charity. The Black woman servant of meagre means in turn provides endless fodder for the kindly white housewife to display her generosity and measured affection, and to instruct her daughters about how to treat the 'help' humanely without letting them get ideas above their station. She is the overlay sheet on which the construction of white femininity depends.

But the passage also recalls Toni Morrison's articulation of the function of Black American characters in white American literature, which she advanced in a series of lectures at Harvard University in 1990, and which were subsequently published by Harvard University Press in 1992 as *Playing in the Dark: Whiteness and the Literary Imagination.* Indeed, Morrison's analysis of the role of white American writers in the social construction of race via the creation and perpetuation of racial stereotypes reverberates throughout Anna's narrative – most notably, when it emerges that it was Anna who taught Gladys Joe and Hy to quilt while she was their mother's servant; that the quilts she made in those years were from the leftover scraps of quilts Pauline was commissioned to make by her white employer; and that it was Anna who founded the quilting circle, after she became Gladys Joe's servant and served 'again [. . .] as the ghostly witness to the American dream'.[31] The belated revelation that the quilting circle was founded by a Black woman whom the novel has only mentioned in passing up to this point throws a pall over the stories of the white women who have preceded it, tempering the sympathy the reader might feel for their different struggles. And in its placement of Anna's story at the end, the novel performs Anna's displacement at the level of form, drawing attention to the role of American literature itself, including feminist fiction, in perpetuating racist oppression. This is made explicit in the prologue to Anna's section, which describes the effects of a white woman's entry into a quilting contest of a quilt she purchased in Hawaii: 'this loss of [the Hawaiian woman's] history by having another woman appropriate it, in turn, increasing [. . .] her own power. On your back. At your expense. You feel it most profoundly.'[32] The appropriation of marginalised women's labour is revealed to be, itself, a longstanding *pattern.*

As this depiction suggests, *How to Make an American Quilt* is also a sustained critique of American imperialism and the use of history to nationalistic ends. Contrary to national monuments, quilts commemorating those lost in battle do 'not glorif[y], just recor[d]'.[33] Such an effort is apparent in the section about Corrina, whose son dies in Vietnam, and particularly in the instructions section that precedes it:

> [Y]ou may not know when [water stains or rodents] threaten your quilt. You could be making dinner for your family [. . .] or doing your part for the war effort in a munitions factory. [. . .] You have done everything the books say to store it properly, to keep it safe from harm. Yet it may not be safe. Do not bleach [. . .] But you know how chemicals can destroy things. Mustard gas can cut a swathe of permanent damage in veterans of the Great War; Agent Orange left its mark on the veterans of Vietnam [. . .] Extremes of temperature can affect the improperly stored quilt, specifically heat. You understand that. Southeast Asia can be brutally moist. You may notice some discoloration.[34]

Via its juxtaposition of mundane instructions with references to the history of chemical warfare, the passage draws attention to the lasting trauma of war, and, in particular, the accrual of trauma in women born in the shadow of one war only to live through two more. The quilt's vulnerability despite its creator's best efforts to protect it becomes a metaphor for the powerlessness of mothers such as Corrina, who '[e]very night [. . .] watched the evening news with a kind of fixed horror', hoping their sons 'are not a statistic in a casualty run-down'.[35]

Otto's juxtaposition of everyday domestic objects and war scenes underscores the unprecedented proximity that Americans felt to this war due to the advent of television, which brought scenes of devastation into the home, and whose reduction of the distance between warzone and 'home' (understood, here, to be both 'nation' and 'dwelling') led to the nomer 'the living room war'. In this, it echoes Martha Rosler's famous photomontage series, *House Beautiful: Bringing the War Home* (1967–72), whose works comprised black-and-white photos of the war taken from *LIFE* magazine overlaid onto colour photos from women's magazines such as *Good Housekeeping* and *House Beautiful* (hence the title of the series). In 'Red Stripe Kitchen', armed soldiers prowl through a pristine red-and-white kitchen. While the soldiers' crouched posture resembles that of someone vacuuming, the kitchen's colour scheme ironically recalls both the blood of battle and the Communist threat the war was intended to vanquish.

Fig. 14.3 Martha Rosler, 'Red Stripe Kitchen', from *House Beautiful: Bringing the War Home* (1967–72). Original in colour; reproduced in black and white with permission from the artist.

In 'Cleaning the Drapes', a housewife vacuums her brightly coloured living room curtains, impervious to the soldiers huddling outside (see Figs. 14.3 and 14.4). The series not only commented on the

Fig. 14.4 Martha Rosler, 'Cleaning the Drapes', from *House Beautiful: Bringing the War Home* (1967–72). Original in colour; reproduced in black and white with permission from the artist.

surreal quality of reading about the war in magazine articles flanked by ads for ordinary household goods. It also forced the viewer to empathise with the thousands of Vietnamese people for whom the war really *was* happening at home, and whom the US government was treating as collateral damage. The contrast between the colourful photos of domestic interiors and the black-and-white photos of war suggested that the American Dream espoused by the All-American Housewife was premised on a vampirical war complex that sucked the life – and colour – from other nations. Like Rosler's series (and anticipating a remarkably similar scene in Don DeLillo's postmodern historiographic novel *Underworld*, published six years after Otto's novel), Corrina's narrative impresses upon the reader the cognitive dissonance that results from absorbing propagandistic images of domestic harmony alongside news bulletins and photo essays portraying mass death. The only way to shut out the violence of war is by emulating the sociopathic housewives of the ads – and to resign one's self to what one of the other characters calls the limited freedoms of 'this homemaker era'.[36]

'... to Show You What Little Progress Has Been Made': Paule Marshall's *Daughters*

Like Finn, the protagonist of Paule Marshall's *Daughters* (1991), Ursa, is a former graduate student seeking to understand her place in history – that of New York City, where she has lived since she was a teenager, and the (fictional) Caribbean island of Triunion, where her father, a politician known as 'the PM', has struggled for decades to improve living conditions without bowing to the pressures of American free-market capitalists. Having dropped out of graduate school after her white supervisor vetoed a project on the relationship between Black Caribbean women slaves and their masters, Ursa has forged a career as a consumer researcher of 'special markets' (read: Black American consumers) before turning to research the effects of urban renewal (read: gentrification) on Black communities in Harlem. The novel opens onto the waiting room of the clinic where Ursa has just had an abortion. As she awaits her release, she recalls snippets of the MA dissertation proposal her supervisor rejected, flashes back to a memory of her father in Triunion lifting her out of the swimming pool of the hotel run by his mistress, Astral, and ruminates over whether her proposed project on Harlem will be funded. In this way, the novel makes clear from the outset the interrelation of women's rights with the history of slavery, the projects of decolonisation, desegregation, and workers' rights, and the politics of urban planning. An American woman at the close of the twentieth century can get an abortion, yes, but other aspects of her existence are contingent on a whole cluster of other class-, race-, and regionally inflected factors.

Daughters is concerned with teasing out these connections and the ways in which progress in the United States has relied on subjugating other nations, just as the improvement of *some* women's lives has often come at the expense of others. This is apparent in a scene following the police's unlawful arrest of the son of Ursa's friend Viney. Viney describes the humiliation of being asked by a policeman whether she is a 'Mrs.' or a 'Ms.', and his subsequent 'stressing [of] the Ms.' every time he addressed her: '*Ms.* Daniels, just to let me know that, yes, I might be a hotshot VP at Metropolitan, I might make twice his salary, but I was still in his book just another welfare mother standing there with her little ADC child and no father in sight.'[37] The title 'Ms.' gained traction in the 1970s, partly thanks to the eponymous feminist magazine launched by Gloria Steinem and Dorothy Pitman Hughes in 1972. Its purpose was to enable women, like men, to withhold their marital status. In the policeman's mouth, however, 'Ms.' becomes a racist pejorative that Viney associates with the pejorative use of 'ADC', or 'Aid to Development Children' – a reference to the Aid to Families with Dependent Children (AFDC) grant programme that enabled states to provide welfare payments to children with absent, unemployed, or deceased parents. The acronym came to be used as a racist dog whistle by conservative politicians in the 1960s, who enlisted it along with the racialised expression 'Welfare Queen' – the pejorative for women who allegedly collected excessive welfare payments, which Ronald Reagan further popularised during his 1976 presidential campaign. Viney's account of the white cop who uses 'Ms.' to cut her down to size by portraying her as a single Black mother growing rich off the state reveals the speed with which acts of resistance are appropriated by their detractors to further penalise those they were intended to liberate.

This concern with progress's capacity to be undone is reflected in the novel's very structure, which in moving between the US and Triunion and between 1990 and the previous four decades, highlights both the tentacular reach of American free-market ideology, and the parallels between seemingly different political eras. Ursa's unspoken question to her mother, 'Why don't you leave him? [. . .] Nobody stays and takes shit anymore. That's passé', conveys the endurance of gender inequality long after the so-called Women's Libbers stopped marching.[38] Likewise, a Black sexagenarian's summary of the mass arrests of activists protesting the erection of a highway overpass through Harlem for white suburban commuters ('It was the sixties all over again') *just pages* before Ursa's discovery that her father has sold Triunion's public land to American luxury real estate developers, conveys the ramifications of the free-market policies implemented by Ronald Reagan's administration, which resulted in the social cleansing of once diverse American cities as well as the establishment of the Caribbean as a tax haven.[39]

As these examples evidence, Marshall's novel is interested in unearthing the myriad ways that systemic inequalities shape individual experience in a manner that both ripples outward and, as the title itself indicates, is transmitted from generation to generation. To this end, Marshall not only switches between narrative modes. She also homes in on objects of seemingly little significance. Ursa is haunted, for example, by the legend of Jane

Cudjoe, a slave girl whose mistress sliced off her nipple upon discovering Jane playing with the mistress's daughter's cast-off toys. Like Thomas Jefferson's impregnation of his slave Sally Hemings, which Otto's narrator Finn cites as one of the 'small footnotes' of history that historians, at least until the 1990s, were loath to interrogate, Jane's narrative is both an example of the 'stuff' that doesn't make it into the history books and an allegory for the historical mistreatment of Black women who dared to ask for more.

A similar subtext is apparent in a page-long description of the wooden valet featuring a built-in ironing board and automatic trouser press that the PM's mistress, Astral, has bought him to use when he visits her. The PM responds to this gift with one word, 'America', before sarcastically remarking that while 'the fella who thought to add on this ironing board is a millionaire today', the gadget can help him (the PM) 'at least look like' one.[40] Domestic appliances, which in television and print advertising well into the 1980s were portrayed as solutions to any and all familial problems, are revealed here to symbolise an American empire that accrues wealth by exporting commodities and its own myth to poorer nations, while highlighting the PM's treatment of Astral herself in utilitarian terms. Via these descriptions of fraught subject-object relations, Marshall demonstrates the enduring need for a feminism that takes into account the complexities of race, class, and an increasingly globalised capitalism.

Conclusion

And so we return to Homes's Elaine Weiss, sitting among the charred remnants of the home to which she has set fire, unaware as yet that her boredom will soon be supplanted by grief at her younger son's murder. Examined alongside Otto and Marshall's texts, Elaine's story appears all the more absurdly predictable. She is, in effect, the logical product of feminism's co-option and dilution, and a warning for readers to resist both the triumphalism of 1990s 'end of history' rhetoric, which obscured the endurance of vast inequalities, and the depiction of history-as-passive-entertainment that pervaded the media landscape of the 1970s, 1980s, and 1990s, which turned the struggles of previous decades into whimsical clichés. Dismissive of nostalgic period dramas, wary of engaging in outright activism, and sceptical of Women's Studies (a source of solace, instead, for her neighbour), Elaine has no recourse but to become a Friedanian stereotype – while her nihilism is best understood as a form of cognitive dissonance in the face of a culture that claims, despite all evidence to the contrary, to have 'solved' inequality.

Otto and Marshall's protagonists, by contrast, suggest the merits of applying the tools of feminist literary scholars and historians to challenge the insularity that nihilism breeds. Their trajectories model an outward-looking approach to the world as a constellation of connected selves and suggest the enduring power of collectivism, regardless of the Communist nations' collapse. This constellatory approach at once bears the traces of domestic craftwork and the influence of the still-nascent Internet (which we might read, in turn, as a digital tapestry), anticipating aspects of postmillennial feminist writing online. The self-conscious literariness of Otto and Marshall's novels attests to the role that writing and attentive reading might play in challenging claims of feminism's obsolescence. As Otto's Finn notes: 'If I learned nothing else in grad school, I learned to be a fairly careful witness.'[41] In 2021, Texas and Georgia passed anti-abortion bills, and in 2022, the Supreme Court overturned both *Roe* and *Casey*. Meanwhile, the United States retreated from Afghanistan, a failed war whose devastating consequences has been compared to that of Vietnam. In the ongoing aftermath of these events, the postmillennial scholar would do well to heed Finn's lessons, too.

Notes

1 A. M. Homes, *Music for Torching* (London: Granta, 1999), p. 215.
2 See Elaine Tyler May, *Homeward Bound: American Families in the Cold War Era* (New York: Basic Books, 1988).
3 See Lynn Spigel, *Make Room for TV: Television and the Family Ideal in Postwar America* (Chicago, IL: Chicago University Press, 1992).
4 George F. Kennan, 'The Sources of Soviet Conduct', *Foreign Affairs* 4.25 (July 1947), pp. 566–82; see also Alan Nadel, *Containment Culture: American Narratives, Postmodernism, and the Atomic Age* (Durham, NC: Duke University Press, 1995), p. 2.
5 For more on the gendered media landscape of the early Cold War era, see Greg Castillo, *Cold War on the Home Front: The Soft Power of Midcentury Design* (Minneapolis, MN: University of Minnesota Press, 2010) and Rachele Dini, *'All-Electric' Narratives: Time-Saving Appliances and Domesticity in American Literature, 1945–2020* (New York: Bloomsbury, 2021), esp. pp. 23–37.
6 Sarah T. Phillips and Shane Hamilton, *The Kitchen Debate and Cold War Consumer Politics* (Boston, MA and New York: Bedford/St Martin's, 2014). See also Joy Parr, 'Modern Kitchen, Good Home, Strong Nation', *Technology and Culture* 43.4 (October 2002), pp. 657–67.
7 See Lizabeth Cohen, *A Consumer's Republic: The Politics of Mass Consumption in Postwar America* (New York: Alfred A. Knopf, 2003), pp. 123–4.

8   Sheila Ballantyne, *Norma Jean the Termite Queen* (New York: Penguin, 1983), p. 4.

9   Ibid.

10 Bendix, 'New BENDIX Tumble Agitator Washer', *Saturday Evening Post*, 22 September 1956, n.p. For more on erotic imagery in mid-century appliance ads, the relationship between appliances and the vibrator, and feminist fiction's engagements with these, see Dini, *'All-Electric' Narratives*, pp. 21–2, 128–9, 218.

11 Simone de Beauvoir, *The Second Sex* [1949], trans. H. M. Parshley (London: Vintage, 1977).

12 Ibid., p. 271.

13 Ibid., p. 304.

14 Ibid.

15 Kelvinator, 'Living Dolls Love Foodarama Living', *Saturday Evening Post*, 1961, n.p.

16 Betty Friedan, *The Feminine Mystique* [1963] (New York: Dell, 1974). See also Daniel Horowitz, *Betty Friedan and the Making of The Feminine Mystique* (Amherst, MA: University of Massachusetts Press, 1998).

17 Combahee River Collective, 'A Black Feminist Statement', in *The Second Wave: A Reader in Feminist Theory*, ed. Linda Nicholson (New York: Routledge, 1997), pp. 63–70.

18 Friedan's words were particularly egregious in their echoing of the rhetoric of McCarthyism: the early 1950s saw the expulsion from government of both those believed (based on no evidence) to be Communist sympathisers, and those believed to be 'sexual deviants'; the latter, it was argued, were uniquely vulnerable to blackmail by Soviet spies looking to infiltrate the government. The latter purge was known as the 'lavender scare'. See May, *Homeward Bound*.

19 Kimberlé Crenshaw, 'Demarginalizing the Intersection of Race and Sex', *University of Chicago Legal Forum* (1989), Iss. 1, Article 8, and 'Mapping the Margins: Intersectionality, Identity Politics, and Violence against Women of Color', *Stanford Law Review* 43.6 (July 1991), pp. 1241–99.

20 Mary Foltz, *Contemporary American Literature and Excremental Culture: American Sh*t* (New York: Palgrave Macmillan, 2020); Sarah Wasserman, *The Death of Things: Ephemera and the American Novel* (Minneapolis, MN: University of Minnesota Press, 2020). See also Rachele Dini, '"The House Was a Garbage Dump": Waste, Mess, and Aesthetic Reclamation in 1960s and 70s "Mad Housewife" Fiction', *Textual Practice* 34.3 (August 2018), pp. 479–505. Available at https://doi.org/10.1080/0950236X.2018.1508069 (1 September 2021).

21 Alison Lurie, *The War Between the Tates* [1974] (London: Abacus, 1989), p. 197.

22 In *The Feminist Bestseller: From Sex and the Single Girl to Sex and the City* (New York: Palgrave Macmillan, 2005), Imelda Whelehan defines the mad housewife genre as a form dominated by middle-class, white, heterosexual

female writers and concerned with the 'intense pressure to perform [...] femininity' (pp. 63–4).

23 Francis Fukuyama, *The End of History and the Last Man* [1992] (New York, Penguin, 2020), p. xi. For a bracing account of feminist fiction's challenge to Fukuyama, see Jane Elliott, *Popular Feminist Fiction as American Allegory: Representing National Time* (New York: Palgrave Macmillan, 2008), and the thesis from which Elliott's book was developed, 'Politics Out of Time: Feminism, Futurity, and the End of History', Rutgers University, 2004.

24 Whitney Otto, *How to Make an American Quilt* [1991] (New York: Picador, 1992), pp. 4–5.

25 Ibid., p. 9.

26 Miriam Schapiro and Melissa Meyer, 'Waste Not, Want Not', *Heresies: Women's Traditional Arts: The Politics of Aesthetics* (Winter 1978), pp. 66–9. Available at https://artcritical.com/2015/06/24/femmage-by-miriam-schapiro-and-melissa-meyer/ (accessed 1 September 2021).

27 Ibid., p. 69.

28 Otto, *How to Make an American Quilt*, p. 133.

29 Ibid., p. 149.

30 James Baldwin, 'Notes for a Hypothetical Novel', *Nobody Knows My Name: More Notes of a Native Son* [1964] (New York: Penguin, 1991), pp. 119–29 (p. 125).

31 Otto, *How to Make an American Quilt*, p. 155.

32 Ibid., p. 132.

33 Ibid., p. 110.

34 Ibid., p. 108.

35 Ibid., p. 115.

36 Ibid., p. 58.

37 Paule Marshall, *Daughters* [1991](New York: Penguin, 1992), p. 330.

38 Ibid., p. 255.

39 Ibid., p. 294.

40 Ibid., p. 371.

41 Ibid., p. 177.

CHAPTER 15

Sexual Rights

Jo Winning

Gender and sexual identities would seem to belong to the most private domains of our lives, personal experiences of desires and embodiments that unfold in our most intimate moments and away from the public gaze or scrutiny. Yet, as we know, across all cultures and historical periods, gender and sexuality are also the site of much contestation and regulation, elements of human subjectivity through which notions of norms and pathologies are deeply embedded. Sexual rights are often hard fought for, sexual and gender minorities needing to stake a claim to the same benefits and legal protections as the heterosexual, cis-gendered majority often unthinkingly enjoy, in order to achieve what the contemporary philosopher Judith Butler describes as 'a livable life', free from persecution and violence and where kinship bonds are recognised.[1] This chapter will explore the relationship between late twentieth-century literature and sexual rights. It will ask what a book can do to advance the political case for sexual rights, as well as show how a book might provide a much-needed textual space for self-imagining and self-determination, for the sexual or gender minority subject literally written out of the socio-cultural mainstream. As Lyndsey Stonebridge notes, there is close correlation between the books that 'give us blueprints for the ways in which it might be possible to live with others in the world' and the writing of 'legal fictions strong enough to make living with others morally tolerable, if not just'.[2]

The 1980s: Political Poetics

Whilst the unfolding of the twentieth century brought gains for LGBT communities in many Western countries, for instance the decriminalisation of consensual sexual acts between men in the 1967 Sexual Offences Act in the UK, it was also a century of often only equivocal progress, in which anti-gay legislations and repressive assaults on basic rights were constantly emerging. In addition, the latter decades of the century brought the global crisis of the HIV/AIDS epidemic, which shaped much of the discriminatory treatment and demonisation of LGBT communities, particularly of gay men. From the 1970s onwards, such complex and testing political terrain galvanised LGBT political activism, and LGBT rights movements emerged around the world. Many forms of writing – literary, political, educational, among others – formed the bedrock of these rights movements, both in terms of self-expression and self-definition, and in terms of community-building and consciousness-raising.

In 1988, in an amendment to the Local Government Act 1986, Margaret Thatcher's Conservative government introduced Section 28, the infamous clause which set a prohibition upon the 'teaching' of homosexuality in schools. The Section read: 'A local authority shall not (a) intentionally promote homosexuality or publish material with the intention of promoting homosexuality; (b) promote the teaching in any maintained school of the acceptability of homosexuality as a pretended family relationship.'[3] Section 28 was introduced by Conservative MPs Dame Jill Knight and David Wilshire, in the wake of a vociferous tabloid newspaper campaign during 1986, which falsely alleged that inner London primary school libraries were stocking a book titled *Jenny Lives with Eric and Martin*, by Danish author Susanne Bösche.[4] Bösche's picture book, published in English in 1983, was an educational text for young children, which introduced them to a gay family: five-year-old Jenny, her father Martin, and his male partner Eric.[5] The furore around the book, and the imposition of controls on schools to prevent the positive representation of lesbian and gay lives and same-sex families, was the culmination of a growing swell of anti-gay rhetoric within Tory government 'messaging', which included Thatcher's own alarmist comments at the 1987 Conservative Party conference, that 'children are being taught they have an inalienable right to be gay. All of those children are being cheated of a sound start in life.'[6] In the context of political resistance, and the burgeoning landscape of lesbian and gay publishing, magazines, community writing workshops, and swiftly expanding readership, literature provided a space for responding to and critiquing the repressions of the dominant culture. In a similar fashion to the second-wave feminist movements, poetry became a medium for mobilising political thought.

In the face of Section 28, working out just what constitutes a family is a theme that sits at the heart of Scottish poet Jackie Kay's debut collection, *The Adoption Papers*, published in 1991, in the wake of Section 28's passing into law.[7] Kay's collection is principally read for its title series, 'The Adoption Papers', which details her own experience as the daughter of a white Scottish birth mother and Nigerian father, who is adopted as a baby by a white Scottish couple. The poems explore the lived experience of adoption, as well as the complexities of dual heritage and racial identity in Scotland in the 1960s and 1970s. As Valerie L. Popp describes, Kay foregrounds the knotted relation between identity and the state through her poetic practice of pulling 'printed state-issued forms of identification: passports, birth certificates, ID cards, and, of course, adoption papers' into the body of her poems.[8] This politically-attuned poetic practice is also strongly present in the other, less-discussed series in the collection, 'Severe Gale 8', which describes the brutal terrain of Thatcher's Britain of the 1980s.[9] Section 28's description of same-sex family relationships as 'pretended' is contested through the richly-textured, intimate reimaginings of family in these poems.

In 'Mummy and Donor and Deirdre', the voices of a lesbian mother, her partner, and their son record the challenges of being a lesbian family in a predominantly heterosexual society. Across the stanzas, we hear the difficulties experienced in primary school by the son who makes friends with a boy called Tunde, who struggles to accept his family arrangement: 'He said my daddy is an underground man / What is your daddy? I said I don't have a daddy; / I have a mummy and a donor and a Deirdre.'[10] The biological mother's voice records the decisions made about not coming out in school settings, in order to protect her son: 'I don't think we'll both go to parents' night. / I don't want things harder than they are. / I want to protect him from the names and the stones.'[11]

Despite the homophobic context, and in a writerly act of resistance to the political climate, the narrative trajectory of the poem also records hope. The biological mother moves from worry about laying low as a family, to remembering the swift, successful, and joyous process of insemination that results in their son: 'I was awful lucky. Third time with a syringe.' And the son's friendship blossoms:

> Today Tunde and I said we won't tell
> anybody else what we tell each other.
> It will all be a secret. I gave him a chocolate.
> He gave me a Monster Munch.[12]

From beneath the visible surface of normative heterosexual families, same-sex desire thrives in the interstices of lived experience. In 'Close Shave', a miner recounts his secret love affair with his barber:

> Our eyes met when he came
> to the bit above my lip. 6 years ago.

> We've only slept the night together twice:
> once when my wife's sister died,
> once when the brother-in-law committed suicide.[13]

The Miners' Strike (1984–5), the major industrial action which defined the increasing class divisions in Thatcher's Britain, is undoubtedly an important context for the poem, but it is sexuality which forms the main theme. The poem's miner describes his time down the pit, working 'so fast it hurts', as 'the only time' he can 'forget' his hidden relationship, which he cannot reveal to his wife or his daughters.[14] Similarly, in 'Pounding Rain', childhood female friends reconnect after years out of touch and heterosexual marriages lived in traditional family settings, and rediscover the sexual desire for each other that was inexpressible in their teenage years:

> Why don't you come round, Trevor would love it.
> He wasn't in. I don't know how it happened.
> We didn't bother with a string of do you remembers.
> [. . . .]
> We sat and stared til our eyes filled
> like a glass of wine. I did it, the thing
> I'd dreamt a million times. I undressed you
> slowly, each item of clothing fell
> with a sigh.[15]

The enjambement in the final stanza above suggests both the lost time between inexpressible adolescent desire to the belated adult moment of its illicit enactment and the unspeakability of this desire in the 1980s context of normative family relationships and heterosexual marriage. Kay's literary foregrounding of the voices of lesbians, gay men, and their families represents a direct response to the social, cultural, and legal 'silencing' of such voices in the enactment of anti-gay legislation. In Kay's hands, the literary form of free verse emphasises the feel of everyday speech, and takes on the political task of representing lives that persist, even in the face of homophobia and state censure.

   The 1980s was a decade notable for the mobilisation and flourishing of LGBT political movements. One iconic group was the grassroots movement AIDS Coalition to Unleash Power (ACT UP), which was founded in New York in 1987 by the author and activist Larry Kramer.[16] From the outset, it sought to use direct action to challenge mainstream social and governmental complacency around HIV/AIDS and the pathologisation of both those infected by the virus and the gay community more generally. Through regular protests and staged actions such as 'die-ins' (protesters lay down in public areas, simulating dead bodies), ACT UP called for supportive legislation and funded biomedical research and more effective treatment protocols for patients with HIV/AIDS. ACT UP groups started across the US, fanning out from New York to other major American cities, and then around the world. ACT UP London was formed in 1989, and, like its sister chapters, undertook multiple protests to raise awareness and demand political change.[17]

The British poet Thom Gunn, born in Kent in 1929 and attached to the group known as 'The Movement' (which included Philip Larkin and Kingsley Amis), relocated to San Francisco in 1954 to live with his partner, Mike Kitay. Gunn documented the unfolding of the HIV/AIDS epidemic in San Francisco in the 1980s in his collection *The Man with Night Sweats* (1992), and reputedly '[admitted] to admiring ACT UP activists'.[18] The poems in Gunn's collection constitute an elegiac series that foreground the occluded lived experience of the epidemic from the intimate perspectives of the lovers and friends of those infected with the virus. Like Kay, Gunn deploys poetry to perform the political act of representation, in particular using the forms of elegy and lyric. Tyler B. Hoffman argues that Gunn's 'professed admiration for ACT UP coupled with his AIDS elegies signals his belief in the need for militancy *and* mourning'.[19] Gunn's understanding that poetic form and socio-political context might co-constitute each other is articulated earlier in his literary critical work: 'Rhythmic form and subject matter are locked in a permanent embrace: that should be an axiom nowadays. So, in metrical verse, it is the nature of the control being exercised that becomes part of the life being spoken about.'[20] In the collection's titular poem, 'The Man with Night Sweats', narrated by a man who experiences the ominous symptom of night sweats and fears he is HIV positive, Gunn begins with a tight metrical ABABCC structure:

> I wake up cold, I who
> Prospered through dreams of heat
> Wake to their residue,
> Sweat, and a clinging sheet.
>
> My flesh was its own shield:
> Where it was gashed it healed.[21]

The potential portent of the night sweat, the terrifying wrench from omnipotent, seemingly indestructible health to the vulnerability of the body to fatal infection, brings about a diminishment in the metrical structure, as if the enormity of the threat of HIV and the pathologising blame of mainstream culture undoes the capacity of metre to contain the poem's content:

> Stopped upright where I am
> Hugging my body to me
> As if to shield it from
> The pains that will go through me,
>
> As if hands were enough
> To hold an avalanche off.[22]

One the most famous AIDS activist slogans from the late 1980s, devised by Avram Finkelstein and colleagues and adopted by ACT UP, was 'Silence=Death'.[23] It was a slogan printed alongside the deeply evocative symbol of the pink triangle. One might argue that for Gunn, putting the experience of HIV/AIDS into poetic language was a political act with this slogan at its heart; that finding a vocabulary through which to narrate the epidemic is a way of repudiating death, defying cultural silence. In 'Still Life', Gunn's narrator describes his shock at seeing a hospitalised, end-stage AIDS patient: 'I shall not soon forget / The greyish-yellow skin / To which the face had set'.[24] The title of the poem plays with the notion of life stilled, ended, as well as the artistic genre. The man in the hospital bed is suspended between life and death, labouring each breath on a ventilator, his natural breathing rhythms mechanistically overtaken by the machine that keeps him alive. The cessation of his capacity to breath for himself, yet his primal urge to fight for his own breath, is reproduced on the page, in a poem riven with enjambement and caesura:

> Lids tight: nothing of his,
> No tremor from within,
> Played on the surfaces.
>
> He still found breath, and yet
> It was an obscure knack.[25]

Gunn's 'Still Life' is a poem about HIV/AIDS, but also a poem which encourages readerly identification, irrespective of sexual identity. Whilst it puts the devastating experience of HIV/AIDS into language, the language it uses to do so is universal. Fighting for breath, we might say, is a fundamental human thing, an embodied experience of end-stage illness that maps across many diseases. As Colin Gillis argues:

> To talk about homosexuality as something 'eccentric' might encourage marginalization. Yet to classify homosexuality in the same category of

lifestyle as heterosexuality could lead to a problematic model for gay subjectivity [... .] Gunn eschews the conventional vocabulary of the AIDS crisis in *The Man with Night Sweats*, in part, to resolve this dilemma. In disavowing this vocabulary, Gunn affirms the similarity between the social problems caused by AIDS and those caused by outbreaks of disease in the past.[26]

As such, the poem offers a point of connection beyond the gay male community. This too is a political act, a call for the recognition of the thoroughly human tragedy of the epidemic.

The 1990s: Playing with Narrative Form

In early 1990, a splinter group from the New York chapter of ACT UP formed the new political movement Queer Nation. Enraged by the continuing political complacency around the HIV/AIDS epidemic, escalating acts of violence against LGBT people, and the ubiquitous homophobia pedalled by mainstream media, Queer Nation espoused direct action politics of a more confrontational nature, including the contentious act of 'outing' celebrities and politicians who hid their sexual identity behind a facade of normative identity. Enacting the use of what Michel Foucault calls 'reverse discourse', the group took both terms, 'queer' and 'nation', and redefined both through the lenses of LGBT identity.[27] As Lauren Berlant and Elizabeth Freeman describe:

> Queer Nation has taken up the project of coordinating a new nationality. Its relation to nationhood is multiple and ambiguous, however, taking as much from the insurgent nationalisms of oppressed peoples as from the revolutionary idealism of the United States. Since its inception in 1990, it has invented collective local rituals of resistance, mass cultural spectacles, an organization, and even a lexicon to achieve these ends.[28]

The 'lexicon' of Queer Nation's political project was closely aligned with the new body of critical thought around gender and sexuality emerging in academic humanities departments in the US and the UK in the late 1980s and early 1990s, pioneered by theorists such as Gloria Anzaldúa, Lauren Berlant, Judith Butler, Teresa de Lauretis, and Eve Kosofsky Sedgwick. Queer theory 'calls into question obvious categories (man, woman, latina, jew, butch, femme), oppositions (man vs. woman, heterosexual vs. homosexual), or equations (gender=sex) upon which conventional notions of sexuality and identity rely'.[29] Importantly, queer politics and queer theory offered a coalitional model for political activism, providing an 'umbrella' under which non-normative heterosexual and bisexual people could also gather. Moreover, the proposed capaciousness of the critical and political term 'queer' sought to allow other vectors of difference, most notably race, to be incorporated into both the theory and politics of gender and sexuality, in a way that had been problematically missing in earlier political movements. As Teresa de Lauretis notes in her introduction to the first collection of queer theory essays, 'we do not know enough about ourselves [...] when it comes to differences between and within lesbians, between and within gay men, in relation to race and its attendant differences of class or ethnic culture, generational, geographical, and socio-political location'.[30]

Queer conceptualisations of gender challenged fundamental ideas that had formed the conceptual bedrock of second-wave feminism through the 1970s and 1980s. It moved beyond the traditional dichotomy between essentialist and social constructionist accounts of sex (the biological body) and gender (a set of culturally prescribed behaviours and norms around masculinity and femininity) that had prevailed within different strands of feminist thought and political action. Judith Butler's *Gender Trouble* (1990) proposed a conceptual model of sex and gender that understood *both* as being socially constructed and, moreover, as being heavily regulated within patriarchal cultures. Within what she defines as the 'heterosexual matrix', sexed bodies, heterosexual desire, and a normative model of masculinity and femininity as polar opposites are entwined and policed, whilst other non-normative expressions of gender and desire are vehemently censured.[31]

Queer theory's reformation of ideas around sex, gender, and sexual desire inspired many literary texts in the 1990s, and offered compelling new paradigms through which to explore the relationship between writing, the body, and sexual identity. Butler's contention that 'the inner truth of gender is a fabrication' and that the notion of a 'true gender is a fantasy instituted and inscribed on the surface of bodies', might well be understood as the premise which led British author Jeanette Winterson to experiment with narratorial gender identity in her fifth novel, *Written on the Body* (1992).[32] Winterson's debut novel, *Oranges Are Not the Only Fruit*, which won the Whitbread Award for First Novel in 1985, established her as one of the foremost late twentieth-century lesbian writers.[33] As Tyler Bradway argues, *Written on the Body*'s title 'echoes queer theory's exposure of the body as a signifying surface, revealing that gender and sexuality are written "on the body" rather than existing in the core of a self'.[34]

Written on the Body is narrated in the first person by a character who never reveals either name or sex. Although we are introduced to other characters by name and hear of the narrator's previous relationships with women and, occasionally, men, the narratorial voice resolutely hovers between genders throughout the text. As Laurie Vickroy argues, such textual ambiguity constitutes a 'discarding [of] conventional and constraining frameworks of identity and narrative form that limit our ways of knowing'.[35] The plot centres around the narrator's convoluted love affair with a married woman, Louise, who undergoes a diagnosis of cancer in the course of the narrative, returns to her husband Elgin, and then disappears from the novel altogether. The book opens with the question, 'Why is the measure of love loss?', and this wistful, elliptical question sets the tone for the narrative, which unfolds into a hybrid text that sits between the forms of philosophical treatise, auto/biographical memoir, and narrative fiction.[36] In many ways, the text's refrain about the nature of love and loss is legible within the context of LGBT politics and the HIV/AIDS epidemic; the following extract, for instance, evokes the political assertion for the legitimacy of same-sex love: 'Love demands expression. It will not stay still, stay silent, be good, be modest, be seen and not heard, no. It will break out in tongues of praise, the high note that smashes the glass and spills the liquid.'[37] However, there is also a deeper, more self-reflexive theme in the text, which proposes on the one hand the complete enmeshment between language, sexual desire, and queerness, and, on the other, suggests the intrinsic importance of queer writing, in all its forms. In the first instance, Louise's intimate touch becomes both linguistic system (language) and writing technology (printing blocks):

> Articulacy of fingers, the language of the deaf and dumb, signing on the body body longing. Who taught you to write in blood on my back? Who taught you to use your hands as branding irons? You have scored your name into my shoulders, referenced me with your mark. The pads of your fingers have become printing blocks, you tap a message on to my skin, tap meaning into my body.[38]

The correlation between sexuality and textuality is extended further in the description of writing on/of the body, which turns the lover's body into a book:

> Written on the body is a secret code only visible in certain lights; the accumulations of a lifetime gather there. In places the palimpsest is so heavily worked that the letters feel like braille. I like to keep my body rolled up away from prying eyes. Never unfold too much, tell the whole story.

> I didn't know that Louise would have reading hands. She has translated me into her own book.[39]

Conversely too, the narrator turns Louise's body into a book in the face of her illness. In the wake of the discovery of Louise's diagnosis, the narrator turns frantically to medical textbooks to read about cancer, admits to becoming 'obsessed with anatomy', and finds 'a love poem to Louise' in the clinical vocabularies of medicine.[40] Suddenly, in a text that has for its first two-thirds eschewed any kind of chapter structure, we are introduced to a series of chapters with anatomical titles which form a central sequence in the novel, and in these chapters the narrator's focus turns to the biological interior of Louise's body, as a way of 'knowing her, more intimately'.[41]

Where Winterson's *Written on the Body* channelled queer theory's disruptions to concepts of the body, desire, and writing, other lesbian writers of the 1990s experimented with narrative form in radically different ways, reframing popular forms such as historical fiction, and playfully 'recovering' lost 'codes' and subcultural languages. British novelist Sarah Waters's debut novel, *Tipping the Velvet*, published in 1998 but written in 1995, signalled a new turn in lesbian writing.

In a 2018 interview celebrating twenty years since its publication, Waters identifies the high-energy LGBT activism of the 1990s as the generative context for her writing:

> I remember the mid-90s as a rather electric time to be gay, and young, and living in London. There was a lot to be angry about, but also a lot to celebrate and relish. Grassroots direct action groups such as OutRage! and the Lesbian Avengers were giving lesbian and gay culture an energy and a political charge. Queer theory was beginning to have an impact on ideas about sex, gender and identity.[42]

Like so many LGBT direct action groups, the Lesbian Avengers was founded in New York in 1992 out of the NY ACT UP chapter. Unlike ACT UP, it sought to make space for the voices of lesbians, which were often overwhelmed by those of their gay male colleagues. A Lesbian Avengers chapter in London grew out of the grassroots mixed group, OutRage!, in 1994. Lesbian Avengers's political actions were designed to be exuberant and provocative. As the *Lesbian Avengers Organising Handbook* describes, members were at liberty to plan their own actions as long as they captured the 'Avenger Phenomenon', which involved shock and strong visual impact, such as 'fire eating, a twelve-foot shrine, a huge bomb, a ten-foot plaster statue, flaming torches, etc'.[43] The group message around actions was 'the more fabulous, witty, and original, the better'.[44] The spectacle of the direct action politics of groups like the Lesbian Avengers is a tangible context for the high-spirited, sexy, and irrepressible narrative of central protagonist Nan King's journey from oyster-seller in Whitstable to cross-dressed star of the music-hall stage, through being a 'kept woman' to a lesbian mistress to eventual political awakening and suffragism in the East End of London. The space of the theatre in *Tipping the Velvet* offers Nan her first taste of queer energy:

> Here you knew yourself to be not just at a show but in a *theatre*; you caught the shape of the stage and the sweep of the seats: and you marvelled to see your neighbours' faces, and to know your own to be like theirs – all queerly lit by the glow of the footlights, and a damp at the lip, and with a grin upon it, like that of a demon at some hellish revue.[45]

Queer theorist Jack Halberstam writes of the 'strange temporalities, imaginative life schedules, and eccentric economic practices' that 'detach queerness from sexual identity'.[46] Halberstam's delineation of what he calls 'queer temporality', in addition to demarcating queer subjectivity from earlier versions of lesbian and gay identity, speaks of the unique relationship that those who stand out of heterosexual societal norms (marriage, reproduction, extended families built on biological ties) have with time. Waters describes the way her novel was written with a temporal bi-location, both in *historical time* – the novel is set between 1889 and 1895 (the year of the Oscar Wilde trial) – but also in the *contemporary moment* of the mid-1990s:

> *Tipping the Velvet* was never intended to be a work of historical realism. Instead, it offers a 1990s-flavoured lesbian Victorian London, complete with its own clubs, pubs and fashions. It conjures up an antique lesbian lingo, using, or cheerfully misusing, some of the words and phrases – 'toms', 'mashers', 'tipping the velvet' itself – that I'd come across in dictionaries of historical slang and in 19th century pornography.[47]

Whatever its nineteenth-century origins, Waters makes the phrase 'tipping the velvet' (meaning oral sex performed on a female partner) central to the narrative arc of her novel. She folds it into Nan's eventual finding of a real relationship with Florence, a diverse and authentic lesbian community to which she can belong, and language to describe lesbian sex:

> I looked again at Florence, and frowned. 'Are they French, or what?' I asked. 'I can't understand a thing they're saying. [. . .] *Tipped the velvet*: what does that mean? It sounds like something you might do in a theatre . . .'

Florence blushed. 'You might try it,' she said; 'but I think the chairman would chuck you out ... ' Then, while I still frowned, she parted her lips and showed me the tip of her tongue; and glanced, very quickly, at my lap. [. . . .] 'How queer you are!' she said mildly. 'You have never tipped the velvet – '

'I didn't say that I'd never done it, you know; only that I never called it that.'[48]

The reclamation of this phrase, its open use as a description of the ordinary, everyday sexual practices of lesbians, and its place in the unashamedly 'happy ending' revision of the stock ending of lesbian novels – torturous loss – indicate just how far LGBT literature had come by the end of the twentieth century.

'Where Does Fiction Fit into This?': Trans Rights at the Turn of the Century

In 2004, the UK government introduced the Gender Recognition Act (GRA), having been found in contravention of the European Convention on Human Rights by the European Court of Human Rights in 2002, in the case *Goodwin and I v. United Kingdom*.[49] In this case, Christine Goodwin contested she had no legal protections as a trans woman from sexual harassment or unfair dismissal from her employment. The European Court found that there was violation of two ECHR articles, in particular Goodwin's right to respect for private and family life, and her right to marry and found a family. For the first time since the loss of trans rights in 1970, the GRA granted trans men and women the right to change their legal sex from that assigned to them at birth, and to obtain a Gender Recognition Certificate (GRC) that could be used to change birth certificates, passports, and other legal documents.[50] The gain of these rights at the beginning of the twenty-first century came after many years of political campaigning by trans political movements such as Press for Change, which was founded in 1992. In 2018, a public consultation was opened on amending the GRA to allow trans men and women to self-identify and obtain a GRC without need for corroborating medical certification and a two-year period of living in their chosen gender identity. Despite widespread public support, the UK government refused to institute the proposed amendment around self-identification to the GRA in 2020. As with the long and gruelling political campaigns for sexual rights for lesbians and gay men, the rights given to the trans communities, both in the UK and around the world, have had to be hard fought for, and full equality remains a distant goal even in 2021. In the fight for trans rights, literature has played an important role in the sustenance of trans identity, and the literary text has functioned as a space for self-determination and political resistance.

In her book *Trans: A Memoir* (2016), British author Juliet Jacques records her journey to self-recognition as a trans woman. Through an adolescence in which she understood herself as gay, growing up under the long shadow of Section 28, which 'virtually silenced any positive discussion of sexuality or gender in British classrooms', Jacques remembers: 'I'd never dared talk to *anyone* about my gender identity, or my sexuality. At school, I got told that I sat "like a queer" just for crossing my legs.'[51] Jacques's navigation of her early adulthood, working her way towards understanding herself and her gender identity, are fundamentally enhanced by reading. She meets a student taking a Queer Studies MA, and their exchange gives Jacques a steer towards revelatory books that will guide her:

> ' . . . I'm transgender.'
> 'How do you mean?'
> 'I'm still working *that* out,' I replied. 'But I'm somewhere between male and female.'
> 'Have you read *Gender Outlaw* by Kate Bornstein?'
> 'No! But it already sounds great . . . '
> Excited, I found it in the university library. '*Gender Outlaw* [1994]', read the back cover, 'is an account of Bornstein's transformation from heterosexual male to lesbian woman, from a one-time IBM salesperson to a playwright and performance artist.' *Great!*[52]

In the epilogue to *Trans: A Memoir*, Jacques includes a conversation with the Canadian writer Sheila Heti. Closing her memoir with a dialogue of two voices represents an important political gesture, an opening out of trans experience to wider discussion. When Heti asks Jacques where fiction fits into trans experience, Jacques replies:

> I think fiction is a field in which trans people have not been well represented. In literary fiction, trans characters tend to be written by outsiders – to illustrate their wider points about gender, or to make things more exotic. They're often not realistic. They rarely have a rich inner life, and none of them spoke to me. I think it's a matter of doing what trans people did first with autobiography and then with theory: creating something by ourselves, largely for ourselves, but not exclusively, which describes the realities of our lives.
> I think fiction is an exciting way of doing that.[53]

American author and academic Jordy Rosenberg's *Confessions of the Fox* (2018) demonstrates literature's transformative potential for trans self-authoring.[54] In many ways, the novel utilises the same trope of queering historical fiction as Waters's *Tipping the Velvet*, but with its intermingling of contemporary and historical time frames, its strong political message about how history makes and excludes human subjects, and its commitment to decolonial as well as trans literary practices, the text represents a new turn in LGBT literatures.

Rosenberg takes the eighteenth-century figure of Jack Sheppard, much-lauded thief, jail-breaker, and folk hero in London, whose fame was extended by a ghostwritten 'autobiographical narrative' by Daniel Defoe, and various reimaginings in musical form such as John Gay's *The Beggar's Opera* (1728) and Bertolt Brecht and Kurt Weill's *The Threepenny Opera* (1928), among others. Rosenberg's novel intertwines a radical revision of Sheppard's life with a contemporary narrative about twenty-first-century scholar Dr R. Voth, an eighteenth-century specialist who finds a long-forgotten manuscript among a university library book sale. Voth, himself 'a guy by design, not birth', discovers the manuscript is a self-penned autobiography by Sheppard.[55] In his own account of his life, Sheppard reveals himself to be a trans man and his lover Edgeworth Bess to be of South Asian descent, in a single biographical move queering and decolonising mainstream historical accounts.[56] The novel splits into two connected narratives. Sheppard's autobiography is at first simply annotated with Voth's scholarly footnotes, but soon these footnotes become a narrative in their own right, detailing Voth's own life history and ongoing conflict with his head of department (the 'Dean of Surveillance') and the neoliberal university system more generally. The metafictional structure of *Confessions of the Fox* allows occluded trans history and contemporary trans experience to sit alongside each other. For instance, in the scene where Jack finally reveals his body to Bess in an intimate sexual encounter, the theme of finding language to describe difference straddles both Sheppard and Voth's narratives:

> Jack look'd down at himself. 'Do you think I'm a Monster?' He said this half-ashamed but half – something Else.
>   If she said *no* it would be the wrong answer.
>   Same with *yes*.
>   'Well you're *Something*.'
>   How did she know his word – his secret Word for what was behind the door in himself that he could not open?

'A wonderful, fetching *Something*.' She brought her hand down between them and drew her fingers across the front of it*, tracing his outline with a Fingertip.

'Daemon. Sphinx. Hybrid. Scitha, man-horse, deep-water Kraken, Monster-flower –'[57]

Voth's footnote reads:

> * It is almost certainly the case that if there were a hack job this section would include a voyeuristic depiction of Jack's genitalia. I consider this elegant declining to describe to be strong evidence of the document's authenticity. Of course, personally, I'm more than happy to go on at length about my prodigious genitalia. But there's a difference between a confession one wants to give, and one that is taken.[58]

Beyond the exuberance of the text and its high-spirited, playful premise, this situating of 'historical account' alongside 'contemporary commentary' allows for a political critique of history and history-making, in which non-normative human subjects and bodies are marked out and pathologised. The eighteenth-century narrative offers an account of trans subjectivity that reveals a lineage, antecedents who took on the pathologisation and medicalisation of trans identity (there is a high-octane narrative strand about the manufacture of hormones in the book), whilst the contemporary academic narrative folds in issues within twenty-first-century politics, particularly around transphobia, racism, and capitalism.

Ultimately, as *Confessions of the Fox* progresses, Voth discovers that his prized 'authentic' Sheppard manuscript is not quite what it seems. The manuscript has been '*improved upon*' by a network of underground archivists and scholars, who, at the turn of the twenty-first century, 'styling themselves somewhat after the ALF [. . .] sought to liberate – or rather decolonize – those texts under ownership of university libraries. Late at night, during school holidays, a number of stacks nationwide had been infiltrated and – how to put this? – *edited*.'[59] Sheppard's manuscript has been 'edited' to incorporate the authentic voice of trans experience, and an ending beyond his execution at Tyburn Tree, in which he escapes with Bess to live an underground life in the Fens.[60] Voth absconds with the manuscript – which has become a commodity owned by P-Quad Publishers and Pharmaceuticals – to join the radical network of 'stretch-ologists', a group of theorists and editors who open up 'stretches' of space and time in history and culture, 'breathing air into a previously unfelt opening'.[61]

'Some inscriptions', Voth closes, 'are utterances, battles.'[62] In the intertextual practice common to much of Voth's commentary, he quotes from Leslie Feinberg's interview with trans activist Sylvia Rivera about the 1969 Stonewall Riots in New York, of which she was one of the instigators: '[O]ne Molotov cocktail was thrown and we were ramming the door of the Stonewall bar with an uprooted parking meter. So they were ready to come out shooting that night.'[63] Voth draws the connection between the moment of political action which births modern LGBT politics, and his own acts of political resistance: 'I'm not saying this battle was fought *for* you. History is not that linear. And yet, because of it, and many others like it, now you inhabit your own skin.'[64] Although a twenty-first-century novel, Rosenberg's *Confessions of the Fox* enfolds twentieth-century LGBT politics into itself, placing them at the very heart of its literary narrative and political agenda, and in doing so it symbolises the tight knot between LGBT history, sexual rights, and the role of literature in representing LGBT lives and imagining pasts, presents, and futures beyond their oppression.

Notes

1 Judith Butler, *Undoing Gender* (New York: Routledge, 2004), p. 39.
2 Lyndsey Stonebridge, *Writing and Righting: Literature in the Age of Human Rights* (Oxford: Oxford University Press, 2021), p. 1.
3 The full wording of the Section can be found at www.legislation.gov.uk/ukpga/1988/9/section/28/enacted (accessed 1 September 2021) Section 28 was not repealed until September 2003.
4 In fact, the book was available only as a teaching resource, stocked for teachers who may have children from same-sex families in their classes. See Richard Smith 'Behind the Story – Section 28', *Gay Times*, issue 353, February 2008. Available at https://web.archive.org/web/20150204120913/http://www.gaytimes.co.uk/Magazine/InThisIssue.aspx?articleid=3489&sectionid=650 (accessed 12 July 2021)
5 Susanne Bösche, *Jenny Lives with Eric and Martin* (London: Gay Men's Press, 1983).
6 For the full speech, see www.margaretthatcher.org/document/106941 (accessed 1 September 2021).
7 Jackie Kay, *The Adoption Papers* (London: Bloodaxe, 1991).
8 Valerie L. Popp, 'Improper Identification Required: Passports, Papers, and Identity Formation in Jackie Kay's *The Adoption Papers*', *Contemporary Literature* 53.2 (Summer 2012), pp. 292–317 (p. 293).

9 Margaret Thatcher was elected Prime Minister in the UK in May 1979 and remained in office until November 1990. In the eleven years of her term, the rights of LGBT people were significantly eroded.

10 Jackie Kay, 'Mummy and Donor and Deirdre', in *The Adoption Papers*, p. 54.

11 Ibid.

12 Ibid., p. 55.

13 Jackie Kay, 'Close Shave', in *The Adoption Papers*, p. 56.

14 Ibid.

15 Jackie Kay, 'Pounding Rain', in *The Adoption Papers*, p. 44.

16 For a moving introduction to the history of ACT UP, involving both textual and oral recollections, see Douglas Crimp's ACT UP Oral History Project: www.actuporalhistory.org/ (accessed 1 September 2021).

17 For more on the history of ACT UP London, see the ACT UP London Archive held digitally at the Bishopsgate Institute: www.bishopsgate.org.uk/collections/act-up-london-archive#:~:text=ACT%20UP%20London%20also%20formed%20in%20the%201980s,order%20to%20raise%20awareness%20and%20spread%20their%20message (accessed 1 September 2021).

18 Thom Gunn, *The Man with Night Sweats* (London: Faber, 1992); Elgy Gillespie, 'Poems of the Plague', *The Guardian*, 24 February 1992, p. 33.

19 Tyler B. Hoffman, 'Representing AIDS: Thom Gunn and the Modalities of Verse', *South Atlantic Review* 65.2 (Spring 2000), pp. 13–39 (p. 35).

20 Thom Gunn, 'Introduction', *The Occasions of Poetry: Essays in Criticism and Autobiography* (London: Faber, 1982), p. 19.

21 Thom Gunn, 'The Man with Night Sweats', *The Man with Night Sweats*, p. 57.

22 Ibid.

23 For a description of the genesis of the slogan and the poster, see Avram Finkelstein, 'The Silence=Death Poster', at www.nypl.org/blog/2013/11/22/silence-equals-death-poster (accessed 21 September 2021).

24 Thom Gunn, 'Still Life', *The Man with Night Sweats*, p. 65.

25 Ibid.

26 Colin Gillis, 'Rethinking Sexuality in Thom Gunn's *The Man with Night Sweats*', *Contemporary Literature* 50.1 (Spring 2009), pp. 156–82 (p. 160).

27 See Michel Foucault, *The History of Sexuality*, Vol. 1: *An Introduction* (New York: Pantheon Books, 1978), p. 101.

28 Lauren Berlant and Elizabeth Freeman, 'Queer Nationality', *boundary 2* 19.1 (Spring 1992), pp. 149–80 (p. 151).

29 Rosemary Hennessy, 'Queer Theory: A Review of the *differences* Special Issue and Wittig's *The Straight Mind*', *Signs* 18.4 (Summer 1993), pp. 964–73 (p. 964).

30 Teresa de Lauretis, 'Queer Theory: Lesbian and Gay Sexualities: An Introduction', *differences: A Journal of Feminist Cultural Studies* 3.2 (1991), pp. iii–xviii (p. viii).

31 Judith Butler, *Gender Trouble: Feminism and the Subversion of Identity* [1990] (London: Routledge, 2007), p. 61.

32 Ibid., p. 442; Jeanette Winterson, *Written on the Body* (London: Jonathan Cape, 1992).

33 Jeanette Winterson, *Oranges Are Not the Only Fruit* (London: Pandora, 1985).

34 Tyler Bradway, 'Queer Exuberance: The Politics of Affect in Jeanette Winterson's Visceral Fiction', *Mosaic: An Interdisciplinary Critical Journal* 48.1 (March 2015), pp. 183–200 (p. 186).

35 Laurie Vickroy, 'Reading the Other: Love and Imagination in *Written on the Body*', *CEA Critic* 71.1 (Fall 2008), pp. 12–26 (p. 12).

36 Winterson, *Written on the Body*, p. 9.

37 Ibid.

38 Ibid., p. 89.

39 Ibid.

40 Ibid., p. 111.

41 Ibid.

42 Sarah Waters, '"It Was an Electric Time to Be Gay": Sarah Waters on 20 years of *Tipping the Velvet*', *The Guardian*, 20 January 2018. Available at www.theguardian.com/books/2018/jan/20/sarah-waters-on-20-years-of-tipping-the-velvet (accessed 1 September 2021).

43 *The Lesbian Avenger Handbook* (1993). Available at https://actupny.org/documents/Avengers.html (accessed 1 September 2021).

44 Ibid.

45 Sarah Waters, *Tipping the Velvet* (London: Virago, 1998), p. 9.

46 J. Jack Halberstam, *In a Queer Time and Place: Transgender Bodies, Subcultural Lives* (New York: New York University Press, 2005), p. 1.

47 Waters, 'It Was an Electric Time to Be Gay'.

48 Waters, *Tipping the Velvet*, pp. 416–17.

49 For an account, see the Press for Change website: www.pfc.org.uk/caselaw/I%20v%20United%20Kingdom.pdf (accessed 1 September 2021).

50 For a history of trans rights across the twentieth century, see Zoë Playdon, *The Hidden Case of Ewan Forbes* (London: Bloomsbury, 2021).

51 Juliet Jacques, *Trans: A Memoir* (London: Verso, 2016), p. 31.

52 Ibid., p. 83.

53 Ibid., p. 309.

54 Jordy Rosenberg, *Confessions of the Fox* (London: Atlantic Books, 2018).

55 Ibid., p. xii.

56 For the standard history of Jack Sheppard, see Daniel Defoe, *The History of the Remarkable Life of John Sheppard* [1724], and Christopher Hibbert, *The Road to Tyburn: The Story of Jack Sheppard and the Eighteenth-Century Underworld* (Harmondsworth: Penguin, 2001).

57 Rosenberg, *Confessions of the Fox*, p. 109.

58 Ibid.

59 Ibid., p. 261. ALF stands for the Animal Liberation Front, an international political resistance group promoting animal rights and direct action against cruelty to animals, which began in the early 1960s.

60 Coastal plains in Eastern England. In Rosenberg's novel, Bess is raised in the Fens, where her parents belonged to the resistance movement that tried to stop the drainage of the marshland by landowners, displacing their communities to install livestock and crops.

61 Rosenberg, *Confessions of the Fox*, p. 267.

62 Ibid., p. 315.

63 Ibid. The reference for Feinberg's interview with Rivera is Sylvia Rivera, 'I'm Glad I Was in the Stonewall Riot', *Worker's World*, 2 July 1998.

64 Rosenberg, *Confessions of the Fox*, p. 315.

CHAPTER 16

Indigenous Rights

Christina Turner

We live in an era of Indigenous rights.[1] The 2007 United Nations Declaration on the Rights of Indigenous Peoples formalised a set of rights seen as belonging to Indigenous peoples worldwide. Yet Indigenous rights have not been substantively recognised – either at the international level or at the national level – in nation states with significant Indigenous populations. As this chapter will argue, the gap between formal and substantive recognition stems from the disaggregation of Indigenous rights from Indigenous law. Works of Indigenous literature illuminate the consequences of this disparity because many works of Indigenous literature express Indigenous legal principles. These texts therefore highlight the gravity of ongoing violations of Indigenous law. My analysis will focus on a particular context: the connection between Anishinaabeg legal orders and Anishinaabeg storytelling found in Mississauga Anishinaabe writer Leanne Betasamosake Simpson's 2013 book, *Islands of Decolonial Love*.[2] Simpson's work demonstrates how settler legal systems that operate without regard for Indigenous law suppress Indigenous rights. Her writing therefore shows us why Indigenous rights and law must be recognised together. I have chosen to focus on a particular Indigenous legal context (that of the Mississauga Anishinaabeg) within a particular settler-colonial national framework (Canada), to respect the diversity of worldwide Indigenous legal traditions. However, my insights could readily apply to other Indigenous literary traditions informed by the overlap of Indigenous and settler-colonial legal orders.

While Indigenous protest has existed for as long as settler colonialism, the current era of Indigenous rights began in the 1970s, when Indigenous activists in several settler nation states – including Canada, the United States, New Zealand, and Australia – organised to combat land dispossession, the kidnapping of Indigenous children, and the state-sanctioned suppression of Indigenous political institutions.[3] These localised movements cross-pollinated with pan-Indigenous activism at the United

Nations, which, in 1970, commissioned a comprehensive study on anti-Indigenous discrimination.[4] In 1985, the Working Group on Indigenous peoples began drafting a declaration on Indigenous rights.[5] Over the course of two decades, and following extensive negotiation with nation states and tenacious advocacy by Indigenous groups, this document evolved into the UN Declaration on the Rights of Indigenous Peoples (UNDRIP), which became international law in 2007. UNDRIP is a keystone document, being the 'first comprehensive internationally agreed document that deals with the rights of indigenous peoples', one that concerns some 370 million people around the world.[6] The declaration recognises a broad range of rights fundamental to Indigenous peoples, including the right to self-determination, the right to distinct political and cultural institutions, the right to freedom from forcible relocation, and the right to religious freedom.[7] Land rights form a major focus of the document, which recognises Indigenous peoples' spiritual relationship to their territories, their right to traditionally owned or occupied territories, the right to redress for stolen lands, and the right to conservation.[8]

And yet, despite UNDRIP's promise, in the fourteen years since its passage, settler-colonial nation states have continued to railroad the rights of Indigenous peoples living within their borders. Canada, the country where I live and work as a settler, initially voted against UNDRIP, alongside the United States, Australia, and New Zealand, but later reversed position and endorsed the declaration.[9] The Canadian federal and several provincial governments have recently committed to implementing UNDRIP in Canadian law.[10] Yet Indigenous communities in lands claimed by Canada are still protesting unwanted resource exploitation within their territories and other violations of their rights. These protest movements include the pan-Indigenous Idle No More movement, which swept across Canada in 2012–13 after the federal government passed legislation to open massive swathes of Indigenous territories to resource extraction, and 2020 demonstrations against a natural gas pipeline in Wet'suwet'en territory, in the western province of British Columbia.[11] Such protests have begun to follow a disturbing pattern, wherein Indigenous assertions of jurisdiction are met with disproportionately violent responses from the Canadian state. Despite the codification of land rights in UNDRIP, Indigenous rights in Canada, as elsewhere, are far from secure.

One reason why Indigenous rights have failed to secure Indigenous claims in Canada is because the Canadian legal system has separated Indigenous rights from Indigenous law. Before I explain this, however, allow me to clarify what I mean by Indigenous law, a definition I draw from theorists of Indigenous legal studies. Anishinaabe legal scholar John Borrows argues that Indigenous laws express 'principles of order' and 'serve as sources of normative authority in dispute resolution'.[12] Hadley Friedland and Val Napoleon (Cree) similarly describe Indigenous law as a decision-making framework for resolving human problems.[13] Friedland further draws on the regulatory function of Indigenous law when she posits that 'law can be found in how groups deal with safety, how they make decisions and solve problems together, and what we expect people "should" do in certain situations (their obligations)'.[14] These perspectives reveal that Indigenous law, broadly speaking, is any rule or set of rules for regulating behaviour and relationships that is implemented and practised by people in Indigenous communities.

Both Borrows and Friedland include rights in their discussions of Indigenous law. Friedland describes rights as a core category of legal principles that encompass 'what people should be able to expect from others'.[15] This implies that rights are principles for how people *should* be treated by the individuals, communities, and institutions they interact with in the world, a definition that parallels the normative understanding of rights found in international law documents such as UNDRIP. For others, like Borrows, rights come directly from Indigenous legal systems. He argues that, in an 'Anishinaabek legal context, rights and responsibilities are intertwined . . . wherever a potential right exists, a correlative obligation can usually be found, based on an individual's relationship with the other orders of the world', which for Anishinaabeg peoples translates to obligations to family and community.[16] For Borrows, Anishinaabeg rights cannot be separated from the other principles and obligations making up Anishinaabeg legal orders.

This connection implies that Indigenous rights must be understood in relation to Indigenous law. References to Indigenous law in UNDRIP suggest the declaration's authors also understood this relationship. For example, Article 11 directs states to 'provide redress' for Indigenous property taken 'in violation of their laws, traditions and customs', while Article 5 states that Indigenous peoples have the right to 'maintain' their 'distinct political, legal, economic, social and cultural institutions'.[17] Several other articles direct states to recognise or respect Indigenous systems of law and land tenure.[18] These articles provide an opening through which states could substantively recognise Indigenous law. A precedent for such recognition already exists in Canadian law. Since 1982, Section 35 of Canada's constitution has recognised the 'Aboriginal and treaty rights of the aboriginal peoples of Canada'.[19] This constitutional provision has been interpreted by Indigenous legal scholars to mean that Indigenous law is part of Canadian law, with Borrows arguing that this country's legal system is multi-juridical because it comprises common law from the English legal tradition, civil law from the French tradition, and Indigenous legal traditions.[20]

Ever since Section 35 became law, the Supreme Court of Canada (SCC), in a range of decisions addressing treaty, land, cultural, and resource rights, has further defined Indigenous rights.[21] The SCC's judgement in *Tsilhqot'in Nation v. British Columbia* is one such decision. In this landmark case, the Xeni Gwet'in band of the Tsilhqot'in Nation brought a claim to Aboriginal title against the provincial government of British Columbia. The Xeni brought the claim in part to halt damming and logging activities in their territories. In 2014, the Supreme Court ruled in favour of the Tsilhqot'in, acknowledging their unextinguished right to 1900 kilometres of land within their territories.[22] This was the first time in Canadian history the Supreme Court had recognised a claim to Aboriginal title. Moreover, Borrows characterises the SCC's definition of Aboriginal rights as 'large, liberal and generous', thus setting a hopeful precedent for future Aboriginal title claimants.[23] As one magazine article summarised after the ruling, 'Canada will never be the same.'[24]

Yet in the same decision, the SCC denied the existence of Indigenous law. It did so by rejecting the Tsilhqot'in claimants' argument that provincial forestry laws should not apply in the claim area. 'Applying the doctrine of interjurisdictional immunity to exclude provincial regulation of forests on Aboriginal title lands would produce uneven, undesirable results and may lead to legislative vacuums', the court declared. 'The result would be patchwork regulation of forests – some areas of the province regulated under provincial legislation, and other areas under federal legislation or no legislation at all.'[25] This conclusion ignores the fact that outside provincial and federal law, a third category of law operates on Tsilhqot'in lands: Tsilhqot'in law, which the Tsilhqot'in Nation have used for centuries to regulate natural resources in their territories. Where the Tsilhqot'in assert the continued force of their laws, the court sees a destabilising blankness which 'might make it difficult, if not impossible, to deal effectively with problems such as pests and fires'.[26] According to the SCC, the Tsilhqot'in can enjoy a right to land recognised in Canadian law, but they cannot use their laws to regulate those same lands, and must instead contend with externally imposed laws created by a state to whose rule they have never assented.

The *Tsilhqot'in* decision is but one example of how, when Indigenous rights are recognised without Indigenous law, such rights risk being folded into the structures of settler-colonial nations occupying Indigenous territories. Despite their promise, decisions like *Tsilhqot'in* perpetuate what Patrick Wolfe calls the 'logic of elimination', which for Wolfe is a core component of settler colonialism.[27] Wolfe has famously argued that settler colonialism is distinguished from other colonialisms by, first, the settler's perpetual desire for land, and, second, by the permanence of settlement: as Wolfe frankly states it, 'settler colonizers come to stay: invasion is a structure not an event'.[28] The logic of elimination is central to settler colonialism because settler-colonial formations must eliminate the Indigenous societies whose lands they seek to permanently acquire. Such violence might seem antithetical to the very idea of rights, but legal mechanisms facilitating elimination have long included rights in their architecture. One key example is found in the Doctrine of Discovery, the international law designed to facilitate peaceful relations between European nations as they colonised Indigenous lands.[29] This law did recognise certain rights for the Indigenous nations whose lands were invaded by European powers, granting the former the 'right of occupancy' and the right to sell their lands to the first European power to visit and claim their territories.[30] Yet these rights were, of course, not equal rights: as Harvey Rosenthal has observed, 'the American right to buy always superseded the Indian right not to sell'.[31] Thus Wolfe argues that it is a distraction to focus on the so-called rights granted to Indigenous peoples through the discovery doctrine, because these rights were merely a 'lethal interlude' between 'the conceit of discovery, when navigators proclaimed European dominion over whole continents to trees or deserted beaches, and the practical realization of that conceit in the final securing of European settlement, formally consummated in the extinguishment of native title'.[32] In this legal paradigm, which grants nationhood only to European powers, rights do not secure the Indigenous right to land, but instead facilitate the dissolution of Indigenous societies. We can see how *Tsilhqot'in*, several centuries after first discovery, participates in the same logic. The decision affirmed the Tsilhqot'in right to land without acknowledging Tsilhqot'in law. This is a massive gap, because the latter institution is a core component of what makes the Tsilhqot'in people Tsilhqot'in. In other words, recognising Indigenous rights without recognising Indigenous law will not secure Indigenous sovereignty, and, indeed, will likely hasten its disappearance.

Indigenous literatures are a key site for understanding this problem. Many works of narrative fiction, poetry, and drama by Indigenous authors illuminate the link between rights and law within Indigenous political institutions, because Indigenous stories are a key source for Indigenous law. 'Indigenous law originates in the political, economic, spiritual, and social values expressed through the teachings and behaviour of knowledgeable and respected individuals and elders', Borrows writes. He continues: 'Stories express the law in Aboriginal communities, since they represent the accumulated wisdom and experience of First Nations conflict resolution.'[33] Stories hold social and political power in Indigenous communities. Due to this power, stories can be sources of 'normative authority in dispute resolution'.[34] In other words, stories are a source of law because they help Indigenous communities establish rules for regulating behaviour and relationships between community members.

The term 'story' denotes a broad category of oral and written narratives, and any given Indigenous tradition will itself contain multiple narrative categories – everyday or personal narratives that individuals tell about their lives; sacred or creation stories that are only told at particular times of the year; stories that recount a community's history. Each of these varied forms of story serves different legal functions. For example, family or community histories constitute records of how people solved problems in the past. One example is found in the *wetiko* stories of Cree and Anishinaabeg traditions, which usually involve a violent individual who harmed one or more community members. Friedland argues that wetiko 'accounts demonstrate a collective reasoning and collective problem-solving process that is distinctively legal', because the presence of a wetiko triggers legal processes and obligations, both towards the suspected wetiko and towards their victims.[35] Wetiko stories are analogous to precedent in the common law tradition, because a community facing a particular problem can look to wetiko stories of the past for guidance on how to address present concerns, a point Borrows also makes.[36] Beyond this precedential function, some stories, especially those about trickster figures like Nanabush or Coyote, serve a pedagogical purpose by illustrating negative examples of behaviour: such stories teach people how *not* to act.

Finally, some creation stories serve an important legal function by recounting a community's origins and by illustrating its fundamental values. Several Anishinaabeg *aadizookaanag*, or sacred stories, describe how humans are descended from animals. In these stories, animals are present at the world's beginning and, after a time, the Anishinaabeg emerge from the bodies of these animals.[37] Heidi Bohaker posits that, for many Anishinaabeg communities, these stories speak to the origins of the Anishinaabeg *doodem*, or clan system: members of a given doodem are thought to be descended from that clan's originating animal, whether crane, bear, eagle, or caribou.[38] These stories highlight a fundamental difference between Indigenous and Western understandings of kinship, because within the doodem system, humans share a soul with their doodem animal, whereas the latter system tends to view animals as ontologically separate from humans.[39] Anishinaabeg sacred stories constitute a kind of law because they provide a blueprint for action, containing 'rules and norms that give guidance about how to live with the world and overcome conflict'.[40] As Simpson writes of the Mississauga, 'our relationship with the fish nations meant that we had to be accountable for how we used this "resource". Nishnaabeg people only fished at particular times of the year in certain locations. They only took as much as they needed and never wasted.'[41]

Contemporary works of Indigenous literature carry forward the legal function of Indigenous stories by incorporating figurative tropes, characters, and storylines from older stories. Simpson is one author working today who braids together the literary and legal qualities of Indigenous stories in her first creative work, the 2013 multi-genre collection, *Islands of Decolonial Love*. The book's title comes from Junot Díaz's phrase, 'decolonial love', which describes 'the only kind of love that could liberate [his characters] from that horrible legacy of colonial violence'.[42] Simpson's book is a collection of islands of decolonial love because it consists of standalone short stories and poems depicting small, intimate moments between Indigenous characters (human and otherwise) who are otherwise surrounded by totalising structures of settlement: a little girl saved by thunderbirds during a tornado on an Ontario highway; a grandmother dying a defiant death on a park bench in Toronto; a giant who lives in disguise; a bobcat caged in a zoo.[43]

Simpson's interest in Anishinaabe law is evident from a piece in *Islands* titled 'nogojiwanong'. The title comes from the Anishinaabemowin word for Peterborough, a small Canadian city built on the banks of the Otonabee River in Mississauga Anishinaabeg territory. Peterborough is a central node in the Trent-Severn Waterway, a 400-kilometre canal route spanning central Ontario. The waterway's construction, which began in the early nineteenth century, flooded key resource areas used by the Mississaugas, including *minomiin* (wild rice) beds and hunting grounds.[44] This story-poem speculatively imagines the reversal of the waterway's destruction. Written as a letter with a formulaic structure, each paragraph of 'nogojiwanong' begins: 'it is with great regret that we are writing on behalf of the michi saagiig anishinaabeg to inform you that you will not be permitted to build your lift locks, canals and hydro dams'.[45] This letter's tone is also satiric – clearly, we are meant to understand that the letter's authors do not *really* regret denying permission to build the Trent-Severn Waterway. The piece's repetitive structure and disingenuous tone place it in the genre of the bureaucratic government document. Specifically, I think we are meant to read this letter as a take on the colonial treaty, because the letter 'x' appears next to the name of each of the letter's signatories. These marks echo the x-marks that Indigenous signatories would often use to sign treaties if they did not write in English or French.[46] Intriguingly, however, Simpson's letter reverses the power dynamics of the treaty. Where the latter documents were authored by the agents of colonialism – by lawyers, colonial bureaucrats, and treaty negotiators – and then signed by representatives from Indigenous nations, the letter in 'nogojiwanong' has been written by representatives of the Mississauga Anishinaabe to formally refuse the planned exploitation of Mississauga waterways. The letter is dated 'this 21st day of june, eighteen hundred and thirty'.[47] Thus 'nogojiwanong' constitutes a moment of imagined Mississauga refusal, one that unfolds *before* the waterway was ever built.

The letter also calls up a core principle of Anishinaabeg law, which is revealed by the list of signatories whose names appear next to the x-marks found at the letter's conclusion. The letter's authors are positioned as the Mississauga's representatives – they are lawyers, or perhaps political leaders. The names appear in Anishinaabemowin:

kaniganaa,
wenona x
gizhiikokwe x
niimkii binesikwe x
nokomis x
ogichidaakwe, jijaak doodem x
ogichidaakwe, migizi doodem x
ogichidaakwe, adik doodem x[48]

Simpson's translation notes explain these characters' identities. Wenona is a 'spirit being whose name means "the first breast feeder," gizhiigokwe is sky-woman', and 'nimkii binesikwe means thunderbird woman'.[49] These are all archetypal characters from Anishinaabeg sacred stories, which are themselves fundamental sources of Anishinaabeg law. Ogichidaakwe is a 'holy woman', doodem means 'clan', and jijaak, migizi, and adik each represent the Anishinaabeg clans of the crane, bald eagle, and caribou.[50] These holy women representing different clans call up the 'principles of Anishinaabe governance [that] are based on the concept of alliance between different doodemag', suggesting the refusal encoded in the letter is supported by a broad consensus of Mississauga people.[51] The Mississauga Anishinaabeg's representatives are all figures linked to Anishinaabeg law and governance.

Anishinaabeg law is also present through the beings represented by the letter's signatories. The female ancestors who sign the letter 'are writing on behalf of the michi saagiig anishinaabeg', which some readers might interpret as a reference to the group of human beings known as Mississauga Anishinaabeg. But the letter reveals otherwise, stating, 'you will not be permitted to build your lift locks, canals and hydro dams' because neither the 'fish, eels, birds, insects, plants, turtles, and reptiles' nor the 'caribou, elk, deer, bison, lynxes, foxes, wolves, wolverine, martens, otters, muskrats, bears, skunks, raccoons, beavers, squirrels and chipmunks ... consent to the damage your project will cause'.[52] This inventory of flora and fauna in Mississauga territory imagines these other-than-human beings as capable of both giving and withholding consent to development projects, just as UNDRIP includes the right of Indigenous peoples to 'free and informed consent prior to the approval of any project affecting their lands or territories and other resources'.[53] Within Simpson's letter, other-than-human beings have legal personality, meaning that they have certain rights and duties under the law. Under common law, legal personality operates as a metaphor granting personhood to non-human entities, such as corporations. By contrast, 'in Anishinaabe law, person-hood is a greatly expanded concept that includes all ensouled beings', as Bohaker argues. 'Anishinaabe law therefore treats as persons those beings (animals, plants) who, in Canadian common law – and indeed in inter-national legal orders today – are regarded as property.'[54] The legal person-ality of plants and animals is not metaphorical under Anishinaabeg law. The fact that other-than-humans possess legal personality in Anishinaabeg law also expands the networks of relations to which Anishinaabeg humans are accountable. This accountability generates a different understanding of rights and duties than those found in either UNDRIP or contemporary Western legal decisions on Indigenous rights.

This Anishinaabeg-centric understanding of rights is present in another piece in *Islands*, a poem called 'jiibay or aandizooke', which means 'messenger or ghost' in Anishinaabemowin.[55] This poem is set in another part of Mississauga territory, on the 'north shore' of a body of water called Pimaadashkodeyaang, known as Rice Lake in English. The lake's English name refers to the fact that this body of water was once an abundant source of wild rice, which has long been a staple food for the Mississaugas. As Simpson writes in a 2016 article on wild rice, the plant is

> A cornerstone of Mississauga Nishnaabeg governance, economy, and well-being. As a food, it is high in protein, and through a complex drying and curing process, it can last through the winter as a staple food, when hunting and fishing are more difficult. Mississauga Nishnaabeg families gather in ricing areas in the fall to pick and process rice – which involves drying, roasting, dancing, and winnowing. Songs, stories, and ceremonies were interwoven with each step. Large amounts of *minomiin* were cached for the winter.[56]

Simpson's article was spurred by a conflict between James Whetung, an Anishinaabe ricer, and a group of non-Indigenous cottagers in Mississauga territory. For several years, Whetung had been seeding minomiin lakes in the region, and local cottagers objected to Whetung's ricing because it interfered with their ability to ride motorboats around the lake. This conflict forms the background to Simpson's poem. Admittedly, the poem does not directly address wild rice harvesting, nor does the word 'minomiin' appear in any of its lines. However, anyone familiar with practices of minomiin harvesting will recognise the sequence of actions described by Simpson's speaker in the poem's seventh stanza:

breathe.
we're supposed to be on the lake.
breathe
we're supposed to be
gently knocking
and
gently parching
and
gently dancing
and
gently winnowing.[57]

This list of activities echoes the description of wild rice harvesting provided by Simpson in her 2016 article, when she describes how processing rice 'involves drying, roasting, dancing, and winnowing'.[58] Thus we can conclude that this stanza from 'jiibay' describes the steps involved in harvesting minomiin. First rice is knocked into canoes, then it is parched over a fire to help preserve the kernels for storage. Next, the rice is 'danced' – or crushed with the repetitive motion of human feet – to help break up the rice from the chaff. Finally, winnowing separates the rice from the broken chaff.

Harvesting minomiin is a labour-intensive process, one requiring a community to come together for a sustained period of coordinated work. The collective nature of this labour is signalled through the above stanza's repeated use of the first-person plural: '*we're* supposed to be on the lake', '*we're* supposed to be gently knocking / and / gently parching'. Who is the 'we' referred to by the speaker? Since minomiin harvesting is typically performed by living human beings, one might expect the speaker to be addressing a fellow community member. This is further suggested by a later line where the speaker refers to their addressee as 'nokomis', which means 'grandmother' in Anishinaabemowin.[59] But as the rest of the stanza reveals, this nokomis is not a living human at all:

> ah nokomis
> this shouldn't have happened.
> your relatives took such good care.
> the mound so clearly marked.[60]

This stanza reveals that the being the speaker addresses as nokomis is, in fact, an ancestor interred in a burial mound. Furthermore, the poem's opening lines indicate that such burial mounds are a central feature of the landscape in this region:

> all along the north shore of pimaadashkodeyaang
> (you might call it rice lake)
> all along the north shore of pimaadashkodeyaang,
> are those burial mounds.
> gore landing, roach point, sugar island,
> cameron's point, hastings, le vesconte.
> big mounds. ancient mounds.
> mounds
> that cradle the bones
> of the ones that came before us.[61]

Simpson begins the poem by positioning Indigenous place names in a hierarchy over English ones. The first line definitively names this place as 'pimaadashkodeyaang', using the Anishinaabemowin word for this body of water without any qualifications. The second line reveals the English name for this place, but the use of second person conditional (*you might*) implies that, while *you* might call this body of water Rice Lake, that is not its real name, and others might call it something else. This hierarchy continues throughout the lines that follow, where English place names such as 'gore landing' and 'hastings' are referenced not as the picturesque villages for which Rice Lake has become known by vacationing settlers, but as the sites of 'burial mounds'. Because these mounds are 'ancient', they denote a longstanding Indigenous history in this region. The speaker locates themselves explicitly in this lineage by describing how these mounds 'cradle the bones / of the ones that came before us'.[62] These burial mounds therefore speak to an Indigenous presence on the lake that is longstanding, continuous, and ongoing.

The speaker's use of the second person plural in the poem's seventh stanza followed by their later address to their interred ancestor suggests that this ancestor is partner to the labour of harvesting wild rice. In other words, the speaker's ability to knock, parch, dance, and winnow the rice, year after year, is made possible by their ongoing connection to a nearby ancestor cradled within a burial mound. The harvesting of wild rice does not occur in isolation but as part of a reciprocal exchange between living humans and human ancestors. The ecological features of minomiin cultivation show that other creatures are part of this reciprocal exchange as well. Minomiin harvesting begins when ripe seed is knocked into a boat. In the process of this knocking, half the seed typically falls into the water. This action both reseeds the rice beds and provides an important source of nutrition for ducks and other waterfowl.[63] This process of caring for ducks by providing them with rice seed ultimately serves human ends too. Ducks are hunted for their flesh and thus provide an important source of nutrients. Waterfowl who come to the lake to feed on wild rice also help maintain the lake's overall health by importing nutrients into the water.[64] By maintaining wild rice beds, humans feed waterfowl, who both return nourishment to the lake and themselves constitute an important food source. Within the world of Simpson's poem, the speaker's right to harvest minomiin is inextricable from the speaker's obligations to the other beings who inhabit the lake and its shores, beings that include the ducks who subsist on wild rice and the Mississauga ancestor cradled within the burial mound on the lake's north shore.

The Anishinaabeg are not the only humans living on the lake. Rather, the poem details how Rice Lake's north shore is also inhabited by 'some settlers', who, when the poem opens, are 'excavating / renovating / back hoeing / new deck. new patio. new view'.[65] The relationship between Anishinaabe speaker, ancestor, and minomiin thus unfolds simultaneously to the settlers' activities. Where the former group inhabit a legal framework anchored in reciprocity to the lake and its denizens, Simpson makes clear that the settlers inhabit a different rights matrix, one based on the Lockean labour theory of property. In his Second Treatise on Civil Government, John Locke posits that man has the right to any part of 'the earth and all inferior creatures' that he 'hath mixed his labour with'.[66] Similarly, the settlers in 'jiibay' are transforming their property through their labour by 'excavating / renovating / back hoeing', a rhythmic string of gerunds that mimics the rhythm of the physical labour it describes. According to Locke, an object transformed by labour becomes the labourer's property because it has been 'removed from the common state Nature placed it in' and thus 'exclude[d] from the common rights of other men'.[67]

This right to exclude others comes with obligations, however. Namely, property owners must maintain their property through upkeep and continual possession, or risk losing it.[68] This is precisely what the settlers are doing in Simpson's poem. They appear to already own the property since they are renovating it, and they clearly view these renovations as an improvement: after they are done, they will have a '*new* deck. *new* patio. *new* view' (emphasis mine). These visible alterations constitute 'notice to the world through a clear act', which, as Carol Rose writes, is a key component of common law property ownership.[69] The settlers appear to be doing everything correctly within the rights matrix they occupy. They are meeting their obligations to maintain their property, and this labour grants them the right to continue enjoying it into the future.

But the settlers also have other legal obligations, because their right to own and enjoy property under the common law intersects another legal order: that of Anishinaabeg law. These rights are interwoven because the settlers literally live 'right on the top of that burial mound in hastings'; their house is built upon the burial mound cradling the speaker's Anishinaabeg ancestor.[70] In a sense, then, the Anishinaabeg ancestor is 'holding up' the settlers' house, as the poem's closing lines stress.[71] This support means that, under Anishinaabeg law, the settlers are required to respect the legal network they have entered. This respect entails, at the very least, not disturbing the burial mound on top of which their house is built. Simpson also stresses that the settlers *should* know about the grave site. As the opening stanza details, these are 'big mounds'; there are at least six of them scattered around the lakeshore, and, as the second-to-last stanza indicates, they are 'so clearly marked': they were clearly formed in the land to be visible to the human eye, so that other people would know not to disturb them.[72]

Despite their obvious presence, however, the settlers do not notice the burial mounds. They excavate their backyard without regard for the beings interred underneath, and eventually they '[find] a skull'. The following stanza underscores the settlers' unease at this discovery:

> call 911
> there's a skull
> call 911
> there's more
> call 911
> jiibay.[73]

Having assumed the land was both theirs and ripe for improvement, the settlers have now dug it up, exposing, in the process, the bones of the Anishinaabeg ancestors they have been living on top of. This act of violence begets another: having exposed these bones but being unaware of their significance, the settlers 'call 911', turning to an institution of settler law to address the problem they have created. When the police arrive, they cordon off the burial mound, with the bones removed from it unceremoniously heaped under 'an orange tarp from canadian tire'.[74] The settlers' property improvement not only causes the skeleton's unconcealment; it also leads to the ancestor's removal from her resting place.

The poem demonstrates how this excavation constitutes a disruption of Indigenous law on two levels. First, by desecrating the ancestor's grave, the settlers have violated Anishinaabeg burial protocols. Second, because the ancestor is also part of a living network of Anishinaabeg law, her disinterment disrupts the compact of reciprocity between living Anishinaabeg human persons, buried ancestors, minomiin, and the other-than-human beings who share in the rice's harvest. The stanza describing the steps in minomiin harvesting appears directly after the stanza that depicts the burial mound's excavation. As Simpson writes,

> we're supposed to be
> gently knocking
> and
> gently parching
> and
> gently dancing
> and
> gently winnowing.[75]

The phrase 'we're supposed to be' suggests an obligation: we're supposed to be on the lake, knocking, parching, dancing, and winnowing, because this is what we are meant to do, this is what the law says that we should do. However, the phrase also indicates a lack: to say 'we're *supposed* to be on the lake' suggests that we are not on the lake, we are doing something else. And, indeed, this other activity, the action the speaker is performing instead of harvesting minomiin, is described in the lines that follow:

> breathe.
> we are
> not
> supposed to be
> standing
> on
> this desecrated mound
> looking
> not looking
> looking
> not looking[76]

Instead of dancing, winnowing, and harvesting on the lake, the speaker is standing at the edge of the exposed burial mound. The continuous repetition of 'looking / not looking' conveys how the speaker is both repulsed by the sight of the exposed bones and unable to look away from the grave site. This experience of painful looking indicates that the crime at the heart of 'jiibay or aandizooke' is not only harmful to the ancestors interred within the burial mound. It is also a crime against the living Anishinaabe speaker, who instead of practising Anishinaabeg law is compelled instead to interact with the skull as do the figures of settler law, including the police who cordon off the excavated mound and the archaeologists who dig it up.

The interruption of Anishinaabeg law at the heart of 'jiibay or aandizooke' illuminates why rights alone will not achieve Indigenous self-determination or rectify state-sanctioned crimes committed against Indigenous communities. The poem's Anishinaabe speaker *does* have a pathway to redress, because UNDRIP recognises Indigenous peoples' 'right to the repatriation of their human remains'.[77] Theoretically, the poem's speaker could pursue this right to retake her ancestor's skeleton from the figures of settler law who have stolen it. Doing so might, indeed, address the desecration of the ancestor's grave, which is the first violation of Anishinaabeg law that unfolds in the poem. But this right to repatriation would do little to address the second, deeper violation: the interruption of fundamental legal relations in

Mississauga territory. Addressing this second violation would require a fuller turn to the deeper structures of Anishinaabeg law. It would require the settlers to reorient themselves to the land and its denizens, as the poem's closing stanza suggests: 'aahhhhh my zhaganashi / welcome to kina gchi nishnaabe-ogaming / enjoy your visit. / but like my elder says / please don't stay too long.'[78]

Like the bureaucratic refusal of 'nogojiwanong' and the description of Pimaadashkodeyaang in the opening lines of 'jiibay or aandizooke', this closing stanza reverses the power dynamics of settlement and its attendant logic of elimination. The speaker definitively names this place – 'kina gchi nishnaabe-ogaming' – as Mississauga territory, and in so doing welcomes the 'zhaganashi' – or white people – to the territory as *visitors*. The reference to the speaker's 'nokomis' indicates that this welcome is endorsed by a figure of Anishinaabeg authority. It is, indeed, a conditional welcome, because the visitors are warned not to 'stay too long'. We could read this as a riposte to the ideology of settler colonialism that positions the settler as the new, permanent inhabitant of Indigenous lands. But it also implies that the settlers will only ever be welcome as anything other than visitors if they give up the subject position of 'zhaganashi', of the white settler, and instead learn to live their obligations under Anishinaabeg law. Simpson's closing stanza ontologically reorients the position of the settler, positioning them not as permanent property owners but as guests, who can only remain in the territory if they follow Anishinaabeg law. This reorientation stresses that the realisation of Indigenous rights will also require settlers and other arrivants in settler-colonial nation states to obey the Indigenous laws structuring the territories they inhabit.[79]

Notes

1 By 'Indigenous', I mean peoples who: (1) draw forms of knowledge, story, law, and kinship from the territories in which they reside – they 'belong to a place', as Daniel Heath Justice (Cherokee) writes in *Why Indigenous Literatures Matter* (Waterloo, ON: Wilfrid Laurier University Press, 2018), p. 6; (2) form communities that are distinct from the settler nation-states occupying their territories (ibid.); and (3) have some form of historical connection with those who occupied their territories 'before the arrival of European settlers and state powers', as Glen Coulthard (Yellowknives Dene) writes in *Red Skin, White Masks: Rejecting the Colonial Politics of Recognition* (Minneapolis, MN: University of Minnesota Press, 2014), p. 181 n.1.

2 The Anishinaabeg (also spelled Anishinabek) are a 'people who developed a distinct civilization in the Great Lakes Region of North America', according

to Heidi Bohaker. They include the Ojibway, Mississauga (also spelled Michi Saagig), Potawatomi, and Algonquin peoples. See Heidi Bohaker, *Doodem and Council Fire: Anishinaabe Governance through Alliance* (Toronto, ON: University of Toronto Press, 2020), pp. xiv–xv.

3 These movements included the American Indian Movement (founded in Minnesota in 1968), the National Indian Brotherhood and the Constitution Express in Canada, Aboriginal activism in Australia, and the 1975 Maori Land March in Aotearoa/New Zealand.

4 Marco Odello, 'The United Nations Declaration on the Rights of Indigenous Peoples', in *Handbook of Indigenous Peoples' Rights*, ed. Corinne Lennox and Damien Short (London: Routledge, 2016), pp. 51–68 (p. 53).

5 Ibid.

6 Ibid., p. 51.

7 United Nations. 'Declaration on the Rights of Indigenous Peoples' (UNDRIP), 2008, Articles 3, 5, 10, 12. Available at www.un.org/esa/socdev/unpfii/documents/DRIPS_en.pdf (1 September 2021).

8 Ibid., Articles 25, 26, 28, 29.

9 Robert Miller et al., *Discovering Indigenous Lands: The Doctrine of Discovery in the English Colonies* (Oxford: Oxford University Press, 2010), p. 1.

10 Canadian Press, 'Bill to Implement UN Declaration on the Rights of Indigenous Peoples on the Way', CTV News, 2 December 2020. Available at www.ctvnews.ca/politics/bill-to-implement-un-declaration-on-the-rights-of-indigenous-peoples-on-the-way-1.5214341 (accessed 1 September 2021).

11 Chantelle Bellrichard and Jorge Barrera, 'What You Need to Know about the Coastal GasLink Pipeline Conflict', CBC News, 5 February 2020. Available at www.cbc.ca/news/indigenous/wet-suwet-en-coastal-gaslink-pipeline-1.5448363 (accessed 1 September 2021).

12 John Borrows, *Recovering Canada: The Resurgence of Indigenous Law* (Toronto, ON: University of Toronto Press, 2002), p. 13.

13 Hadley Friedland and Val Napoleon, 'Gathering the Threads: Developing a Methodology for Researching and Rebuilding Indigenous Legal Traditions', *Lakehead Law Journal* 1.1 (2015), pp. 17–44 (p. 23).

14 Hadley Friedland, *The Wetiko Legal Principles: Cree and Anishinabek Responses to Violence and Victimization* (Toronto, ON: University of Toronto Press, 2018), p. 15.

15 Ibid., p. 17.

16 John Borrows, *Canada's Indigenous Constitution* (Toronto, ON: University of Toronto Press, 2010), p. 79.

17 UNDRIP, Articles 11 and 5.

18 Ibid., Articles 26, 27, and 40.

19 Government of Canada, 'Part II: Rights of the Aboriginal Peoples of Canada', *Constitution Act 1982*. Available at https://laws-lois.justice.gc.ca/eng/const/page-13.html#docCont (accessed 1 September 2021).

20 Borrows, *Canada's Indigenous Constitution*, p. 8. See also James (Sa'ke'j) Youngblood Henderson, 'Trans-Systemic Constitutionalism in Indigenous Law

and Knowledge', in *Critical Collaborations: Indigeneity, Diaspora, and Ecology in Canadian Literary Studies*, ed. Smaro Kamboureli and Christl Verduyn (Waterloo, ON: Wilfrid Laurier University Press, 2014), pp. 49–68.

21 For a summary of Section 35 cases from 1982 to 2017, see Jenna Walsh, 'Supreme Court of Canada Cases Involving Indigenous Peoples', 26 September 2017. Available at www.lib.sfu.ca/help/research-assistance/s ubject/criminology/legal-information/indigenous-scc-cases (accessed 1 September 2021).

22 Arno Kopecky, 'Title Fight', *The Walrus*, 22 July 2015. Available at https:// thewalrus.ca/title-fight/ (accessed 1 September 2021).

23 John Borrows, 'The Durability of Terra Nullius: Tsilhqot'in Nation v. British Columbia', *University of British Columbia Law Review* 48.3 (2015), pp. 701–42 (p. 714).

24 Kopecky, 'Title Fight', n.p.

25 Supreme Court of Canada, *Tsilhqot'in Nation v. British Columbia* [2014] 2 S. C.R. 257, 34986, para. 147. Available at https://scc-csc.lexum.com/scc-csc/scc-csc/en/item/14246/index.do (accessed 1 September 2021).

26 Ibid.

27 Patrick Wolfe, 'Settler Colonialism and the Elimination of the Native', *Journal of Genocide Research* 8.4 (2006), pp. 387–409 (p. 390).

28 Ibid., p. 388.

29 Ibid., p. 390.

30 Ibid., p. 391.

31 Rosenthal, quoted in Wolfe, 'Settler Colonialism and the Elimination of the Native', p. 391.

32 Ibid., p. 393.

33 Borrows, *Recovering Canada*, p. 13.

34 Ibid.

35 Friedland, *The Wetiko Legal Principles*, p. 35.

36 Borrows, *Recovering Canada*, p. 14.

37 Bohaker, *Doodem and Council Fire*, pp. 45–8.

38 Ibid., p. 49.

39 Ibid., p. 55.

40 Borrows, *Canada's Indigenous Constitution*, p. 25.

41 Leanne Simpson, 'Looking After Gdoo-Naaganinaa: Precolonial Nishnaabeg Diplomatic and Treaty Relationships', *Wicazo Sa Review* 23.2 (2008), pp. 29–42 (p. 34).

42 Junot Díaz, quoted in Leanne Betasamosake Simpson, *Islands of Decolonial Love: Stories & Songs* (Winnipeg, MB: ARP Books, 2013), p. 7.

43 See Simpson, *Islands*, pp. 17, 71, 95, 97.

44 Leanne Betasamosake Simpson, *As We Have Always Done: Indigenous Freedom Through Radical Resistance* (Minneapolis, MN: University of Minnesota Press, 2017), p. 4.

45 Simpson, *Islands*, p. 114.

46 Bohaker, *Doodem and Council Fire*, p. 31.

47 Simpson, *Islands*, p. 114.
48 Ibid., p. 115.
49 Ibid., p. 114.
50 Ibid.
51 Bohaker, *Doodem and Council Fire*, p. xv.
52 Simpson, *Islands*, p. 114.
53 UNDRIP, Article 32.2.
54 Bohaker, *Doodem and Council Fire*, p. 27.
55 Simpson, *Islands*, p. 69.
56 Leanne Betasamosake Simpson, 'Land & Reconciliation', *Electric City Magazine* 7 (January 2016). Available at https://watershedsentinel.ca/articles/ land-reconciliation/ (accessed 1 September 2021).
57 Simpson, *Islands*, p. 68.
58 Simpson, 'Land & Reconciliation', n.p.
59 Simpson, *Islands*, p. 68.
60 Ibid., p. 69.
61 Ibid., p. 67.
62 Ibid., p. 67.
63 Robin Wall Kimmerer, *Braiding Sweetgrass: Indigenous Wisdom, Scientific Knowledge and the Teachings of Plants* (Minneapolis, MN: Milkweed Editions, 2013), p. 188.
64 M. Boyd et al., 'Holocene Paleoecology of a Wild Rice (Zizania Sp.) Lake in Northwestern Ontario, Canada', *Journal of Paleolimnology* 50.3 (2013), pp. 367–77 (p. 375).
65 Simpson, *Islands*, p. 67.
66 John Locke, 'Concerning the True Original Extent and End of Civil Government', *Two Treatises of Government* (London: Thomas Tegg et al., 1823), para. 26.
67 Ibid.
68 As Sarah Keenan notes, under English common law 'even a lord with his paperwork in perfect order could effectively lose his title if he allows his land to be possessed by a squatter for 12 years or more'. See Keenan, 'From Historical Chains to Derivative Futures: Title Registries as Time Machines', *Social & Cultural Geography* 20.3 (2018), pp. 283–303 (p. 286).
69 Carol M. Rose, 'Possession as the Origin of Property', *University of Chicago Law Review* 52.1 (1985), pp. 73–88 (p. 77).
70 Simpson, *Islands*, p. 67.
71 Ibid., p. 69.
72 Ibid.
73 Ibid., pp. 67–8.
74 Ibid., p. 69.
75 Ibid., p. 68.
76 Ibid., p. 68.
77 UNDRIP, Article 12.
78 Simpson, *Islands*, p. 69.

79 I use 'arrivant' to 'signify those people forced into the Americas through the violence of European and Anglo-American colonialism and imperialism around the globe', as Jodi Byrd (Chickasaw) writes in *The Transit of Empire: Indigenous Critiques of Colonialism* (Minneapolis, MN: University of Minnesota Press, 2011), p. xix. Byrd borrows this term from African Caribbean poet Kamau Brathwaite. I use this term to avoid collapsing all non-Indigenous peoples in Turtle Island into the term 'settler', which would erase crucial power differences between what Justice calls 'intentional colonizing settlers' from Europe and 'conscripted and enslaved populations from Europe, Africa, the Pacific, and other regions' (p. 6). The terms 'Indigenous', 'settler', and 'arrivant' denote relational positions rather than essentialist identity categories.

CHAPTER 17

Environmental Rights

Jos Smith

The philosophy, literature, and politics of 'nature' have histories that are deep and that have long been intertwined with one another: Keith Thomas's *Man and the Natural World* (1983) gives perhaps the most comprehensive account of their emergence *together* into the modern understanding that was inherited by the conservation and environmental traditions of the nineteenth century; and Derek Wall's *Green History* (1993) offers an anthology of key writings from this long history that extends into more recent environmental politics. From Romantic landscape tourism to amateur field science, from campaigns against cruelty to animals to working-class rambling clubs, environmentalism is founded on a long and intricate weave of values, pursuits, aesthetics, and politics that range from liberal to fascist, conservative to anarchist, and which have often overlapped in the most surprising of ways. However, what John McCormick describes as the 'New Environmentalism' arose in the late 1960s to plot a new course.[1] Influenced by the anti-Vietnam War protests and the Campaign for Nuclear Disarmament (and inspired by the Civil Rights movement), the New Environmentalism saw the beginnings of an international collaborative reorientation and, as a result, a slow steering of the movement from the conservative preoccupation with preservation and national heritage towards the more cosmopolitan march on alternative global futures that we have today. This chapter focuses on this turning point, following environmentalism's trajectory from a national into a global movement. As it does so, however, it thinks critically about the nature of that global politics too, tracing a subsequent turn from the early optimism of the 'Global North' to the environmental literature and politics of poorer and more vulnerable countries. The aim is not to give the whole picture – there are aspects of the movement such as wildlife campaigning, for example, that would require their own extensive study – but, rather, to look at these two moments of significant alteration in the general direction and to reflect on the role of literary work, its capacity for agency, and its ability to illustrate and provoke changes in thought and action.

In the early 1960s, few in America could have missed the controversial coverage of Rachel Carson's *Silent Spring* (1962) and its dire warning about the dangers of synthetic agricultural pesticides. Her previous book had been a bestseller for eighty-six weeks, and after public denial of *Silent Spring*'s scientific argument by pesticide companies – and even the Department for Agriculture – President Kennedy appointed a 'Special Panel of the President's Scientific Advisory Committee'. Carson was vindicated, and the 'Special Panel' provided support for subsequent attempts at legislation banning the use of DDT.[2] Later, British and American publics were faced with a sequence of extraordinary news stories of industrial accidents, oil spills, and pollution.[3] Such controversies were not all firsts, as is often claimed, but their proximity and succession throughout the 1960s was met by a context of lively outrage and an eagerness to take to the streets in the student peace movement.

This came to a head in a very deliberate mobilisation of popular support, led by Senator Gaylord Nelson, around the first Earth Day on 22 April 1970. Millions of people were involved in teach-ins at 1,500 US colleges and in events at over 10,000 schools, churches, temples, city parks, and in front of corporate and government offices.[4] There were thousands of marches, talks, and debates; the cast of *Hair* performed 'The Age of Aquarius' to open one teach-in at the University of Michigan, where a guerrilla theatre group also put a 1959 Ford sedan on trial for crimes against the environment; traffic was banned from New York's 5th Avenue for two hours allowing 100,000 pedestrians to fill the streets; and 10,000 people surrounded the Washington Monument for twelve hours of revelry.[5] In the same year, Greenpeace published their first pamphlet concerning underground nuclear testing in Alaska, and Friends of the Earth, which had been founded by David Brower in 1969, published *The Environmental Handbook*, which sold two million copies before the end of April.[6] There was a groundswell of public outrage fuelling the events around Earth Day, but also an exuberance and optimism at the coalescing of a movement for change, an optimism that would find its political counterpart in the UN Conference on the Human Environment in Stockholm in 1972, which initiated the world's first major international efforts at a global environmental politics. To fulfil some of this optimism, however, the movement would have to face some of the paradoxes of its foundations.

Wilderness and Modernity

The Sierra Club (formed in 1892) was an American society founded to protect wilderness areas from the excessive exploitation of logging and mining companies. While it was begun by 'mainly affluent, leisured "outdoorsmen" hooked on fishing, hunting, or camping', one of its earliest members, the nature writer John Muir, would invest their work with a religious zeal, writing of the 'God of the Mountains' and describing those who would profit from their exploitation as 'temple destroyers'.[7] Muir was a literary philosopher of nature, in the tradition of Rousseau, Wordsworth, Emerson, and Thoreau, but he had the ear of political power too, and once invited President Roosevelt to visit him in Yosemite Valley in 1903. Mark Dowie describes how 'Muir told the president that everything he saw around him should be protected by legislation as a cathedral where people could experience the wild in their souls and rejuvenate themselves after months in the urban jungles of America.'[8] In response, Roosevelt would introduce a bill to protect Yosemite from the forms of conservative, 'wise-use' resource exploitation that were permitted even in national parks.

Muir's nature writing helped to give the Sierra Club an uplifting moral language for its ambitions while his campaigning gave it genuine political influence. The two supported each other and together they helped to institute a powerful and lasting legacy of national heritage based on a reverence for 'Nature' as that which stands beyond the clutches of modernity. For these reasons, the Sierra Club has been an important foundation stone for environmental politics, rooting it in romantic philosophy and aesthetics; but also for these reasons, it has haunted environmental politics with a persistent ideology that holds 'Nature' and modernity at odds in ways that it has been difficult to outgrow.

The Sierra Club served as an incubator for the younger environmentalists coming of age in the late 1960s. Individuals who would go on to found Greenpeace and Friends of the Earth were closely involved with the Club, but each broke free to pursue a more radical agenda that complicated this opposition of 'Nature' and modernity. Greenpeace was begun by a group including Irving and Dorothy Stowe, who, after founding the first Canadian branch of the Sierra Club in British Columbia, began plans to oppose the American testing of nuclear weapons underground on the island of Amchitka at the north-western tip of Alaska. After publicising plans to sail a boat – the *Greenpeace* (a name suggesting the alliance between the peace movement and the environmental movement) – into the area where the testing was to take place, the Sierra Club withdrew its support and questioned the legitimacy of the BC branch. They felt that the issue was not strictly concerned with advocacy for 'Nature' itself in the reified sense it had for the wilderness protection movement, and, as a result, they were 'not prepared to launch a seagoing protest against the American government'.[9]

David Brower had been the Sierra Club's executive director since 1952, but he too fell out with the organisation to establish Friends of the Earth in San Francisco in 1969. Brower was a champion of Thoreau and Muir, and alongside tireless lobbying and campaigning against dam building, he had edited books in the Sierra Club's Exhibit Format series that reproduced nature writing alongside photography by Ansel Adams. However, he felt the Sierra Club had become 'seduced away from their original intentions by the argument that conservation . . . should stem from realistic, science-based principles', much like the 'wise-use' agenda Muir had resisted in Yosemite.[10] In response, Brower was keen to turn towards the youth movement and its more diverse and global agenda. Friends of the Earth would still be concerned with national parks, but they also took on recycling, the fur trade, whaling, and air pollution, and their tactics were – like those of Greenpeace – more direct.

As William Cronon has so careful demonstrated, there is an ideology embedded within the literature and politics of the wilderness protection movement which casts wilderness as 'the ultimate landscape of authenticity', a refuge, 'the last remaining place where civilization, that all too human disease, has not fully infected the earth'.[11] In doing so, however, it simultaneously denies the fact that it is 'profoundly a human creation', a 'cultural invention' based on that reified and romantic understanding of 'Nature' as pristine, untrammelled.[12] It naturalises an aestheticised account of nature, something which can seem paradoxical, but in the slippage of memory there is an act of erasure that has had very real consequences. As Greg Garrard has shown, Muir's tireless advocacy for the protection of Yosemite Valley saw it designated as an 'uninhabited wilderness', but this also led to the forced removal of Ahwahneechee and settler white mining communities.[13] Wilderness might be a condition of nature to protect, but it has also become a regime to impose on the landscape as well.

In their introduction to a volume of essays dedicated to the relationship between socialism and ecology in British literature, John Rignall and H. Gustav Klaus turn to Raymond Williams, who noted the 'missing dimension of human labour in the discussion of nature' in his 1971 lecture, 'Ideas of Nature'.[14] Williams was at the time writing *The Country and the City* (1973), a book that shows at length, in a British context, the imposition of a nostalgic, nationalist literary aesthetics on rural areas, occluding the material realities of people living in those areas. One of the consequences of this 'missing dimension', Rignall and Klaus point out, is an environmental politics that continues, perhaps a little unconsciously, in 'the footprints of conservative thinkers', often reproducing a retrospective discourse of 'irretrievable loss'.[15]

Such a position creates its own self-fulfilling narrative of tragic impasse, beyond which there is no going without breaking down and complicating the monolithic and romantic opposition of wilderness to modernity. To do so is, on the one hand, to find human histories in the wilderness (including those that may have been erased to create that wilderness) and, on the other hand, to find in modernity hope for the future.[16] It was this pivot towards the latter that came to characterise the New Environmentalism's shift away from the old conservation tradition. The break was not clean, of course, and threads of wilderness protection have persisted in contemporary environmentalism, even in forms of radical environmental activism nourished by certain key literary texts.

The novelist and nature writer Edward Abbey is one example of this persistence. In 1975, Abbey published The Monkey Wrench Gang, a divisive and now dated novel, but one that captures like no other the difficulties of an environmental politics caught in this tension between the conservatism of wilderness protection and the youthful energy of the New Environmentalism. The novel sees an unlikely alliance between a group of eccentric misfits who share a common outrage at the strip mining, pipelines, power plants, and cattle companies that are encroaching on their cherished wilderness areas. The Glen Canyon Dam becomes the focus of their 'healthy hatred', and inspired by stories of the Luddites, they turn to sabotage, amassing caches of monkey wrenches, wrecking bars, bolt cutters, blasting caps, and, of course, 'Du Pont Red Cross Extra' dynamite. The novel begins with the climax of their activities. On the day of the dam's official opening, amid the banners, bunting, and marching bands, a bomb sees the dam collapse with a 'sheet of red flame stream[ing] skyward'.[17]

In 1980, the novel directly inspired Dave Foreman, a lobbyist in Washington for the Wilderness Society, to resign and found Earth First!, an activist group intended, as Foreman claimed, to 'make the Sierra Club look moderate'.[18] The claim is a significant one, suggesting an intensification of their values rather than the new direction of Greenpeace and Friends of the Earth. Foreman would go on to produce a manual for 'ecotage' called Ecodefense: A Field Guide to Monkeywrenching (1985), which contained instructions for dismantling animal traps, burning and felling billboards, tree-spiking (inserting long nails into trees marked for felling to damage saw blades), and even attacking the corporate offices of offending companies.

The position of Earth First! is that mainstream politics has become a dead end. Derek Wall has described it as a 'product of political closure', drawing in those tired of the slow bureaucracy of more formal green organisations and finding the turn to direct action 'personally empowering'.[19] It is hard, then, to come to terms with the actual politics of Abbey and Earth First! One of Abbey's characters prays for a natural disaster while another suggests that 'our only hope is catastrophe'.[20] As Greg Garrard points out, in the end, there is an unsettling alignment of Abbey's characters with 'paranoid survivalist militias'.[21] Reverence for wilderness in both Abbey and Earth First! has often come hand in hand with alarmist fears about 'overpopulation', and Penny Kemp and Derek Wall have noted that extreme factions of Earth First! have publicly espoused positions of 'neo-Malthusian praise for diseases like AIDS, for famine and for other maladies that reduce human numbers'.[22]

No one would wish to discredit the ordinary pleasure taken in woods, mountains, deserts, and so on, nor the desire to protect them, but the evangelism that can take hold of the idea of embattled wilderness can lend itself to profound misanthropy that wants no part in history. Yet no wilderness is exempt from history. Quite the opposite in fact: 'wilderness' as a frame is often the contortion of a *historical* landscape. Such a contradiction sits awkwardly at the foundations of environmental politics, and the New Environmentalism's turn towards international modernity has had to contend with this difficult wrench away from this nostalgic backward gaze.

Whole Earth Utopianism

In California, the late 1960s had seen the emergence of another influential counterculture figure. Stewart Brand had made a name for himself petitioning NASA to publish the first photograph of the earth from space. He believed that the image would trigger a leap in human consciousness, and he was, in many ways, quite right.[23] Friends of the Earth and Earth First! were just two of the names of environmental groups that would come to adopt this new planetary register. Brand used the photographs, as they emerged, on the cover of his *Whole Earth Catalog*, a magazine with the tagline 'access to tools'.[24] Informed by ecological science and the systems theory of Buckminster Fuller (who was featured in the first issue), it was intended simply to equip its readers to take an active role in shaping the future of what Fuller was calling 'Spaceship Earth' (drawing on the economist Barbara Ward).[25]

'We are as gods and we might as well get good at it', the first issue claimed. '[A] realm of intimate personal power is developing . . . power of the individual to conduct his own education, find his own inspiration, shape his own environment.'[26] Like Earth First!, its particular position on environmental politics offered a personally empowering form of liberalism, an alternative to the top-down model of governmental legislation and environmental regulation, but this was where the similarity ended. Predicated on technological optimism and experimental living, its focus was on ecology as a malleable system oriented towards future possibilities, something which couldn't have been further from the retrospective conservatism of the wilderness protection movement. In many ways more interested in the ecology of urban areas than of natural landscapes, the *Catalog* collected together ideas for design, energy, architecture, food systems, waste, and communications, to promote what Andrew Kirk has called a 'pragmatic environmental sensibility'.[27]

If the celebratory prose of nature writing like Muir's was the literary form most closely aligned with wilderness protection, then the politics of the new 'Whole Earth' environmentalism would find its literary voice in science fiction. Brand published stories by Ursula K. Le Guin and Ernest Callenbach alongside ideas for alternative living not only because science fiction tended to be future-oriented but because, to quote Le Guin herself, the genre offered 'thought-experiments' that challenged conventional ways of thinking; it too was 'a good tool, an enlargement of consciousness'.[28]

No novel better captures the *Catalog*'s sense of hopeful, West Coast, DIY possibility than Ernest Callenbach's *Ecotopia* (1975). The vast majority of science fiction working with environmentalism in mind has been dystopian in nature, but Callenbach's novel is significant for the way it captures a pivot in orientation towards the future – and of course towards modernity itself – as a site of possibility at this watershed moment. 'Ecotopia' describes a large area – formerly Washington, Oregon, and California – that has devolved from the United States in a 'fratricidal breach' to create a society based on the idea of a 'stable-state ecosystem'.[29] In a familiar trope of utopian novels, it sees a sceptical reporter, William Weston, cross 'the forbidding Sierra Nevada mountains that guard the closed borders' to report on Ecotopia's decades of 'social experimentation', only to find himself slowly persuaded by their way of life (note the telling reversal of Muir's direction of travel).[30] The Ecotopians live in quiet, traffic-free cities where electric public transport and bicycles cut across 'gurgling and splashing creeks' lined with 'rocks, trees, bamboos, ferns'.[31] They recycle everything, 'metal, glass, or paper and plastic refuse in the appropriate bin' and all food waste, sewage, and garbage is 'turned into organic fertilizer and applied to the land', and they have adopted a variety of sustainable energy solutions – solar, geothermal, tidal, and wind.[32] Their attitude to technology is simply selective and decisions are made based on its impact on human well-being and 'the local biosphere' (note the technical terminology from ecological science supplanting reverence for 'Nature').[33]

On the subject of politics itself, Weston is told by the Minister for Food that 'you will find many things happening without government authorization'. Instead, committees 'operate with scientific advice, of the most sophisticated and independent type imaginable'.[34] This privileging of science over politics in questions of governance was characteristic of a generation who had seen Rachel Carson denounced and then vindicated. Kurt Vonnegut, speaking at an Earth Day event in New York in 1970, was referring to President Nixon when he told crowds: 'I'm sorry he's a lawyer; I wish to God that he was a biologist.'[35] And, as Wall points out, in 1974, professor of agricultural sciences René Dumont ran for the French presidency, as did professor of biology Barry Commoner in the US in the 1980s, both on radical green agendas.[36]

If *Ecotopia* fails to *fully* articulate a political vision for the New Environmentalism, it is in the way it is haunted by the contradiction of its devolution, at once reaching towards a stable-state 'whole earth' systems model of sustainability, but, in doing so, being forced to erect 'closed borders'.[37] The book is premised on a breakdown of communications between the United States and Ecotopia (this is why Weston is sent to report), and, as a result of that, it never has to grapple with the problem of international politics and the relational compromises that must be met to achieve political agency on a larger scale. In *Sense of Place and Sense of Planet*, Ursula K. Heise has described a tension between the increasingly global interests of late twentieth-century political and economic history and the 'excessive investment in the local' in much of the environmental literature of the period:

> The challenge that deterritorialization poses for the environmental imagination is to envision how ecologically based advocacy might be formulated in terms that are premised no longer primarily on ties to local places but on ties

to territories and systems that are understood to encompass the planet as a whole.[38]

The very experiment that *Ecotopia* represents is made possible only by its withdrawal from what Heise comes to call 'eco-cosmopolitanism', that is, 'an environmental world citizenship'.[39]

The optimism of Brand and Callenbach was qualitatively different from that created by Earth Day in 1970. Where Brand and Callenbach seemed to withdraw from the mainstream to experiment with alternatives, the optimism of Earth Day was founded on outrage and a commitment to make change in national and international politics.[40] The groundswell of popular support was given international political credence two years later when the UN held its Conference on the Human Environment in June 1972, where McCormick has described a similar sense of 'excitement and anticipation', 'hope that lofty declarations would be converted into action'.[41]

Today we might choose to be circumspect about such optimism, especially when we remember that the Vietnam War continued into the mid-1970s despite the intensified efforts of the peace movement in 1968. Le Guin gave voice to some of this circumspection at the time. If Callenbach excites with pragmatic solutions, then Le Guin challenges with uncomfortable questions. She has described her role throughout the 1960s in 'helping to organise and participating in non-violent demonstrations, first against atomic bomb testing, then against the pursuance of the war in Viet Nam'. During this time, she writes, 'it was becoming clear that the ethic which approved the defoliation of forests and grainlands and the murder of non-combatants in the name of "peace" was only a corollary of the ethic which permits the despoliation of natural resources for private profit'.[42]

We see this most bluntly in her novel *The Word for World Is Forest* (1972), written in 1968 when she was briefly living in the UK, cut off from her usual activist networks. The novel describes a violent conflict among future 'yumens', the colonial 'Terra' who have come to the planet Athshe (renamed initially as New Tahiti, then World 41) to raid its forests for timber, deploying high-yield, profitable forestry methods, and the enslaved Athsheans. Written after this novel but published a year before it in 1971, *The Lathe of Heaven* takes a subtler approach to the question of 'whole earth' political agency, set, unusually for Le Guin, on Earth in the near future. George Orr, an ordinary working man – a man who 'ranks right in the middle of the graph' – finds that his dreams have the capacity to change reality. Le Guin has a sophisticated understanding of psychoanalysis and dream science so the catch is that he cannot control his dreams, meaning that it is more a curse than a blessing. Orr simply does not want the responsibility of dreaming the world anew. In a trope that may seem familiar now, he 'daydreams about having a place in the Wilderness Areas, you know, a place in the country like in the old novels [. . .] a cabin somewhere outside the cities'.[43]

He becomes the patient of a Dr Haber who *does* want such a responsibility (or at least the power that comes with it) and who sees the potential to change the world for the better by working (with) Orr using a dream-influencing machine called 'the Augmentor'. Dream by dream, Haber promotes himself to greater power until Portland – where the novel is set – becomes the 'capital of the planet' and the home of the 'World Planning Center' of which he is the head.[44] The fact that Haber's personal and professional desires seem to be satisfied alongside his more noble political ambitions has led most critics to read the novel as a fairly straightforward allegory opposing a selfless Taoist humility (Orr) with a modern Western will to power (Haber).

Fredric Jameson has complicated this rather too easy moral opposition, pointing out that 'the fable comes down rather hard' on Haber.[45] Jameson places Orr in a 'Thoreauvean tradition' of 'conventional liberalism' – the individual digging in to his 'cabin' in the 'Wilderness Areas' against the pressures of modernity – and while, admittedly, he casts this in a favourable light in contrast to what he calls the 'imperial liberalism' of Haber, he warns that both are forms for which we might reserve some scepticism.[46]

The truth is that both Orr and Haber commit atrocities with their world-dreaming. Orr's desire for a quiet life in the Wilderness Areas is a response to feeling overcrowded, and results in a dream addressing the problem of 'overpopulation' by retroactively introducing 'The Plague Years' – when chemical pollutants in the atmosphere combine to form virulent carcinogens and reduce the global population from seven billion to one billion.[47] Haber suggests that Orr's fear of 'overpopulation' might be a 'metaphor, for this feeling of unfreedom', adding that 'perhaps an excessive dread of overpopulation . . . reflects not an outward reality, but an inward state of mind' (a withering critique of a subject at the fore of environmental discourse at the time).[48]

Later, reality itself is nearly pulled apart into groundless chaos when Haber transfers Orr's power to himself. 'To do any good at all', Orr reflects, 'just believing you're right and your motives are good isn't enough. You have to . . . be in touch. He [Haber] isn't in touch. No one else, no thing even, has an existence of its own, for him; he sees the world only as a means to his end.'[49] The novel might be read as articulating a conundrum about individual agency in an increasingly deterritorialised world, a wrenching apart of the liberal and the neoliberal, finding both insufficiently equipped to really take responsible action and certainly falling short of Heise's ideal of 'eco-cosmopolitanism'. More sceptical of the idea of the 'Whole Earth' utopianism than Callenbach, Le Guin's two novels of 1971 and 1972 anticipate some of the coming challenges that environmental politics would have to face if it was going to stay 'in touch' with the world it sought to represent.

Environmentalism of the Poor

There were two key issues that dominated the UN Conference on the Human Environment in 1972 (wilderness protection was not one of them). The first was pollution (acidity of rain, in fact, but other pollutions too). The other key issue was international relations between 'More Developed' and 'Less Developed' countries. Many leaders from the 'LDCs' voiced concern about the imposition of neocolonial regulations that would stem the development of burgeoning economies. China was among the countries that spoke out most forcefully against this kind of Western rhetoric, arguing that 'each country has the right to determine its own environmental standards'.[50] An unfortunate consequence of this debate was a growing suspicion that environmentalism was a pursuit reserved for wealthy countries, something that has been challenged and corrected as the environmentalism of the 'Global South' has drawn critical attention, and as Indigenous voices have found their way onto the political world stage.[51]

In 2014, Marshallese poet and climate activist Kathy Jetñil-Kijiner spoke before the politicians gathered in New York at the United Nations Secretary-General's Climate Summit. She began by retelling a legend from home about a canoe race between ten brothers: 'Their mother, holding a heavy bundle, begged each of her sons for a ride on their canoe. But only the youngest listened and took her along for the ride, not knowing that his mother was carrying the first sail. With this sail he won the race and became chief.'[52] Speaking on behalf of 'Indigenous mothers like me', she added, 'I ask world leaders to take us all along on your ride. We won't slow you down.'[53] Knotted inside this concisely articulated fable is an argument about the error of blinkered self-confidence, its misguided certainty overlooking an older maternal wisdom as inconvenient baggage that will have them lose the race. What can be learned from the 'Indigenous mothers like me', then, that equates to the sail that wins the race?

In *Varieties of Environmentalism* (1997), Ramachandra Guha and Joan Martínez Alier challenged the narrowness of the environmentalism of the 'Global North' for overlooking alternative conceptualisations of 'the environment' and for assuming that its own conceptualisation was in some way universal. Perhaps drawing on the debates of the 1972 UN conference, this environmentalism was thought to be 'post-materialist': the conservation of wildlife and protected landscapes was an indication of a country's high level of development, that it was economically prosperous and stable enough to focus its attentions on nature as a space of leisure, contemplation, restorative good health, and, of course, of altruistic guardianship, as one with the security of home ownership might turn their attention to the garden.[54] With this in mind, countries of the South were seen to be 'too poor to be Green'.[55]

However, certain high-profile battles complicate this position, and *another* environmentalism, what they call an 'environmentalism of the poor', has come into view.[56] For example, in Nigeria in the 1990s, the playwright Ken Saro-Wiwa and the Movement for the Survival of the Ogoni People saw a minority ethnic group stand up against the extreme pollution of the Niger Delta by the crude oil extraction of the Anglo-Dutch company Royal Shell, supported by the Nigerian federal government. The pollution caused by drilling and badly maintained pipelines was having a catastrophic impact on the land, livelihood, and physical health of the Ogoni people in ways that were obscured and denied by Royal Shell. Famously, the battle resulted in the execution of Saro-Wiwa in 1995.

Guha and Alier argue that development goals among countries in the 'Global South' must not be met at any cost. Founded on the idea of environmental justice, an environmentalism of the poor will campaign for an accommodation within such goals of 'a decentralisation of power structures, local and more equitable resource management, and the use of sustainable cultural practices leading towards a new self-reliance'.[57] Of course, the appeal of such amendments to ambitious governments aiming to broker high-powered deals with large multinational corporations is rather like that of the appeal of the mother with her bundle to the brothers facing their canoe race.

Increasingly, the environmentalism of the 'Global North' is recognising value in the environmentalism of the poor and its fight for justice, because to do so is to recognise nature not only as a site of leisure and wildlife but also as a site of livelihood, dwelling, and cultural meaning. It forces environmental politics to operate within *both* the fine grain of local distinctiveness *and* the sweeping gestures of global politics. Of course, this also means facing past injustices and, as postcolonial ecocritics have been arguing for some time, acknowledging that the exploitations of colonialism and the exploitations of nature (as Le Guin illustrates in *The Word for World Is Forest*) are part and parcel of the same historical narrative.

The Marshall Islands, twenty-nine low lying atolls where Jetñil-Kijiner is from, were subject to US nuclear bomb testing in the 1940s and 1950s. Sixty-seven nuclear bombs were detonated in and over the islands at the time, and subsequently 3.1 million cubic feet of radioactive soil and debris were fixed in the ground under a massive concrete structure called the Runit Dome in Enewetak Atoll, known locally as 'the Tomb'.[58] In her film poem 'Anointed' (2018), Jetñil-Kijiner travels by canoe out to the island and is filmed reciting the poem on top of the huge dome, a poem that addresses the island in the form of an elegy: 'How shall we remember you? / You were a whole island, once. You were breadfruit trees heavy with green globes of fruit whispering promises of massive canoes.'[59]

Dina El Dessouky has explored the dissonance between American accounts of this nuclear testing and the experience of the islanders themselves in her reading of Jetñil-Kijiner's long poem 'History Project' (2012), arguing that where culture and place are 'co-constitutive of Indigenous identity', the poisoning of landscape and bodies is the poisoning of a whole way of life, its livelihood, culture, and identity.[60] Nuclear testing like this is an example of what Rob Nixon has described as 'slow violence', an 'environmentally embedded violence that is often difficult to source, oppose, and once set in motion, to reverse'.[61] The 'slowness' of such violence also makes it difficult to assign responsibility and is easy to deny.

Climate change is another example of slow violence; the Marshall Islands are on the frontline for some of the worst effects of sea level rise as a result of climate change, low lying as many of them are. This connection intensifies the historical relationship between colonialism and climate change that is another important aspect of the environmentalism of the poor. As Elizabeth DeLoughry has observed in the current criticism about the Anthropocene, 'a lack of engagement with postcolonial and Indigenous perspectives' has produced a discourse claiming 'the novelty of the crisis rather than being attentive to the historical continuity of dispossession and disaster caused by empire'.[62] Kyle Powys Whyte makes a similar point when, responding to calls for more dystopian science fiction to illustrate the coming catastrophe, he points out that there are communities of Indigenous people in North America who 'already inhabit what our ancestors would have understood as a dystopian future'.[63]

In a film project funded and supported by glaciologist Jason Box, activist Bill McKibben, and the grassroots climate action group 350.org, Jetñil-Kijiner travelled to Greenland in 2018 to work with the poet Aka Niviana. They recorded the collaboratively written film poem 'Rise', which describes the thawing of Greenland and the related sea level rise for the Pacific Islands. The two stand back-to-back on a glacier: 'Let me show you the tide, coming for us faster than we'd like to admit. Let me show you airports under water', says Jetñil-Kijiner. 'Can you see our glaciers groan with the weight of the world's heat?' asks Niviana.[64]

One of the key forms that Indigenous climate politics is taking is emerging in transnational work of this kind, what Dessouky calls 'alternative global alliances', 'relational and planetary coalitions'.[65] Their 'eco-cosmopolitanism' amplifies messages spoken in isolation by seeking to speak them together in solidarity. Writing about the making of this film for *The Guardian*, Bill McKibben notes that for places on the frontline of climate change, 'There is no distance any more: the isolation that once protected places like Greenland or Micronesia no longer offers any buffer.'[66] The poets' collaboration turns this breakdown of distance into a tool for political efficacy too, as their collaborative and interdisciplinary message reaches its audiences online. In such work, there is a grounding of environmental politics in *place*, not 'Nature'; but place as it is constellated among many other places; not global in the sense of being deterritorialised, lurching towards a premature 'whole earth' community, but transnational in the sense of being allied, heard, and witnessed.

Notes

1 John McCormick, *The Global Environmental Movement* (Chichester: John Wiley & Sons, 1995).

2 Ibid., pp. 65–7.

3 For example, in 1966, in Aberfan, Wales, a mining spoil tip collapse would see the deaths of nearly 150 children and adults; in 1967, over 100,000 tonnes of crude oil were spilled, both off the coast of Cornwall in the UK and off the coast of Santa Barbara in the US; then in 1969, in Cleveland, the Cuyahoga River was so badly polluted that it actually caught fire.

4 Adam Rome, 'The Genius of Earth Day', *Environmental History* 15.2 (April 2010), pp. 194–205.

5 Ibid., p. 199; McCormick, *The Global Environmental Movement*, p. 79.

6 Rex Weyler, *Greenpeace: An Insider's Account* (London: Rodale, 2004), p. 69.

7 Quoted in Mark Dowie, *Losing Ground: American Environmentalism at the Close of the Century* (Cambridge, MA: MIT Press, 1995), p. 17.

8   Ibid.
9   Weyler, *Greenpeace*, pp. 68–9.
10 Robert Lamb, *Promising the Earth* (London: Routledge, 1996), p. 23.
11 William Cronon, 'The Trouble with Wilderness; or, Getting Back to the Wrong Nature', in *Uncommon Ground: Rethinking the Human Place in Nature*, ed. Cronon (New York: Norton, 1995), pp. 69–90 (pp. 80, 69).
12 Ibid., p. 69.
13 Greg Garrard, *Ecocriticism* (London: Routledge, 2011), p. 78.
14 John Rignall and H. Gustav Klaus, 'Introduction', in *Ecology and the Literature of the British Left: The Red and the Green*, ed. Rignall, Klaus, and Valentine Cunningham (London: Routledge, 2012), pp. 1–12 (p. 10).
15 Ibid., p. 7.
16 Lauret Savoy's *Trace: Memory, History, Race, and the American Landscape* (Berkeley, CA: Counterpoint, 2015) is an example of nature writing doing just this: promising an important departure for the form.
17 Edward Abbey, *The Monkey Wrench Gang* (London: Penguin, 2004), pp. 32, 71, 5–6.
18 Quoted in James M. Cahalan, *Edward Abbey: A Life* (Tucson, AZ: University of Arizona Press, 2001), p. 192.
19 Derek Wall, *Earth First! and the Anti-Roads Movement: Radical Environmentalism and Comparative Social Movements* (London: Routledge, 1999), pp. 189, 106.
20 Abbey, *The Monkey Wrench Gang*, pp. 37, 42.
21 Garrard, *Ecocriticism*, p. 68.
22 Penny Kemp and Derek Wall, *A Green Manifesto for the 1990s* (Harmondsworth: Penguin, 1990), p. 11.
23 Where exactly that 'leap' would take human consciousness is less clear. Dennis Cosgrove has given a thoughtful analysis of these first images in the final chapter of his *Apollo's Eye: A Cartographic Genealogy of the Earth in the Western Imagination* (Baltimore, MD: Johns Hopkins University Press, 2001).
24 Stewart Brand, *Whole Earth Catalog* (Fall 1968).
25 R. Buckminster Fuller referred to 'Spaceship Earth' in the title of his *Operating Manual for Spaceship Earth* (New York: Lars Müller, 2008).
26 Ibid., p. 2.
27 Andrew G. Kirk, *Counterculture Green: The Whole Earth Catalog and American Environmentalism* (Kansas: University Press of Kansas, 2007), p. 8.
28 Ursula K. Le Guin, *The Language of the Night: Essays on Fantasy and Science Fiction* (New York: Putnam Adult, 1979), p. 119.
29 Ernest Callenbach, *Ecotopia* (New York: Bantam, 1990), p. 2.
30 Ibid., p. 4.
31 Ibid., p. 13.
32 Ibid., p. 18.
33 Ibid., p. 112.
34 Ibid., p. 21.

35 National Staff of Environmental Action, ed., *Earth Day – The Beginning: A Guide for Survival* (New York: Arno Press, 1970), p. 64.

36 Derek Wall, *Green History: A Reader in Environmental Literature, Philosophy, and Politics* (London: Routledge, 1993), p. 5.

37 Callenbach, *Ecotopia*, p. 3.

38 Ursula K. Heise, *Sense of Place and Sense of Planet: The Environmental Imagination of the Global* (Oxford: Oxford University Press, 2008), p. 10.

39 Ibid.

40 Through a series of personal interviews, Adam Rome has shown how Earth Day helped influence a whole new generation to turn to political lobbying and to work within mainstream politics to affect change (Rome, 'The Genius of Earth Day').

41 McCormick, *The Global Environmental Movement*, p. 119.

42 Ursula K. Le Guin, *The Word for World Is Forest* (London: Gollancz, 2014), p. 7.

43 Ursula K. Le Guin, *The Lathe of Heaven* (London: Gollancz, 2001), p. 45.

44 Ibid., p. 126.

45 Fredric Jameson, *Archaeologies of the Future: The Desire Called Utopia and Other Science Fictions* (London: Verso, 2005), p. 78.

46 Ibid.

47 Le Guin, *The Lathe of Heaven*, p. 67.

48 Ibid., p. 58.

49 Ibid., p. 155.

50 McCormick, *The Global Environmental Movement*, p. 121.

51 See, for example, Scott Slovic, Swarnalatha Rangarajan, and Vidya Sarveswaran, eds., *Ecocriticism of the Global South* (New York: Lexington Books, 2015).

52 A fuller account of the story of Lōktañūr is given is given in Kathy Jetñil-Kijiner, *Iep Jāltok: Poems from a Marshallese Daughter* (Tucson, AZ: University of Arizona Press, 2017), p. 7.

53 'Statement and poem by Kathy Jetnil-Kijiner, Climate Summit 2014 – Opening Ceremony'. Available at www.youtube.com/watch?v=mc_IgE7TBSY (accessed 8 September 2020).

54 Ronald Inglehart, quoted in Ramachandra Guha and Joan Martínez Alier, *Varieties of Environmentalism: Essays North and South* (London: Taylor and Francis, 1997), p. 4.

55 Ibid., p. 7.

56 Ibid., p. 3.

57 Ibid., p. 10.

58 Susanne Rust, 'How the US Betrayed the Marshall Islands, Kindling the Next Nuclear Disaster', *LA Times*, 10 November 2019. Available at www .latimes.com/projects/marshall-islands-nuclear-testing-sea-level-rise/ (accessed 7 September 2020).

59 Kathy Jetñil-Kijiner, 'Dome Poem Part III: "Anointed" Final Poem and Video'. Available at www.kathyjetnilkijiner.com/dome-poem-iii-anointed-final-poem-and-video/ (accessed 8 September 2020).

60 Dina El Dessouky, 'Fish, Coconuts and Ocean People: Nuclear Violations of Oceania's "Earthly Design"', in *Ecocriticism of the Global South*, ed. Slovic, Rangarajan, and Sarveswaran, pp. 109–22.

61 Rob Nixon, *Slow Violence and the Environmentalism of the Poor* (Cambridge, MA: Harvard University Press, 2013), p. 7.

62 Elizabeth DeLoughrey, *Allegories of the Anthropocene* (Durham, NC: Duke University Press, 2019), p. 2.

63 Kyle Powys Whyte, 'Our Ancestors' Dystopia Now: Indigenous Conservation and the Anthropocene', in *The Routledge Companion to the Environmental Humanities*, ed. Ursula K. Heise, Jon Christensen, and Michelle Niemann (London: Routledge, 2017), pp. 206–15 (p. 207).

64 Bill McKibben, 'High Ice and Hard Truths: The Poets Taking on Climate Change', *The Guardian*, 12 September 2018. Available at www.theguardian.com/environment/2018/sep/12/high-ice-hard-truth-a-poetry-expedition-to-greenlands-melting-glaciers-bill-mckibben (accessed 8 September 2020).

65 Dessouky, 'Fish, Coconuts and Ocean People', p. 111.

66 McKibben, 'High Ice and Hard Truths'.

CHAPTER 18

Neoliberalism

Peter Boxall

How does the late twentieth-century novel offer a critical response to the pervasive phenomenon of neoliberalism?

We might begin to address this question by attending to a key moment in Philip Roth's novel *The Human Stain* (2000), in which the protagonist, Coleman Silk, pays a visit to the small-town American university at which he was once Dean of Humanities. He has not been back to the campus since he retired in disgrace, having been accused, falsely as he sees it, of using a racist slur against two African American students. As he walks towards the campus, he overhears a discussion between a number of male faculty members sitting in the sun on a park bench. The topic of conversation is the ongoing sexual scandal surrounding Bill Clinton and Monica Lewinsky, the scandal which is one of the reference points of the novel's title, the human stain in question being in part the famous stain left by the presidential semen on Lewinsky's dress. The conversation, in its repellent bantering misogyny, turns around what it was that attracted Clinton to Lewinsky. He could see the kind of person she was, the men agree, 'a total narcissist', an 'exhibitionist, corrupted by privilege'. He could read her – 'if he can't read and outfox Monica Lewinsky, the guy *shouldn't* be president'. It was not, they speculate, that he was blinded by her or seduced by her – on the contrary it was her very obvious limitations that attracted him to her. 'That she was totally corrupt and totally innocent, of course he saw it. The extreme innocence was the corruption.'[1] Innocence is somehow equated, in the figure of Lewinsky, with corruption, a woven combination of opposites that is replicated across a number of the political contradictions that Lewinsky seems, to these men, to embody. 'That was her force', one of the men says, that combination: 'That she had no depth, that was her charm at the end of his day of being commander in chief. The intensity of the shallowness was its appeal. Not to mention the shallowness of the intensity.'[2]

This moment touches on many of the questions that propel *The Human Stain*, and that preoccupy the later twentieth-century novel more generally, as it is shaped by the collective forces of neoliberalism. The passage is in part about the politics and aesthetics of reading. Clinton can read Lewinsky, he can understand her specific combination of innocence and corruption, because his job requires him to be an analyst – a close reader – of the forms which corruption and innocence take in the late twentieth century. 'He could read her', one of the men says. 'If he can't read Monica Lewinsky, how can he read Saddam Hussein?'³ The logic here is that a president who can't negotiate a trivial incident – a tame affair with an intern – could hardly be expected to manage a matter of major geopolitical significance – the relation between Clinton's administration and Saddam Hussein's regime, as it influences the globally critical balance of power in the Middle East. Of course, Clinton should be able to read Lewinsky; he devotes his exhausting days as commander in chief to the task of critical analysis, whose stakes are immeasurably higher than those which determine the quaint intricacies of his heavy petting with Monica. But, at the same time, the scale which underlies this rhetoric, which opposes the weightily geopolitical to the trivially domestic, is disturbed or deranged by the prospect of Lewinsky herself, who seems to require a different model of reading, both of Clinton and of us. She collapses the distinction between the innocent and the corrupt, between the shallow and the intense, Roth's novel suggests, because she herself, in her relation to Clinton, is the symptom of a loss of historical perspective, in which we can no longer easily distinguish between the superficial and the profound, between surface and depth.

To read Monica Lewinsky's shallow intensity, to understand how intensity can be shallow, and shallowness can be intense, Roth's novel suggests, requires us to rethink the antinomial relationship between these terms. And if this moment touches on the novel's concern with reading, it activates too its wider thematic and political focus – the means by which the deep psychic and historical structures that determine identities are attached to the surfaces in which those identities present themselves to the world, and specifically the ways in which identity relates to the colour of one's skin. Coleman Silk is forced out of his university position, by his own account, because he was falsely accused of racism against two African American students; the irony as he sees it is that he himself, despite his self-presentation as a white Jew, is in fact an African American. The university administration's reading of the 'racist' incident – according to which a powerful white man abuses his privilege to discriminate against African American students – thus masks an entirely different set of active forces, which have led Coleman to disguise his own racial identity in order to gain access to the white enclave of the university administration, the very racist enclave that is now preparing to expel him for his perceived racism. The novelist-narrator of *The Human Stain*, Nathan Zuckerman, is fascinated by this turn of events and drawn to the writerly task of recovering Coleman's African American history from the white Jewish cloak which has occluded it, in part because it allows him to reflect on the way in which legible surfaces relate to the deep histories they contain. It is when Zuckerman visits Coleman in his house on a warm evening early in the novel that this act of narrative reclamation is set in motion, this adjustment of the relation between the surface and the depth. Zuckerman finds Coleman in a loose and euphoric mood, listening to jazz with his shirt off, and is drawn to him, erotically and intellectually, in a way that leads him to undertake one of the several close readings of Coleman's body that recur throughout the novel. There is an intense homoerotic quality to the meeting, at which Coleman and Zuckerman end up dancing in each other's arms to Frank Sinatra, and this eroticism is grounded in Zuckerman's fascinated attention to the 'suntanned surface' of Coleman's body.[4] 'Coleman wore a pair of denim shorts and sneakers', Zuckerman says, and nothing else:

> From behind, this man of seventy-one looked to be no more than forty – slender and fit and forty. Coleman was not much over five eight, if that, he was not heavily muscled, and yet there was a lot of strength in him, and a lot of the bounce of the high school athlete was still visible, the quickness, the urge to action.[5]

Zuckerman is drawn to a close examination of this lithely compact body, just as Coleman's various lovers are throughout the novel – as his lover Steena later thinks, 'there was nothing about his body that she had not microscopically absorbed, nothing about this extensive surface imprinted with his self-cherishing evolutionary uniqueness [...] that she had not registered' – but even as he is so drawn, he is intrigued not only as a potential lover but also as a reader. Looking at the suntanned skin, Zuckerman sees also a 'small, Popeye-ish, blue tattoo situated at the top of his right arm, just at the shoulder joining – the words "U.S. Navy" inscribed between the hooklike arms of a shadowy little anchor and running along the hypotenuse of the deltoid muscle'.[6] Text and muscle

come together here, the body offering itself up to be read, as Jeanette
Winterson stages the joining of body and text in her influential 1992 novel,
Written on the Body. But Zuckerman, novelist that he is, is struck by the
sense that this image of skin as text does not suggest legibility, but rather
obscurity, the uncertain seam between skin and history in which the secret
of Coleman's race is hidden. The tattoo, Zuckerman thinks to himself, as
he is drawn, unknowing, into the task of novelising Coleman's past, is a

> tiny symbol, if one were needed, of all the million circumstances of the other
> fellow's life, of that blizzard of details that constitute the confusion of
> a human biography – a tiny symbol to remind me why our understanding
> of people must always be at best slightly wrong.[7]

Zuckerman is drawn erotically and intellectually to the task of reading
Coleman's body. But if he is compelled in this way, it is the case, too, that
the terms in which Zuckerman, and Roth, understand the capacity of the
novel to establish a legible relation between surface and depth have been
profoundly recast by the historical forces that have taken us to this
strangely disoriented end of the millennium, at which surface and depth,
the shallow and the intense, enter into new relations with one another.
Zuckerman's reflection here on the unknowability of other people has
a rich novelistic heritage. We can hear, in this invocation of the 'blizzard of
details' that constitute a life, an echo of George Eliot's reflection on the
sublime variousness of the world, in her 1871-2 novel *Middlemarch*. 'If we
had a keen vision and feeling of all ordinary human life', Eliot's narrator
writes, 'it would be like hearing the grass grow and the squirrel's heart beat,
and we should die of that roar which lies on the other side of silence.'[8] The
blizzard of details, for Zuckerman and for Eliot's narrator, does not make
for rich narrative experience, but overwhelms narrative altogether. And we
can hear, too, an echo from an earlier moment in the history of the novel,
from Jane Austen's *Emma* (1815). Austen's novel narrates Emma's progression from blindness to insight, from error to rectitude, as this takes the
form of her gradual realisation that she loves her avuncular family friend
Mr Knightley. It is in satisfied recognition of this progress towards revelation that Mr Knightley declares, at the end of the novel, 'My Emma, does
not every thing serve to prove more and more the beauty of truth and
sincerity in all our dealings with each other?'[9] But even as Mr Knightley
celebrates the beauty of natural truth telling, Austen's narrator gently
corrects him. 'Seldom', the narrator says, 'very seldom, does complete
truth belong to any human disclosure; seldom can it happen that something is not a little disguised, or a little mistaken.' Austen's narrator, like

Roth's nearly two centuries later, acknowledges that 'our understanding of people must always be at best slightly wrong'.[10]

The uncertain relation between seeing and mis-seeing is woven into the very mechanics of the novel form. But if one can feel the presence of Austen and Eliot at this moment in *The Human Stain*, as Zuckerman studies Coleman's smooth 71-year-old skin, one can see, too, that Roth's novel is witnessing a deep transformation in the way that prose fiction, under late twentieth-century conditions, responds to the faultiness of its own medium. For Austen, for Eliot, the novel functions as a machine that converts the uncontainable variety of reality – the blizzard of details – into a narrative shape. Its magic is that it can make of the uncertain relation between word and thing the means to produce the most vivid pictures of reality, the means, as Eliot puts it, to undertake the 'difficult task of knowing another soul'.[11] Austenian irony, narrative irony more generally, is powered by the sense that language is always at a remove from reality, always double, that it very seldom constitutes a medium of complete truth; but it wins from its doubleness its own kind of novelistic truth. There is a mismatch between surface and depth, between what we say and what we mean. But the novel of interiority has allowed us to make a home for ourselves in a world from which we are always partly estranged. At this moment in *The Human Stain*, though, as Zuckerman recognises that Coleman's skin presents to him a text that he cannot read – as a history of racism remains detached from the forms in which it is written – Roth exposes a malfunction of the terms in which surface and depth have adhered to one another in the work of prose fiction, a sudden expiry of the novel's capacity to map the relations between the trivial and the profound, the shallow and the intense.

One cannot understand the novel of the later twentieth century without addressing this problem, this refiguring of the relations between surface and depth, shallowness and intensity; and one cannot measure the stakes of this refiguring without reckoning with the economic, political, and aesthetic effects of the new cultural-economic logic that rises to dominance in the 1970s, and that has come to be known by the name of neoliberalism. We can see the outline of this relation, between the dawn of neoliberalism and the history of the novel form, by overhearing a conversation between Muriel Spark and David Harvey concerning the effects of the various economic crises that cluster around 1973. In works such as *The Condition of Postmodernity* (1989) and *A Brief History of Neoliberalism* (2005), Harvey has developed an influential account of the ways in which the economic transformations that occur in the early 1970s – most notably the US withdrawal in 1971 from the Bretton Woods agreement that kept the US dollar pinned to a notional gold standard – have given rise to a neoliberal cultural logic. The Bretton Woods agreement, established in the immediate aftermath of the Second World War, was a mechanism, Harvey explains, for the development of what he calls 'embedded liberalism'.[12] This is the form of liberal economics in which advanced economies balance the free movement of capital against the requirement, established in the wake of the war, that nation states cooperate with one another to regulate markets. The logic of neoliberalism, however, as it develops from the early 1970s, requires that capital is increasingly freed from any of the regulatory frameworks imposed upon it by the state. The fundamental principle of neoliberalism, for Harvey, is that the market should operate with maximum freedom and minimum constraint, because 'market exchange', as Paul Treanor puts it, becomes 'an ethic in itself, capable of acting as a guide to all human action, and substituting for all previously held ethical beliefs'.[13] The post-war consensus that the sovereign state should impose some kind of social control over the global economy thus gives way to the belief that the social good is actually guaranteed not by political intervention but by free market economics, and so to the increasing compulsion to free capital from any shackles that governments might lay upon it, and from any forms in which it might be weighed down. If the political forces operating in the immediate post-war period gave rise to a form of embedded liberalism, then the 'neoliberal project', Harvey writes, 'is to disembed capital from these constraints', a disaggregation of capital from its material forms that is given its clearest manifestation in the breakdown of the Bretton Woods agreement.[14] 'Since 1973', Harvey writes in *The Condition of Postmodernity*, 'money has been "de-materialized" in the sense that it no longer has a formal or tangible link to precious metals [. . .] or for that matter to any other tangible commodity'. The 'de-linking of the financial system', he goes on, 'from active production and from any material monetary base calls into question the reliability of the basic mechanism whereby value is supposed to be represented'.[15]

Neoliberalism for Harvey, then, is the economic process whereby capital is freed from the constraints of nation states, in order to act as its own kind of sovereign agent. But if neoliberalism is an economic project, it is also a political one, whose effects can be felt in every area of cultural life – a fact that is given novelistic expression by Muriel Spark, remarkably early in the history of neoliberalism, in her 1976 novel *The Takeover*. Written in a self-consciously fragile realist mode, this novel seeks to understand how the economic crises of 1973, and the neoliberal structures that arose from them, might have effects on a wider logic of representation. Spark's novel, dramatising the troubles of a group of moneyed expats struggling to understand the impact of the 1973 oil crisis on their wealth and privilege, is a response to the narrator's perception that the breakdown of Bretton Woods has brought about 'the deterioration of money in general', 'the collapse of money as a concept'.[16] In seeking to respond to this collapse, what the novel both explores and in its own way demonstrates, is that Harvey's 'de-linking' of capital 'from any monetary base' has an equivalent in a delinking of word from world, of text from body, a dismantling of the representational forms that allowed us to embed our sense of value and of signification in a reliable correspondence between thought and thing. What the collapse of Bretton Woods brings about, the narrator says, is a total transformation in the psychic structure of reality. The truth that the moneyed friends are trying to grasp is that 'a complete mutation of our means of nourishment had already come into being where the concept of money and property were concerned, a complete mutation not merely to be defined as a collapse of the capitalist system, or a global recession, but such a sea change in the nature of reality as could not have been envisaged by Karl Marx or Sigmund Freud'.[17]

Harvey and Spark here are both responding to the same phenomenon – the perception that the freedom of capital from its material forms produces a shift in the way that reality is perceived and constituted. And the way that we understand the relationship between neoliberalism and the novel is determined by how we read the novel's reaction to this shift, how we think the novel gives expression at a superstructural level to transformations in the economic base. In Spark's novel this takes the form of a peculiar wobble in the quality of the realism, an anti-mimetic effect brought about by the 'complete mutation' in representational forms caused by the 'collapse of money as a concept'. As the character Hubert puts it, when the 'concepts of property and material possession' are revealed to be a product of 'lying, deception and fraud', then our broader mechanisms of faithful representation are also disabled. If everything is fraud and deceit, then 'deceit has no meaning, lies do not exist, fraud is impossible'.[18] We see the beginning of the process which leads us to the world of 'alternative facts' and 'fake news' that characterises our own grievous moment in the history of neoliberalism. Rudy Giuliani notoriously declared in August 2018, when explaining why Donald Trump should not testify to the Mueller inquiry, that 'truth isn't truth';[19] Hubert in *The Takeover* offers an early echo of this chilling sentiment, asserting that 'truth is not literally true'.[20] Spark's response to the untruthfulness of the truth is to develop a realist narrative mode that oversees a malfunction in the reality effect – and one can see that the novel form more generally, in the passage from the 1970s to the turn of the century, offers itself as a vehicle with which to explore the crisis in representation set in motion by the neoliberalisation of capital. All of the major developments in the history of the novel in this period are touched by this close relation between narrative form and the anti-representational logic of neoliberalism. From J. G. Ballard's *Crash*, to Angela Carter's *The Bloody Chamber*, to Salman Rushdie's *Midnight's Children*, to Don DeLillo's *White Noise*, to Toni Morrison's *Beloved*, to Chris Kraus's *I Love Dick*, the formal inventiveness of the novel is powered, to some degree, by the energy that is released by the freeing of capital from its material base. As the narrator of Martin Amis's grotesque novel *Money* (1984) puts it, the epistemological crisis that novel enacts began 'when money went wrong' in 1973.[21] Realities are performative, as Chris puts it in Kraus's *I Love Dick* (1997), because 'money's abstract'.[22] Or as DeLillo's narrator puts it in *Underworld* (1997), 'capital burns off the nuance in a culture', exposing us to the 'attenuating influence of money that's electronic and sex that's cyberspaced'.[23]

The later twentieth-century novel can thus seem to act as the cultural expression of an underlying neoliberal logic. The free market economic forces that decouple capital from its material base are mirrored in the anti-representational narrative forces that decouple textual surface from historical or psychological depth. Through the later decades of the twentieth century, as the effects of this decoupling were making themselves felt, critics from Jean-François Lyotard to Fredric Jameson developed a theoretical language that sought to account for it, that sought to make it expressive – the theoretical language that anatomised what Lyotard called the 'postmodern condition'.[24] Intense shallowness became known, in Jameson's famous formulation, as the 'waning of affect'.[25] The loss of material traction that is manifest in the abstraction of money is mirrored in a wider cultural sign system, not only in the simulacral effects explored in novels such as Thomas Pynchon's *The Crying of Lot 49* or DeLillo's *White Noise*, but in artworks by Andy Warhol such as *Atomic Bomb, Red Explosion* or *Campbell's Soup Cans*, or self-referential film, from Ingmar Bergman's *Persona* to Quentin Tarantino's *Pulp Fiction*. But as critics from across the humanities and social sciences seek to account for neoliberalism today, they find themselves dissatisfied with what quickly became the orthodoxies of postmodernism, and in need of a means of approaching the neoliberal condition that is not a simple submission to the forms of intense shallowness that it seems to produce. With the waning of postmodernism in the early decades of the twenty-first century, it has become necessary to rethink the relation between neoliberalism and the cultural forms which give expression to it. It is not enough, critics such as Walter Benn Michaels have argued, for the postmodern novel to offer a critical response to neoliberal conditions that is also a symptom of such conditions – not enough to be content with a performance of intense shallowness as our only means of responding to the forces that are rendering our cultural experience shallow. Such a tight relation between the 'economic system' and the 'cultural "structure of feeling"' does not give rise, Michaels argues, to a postmodern mode of critique, so much as it signals the end of critique altogether, the folding of the novel into the neoliberalism that it sets out to diagnose. The humanities departments that teach these novels, he writes, are not the 'hotbeds of leftism' that they believe themselves to be, but are more like the 'research and development division of neoliberalism'.[26] Some of the most celebrated novels of the period – from Morrison's *Beloved*, to Jonathan Franzen's *Corrections*, to Roth's *The Plot Against America* – for all their differences, have something in common, something which allows us to group these texts together under the heading of what Michaels calls the 'neoliberal novel'. What they share, he suggests, is their tendency to endorse a neoliberal economic logic through a failure to critique it. These novels, he writes, trade in personal stories of individual suffering or trauma or pleasure – Monica and Bill making out in the Oval Office rather than American power protecting its economic interests in the Middle East – because the novel of the period has reneged on its duty to expose the real economic drivers of our cultural condition. The recent explosion of books about historical injustice – novels exploring the trauma of the Holocaust or of slavery – has come about, he argues in a cheaply provocative essay, because shared historical suffering is a distraction from real contemporary inequality. 'No move is more characteristic of the neoliberal novel', he writes, 'than the substitution of cultural difference for [. . .] class difference.'[27]

Michaels's response to this perception – that the neoliberal novel has lost its critical power – is to suggest that the novel itself is bankrupt, obsolete. He hopes that the economic crash of 2008 will spell the end of neoliberal triumphalism, and with it the end of the neoliberal novel. 'Maybe', he suggests, an 'upside of the collapse of a Thatcherite economy will be the disappearance of this entirely Thatcherite genre.' There'll be 'no more books like *The Corrections*'. There'll be 'no memoirs, no historicist novels', and 'a lot of other novels will have to go, too'.[28] Michaels welcomes a bonfire of the novel vanities. But for other more sober-minded critics and theorists, the clear and pressing problem of the critical failures of the novel under neoliberalism requires not a bonfire but a new way of understanding critique, and the novel's contemporary capacity to perform it. There is a wave of scholars writing now who are seeking, after the decline of the languages of postmodernism, to develop new critical ways of understanding both neoliberalism itself, and the art forms that have arisen in response to it. The contemporary proliferation of new forms of reading – surface reading, mere reading, distant reading – is a part of this new wave, a response to the perception that the dominance of a neoliberal logic does not mean that our art forms have become complicit with the marketplace, so much as it requires us to develop new ways of understanding how art and economics are interwoven. It might suggest, as Rita Felski has argued, that we are entering into a new era of critical thinking that she characterises as 'post-critique'; or it might prompt us, like Sianne Ngai, to the conclusion that we need a new set of aesthetic categories with which to grasp our contemporary modes of expression.[29] For Mitchum Huehls, in an implicit rejoinder to Michaels's scepticism about the contemporary novel's capacities for critical work, it is 'too easy' to conclude that the contemporary novel has become 'merely symptomatic of neoliberalism's capacious grasp'. It seems to him more likely that 'many contemporary authors who at first glance might appear to be abandoning politics are actually entirely rethinking what politics looks like in our neoliberal age'.[30] Shallowness has not become simply identical with intensity, this thinking goes, but has entered into a different relationship with it, which can only be seen through a fresh critical lens. As Rachel Greenwald Smith has influentially argued, it may be that 'one of the most important legacies of postmodernist experimentation might in fact be the denaturalization of this binary'. It is not that affect has waned, but that it has migrated. 'What if what we see in postmodernist fiction are fleshed-out non-humans, warmth without depth, embodiment as a form of surface subjectivity?'[31] It's not, perhaps, that the novels of the late twentieth century 'will have to go', but that we need a new means of reading them, as Bill needs to find a way of reading Monica's shallow intensity, as Zuckerman reaches for a means of reading Coleman's tanned skin or his tattoo declaring his allegiance to the US navy.

To begin to imagine such a mode of reading, we might take as an example James Kelman's stunning 1994 novel, *How Late It Was, How Late*. This is a novel concerned, both centrally and elliptically, with the condition of lateness, with the *fin-de-millennial* perception that we have reached a late stage, culturally, politically, economically. The protagonist, Sammy, an impoverished ex-convict living precariously in Glasgow and trying to stay out of the way of the police, comes back repeatedly to his feeling that it is late, that things are late. 'Ah, fuck it', he thinks, 'life, it can be awkward. And time passes. Then it's too late.'³² 'It's getting a bit late for games, and he's getting a bit too auld to be playing them anyway.'³³ 'A bus was coming; he put out his hand; too late. There ye are; fucking time; fucking late again.'³⁴ Kelman's novel is set in a late medium; but this is not quite the lateness that Harvey diagnoses. There is no grand DeLillian theorising, no attempt to give a critical quality to this late time. Rather, the novel depicts lateness as complete, borderless disorientation. A groping in the dark. The novel opens in media res with the story, told exclusively in Sammy's demotic third person, of a fight. Sammy wakes up on the street after a long and heavy drinking binge, to find himself surveilled by two plain-clothes policemen. He walks up to them and punches one of them, inadvisedly perhaps, whereupon he is taken into a close and severely beaten. 'They had him', he says, 'they fucking had him, the two of them, one hand gripping the back of his neck and another on his left wrist and another yin twisting his right arm all the way up his fucking back and it was pure fucking agony like it was getting wrenched off man.'³⁵ We don't see the beating that Sammy is given. 'Ye're as well drawing a curtain here', he says, 'nay point prolonging the agony.'³⁶ But it is so horrific, so grotesquely violent, that it nearly kills him. He wakes in a prison cell in terrible pain and confusion, with strange effects in his vision. 'His fucking eyes', he thinks, 'there was something wrong with them, like if it had still been daylight and he was reading a book he would have had double-vision or something.'³⁷ He passes out, and when he reawakens he can no longer see: 'Then he scratched his cheek. Just at the bone beneath where his right eye should have been, then closing the eye and putting his finger on the lid, then opening it and closing it and for fuck sake man nothing, he couldnay see nothing.'³⁸

The rest of the novel takes place in the darkness to which that beating delivers Sammy, and our understanding of the novel's critical and aesthetic texture, its relation to the lateness in which it is set, is determined by that darkness. Sammy's blindness is an effect of state violence; and in a sense this in itself serves a critical function, offering the kind of brutal depiction of the violence of neoliberal inequality that Michaels suggests the contemporary novel has largely forsaken. *How Late* is one of the more powerful dramatisations of state violence written in the last half century (one of the others being Kelman's later novel, *Translated Accounts*). There are few novels which live through the subjection of the poor and the precarious to the brutality of the neoliberal state with such intensity. But if that is so, what is so extraordinary about this novel is that the terms in which it dissects the violence of late culture are also, and at every moment, symptomatic of that lateness. There is no critical move outside of the condition to which Sammy is condemned, no Lukácsian corrective, no moment of redress. This is a narrative voice, descendant of the alienated voice in Kafka or in Beckett, that can find no traction, no alternative to the logic which grips it, as those policemen grip Sammy at the opening of the novel, preparing to beat him nearly to death. Like Gregor Samsa waking to find himself transformed from salesman to cockroach, Sammy does not even exhibit much surprise at the loss of his sight, or at the terrible damage done to his body. 'The auld life was definitely ower now man', he thinks, 'it was finished, fucking finished';[39] but he contemplates the end of his old life from a kind of distance, as Gregor contemplates the end of his, as Gregor wonders dispassionately how he is going to get to work now he is an insect. 'Now he was chuckling away to himself', Sammy says, in the first hours of his blindness: 'How the hell was it happening to him! . . . he started thinking about it; this was a new stage in life, a development. A new epoch!'[40]

There is, then, despite its intensity, a certain affectlessness to this novel as Sammy chuckles to himself at the condition he is in, a certain disconnect that is the cause and effect of the violence it witnesses. And if Sammy's own relation to his beaten body is disjointed in this way, then the story that the novel goes on to tell is a story of affectlessness, a story of the dismantling of the apparatuses of embodied perception that is the work of the neoliberal state. One of the plotlines of the novel concerns Sammy's attempt to apply for disability benefit, as his blindness makes it impossible for him to work. He visits the doctor who is responsible for registering him as blind, explaining to him that he can't work on building sites if he can't see. 'A lot of things ye do are up high doctor', he says, 'eh . . . there isnay any floors; nay walls, nay ceilings. Ye're in the middle of building them so . . . they're not there yet. Sammy shrugged. If ye cannay see ye're liable to fall off.'[41] This is a peculiarly moving moment in the novel. The lack of walls and ceiling, the unmade state that Sammy describes, names both the partly built environment of the labourer's workplace, and the condition to which blindness has delivered him, that sense that his body's place in the world has been suddenly erased. His visit to the doctor is an appeal to the state – the state, of course, whose law-enforcers blinded him in the first place – to help him to embed himself again in a fully built environment, with walls and ceilings, and to help him embed himself in his own body. It is a first principle of the democratic condition, as John Locke famously tells us, that we all have a property in our own person. But the response of the doctor to Sammy's plea is a radical denial of this democratic principle, and a symptom of a failure of the bonds that tie bodies to minds, that ground ideational structures in material things. He refuses to acknowledge that Sammy is blind, as if the state cannot accept the consequences of its own actions, or as if it insists upon deepening that violence by failing to endorse the victim's experience and perception of it.

The refusal of the state to recognise Sammy's condition is a corollary of the alienation that the novel performs in its own voice – the enclosure of the narrative in a consciousness that cannot fling itself clear of its own closed circuitry. The sealed nature of the narrative voice lives out the sense that there is no way that Sammy can show the inside of his head to others to demonstrate how he is feeling, how he is perceiving the world. As Sammy's self-appointed 'rep' Ally puts it later in the novel, it is hard to prove that you are blind, when other people cannot know what or if you are seeing. 'See I mean', he says, 'if it was a straightforward loss of what we might call an objective function, like a limb or something, then fair enough but the eyes are something else.'[42] What *How Late* suggests is that, under late conditions, we cannot share our view of the world. We cannot give ourselves to others to be read, as Coleman cannot give himself to Zuckerman to be read. Harvey's 'decoupling' of capital from material that is the signature of late historical time has allowed the material world more generally to float free from the forms in which we measure and value it, and so those who fall victim to the state can gain no purchase on their own material conditions. The intensity of their suffering remains shallow. The peculiar alienation of the narrative voice in Kelman's novels, like the dismantlement of Spark's realism in *The Takeover*, is a symptom of this shallowness. But if this is the case, what Kelman's novel tells us, so loudly it deafens us, is that shallowness, loss of traction, is itself an affect, even if one that requires us to develop a new way of understanding how perception materialises itself. This altered affect is given an arresting form early in the novel, as Sammy awakens to his blindness. 'He shifted his head', the narrator says, 'and felt the pillow damp on his face.'[43] While he has been sleeping, liquid has been running from his eyes, but of course he can't see it, so he doesn't know what the liquid is, what it is that has been leaking from him. 'He hadnay been greeting', he thinks, 'just water must have been running out.' 'Maybe it was fucking pus', he thinks, 'Maybe it was fucking yellow fucking mucus pus or something, rancid fucking liquid shit running out his body, out his eyes.' His distance from his body is such that he cannot imagine what his own materiality consists of. But then he hits on another idea, a way of thinking about sight that resonates through *How Late*, and perhaps through the novel of the period more generally. 'Maybe', he says, 'it was the thing that gave ye sight, and now he didnay have sight the thing had turned into pus, and here it was getting discharged, excess body baggage.'[44]

The weightless concept of sight, here, is given a kind of substance, a kind of embodied thinghood, just at the moment when our modes of perception are most divorced from the material world that we fail to look upon. The novel – Kelman's novel, but also perhaps the novel more generally – is in a certain sympathy with Sammy's blindness. The novel is a blind medium, a medium that has to do without the visual, that transmits its thoughts in words directly to the mind. The enclosure of the narrative within the precinct of Sammy's thoughts is a mark of this privation. But if narrative is blind, it is itself a substance that conjures the most intense forms of seeing, a kind of thing that gives ye sight. Writing at the end of the century, writing in the gloaming of the millennium, Kelman suggests that the real violence of late capitalism is that it destroys the apparatuses we have to see it with, to appraise or critique its affects. But if this is so, the novel contains within itself also a kind of substance, the substance perhaps of fiction itself, which is its own form of seeing, a seeing that adjusts the relations between the subject and the object, between the shallow and the intense. If we are to discover in our time a means of reading the relation between neo-liberalism and the novel, we have to find a way of seeing fiction, fiction as an agent at work in the world, casting its own slant of light.

Notes

1 Philip Roth, *The Human Stain* (London: Vintage, 2001), p. 148.
2 Ibid.
3 Ibid., p. 147.
4 Ibid., p. 21.
5 Ibid., p. 15.
6 Ibid., pp. 113, 22.
7 Ibid., p. 22.
8 George Eliot, *Middlemarch* (London: Penguin, 1994), p. 194.
9 Jane Austen, *Emma* (London: Penguin, 1996), p. 365.
10 Ibid., p. 354.
11 Eliot, *Middlemarch*, p. 119.
12 David Harvey, *A Brief History of Neoliberalism* (Oxford: Oxford University Press, 2005), p. 11.

13 Quoted in ibid., p. 3.
14 Ibid., p. 11.
15 David Harvey, *The Condition of Postmodernity: An Enquiry into the Origins of Cultural Change* (Oxford: Blackwell, 1990), p. 297.
16 Muriel Spark, *The Takeover* (London: Macmillan, 1976), pp. 10, 147.
17 Ibid., p. 97.
18 Ibid., p. 138.
19 Giuliani's comment can be seen here: https://www.youtube.com/watch?v=C ljsZ7lgbtw (accessed 1 September 2021).
20 Spark, *Takeover*, p. 138.
21 Martin Amis, *Money* (London: Vintage, 2011), p. 7.
22 Chris Kraus, *I Love Dick* (London: Serpent's Tail, 2016), p. 71.
23 Don DeLillo, *Underworld* (London: Picador, 1999), p. 785.
24 See Jean-François Lyotard, *The Postmodern Condition: A Report on Knowledge* (Manchester: Manchester University Press, 1984).
25 Fredric Jameson, 'Postmodernism, or the Cultural Logic of Late Capitalism', *New Left Review* 1.146 (July/August 1984). Available at https://newleftreview .org/issues/i146/articles/fredric-jameson-postmodernism-or-the-cultural-logic-of-late-capitalism, n.p. (accessed 1 September 2021).
26 Walter Benn Michaels, *The Trouble with Diversity: How We Learned to Love Identity and Ignore Inequality* (New York: Holt, 2006), p. 200.
27 Walter Benn Michaels, 'Going Boom', *BookForum* (February/March 2009). Available at https://www.bookforum.com/print/1505/the-economic-collapse-points-up-how-little-our-literary-world-has-to-say-about-social-inequality-32 74, n.p. (accessed 1 September 2021).
28 Michaels, 'Going Boom', n.p.
29 See Rita Felski, *The Limits of Critique* (Chicago, IL: University of Chicago Press, 2015), and Elizabeth S. Anker and Rita Felski, eds., *Critique and Postcritique* (Durham, NC: Duke University Press, 2017). See also Sianne Ngai, *Our Aesthetic Categories: Zany, Cute, Interesting* (Cambridge, MA: Harvard University Press, 2012), and *Theory of the Gimmick: Aesthetic Judgement and Capitalist Form* (Cambridge, MA: Harvard University Press, 2020).
30 Mitchum Huehls, *After Critique: Twenty-First-Century Fiction in a Neoliberal Age* (Oxford: Oxford University Press, 2016), p. xi.
31 Rachel Greenwald Smith, 'Postmodernism and the Affective Turn', in *Twentieth Century Literature* 57.3/4 (2011), pp. 423–46 (p. 428).
32 James Kelman, *How Late It Was, How Late* (London: Secker, 1994), p. 151.
33 Ibid., pp. 204–5.
34 Ibid., p. 246.
35 Ibid., p. 6.
36 Ibid.
37 Ibid., p. 9.
38 Ibid., p. 10.
39 Ibid., p. 11.

40 Ibid.
41 Ibid., p. 223.
42 Ibid., p. 295.
43 Ibid., p. 23.
44 Ibid., p. 24.

Further Reading

Liberalism

Sascha Bru, *Democracy, Law and the Modernist Avant-Gardes: Writing in the State of Exception* (Edinburgh: Edinburgh University Press, 2009)

John Carey, *The Intellectuals and the Masses: Pride and Prejudice among the Literary Intelligentsia, 1880–1939* (London: Faber, 1992)

Christos Hadjiyiannis, *Conservative Modernists: Literature and Tory Politics in Britain, 1900–1920* (Cambridge: Cambridge University Press, 2018)

Janice Ho, 'The Crisis of Liberalism and the Politics of Modernism', *Literature Compass* 8 (2011): 47–65

Michael Levenson, *Modernism and the Fate of Individuality: Character and Novelistic Form from Conrad to Woolf* (Cambridge: Cambridge University Press, 1991)

Michael North, *The Political Aesthetic of Yeats, Eliot, and Pound* (Cambridge: Cambridge University Press, 1991)

Rachel Potter, *Modernism and Democracy: Literary Culture, 1900–1930* (Oxford: Oxford University Press, 2006)

Nathan Waddell, *Modernist Nowheres: Politics and Utopia in Early Modernist Writing, 1900–1920* (Basingstoke: Palgrave Macmillan, 2012)

Communism

Ulka Anjaria, *Realism in the Twentieth-Century Indian Novel* (Cambridge: Cambridge University Press, 2012)

Andy Croft, *Red Letter Days: British Fiction in the 1930s* (London: Lawrence & Wishart, 1990)

Ben Harker, *The Chronology of Revolution: Communism, Culture, and Civil Society in Twentieth-Century Britain* (Toronto: University of Toronto Press, 2021)

Nick Hubble, *The Proletarian Answer to the Modernist Question* (Edinburgh: Edinburgh University Press, 2017)

Benjamin Kohlmann, *Committed Styles: Modernism, Politics, and Left-Wing Literature in the 1930s* (Oxford: Oxford University Press, 2014)

Benjamin Kohlmann and Matthew Taunton (eds.), *A History of 1930s British Literature* (Cambridge: Cambridge University Press, 2019)

Janet Montefiore, *Men and Women Writers of the 1930s: The Dangerous Flood of History* (New York: Routledge, 1996)

Natasha Periyan, *The Politics of 1930s British Literature: Education, Class, Gender* (London: Bloomsbury, 2018)

Glyn Salton-Cox, *Queer Communism and the Ministry of Love* (Edinburgh: Edinburgh University Press, 2018)

Matthew Taunton, *Red Britain: The Russian Revolution in Mid-Century Culture* (Oxford: Oxford University Press, 2019)

Fascism

Michael Denning, *The Cultural Front: The Laboring of American Culture in the Twentieth Century* (London: Verso, 2011)

Priyamvada Gopal, *Insurgent Empire: Anticolonial Resistance and British Dissent* (London: Verso, 2019)

David Renton, *Fascism: History and Theory* (London: Pluto Press, 2020)

Elinor Taylor, *The Popular Front Novel in Britain, 1934–1940* (Leiden: Brill, 2018)

Suffragism

Katharine Cockin, Glenda Norquay, and Sowon S. Park (eds)., *Women's Suffrage Literature* (London and New York: Routledge, 2007)

Maria DiCenzo with Lucy Delap, and Leila Ryan, *Feminist Media History: Suffrage, Periodicals and the Public Sphere* (Basingstoke: Palgrave Macmillan, 2011)

Barbara Green, *Spectacular Confessions: Autobiography, Performative Activism, and the Sites of Suffrage, 1905–1938* (London: Macmillan, 1997)

Sandra Stanley Holton, *Feminism and Democracy: Women's Suffrage and Reform Politics in Britain, 1900–1918* (Cambridge: Cambridge University Press, 1986)

Jill Liddington and Jill Norris, *One Hand Tied Behind Us: The Rise of the Women's Suffrage Movement* (London: Rivers Oram, 2000)

Carolyn Christensen Nelson (ed.), *Literature of the Women's Suffrage Campaign in England* (Peterborough, ON; Plymouth: Broadview Press, 2004)

Glenda Norquay (ed.), *Voices and Votes: A Literary Anthology of the Women's Suffrage Campaign* (Manchester: Manchester University Press: 1995)

Sowon S. Park, 'The First Professional: The Women Writers' Suffrage League', *Modern Language Quarterly* 58.2 (1997), 185–200

June Purvis and Sandra Stanley Holton (eds.), *Votes for Women!* (London: Routledge, 2000)

Lisa Tickner, *The Spectacle of Women* (London: Chatto & Windus, 1987)

Pacifism

Charles Andrews, *Writing Against War: Literature, Activism, and the British Peace Movement* (Evanston, IL: Northwestern University Press, 2017)

Grace Brockington, *Above the Battlefield: Modernism and the Peace Movement in Britain, 1900–1918* (New Haven, CT: Yale University Press, 2010)

Josephine Eglin, 'Women Pacifists in Interwar Britain', in *Challenge to Mars: Essays on Pacifism from 1918 to 1945*, ed. Peter Brock and Thomas P. Socknat (Toronto: University of Toronto Press, 1999), pp. 149–68

David Martin, *Pacifism: An Historical and Sociological Study* (London: Routledge & Kegan Paul, 1965)

R. K. S. Taylor and Nigel Young, *Campaigns for Peace: British Peace Movements in the Twentieth Century* (Manchester: Manchester University Press, 1987)

R. S. White, *Pacifism and English Literature: Minstrels of Peace* (Basingstoke: Palgrave Macmillan, 2008)

Partitions

Stefano Bianchini, Sanjay Chaturvedi, Rada Iveković, and Ranabir Samaddar (eds.), *Partitions: Reshaping States and Minds* (Abingdon: Frank Cass, 2005)

Urvashi Butalia, *The Other Side of Silence: Voices from the Partition of India* (London: C Hurst & Co., 2000)

Joe Cleary, *Literature, Partition and the Nation-State: Culture and Conflict in Ireland, Israel and Palestine* (Cambridge: Cambridge University Press, 2001)

Arie M. Dubnov and Laura Robson (eds.), *Partitions: A Transnational History of Twentieth-Century Territorial Separatism* (Stanford, CA: Stanford University Press, 2019)

Ghislaine Glasson Deschaumes and Rada Iveković (eds.), *Divided Countries, Separated Cities: The Modern Legacy of Partition* (New Delhi: Oxford University Press, 2003)

Smita Tewari Jassal and Eyal Ben-Ari (eds.), *The Partition Motif in Contemporary Conflicts* (New Delhi: Sage Publications, 2007)

Yasmin Khan, *The Great Partition: The Making of India and Pakistan* (New Haven, CT: Yale University Press, 2007)

Radhika Mohanram and Anindya Raychaudhuri (eds.), *Partitions and their Afterlives: Violence, Memories, Living* (London: Rowman & Littlefield International, 2019)

Gyanendra Pandey, *Remembering Partition* (Cambridge: Cambridge University Press, 2001)

Anindya Raychaudhuri, *Narrating South Asian Partition: Oral History, Literature, Cinema* (New York: Oxford University Press, 2019)

Federalism

Étienne Balibar, *We, the People of Europe?: Reflections on Transnational Citizenship*, trans. James Swenson (Princeton, NJ: Princeton University Press, 2004)

Duncan Bell, *The Idea of Greater Britain: Empire and the Future of World Order, 1860–1900* (Princeton, NJ: Princeton University Press, 2007)

Adom Getachew, 'Revisiting the Federalists in the Black Atlantic', in *Worldmaking After Empire: The Rise and Fall of Self-Determination* (Princeton, NJ: Princeton University Press, 2019), pp. 107–41

Paul Q. Hirst (ed.), *The Pluralist Theory of the State: Selected Writings of G. D. H. Cole, J. N. Figgis, and H. J. Laski* (London: Routledge, 1989)

Samuel Moyn, 'Fantasies of Federalism', Review of: Frederick Cooper, *Citizenship Between Empire and Nation: Remaking France and French Africa, 1945–1960* (Princeton University Press, 2014) and Gary Wilder, *Freedom Time: Negritude, Decolonization, and the Future of the World* (Duke University Press, 2015), in *Dissent* (Winter 2015), n.p.

Or Rosenboim, 'The End of Imperial Federalism?' and 'Federal Democracy for Welfare', in *The Emergence of Globalism: Visions of World Order in Britain and the United States, 1939–1950* (Princeton, NJ: Princeton University Press, 2019), pp. 100–29 and 130–67

Mark J. Rozell and Clyde Wilcox, *Federalism: A Very Short Introduction* (Oxford: Oxford University Press, 2019)

Mahendra Prasad Singh and Veena Kukreja, *Federalism in South Asia* (New York: Routledge, 2014)

Quinn Slobodian, 'A World of Federations', *Globalists: The End of Empire and the Birth of Neoliberalism* (Cambridge, MA: Harvard University Press, 2018), pp. 91–120.

Michelle A. Stephens, *Black Empire: The Masculine Global Imaginary of Caribbean Intellectuals in the United States, 1914–1962* (Durham, NC: Duke University Press, 2005)

R. L. Watts, *New Federations: Experiments in the Commonwealth* (Oxford: Clarendon Press, 1966)

Cold War

Greg Barnhisel, *Cold War Modernists: Art, Literature, and American Cultural Diplomacy* (New York: Columbia University Press, 2015)

David Caute, *The Dancer Defects: The Struggle for Cultural Supremacy During the Cold War* (Oxford: Oxford University Press, 2003)

Peter Finn and Petra Couvée (eds.), *The Zhivago Affair: The Kremlin, the CIA, and the Battle Over a Forbidden Book* (London: Vintage, 2015)

Andrew Hammond (ed.), *Cold War Literature: Writing the Global Conflict* (London: Routledge, 2006)

Eric Hobsbawm, *The Age of Extremes: The Short Twentieth Century, 1914–1991* (London: Michael Joseph, 1994)

Amanda Laugesen, *Taking Books to the World: American Publishers and the Cultural Cold War* (Amherst, MA: University of Massachusetts Press, 2017)

Monica Popescu, *At Penpoint: African Literatures, Postcolonial Studies, and the Cold War* (Durham, NC: Duke University Press, 2020)

Frances Stoner Saunders, *Who Paid the Piper?: The CIA and the Cultural Cold War* (London: Granta, 1999)

Stephen Voyce, *Poetic Community: Avant-Garde Activism and Cold War Culture* (Toronto: University of Toronto Press, 2013)

Patrick Wright, *Iron Curtain: From Stage to Cold War* (Oxford: Oxford University Press, 2007)

Irish Nationalism

Angela Bourke et al. (eds.), *The Field Day Anthology of Irish Writing*, Vols. 4 and 5: *Irish Women's Writings and Traditions* (Cork: Cork University Press, 2002)

Joe Cleary, *Literature, Partition and the Nation-State: Culture and Conflict in Ireland, Israel and Palestine* (Cambridge: Cambridge University Press, 2001)

Michael G. Cronin, *Impure Thoughts: Sexuality, Catholicism and Literature in Twentieth-Century Ireland* (Manchester: Manchester University Press, 2012)

Seamus Deane, *Strange Country: Modernity and Nationhood in Irish Writing since 1790* (Oxford: Oxford University Press, 1998)

Seamus Deane (ed.), *The Field Day Anthology of Irish Writing*, Vols. 1–3 (Derry: Field Day, 1991)

Seán Kennedy (ed.), *Beckett and Ireland* (Cambridge: Cambridge University Press, 2010)

David Lloyd, *Anomalous States: Irish Writing and the Post-Colonial Moment* (Dublin: Lilliput, 1993)

Emer Nolan, *Five Irish Women: The Second Republic, 1960–2016* (Manchester: Manchester University Press, 2019)

Marilynn Richtarik, *Acting Between the Lines: The Field Day Theatre Company and Irish Cultural Politics, 1980–1984* (Oxford: Clarendon Press, 1994)

Clair Wills, *That Neutral Island: A Cultural History of Ireland During the Second World War* (London: Faber, 2007)

Black Nationalism

Keisha Blain, *Set the World on Fire: Black Nationalist Women and the Global Struggle for Freedom* (Philadelphia, PA: University of Pennsylvania Press, 2018)

Robert Carr, *Black Nationalism in the New World: Reading the African-American and West Indian Experience* (Durham, NC: Duke University Press, 2002)

Cheryl Clarke, *'After Mecca': Women Poets and the Black Arts Movement* (New Brunswick, NJ: Rutgers University Press, 2004)

Patricia Hill Collins, *From Black Power to Hip Hop: Racism, Nationalism, and Feminism* (Philadelphia, PA: Temple University Press, 2006)

Peniel E. Joseph, *Waiting 'Til the Midnight Hour: A Narrative History of Black Power in America* (New York: Henry Holt & Co., 2006)

Jeffrey O. G. Ogbar, *Black Power: Radical Politics and African American Identity* (Baltimore, MD: Johns Hopkins University Press, 2005)

Amy Abugo Ongiri, *Spectacular Blackness: The Cultural Politics of the Black Power Movement and the Search for a Black Aesthetic* (Charlottesville: University of Virginia Press (2009)

Melanye Price, *Dreaming Blackness: Black Nationalism and African American Public Opinion* (New York: New York University Press, 2009)

Barbara Ransby, *Making All Black Lives Matter: Reimagining Freedom in the Twenty-First Century* (Berkeley, CA: University of California Press, 2018)

James Smethurst, *The Black Arts Movement: Literary Nationalism in the 1960s and 1970s* (Chapel Hill: University of North Carolina Press, 2005)

Caribbean Nationalisms

J. Dillon Brown and Leah Reade Rosenberg (eds.), *Beyond Windrush: Rethinking Postwar Anglophone Caribbean Literature* (Jackson: University Press of Mississippi, 2015)

Alison Donnell, *Twentieth-Century Caribbean Literature: Critical Moments in Anglophone Literary History* (London and New York: Routledge, 2006)

Brent Hayes Edwards, *The Practice of Diaspora: Literature, Translation, and the Rise of Black Internationalism* (Cambridge, MA: Harvard University Press, 2003)

Curdella Forbes, *From Nation to Diaspora: Samuel Selvon, George Lamming and the Cultural Performance of Gender* (Kingston: University of the West Indies Press, 2005)

Kate Houlden, *Sexuality, Gender and Nationalism in Caribbean Literature* (London and New York: Routledge, 2016)

George Lamming, *The Pleasures of Exile* (London: Michael Joseph, 1960)

Michael Niblett, *The Caribbean Novel Since 1945: Cultural Practice, Form, and the Nation- State* (Jackson: University Press of Mississippi, 2012)

Kenneth Ramchand, *The West Indian Novel and Its Background* (London: Faber, 1970)

Leah Rosenberg, *Nationalism and the Formation of Caribbean Literature* (London and New York: Palgrave Macmillan, 2007)

Patricia Saunders, *Alien-Nation and Repatriation: Translating Identity in Anglophone Caribbean Literature* (Lanham, MD: Lexington, 2007)

African Nationalisms

Jacques Chevrier, *Littératures francophones d'Afrique noire* (Aix en Provence: Edisud, 2006)

Maryse Condé, *Segu*, 1st edition (New York: Ballantine, 1988)

David C. Conrad and Djanka Tassey Condé (eds.), *Sunjata: A New Prose Version* (Indianapolis: Hackett, 2016)

Fatou Diome, *The Belly of the Atlantic* (London: Serpent's Tail, 2006)

Frantz Fanon, *The Wretched of the Earth*, trans. Richard Philcox, intro. Jean-Paul Sartre and Homi K. Bhabha (New York: Grove Press, 2004)

Ahmadou Kourouma, *Waiting for the Wild Beasts to Vote* (London: Heinemann, 2003)

Achille Mbembe, *Necropolitics*, trans. Steve Corcoran (Durham, NC: Duke University Press, 2019)

Ato Quayson, *Strategic Transformations in Nigerian Writing: Orality and History in the Work of Rev. Samuel Johnson, Amos Tutuola, Wole Soyinka and Ben Okri* (Oxford: James Currey, 1997)

Léopold Sédar Senghor, *On African Socialism* (New York: Praeger, 1964)

Ngũgĩ wa Thiong'o, *Decolonising the Mind: The Politics of Language in African Literature* (Woodbridge: James Currey, 1986)

Apartheid

David Attwell, *Rewriting Modernity: Studies in Black South African Literary History* (Pietermaritzburg: University of KwaZulu-Natal Press, 2005)

David Attwell and Derek Attridge (eds.), *The Cambridge History of South African Literature* (Cambridge: Cambridge University Press, 2012)

Steve Biko, *I Write What I Like: A Selection of Writings* (London: Heinemann Educational Books, 1989)

Michael Chapman, *Southern African Literatures* (London: Longman, 1996)

Gareth Cornwell, Dirk Klopper, and Craig MacKenzie (eds.), *The Columbia Guide to South African Literature in English Since 1945* (New York: Columbia University Press, 2010)

Christopher Heywood, *A History of South African Literature* (Cambridge: Cambridge University Press, 2004)

Peter Horn, *Writing my Reading: Essays on Literary Politics in South Africa* (Amsterdam: Rodopi, 1994)

Matthew P. Keaney, "'I Can Feel My Grin Turn to a Grimace": From the Sophiatown Shebeens to the Streets of Soweto on the pages of *Drum, The Classic, New Classic*, and *Staffrider*', unpublished MA dissertation, George Mason University, 2011

Peter D. McDonald, *The Literature Police: Apartheid Censorship and its Cultural Consequences* (Oxford: Oxford University Press, 2010)

Mbulelo V. Mzamane, 'The Impact of Black Consciousness on Culture', in B. Pityana, M. Ramphele, et al. (eds.), *Bounds of Possibility: The Legacy of Steve Biko and Black Consciousness* (Cape Town: David Philip, 1991), pp. 179–93

Njabulo Ndebele, *South African Literature and Culture: Rediscovery of the Ordinary* (Pietermaritzburg: University of KwaZulu-Natal Press, 1994)

Lewis Nkosi, *Home and Exile and Other Selections* (London: Longmans, Green & Co., 1965)

Lily Saint, *Black Cultural Life in South Africa: Reception, Apartheid, and Ethics* (Ann Arbor: University of Michigan Press, 2018)

Women's Rights

Teresa Amott and Julie Matthaei, *Race, Gender, and Work: A Multicultural Economic History of Women in the Unites States* (Boston, MA: South End Press, 1996)

Vicki Coppock, Deena Haydon, and Ingrid Richter, *The Illusions of 'Post-Feminism': New Women, Old Myths* (1995; London and New York: Routledge, 2014)

Leslie Feinberg, *Transgender Warriors: Making History from Joan of Arc to Dennis Rodman* (Boston, MA: Beacon Press, 1996)

Sarah Gamble, *The Routledge Companion to Feminism and Postfeminism* (London: Routledge, 2004)

Henry Louis Gates, Jr. (ed.), *Reading Black, Reading Feminist: A Critical Anthology* (New York: Penguin, 1990)

Stéphanie Genz and Benjamin A. Brabon (eds.), *Postfeminism: Cultural Texts and Theories* (2009; Edinburgh: Edinburgh University Press, 2018)

Rosalind Gill and Christina Scharff (eds.), *New Femininities: Postfeminism, Neoliberalism and Subjectivity* (New York: Palgrave Macmillan, 2013)

Daniel Horowitz, *Betty Friedan and the Making of The Feminine Mystique: The American Left, the Cold War, and Modern Feminism* (Amherst: University of Massachusetts Press, 1998)

Michelle M. Nickerson, *Mothers of Conservatism: Women and the Postwar Right* (Princeton, NJ: Princeton University Press, 2012)

Yvonne Tasker and Diane Negra (eds.), *Interrogating Postfeminism: Gender and the Politics of Popular Culture* (Durham, NC: Duke University Press, 2007)

Myka Tucker-Abramson, *Novel Shocks: Urban Renewal and the Origins of Neoliberalism* (New York: Fordham University Press, 2019)

Robyn R. Warhol and Diane Price Herndl, *Feminisms: An Anthology of Literary Theory and Criticism* (New Brunswick, NJ: Rutgers University Press, 1991)

Sexual Rights

Judith Butler, *Bodies that Matter: On the Discursive Limits of Sex* (London: Routledge, 2011)

Devon W. Carbado, Dwight A. McBride, and Donald Weise (eds.), *Black Like Us: A Century of Lesbian, Gay and Bisexual African American Fiction* (New Jersey: Cleis Press, 2020)

Elaine Hobby and Chris White, *What Lesbians do in Books: Essays on Lesbian Sensibilities in Literature* (London: Women's Press, 1992)

Mark Lilly, *Gay Men's Literature in the Twentieth Century* (New York: New York University Press, 1993)

Jodie Medd (ed.), *The Cambridge Companion to Lesbian Literature* (Cambridge: Cambridge University Press, 2015)

Eve Kosofsky Sedgwick, *Epistemology of the Closet* (Oakland, CA: University of California Press, 2008)

Alan Sinfield, *The Wilde Century: Effeminacy, Oscar Wilde and the Queer Moment* (London: Cassell, 1994)

Urvashi Vaid, *Irresistible Revolution: Confronting Race, Class and the Assumptions of LGBT Politics* (New York: Magnus Books, 2012)

Jeffrey Weeks, *Against Nature: Essays on History, Sexuality and Identity* (London: Rivers Oram Press, 1991)

Indigenous Rights

Jordan Abel, *NISHGA* (Toronto: McClelland & Stewart, 2021)

Janice Acoose et al., *Reasoning Together: The Native Critics Collective* (Norman, OK: University of Oklahoma Press, 2008)

John Borrows, *Recovering Canada: The Resurgence of Indigenous Law* (Toronto: University of Toronto Press, 2002)

Glen Coulthard, *Red Skin, White Masks: Rejecting the Colonial Politics of Recognition* (Minneapolis: University of Minnesota Press, 2014)

Daniel Heath Justice, *Why Indigenous Literatures Matter* (Waterloo, ON: Wilfrid Laurier University Press, 2018)

Keavy Martin, *Stories in a New Skin: Approaches to Inuit Literature* (Winnipeg: University of Manitoba Press, 2012)

Beth Piatote, *Domestic Subjects: Gender, Citizenship, and Law in Native American Literature* (New Haven, CT: Yale University Press, 2013)

Mark Rifkin, *Beyond Settler Time: Temporal Sovereignty and Indigenous Self-Determination* (Durham, NC: Duke University Press, 2017)

Leanne Betasmosake Simpson, *Dancing on Our Turtle's Back: Stories of Nishnaabeg Re-Creation, Resurgence and a New Emergence* (Winnipeg, MB: ARP Books, 2011)

Cheryl Suzack, *Indigenous Women's Writing and the Cultural Study of Law* (Toronto, ON: University of Toronto Press, 2017)

Environmental Rights

William Cronon (ed.), *Uncommon Ground: Rethinking the Human Place in Nature* (New York: W. W. Norton, 1995)

Elizabeth DeLoughrey, *Allegories of the Anthropocene* (Durham, NC: Duke University Press, 2019)

Ramachandra Guha and Joan Martínez Alier, *Varieties of Environmentalism: Essays North and South* (London: Taylor & Francis, 1997)

John McCormick, *The Global Environmental Movement* (Chichester: John Wiley & Sons, 1995)

Rob Nixon, *Slow Violence and the Environmentalism of the Poor* (Cambridge, MA: Harvard University Press, 2013)

John H. Rignall, H. Gustav Klaus, and Valentine Cunningham (eds.), *Ecology and the Literature of the British Left: The Red and the Green* (London: Routledge, 2012)

Scott Slovic, Swarnalatha Rangarajan, and Vidya Sarveswaran (eds.), *Ecocriticism of the Global South* (New York: Lexington Books, 2015)

Keith Thomas, *Man and the Natural World: Changing Attitudes in England, 1500– 1800* (London: Penguin, 1984)

Derek Wall, *Green History: A Reader in Environmental Literature, Philosophy, and Politics* (London: Routledge, 1993)

Neoliberalism

Anne Applebaum, *Twilight of Democracy: The Failure of Politics and the Parting of Friends* (London: Penguin, 2020)

Walter Benn Michaels, 'Neoliberal Aesthetics: Fried, Rancière and the Form of the Photograph', *Nonsite.org*, issue 1 (2011), available online at https://nonsite .org/neoliberal-aesthetics-fried-ranciere-and-the-form-of-the-photograph

Mark Fisher, *Capitalist Realism: Is There No Alternative* (Ropley: Zero Books, 2009)

Mitchum Huehls and Rachel Greenwald Smith (eds.), *Neoliberalism and Contemporary Literary Culture* (Baltimore, MD: Johns Hopkins University, 2017)

Sianne Ngai, *Theory of the Gimmick: Aesthetic Judgment and Capitalist Form* (Cambridge, MA: Harvard University Press, 2020)

Mathias Nilges, *How to Read a Moment: The American Novel and the Crisis of the Present* (Evanston, IL: Northwestern University Press, 2021)

Rachel Greenwald Smith, *Affect and American Literature in the Age of Neoliberalism* (Cambridge: Cambridge University Press, 2015)

Rachel Greenwald Smith, *On Compromise* (Minneapolis, MN: Graywolf Press, 2021)

Manfred B. Steger and Ravi Roy, *Neoliberalism: A Very Short Introduction* (Oxford: Oxford University Press, 2010)

Slavoj Žižek, *Living in the End Times* (London: Verso, 2011)

Index

Abani, Chris, 11, 208
Abbey, Edward
  Monkey Wrench Gang, The, 294
Abbey Theatre, 154–155
Abel, Elizabeth, 65
Abortion, access to, 234, 237, 248
Abstraction
  US Cold War funding, 139
Achebe, Chinua, 11, 197
  Things Fall Apart, 199, 201
Ackland, Valentine, 38
ACT UP, 254–255, 257
Activism, generally, 5, 8
Adam, Ruth
  There Needs No Ghost, 98
Adams, Ansel, 293
Adorno, Theodor, 1, 2–3, 6, 154
  alienation in modernist literature, 2
  'Commitment', 37, 43, 51, 136–137
  'Freudian Theory and the Pattern of Fascist
    Propaganda', 64–65, 66
Africa
  African Diaspora, 208–209
  African nationalisms, 10–11, 197–210, 219
  Afropolitanism, 5, 11, 208–209
  Apartheid *see* Anti-apartheid movement;
    Apartheid
  Berlin/Congo Conference, 120, 198
  decolonisation, 10–11, 199–210
  epic form, 203–207
  globalisation's effects, 207–210
  imposed nationhoods, 198–199
  literary nationalism, 200–202, 208
  migritude novels, 209
  oral traditions, 222
  Pan-African Conference, 189
  Pan-African movement, 180, 183, 184, 189–192
  postcolonial novels, 199–202
  'wake works', 209–210
African Writers Association, 223
Agamben, Giorgio, 3

Aid to Development Children (ADC), 246
AIDS epidemic, 12–13, 238, 252, 254–257, 259, 295
  ACT UP, 254–255, 257, 260
Akomfrah, John
  Handsworth Songs, 209
  Nine Muses, 209
Aldermaston Marches, 136
Aldington, Richard, 92
Aldrich, C. R.
  *Primitive Mind and Modern Civilization,
    The*, 201
Ali, Dusé Mohamed, 189
Ali, Rabia Umar
  Empire in Retreat, 114
Alienation
  Cold War, 135, 236
  colonial, 202
  modernist novel and, 2
  neoliberal writing, 319
All-India Progressive Writers' Association
  (AIPWA), 41
Allatini, Rose
  Despised and Rejected, 91
Allen, Clifford, 89
Allen, Walter, 142
Allfrey, Phyllis Shand, 185
  Cabinet, The, 126
  Orchid House, The, 191
Allison, Dorothy
  Bastard Out of Carolina, 238
Amis, Kingsley, 255
Amis, Martin
  Money, 314
Anand, Mulk Raj
  AIPWA manifesto, 41
  anti-colonialism, 42–43
  conversion narrative, 41–46, 51
  Marxism, 6, 37, 41–46
  modernism, 41–42
  Socialist Realism, 41–42
  Untouchable, 42–46, 51

Authors

Edward Albee edited by Stephen J. Bottoms
Margaret Atwood edited by Coral Ann Howells (second edition)
W. H. Auden edited by Stan Smith
Jane Austen edited by Edward Copeland and Juliet McMaster (second edition)
James Baldwin edited by Michele Elam
Balzac edited by Owen Heathcote and Andrew Watts
Beckett edited by John Pilling
Bede edited by Scott DeGregorio
Aphra Behn edited by Derek Hughes and Janet Todd
Saul Bellow edited by Victoria Aarons
Walter Benjamin edited by David S. Ferris
William Blake edited by Morris Eaves
Boccaccio edited by Guyda Armstrong, Rhiannon Daniels, and Stephen J. Milner
Jorge Luis Borges edited by Edwin Williamson
Brecht edited by Peter Thomson and Glendyr Sacks (second edition)
The Brontës edited by Heather Glen
Bunyan edited by Anne Dunan-Page
Frances Burney edited by Peter Sabor
Byron edited by Drummond Bone
Albert Camus edited by Edward J. Hughes
Willa Cather edited by Marilee Lindemann
Catullus edited by Ian Du Quesnay and Tony Woodman
Cervantes edited by Anthony J. Cascardi
Chaucer edited by Piero Boitani and Jill Mann (second edition)
Chekhov edited by Vera Gottlieb and Paul Allain
Kate Chopin edited by Janet Beer
Caryl Churchill edited by Elaine Aston and Elin Diamond
Cicero edited by Catherine Steel
J. M. Coetzee edited by Jarad Zimbler
Coleridge edited by Lucy Newlyn
Coleridge edited by Tim Fulford (new edition)
Wilkie Collins edited by Jenny Bourne Taylor
Joseph Conrad edited by J. H. Stape
H. D. edited by Nephie J. Christodoulides and Polina Mackay
Dante edited by Rachel Jacoff (second edition)
Daniel Defoe edited by John Richetti
Don DeLillo edited by John N. Duvall
Charles Dickens edited by John O. Jordan
Emily Dickinson edited by Wendy Martin
John Donne edited by Achsah Guibbory
Dostoevskii edited by W. J. Leatherbarrow

Topics

www.ingramcontent.com/pod-product-compliance
Ingram Content Group UK Ltd.
Pitfield, Milton Keynes, MK11 3LW, UK
UKHW042154280225
455719UK00001B/338